Phineas F. Bresee:
A Prince in Israel

A Biography

By

Rev. E. A. Girvin

The steps of a good man are ordered by the Lord;
and he delighteth in his way. Psa. 36:23

Nazarene Publishing House
Kansas City, Missouri

PHOTOLITHOPRINTED BY CUSHING - MALLOY, INC.
ANN ARBOR, MICHIGAN, UNITED STATES OF AMERICA

Contents

CHAPTER VIII

CHAPTER IX

CHAPTER X

CHAPTER XI

CHAPTER XII

CHAPTER XIII

CHAPTER XIV

CHAPTER XV

CHAPTER XXIV

CHAPTER XXV

CHAPTER XXVI

CHAPTER XXVII

CHAPTER XXVIII

CHAPTER XXIX

CHAPTER XXX

CHAPTER XXXI

CHAPTER XXXII

CHAPTER XXXIII

CHAPTER XXXIV

CHAPTER XXXV

CHAPTER XXXVI

CHAPTER XXXVII

CHAPTER XXXVIII

CHAPTER XXXIX

CHAPTER XL

CHAPTER XLI

CHAPTER XLII

CHAPTER XLIII

CHAPTER XLIV

CHAPTER XLV

A Prince in Israel

INTRODUCTION

In presenting to the public this biography, I keenly realize my inability to meet the requirements of such a work, the incompleteness of the materials at my command, and the impossibility at this time of obtaining a proper historical perspective. When a worthy and comprehensive biography of Dr. Bresee shall be written — and the time will surely come when such a work will be accomplished — a vast quantity of materials now in existence, but not within my reach, will be availed of in the preparation of such a biography. To do justice to the life of a man so great as Phineas F. Bresee, years should be spent in gathering data. From those who were most intimately associated with him, should be elicited the great wealth of rich biographical material which lies dormant in their memories. His letters, hundreds and perhaps thousands of which are scattered over this country, should be collected. This data, including the thousands of sermon outlines which he left behind him, should be subjected to the most painstaking scrutiny. To digest and analyze such a mass of facts, sift therefrom that which might be most suitable for historical purposes, and incorporate it into the finished product of a biography, would call for the very highest intellectual powers on the part of the historian, and would require many years of careful research, compilation and literary labor. I have had neither the ability, the data, nor the time which are requisite to the proper performance of this task. On the other hand, I have had many things in my favor as a biographer. Chief among these was my intimate friendship with Dr. Bresee for more than a quarter of a century, my close association with his family since his decease, and the fact that for three years or more prior to his death, I enjoyed the privilege of taking down in shorthand, as the words fell from his own lips, the story of his life. We devoted many evenings to this work. Our custom was to go up into his study, and he, while lying on the lounge, would review his eventful career. Frequently during the course of these reminiscences, he would pause for the purpose of commenting informally upon some of the persons and incidents included in his narrative.

It was also my privilege to converse with him on a vast range of topics. While much of our conversation was of a private and personal nature, and much more related to the deep things of God, and to the progress of the great work in which we were both so vitally interested, still Dr. Bresee would give frequent expression to his views of current events.

I conducted a voluminous correspondence with him in the earlier years of the Nazarene movement, but all his letters to me were destroyed in the San Francisco earthquake and fire of 1906, and between that time and the date of my coming to Los Angeles in 1911, our correspondence diminished both in frequency and importance.

When the complete biography of Dr. Bresee shall be written, this book will be only one — though perhaps the chief one — of the documents used by the writer of the greater and more comprehensive work. John Morley states in his introduction to the life of Gladstone, that during the preparation of that work three hundred thousand papers passed through his hands, and that in addition to them, he had had access to a diary kept by Gladstone for forty years.

When Dr. Bresee was born, this country was in a comparatively primitive condition. The great inventions which make it what it is today, were then nearly all unknown. The Mexican war was still in the future. He came to manhood before the great Civil war began. During that conflict, he was a radical Union man, and made a practice of draping his pulpit with the American flag, thus offending many Southern sympathizers, who otherwise would have been his fast friends. He was a deeply interested spectator of all the great events which took place in the world during the nearly seventy years that elapsed from the time of his boyhood to his death in 1915. His views were pronounced on all the great questions which arose during that period.

I never knew any other man who exerted so profound a personal influence upon his associates. Those who were brought into close contact with him were unconsciously to him, and unconsciously to themselves, deeply changed by their association with him. This was especially true in regard to the safeness and saneness of his judgment, his remarkable intensity of soul, and his constant insistence that holiness must always have the right-of-way. In fact, the entire Nazarene movement became imbued with these three characteristics. As Dr. Bresee so often said, the Nazarenes are the rough riders of the holiness movement. They have desperation and intensity. Holiness occupies the central place in their doctrine, polity, experience and propaganda. The work has also been peculiarly free from extravagance and fanaticism.

Words are weak for portraying a great personality. Life, character, disposition, motive, are subtle things, which largely defy analysis. Phineas F. Bresee was one of the greatest men who have arisen in the church of Christ through all the ages; and great men are seen from so many view-points that to adequately depict them as they really were, is impossible.

From early childhood, he had the settled conviction that his life work would be that of a preacher. Later, when God called him to the ministry, he had no difficulty in recognizing the genuineness of the call.

That he was divinely appointed for a great work; that he was physically and mentally endowed for a long, active and arduous career; that he was prepared and fitted by heredity, environment, training, and the stern discipline of his earlier ministry, for leadership in the mighty movement of organized holiness, is as infallibly true as the divine call of any of the men of God who have led the Church to victory in all the centuries.

God gave this man a dominating personality, and put

17

the stamp of greatness upon him so indelibly and conspicuously as to compel recognition by all with whom he was brought into close association.

The purpose of God was that he should endure hardness; that he should bear heavy burdens of responsibility; that he should labor long and incessantly in the cause of Christ; that he should make many and trying sacrifices; and that he should suffer numerous and grievous afflictions for Jesus' sake. But it was also divinely planned that he should prevail over his enemies; that he should meet with almost unbroken success in the holy conflict; that he should win many glorious victories; that he should be tenderly loved and revered by multitudes of the Lord's people; and that he should be honored during his lifetime and by his contemporaries as few great men have ever been before.

In order to meet the requirements of such a career, it was necessary that he should possess unusual physical strength, and powers of endurance that are rarely found in mortal man. Although of only medium height, his deep chest, broad shoulders and heavy frame, gave evidence of a powerful physique. So strong was he that during all the toil and hardships of the first forty years of his ministry, he rarely felt fatigue.

There is a strength which is coarse and incapable of feeling the finer things of life, or seeing the invisible beauties and glories which ever envelop us. But, although Phineas F. Bresee was big and brave and strong, his soul was as delicately poised and as sensitive to environment as an aspen-leaf.

He was nearly fifty-seven years of age when he undertook the trying task of organizing the Church of the Nazarene. It is now difficult for us to realize the true nature and vast extent of that undertaking. The church began with only a handful of members. But it was the beginning, not only of an individual church, but of a denomination and a movement. Its material necessities had to be attended to. A place of worship had to be built. A church polity had to be adopted. Dr. Bresee's task was not that of conserving a great work, but of building it from the very foundations.

18

Membership increased so rapidly that the tabernacle, as it was called, was soon enlarged. To his rapidly increasing pastoral duties were added those of legislator, editor, educator and financier. And, as other churches sprang up, the activities of superintendency grew apace. As the years passed by, his labors constantly increased, and at a time of life when most men are making arrangements to retire from active service, he was doing the labor of at least three ordinary men.

It was also requisite to his life work that he should be endowed with rare intellectual gifts, and so he was endued in a high degree with five mental traits which are thus combined in one individual only a few times in a century. These were: retentive memory, vivid imagination, keen analysis, marked synthetic ability, and the power of analogy. As a result of these and other rich gifts, he possessed that three-fold personality of poet, orator and philosopher, which has characterized every great preacher of ancient and modern times.

Seldom, indeed, is the possessor of these endowments also practical and sagacious; but Phineas F. Bresee was a strong executive and man of affairs, knowing how to manage men, master difficult situations, and thus bring things to pass for the glory of God. None could fly higher than he, or soar longer in the vast altitudes of vision, thought, and rapturous personal experience; but he was also at home on the ground. His judgment was singularly calm, and dispassionate. He róse into the upper regions at his own volition, but was never swept off his feet by any sudden gust of passion or wind of doctrine.

But, even more essential than his powers of mind and body, were a moral nature fitted to the mighty ministry into which God had called him, a soul commensurate with his service, and a spiritual life and experience, so maintained and developed by the indwelling Christ, as to respond to all the demands made upon them.

At this time I will not attempt to depict the great soul of Dr. Bresee, or to describe his Christian personality. In subsequent chapters, I will essay a characterization of the man, with whom I was brought into close and tender touch for so long a period. Suffice it to say here that he was unswerving in his loyalty to God and men. He was a faithful friend. His character was beautiful for its simplicity and deep appreciation of love and kindness. He sympathized with those who failed, was a stranger to envy, and was full of admiration for his brethren in the ministry. He was so humble that he did not realize his own strength, greatness and self-sacrifice. To use his own words, in speaking of the Regnant Man, "It was his to be kind, gentle, patient, to be buffetted and bear the burdens of men; to weep with those that wept, and to love and care for them for whom nobody else cared; to be like a river, which never competes with other streams, but opens its bosom, takes them into its life, and bears them to the great sea."

He was converted when a boy, became a circuit preacher in the Methodist church in his early youth, and was sanctified in the prime of his manhood. From the time that he came into the experience of holiness, he was a constant and flaming evangel of that glorious life and doctrine. He had a mighty passion for souls. He was filled with a burning desire to lead men and women into the kingdom of God; to induce believers to plunge into the fountain of Jesus' blood and be made every whit whole. Nothing could divert him from this one thing. He stood for holiness. He favored everything that was consistent with holiness, and opposed with all his might everything that was against it. In 1895, he began the work of the Church of the Nazarene with a handful of faithful believers. During the twenty years that intervened between that time and his death, the church of which he was the honored and beloved leader, had become a host of nearly thirty-two thousand, extending all over the American continent, with approximately eight hundred local churches, a great Publishing House, several Colleges and Universities, and scores of missionaries in every quarter of the world.

A Prince In Israel

PHINEAS F. BRESEE:
A PRINCE IN ISRAEL

CHAPTER I.

Birth and Childhood — Education — Parentage and Ancestry
— Conversion — Called to Preach.

Phineas F. Bresee was born on the 31st of December, 1838, in the town of Franklin, Delaware county, New York. Franklin is perhaps six or eight miles square, and is situated in a beautiful little valley, through which flows a charming stream called the Ouleout. Here it was that the boy Phineas fished and swam with his childish playmates.

He was born in a log house, about five miles from the village of Franklin. The whole district including his birthplace, took the name of the town of Franklin.

Doctor Bresee says of his early childhood: "I remember when I was a year old that my parents moved from where I was born to the house where I lived until I was about

Early Memories twelve years of age. With an ox team and a sled, they went over a cross road not often traveled. It was early in the spring, when most of the snow was on the ground, and just as they were going from the rough road to the turnpike, the oxen got frightened and turned to the left, off the road into the brush. I remember my father jumping off the sled and getting the oxen back into the road. I can see the scene yet. I remember when I was two years old, having a little red flannel dress with my legs bare, and burning my right thigh against the stove. My mother put cream on it, and it felt cool and nice.

"I remember before I was three years old, playing with my little brother, two years younger than I, who died when he was about a year old.

"My parents sent me to school when I was only three years of age. I came home one evening with my little primer. It had pictures in it, and I said: 'Oh, Ma! I have got clear over to the wolf.' I was so proud. I remember that still. We lived in that house, about half a mile from the valley road, until I was twelve years old."

It was a very picturesque country, and the love of natural beauty which characterized Phineas F. Bresee throughout his life, was doubtless intensified by the lovely environment of his earliest years.

From the days of his tender childhood he was taught to work on the farm, to drive horses and oxen, to attend to the cows, and to do every kind of farm work. He did not go to school very much of the time, but when he did, he attended the District School. At the age of twelve he had learned the ordinary rudimentary things. He could read and write, and knew something of arithmetic and geography. He took up the latter study before he could read. He and his schoolmates read United States history in the school. In those days he was not a good reader, but knew by heart all the things that were read in the district school. Of this stage of his boyhood, he says: "I could read first-rate the things that they ordinarily read, because I knew them by heart, but once in a great while the teacher would take a notion to have them read out of a newspaper, or some other printed matter, and I made bad work of it."

Among the wealthy people at Oneonta, which is situated on the other side of the mountains from where Phineas F. Bresee was born, were the Huntingtons and E. R. Ford. One day, the latter approached the father of Phineas, and told him that he wanted to sell or trade him a magnificent place that he owned over on the Charlotte river, which was between Oneonta and Davenport, just on the edge of the town of Davenport, and about on a line between Oneonta and Davenport. The result was that the Bresee family acquired the Ford property, turning in their farm as part payment. The new place was much more valuable than their former

24

home, and was one of the most beautiful places in all that section of country. There were so many buildings on it, that it was like a little village. Of this farm, where he lived so many years and did so much hard work, Doctor Bresee says: "There was a real good house, fine outbuildings, a wagon-house and barn, a cowhouse, a cheese and milkhouse, a corn-house, and hoghouses, all nicely painted like a little village. The dwelling was white and all the other buildings were trimmed with white. E. R. Ford's brother, Jacob, lived on this place, but did not make a success of it, and the probability is that Mr. Ford got out of heart with his brother and sold it. At any rate, we moved there just after I was twelve years old. I did not go to school much of the time while there, although there was a schoolhouse right on our place. The fact was, I was getting too smart to go to a little district school, with some young woman teacher who didn't know as much about arithmetic and algebra as I did. I think I had commenced the study of algebra. In fact, I could have gone to school to very fine advantage to almost anybody; for I couldn't spell. I never could spell. I never knew anything about grammar. The only kind of books that we had were the spelling book, the arithmetic, etc. Every winter I studied in the beginning of the spelling book about the consonants, the vowels, the diphthongs, and those things, and I never could learn them; so that a little smattering of the forepart of the spelling book, and the arithmetic, and a little reading and history, etc., was about all the education I had."

For two winters he attended a little school called an academy, at Oneonta. It was a sort of a select school, taught by Isaac T. Dann, a man of considerable talent and education. At that school, young Phineas got a start in Latin Grammar, which was the first idea he ever had of grammar of any kind. He also learned a little algebra, geometry, trigonometry, and other rudimentary things. Later for a very short time he attended the academy at Franklin village, conducted by Doctor Kerr, a man of culture, and a good teacher. The strain, however, of studying and doing farm work at the same time, was too much for Phineas, and his health gave way. That was the end of his education, so far as regular attendance at school was concerned. While he attended the Franklin academy, he became very studious, and after that he spent much time in the study of Latin, Greek, and other branches.

Of this period of his life Doctor Bresee says: "I worked on the farm very hard. My father was an exceedingly hard worker. I worked there most of the time for about four years, after which my father sold out, and we went to West Davenport, where he bought a few things in a store. It was the only store there, a kind of a general merchandise country store. My father bought a half interest in it, and in the contract of purchase, it was agreed that I was to serve as a clerk in the store."

It was while working here that Phineas was converted, but the narration of this great event in his career will be given in another place.

The name of Doctor Bresee's father was Phineas Philips Bresee. He was born in Schohanie county, New York, in 1813. He was of French and Dutch ancestry, and was

Parentage and Ancestry descended from some of the Huguenot refugees who came to America to escape from religious persecution. The family settled in New York at an early date. The name Bresee is of French origin, and signifies "Coals." The father of Phineas Philips Bresee had a large number of children, and was persuaded by his aunt, Mrs. Philips, to give her his youngest child, then in infancy. This little baby was Doctor Bresee's father. He was adopted and brought up by his aunt. Her husband's name was Phineas Philips, a man of considerable standing and wealth. He was a prominent citizen, and was generally called "Governor." The adopted boy was named after him. Not long after his adoption, the aunt of Phineas Philips Bresee died, and her husband married another woman, who had two children of her own, one of

26

whom married and continued to live in the old home. Doctor Bresee's father lived to be eighty-three years of age, and died in Los Angeles, Cal. He spent many years of his life with his distinguished son. Doctor Bresee thus characterized his father: "My father was a very hard working man. He was full of fiber, vitality and life. He had a saw mill right below our house, and he would work on the farm in the daytime and run his saw mill at night. He had a very productive place, but it was stony and hilly."

When a very young man, Phineas Philips Bresee married Miss Susan Brown, both being earnest Christians and members of the Methodist Episcopal church. She had removed from Connecticut to New York in her early childhood, and lived in the town of Merideth, adjoining Franklin. She was converted in her girlhood, and was a very devoted, earnest Christian all her life. There were three children born of this marriage. Phineas was the second child. Mrs. Susan Bresee was born in 1812, and died in Los Angeles in 1902.

In February, 1856, a protracted meeting was held in the little Methodist church, of which the parents of Doctor Bresee were members. The meeting was conducted by the pastor in charge, Rev. Smith. There were two *Conversion* pastors, and the name of the junior was Rev. George Hearn, a young Englishman, and an unmarried man. The church was really a circuit, which extended up and down the Charlotte river. In those days a married man and a single man traveled together on a circuit. This was not an invariable rule, but was the case in a large majority of instances. These two pastors held the meetings, and one day Brother Smith came to the store where Phineas was working, and spoke a few words to him about his soul. This was the means of bringing him under conviction, and he determined before night that he would go to the meeting and seek salvation. Doctor Bresee's own account of his conversion is as follows: "I went and he preached. I thought he never would get through and give

27

me a chance to go to the altar, but he did, finally, after preaching and exhorting. Nobody had been to the altar up to that time in the meeting, but he gave a chance and I went immediately and others followed. The meeting continued until Sunday. I think this was Friday night. On Sunday, there was an old minister there from New York city, by the name of Lull. They called him old Father Lull. He was a man of considerable genius and ability, and he preached in the morning. After the morning service they had a class-meeting, which was the custom in those early days; and it was during that classmeeting that I was converted, and I realized that the peace of God came into my soul at that classmeeting. I at once began to try and do Christian work. My soul was filled with great intensity for doing the work of the Lord, and I began to hold prayermeetings, talk to and exhort the people, and do all I could to push along the work. After a few months, Brother Smith gave me a license to exhort, which I proceeded not to use. I was very bashful and modest, though I tried to work and do things. He made several appointments for me, which I did not go to fill. I never had used my license for any special service, or regular public service until the next spring, when my father sold the store. I always felt called to preach from the time I was born, or began to know anything. I remember when I was a very little boy, that the leading man in the community, who lived right down near where the turnpike road turned off from the Ouleout road, spoke to me on the subject. He was Captain Miller, a large man with a good deal of dignity. He put his hand on my head, and said: 'Now what are you going to do when you are a man?' I was too embarrased to answer, but he asked me one question after another, and he said: 'You will be a minister, won't you?' And I suppose there was some response in my face. He said: 'Oh, yes; that is it. That is the noblest calling of all.' And I always wondered that everybody did not know. I thought he was smart, and that he knew that I was to be a preacher, and I wondered that everybody did n't know.

When I was just a little boy, it was as clear to me that I was to be a preacher, as it ever has been since. But by my father's contract, I was tied up in this arrangement at the store for five years from the time we began there, of which three years probably were still to run. I thought it over, and in praying about it, I said: 'Well, Lord, I am tied up here. If Thou wilt open the way, I will go.' I don't suppose it was more than two weeks until my father sold out, and I was left free to go. My father soon arranged to move to Iowa. Some of my friends insisted that I should preach before I went, and they made me an appointment down at a place called the Hemlocks, about two miles and a half from West Davenport, where there was a regular meeting on Sunday afternoons. It was the appointment of the junior preacher, but it was announced that I would preach. So I went down there with the junior preacher and preached, or tried to. That was my first sermon. I tried to preach from the text: 'My soul has escaped out of the snare of the fowler. The snare has broken and the bird has escaped.' It is in one of the Psalms. That was my first text and my first sermon. That is the one that I told the boys about, that embraced so much, that it had in it everything I knew. I was just a boy. It began away back before the creation of the world, came down through the Garden of Eden, along down to the fall, and down through the ages to the Incarnation and the Atonement, and then on through the years until the time I was born, my conversion, then on to the judgment, and on through eternity. Although I put everything I knew in it, it was only about twenty minutes long. I wondered what in the world a fellow would ever preach about at another sermon, for I had everything in that. I came to Iowa with one sermon."

A matter of some interest in connection with Doctor Bresee's middle name, is the fact that his parents called him "Phineas," and he was baptized by that name. When he grew up to manhood, he found himself without any middle name, and "Phineas" being such a common name in his family, he wanted something distinctive, and after talking it over with his parents, he insisted, and they agreed, that he should take "Franklin," the name of the town in which he was born, for his middle name.

CHAPTER II.

Early in 1857, the father of Doctor Bresee, accompanied by his son-in-law, Giles H. Cowley, went to Iowa, with the intention of moving there if they were pleased with the country. While there, they bought a farm out on the prairie, after which the father returned to New York state, with the object of coming to Iowa later with his family. The son-in-law remained in Iowa, where in June he was joined by Phineas, the rest of the family removing there later in the summer, when they all settled on the prairie and lived in a log house. Doctor Bresee described the scene as follows: "Oh, how beautiful the prairies looked to me in June — great stretches of them, with nothing but green grass and flowers, waving in the breezes. I never will forget when I first saw those prairies. We lived there and worked on the farm two or three months. My brother-in-law and I boarded at a place where it was hard to get enough to eat, but we used to go out after dinner and eat watermelons and trout, and fill up. It was just astonishing how much fun we had that summer. We used to say that once in awhile the old lady where we boarded would try to have something extra, and that she képt an old rooster there, and when she wanted to make chicken for us, she would take the old rooster and lead him around a ditch, and when she wanted to make it extra good, she would lead him through. We lived there and worked those months. Then my father and mother and sister came, and they lived there."

It was in the fall of 1857, that Phineas went on his first circuit. Their farm was about six or seven miles west of Millersburg, on the road that went directly west through the state. The next town, fourteen miles west of them, was Montezuma. Much of Iowa was a wilderness in those

31

days, and was unsettled prairie. Their home was along the fringes of civilization. Comparatively little religious work was being done. Here and there a meeting was held in a schoolhouse or a private home. A church was a rare thing, but there were a few scattered over the country, and in some of the towns. A pressing demand existed for somebody to hold meetings, and Phineas immediately responded to that demand. The people finding out that he was an exhorter, called on him to preach. Occasionally, when he did not have a meeting at the church of which he was a member, he would go to Millersburg, where at that time there was a Methodist class, and later he united with this class. I will quote from Doctor Bresee as to this occasion: "On Saturday I went to the quarterly meeting. We walked seven miles to Millersburg, through the dust and dirt of the road. I arrived towards night. The Saturday morning meeting and the quarterly conference were both past. William Simpson, a distant relative of Bishop Simpson — a second cousin I think — who was a man of sterling worth and character and of good ability, was a frontier preacher at that time. He was one of the early preachers in Iowa, and a great, strong fellow, six feet high, with black hair, and a big heart. He was the Presiding Elder. I think that he had called upon the preacher to give the message on Saturday morning. He was telling me about it, and he said that the sermon had one redeeming quality — it was short. But he insisted on my preaching Saturday night. They had a custom in those days of appointing some boy preacher to fill the pulpit on Saturday nights, at the quarterly meeting. I thought I had to do as I was told, so I tried to preach. I preached from the text about the healing of the man with the weak ankles, where Peter and John were going up into the temple. I had a good time, and evidently Simpson was greatly pleased with me. Seemingly I was a promising young lad, and those old fellows always had their eyes out for the boys, to get them. As I heard Bishop Janes say one day when he was preaching with all his might on the ministry — sud-

32

denly pausing in his sermon: 'Brother, brother, get hold of the boys; get hold of the boys. Get them out on the circuit before these college presidents and professors get hold of them.' They worked on that principle.

"So Simpson said that he was going to hold a campmeeting over along the Iowa river, at Kosta, early in the fall of 1857, and he insisted that I should come to that campmeeting.

He said that he would have the class at Kosta recom-*Kosta* mend me to that quarterly conference, and would have me licensed to preach, and recommended to the Annual Conference, and that I should unite with the Conference. It was necessary for him to take that course, because the quarterly conference at Kosta, of which I speak, had adjourned. Simpson arranged with the preacher to do that, and I did n't hear anything more of it. I went to the campmeeting about twenty miles over on the Iowa river. There were a live set of Methodists over there, at Kosta, a strong class of really hallelujah people. So Simpson put me up to preach, and I tried to preach the best I could. However, the people who belonged to the class at Millersburg, and who did n't know anything about me, or know me at all, but had only seen me two or three times, said that, although they were not acquainted with me, still if I could preach any, they needed me very much in that country, and that it was not worth while to recommend me to this other quarterly conference, because they had plenty for me to do there. Accordingly they refused to recommend me. So when Simpson came to the campmeeting, I was there, and he found no recommendation; but in those days they had a way of doing things, anyway. He said that it did n't make any difference; he was going to recommend me, and he recommended me to the quarterly conference, and had me licensed and recommended to the Annual Conference; after which they requested that I be sent to that circuit as the junior preacher, which was done."

Rev. A. C. Barnhart was the preacher in charge. He was a man of great hortatory force and a very good man. Although not a great preacher, he could exhort and pray, and sing his way through. This was a four weeks' circuit. It extended from some place between Marengo and Iowa City, west, for about fifteen or twenty miles, up the Iowa river, then directly west across the prairies an equal distance, and then extended south to Brooklyn. At that point it turned east again and went down into Iowa county to Williamsburg, and then back to Marengo. This was the Marengo circuit. Marengo was the county seat of Iowa county.

In the northwest part of that circuit there lived a man named Jones. The place was so isolated that it was commonly called "Davy Jones' Locker." Nevertheless, the people would gather together there to attend meet-
Davy ings. It looked as if there was not another human
Jones' being living within the range of vision anywhere
Locker in the neighborhood. However, many of the set-
tlers who lived in little cottages which were out of sight, would come with their oxen, wagons, horses, guns, babies and older children, and people would gather from far and near. During the service, Mrs. Jones would prepare dinner for them all. Although the Jones family lived in a log house, amid somewhat primitive conditions, rousing religious services were held there, and the Lord greatly blessed the efforts of the young preacher. In June, 1908, when Doctor Bresee, fifty years after the meetings held in the log house of Brother Jones, was dedicating the Pentecostal Church of the Nazarene at Berkeley, Cal., he told in his sermon about something that had occurred at one of these meetings in Davy Jones' Locker. At the conclusion of the service, an old gentleman came forward, and said that his name was Jones, that he was the son of the Jones that lived in the old log house, and that he was a small boy when Doctor Bresee was on that circuit. He stated that his mother had written to him not long before to the effect that Doctor Bresee was somewhere on the Pacific Coast, and that if he ever discovered his whereabouts, he was to bear her remembrances to him.

Doctor Bresee held protracted meetings all over the circuit in 1857 and 1858, and a great revival took place at Marengo. Among those who were converted, was Judge Miller, one of the most prominent men in the *Revival* community. He happened to come to a testimony *at* meeting, where Brother Barnhard was calling on *Marengo* different persons to tell what they thought about salvation, and he asked the Judge, who was not a Christian man, to tell what he thought. He replied that he did not know as he believed in religion at all, and then sat down. As he afterward related his experience, the Devil said: "Now, you know you are a liar. You know you believe in religion." He said that Satan tormented him in this way until he got under conviction and was powerfully converted.

Doctor Bresee narrated a rather amusing incident which occurred at one of the protracted meetings at Brooklyn. To put it in his words: "Brother Barnhard went ahead to begin the services, and I was to fill the appointment and come later. A few days after he opened the meeting, I came and stopped at the hotel. They were Methodist people. I saw these same people many years afterward, and we had quite a laugh over what occurred.

"As I sat in the hotel parlor, I remarked, 'Well, Brother Barnhard, how does the meeting go?' He said, 'Pretty well.' I said, 'I had such a strange dream about you.' He said, 'What was it?' 'Well,' I said, 'I dreamed that you and I went fishing, and were fishing along down the brook, with our hands, catching some fishes, quite nice fish, and all at once you stirred up a snake, and it stood right up before you, and ran out its tongue at you, and you had a tremendous fight with that snake.' 'Well,' he said, 'That is a true vision. I have caught some fish, and I have seen the snake.' He referred to a certain woman that was in the meeting, and gave me a little description of the occurrence. Who heard us talking we never knew, but our conversation was overheard, and that woman was told about it. As a result, she got up in the meeting and abused Barnhard, just as the snake had attacked him in my dream."

In the autumn of 1858, Dr. Bresee was sent to Pella. This town had been founded by a Holland colony, led by a distinguished exile from Holland, who induced a large number of Hollanders to come to this country. With them he established on the prairie a town which has now become quite a city. It was then a place of three or four thousand inhabitants, with one little Methodist church. It was what was called a half station. There was preaching in town every Sunday morning and night, and in the surrounding country there were afternoon appointments. Doctor Bresee was there two years. It was a difficult appointment because of the Dutch element, and the comparatively small number of English-speaking people. Around the Baptist college there had gathered quite a number of the members of that denomination, so that the English-speaking people of the place were quite predominantly Baptist, and the Methodist work was difficult. Nevertheless, God blessed the young preacher and gave him revivals during the two years of his pastorate in Pella.

Sent to Pella

CHAPTER III.

Marriage and Early Ministry in Iowa — Sent to Grinnell —
The Civil War — The Galesburg Circuit — Hard-
ships and Privations — A Great Crisis —
Success in the Work.

At the close of his pastorate in Pella, in the latter part of
the year 1860, and shortly before the session of the conference, Doctor Bresee returned to New York, where he was
united in marriage to Miss Maria E. Hibbard. She belonged
to a prominent Methodist family, and was distantly related
to the somewhat renowned Uncle Billy, whose son, Dr. F. G.
Hibbard, a leader in Methodism, wrote "Hibbard on Baptism," and other works. Mrs. Bresee's family lived in Davenport, N. Y., near where the parents of Phineas had taken
up their residence five or six years previous, so that the acquaintance, which ripened into love and matrimony, began
at that time. The Hibbard residence was only about three
miles from the store where Phineas worked, and the little
church which he attended was closely allied to that of
which she was a member, was a part of the same general charge, and was under the same preacher. At the time
of Doctor Bresee's conversion, the two families were brought
into quite intimate relationship. Mrs. Bresee's brother Nat,
and Phineas, became very warm friends, and the latter frequently visited the home of the former before going to Iowa.
However, Phineas and Maria were not engaged until a few
months before their marriage. Of this period, Doctor Bresee says: "While in Iowa, I corresponded with my wife's
brother, but I did not correspond regularly with her until
I made up my mind that I would propose marriage to her.
I began to write to her with that object in view. We became
engaged by letter. I had become very intimately acquainted
with her family and was often at the house with her brother
Nat, and he frequently came to my house. He was a magnificent fellow, a beautiful character. He joined the army,
came home after the Civil war, in rather broken health, and

37

died after our marriage. My wife's whole family were Christians. Her father was a class leader and Sunday school superintendent. His name was Horace Hibbard. He was regarded as one of the most staunch and prominent Methodists in that part of the state. My wife's mother was a very model woman. They had five children, who were all very earnest and active Methodists. The family was one of the best in that whole land, and was so regarded. They had a very nice home on a farm about half a mile from Davenport Center, overlooking the Charlotte Valley. One of Mrs. Bresee's nephews still lives there."

Two or three weeks after their marriage, the young couple went to Iowa. It meant a great deal to Mrs. Bresee to leave a fine home and go out on the frontier. Her parents, *Return to Iowa* although approving the marriage, were opposed to her making the sacrifice, and her mother reminded her of the fact that she was of a diffident nature and slow to make warm and intimate friends. She told her that if she went to Iowa, she would leave all her friends behind her, and would be compelled to live among strangers. But Maria, like Rebecca of old, did not hesitate to leave her father's house and those who were near and dear to her, to respond not only to the dictates of her heart, but also to what she regarded as the will of her Savior, of whom she was a devoted follower. Phineas took his bride to the home of his parents for a little visit, and from there they went to the annual conference, which was held at Oskaloosa, Iowa.

He had been a member of the conference three years, and was sent to Grinnell. The place took its name from J. B. Grinnell, who was a member of Congress and a great Abolitionist. He went from New England to Iowa, *Appointed to Grinnell* and founded the town and college of Grinnell. It was a place of a thousand or fifteen hundred inhabitants. Brother Bresee was assigned to a circuit, with five or six appointments, which made it necessary to preach three times every Sunday.

While there, the Civil war began, and it was a time of great hardship. Heretofore the money in use had consisted of currency issued by the state banks, but shortly after the

The Civil War
beginning of hostilities, it became practically worthless. Under these circumstances, it was extremely difficult to obtain the necessaries of life, and business was almost paralyzed. For a time the people had to get along the best they could without money. It was

under these circumstances that Mrs. Bresee was compelled to use a little gold dollar, which had been presented to her by her husband, for the purpose of buying postage stamps to enable her to correspond with her family in New York state. Of course, there was great excitement, and war conditions were not favorable to spiritual life. Nevertheless, the young preacher met with a fair degree of success, and there were revivals at most of his appointments. I can not better bescribe these times than by quoting from Dr. Bresee:

"The first soldiers were called out that year. One of the first who volunteered in this part of the country, was a member of our church, and the people were horrified at the idea of a man leaving his family and children and going to the war. I will never forget the awful feeling. We stayed at Grinnell one year. We lived largely on faith. You would hardly believe that one sack of flour, with a few pounds of buckwheat to make pancakes, did us that year. My wife had clothes enough when she was married, so that she did not have to buy more. I did not need anything much, and we got on. Still we were in debt somewhat when we left that circuit, a thing that I never allowed to occur again. Although the people did not support us so that we could keep out of debt, they strenuously believed that it was bad in a preacher not to pay his debts, which is true. But when a minister got in debt for something to live on, because the people did n't pay him, it was not an unforgivable crime. They desired my return very much to that circuit, but the war had already begun, and one of the appointments was made up largely of Southern people. They were very strong in their feeling of sympathy with the Rebellion, and I was very strong in my loyalty, and anti-slavery conviction. Hence, I did not feel that it was best for the church on that charge for me to go back. I had already more or less grieved these people by my preaching of what they regarded as Abolition doctrine, and I saw that it would be very difficult for me to get along with them. So I told the Presiding Elder that I did not want to go back. He intimated to me that I might get a poorer appointment." This turned out to be a true prophecy, as we will see.

When the appointments were read at conference, young Bresee was sent to what was called the Galesburg circuit, which was made up of the "tail ends" of two or three other circuits. It was out on the prairie, without center or circumference, having no churches and no parsonage. There were half a dozen places for preaching, mostly in schoolhouses. The little hamlet which gave its name to the charge, had in it perhaps twenty persons, living in a cluster of four or five houses. Of this crisis in his ministry, Doctor Bresee says: "The appointment, of course, seemed to me considerable of a hardship, as I had appeared to have had very fair success and much better appointments. I felt grieved about it, though I did not give any expression to the feeling. It was in going there that there came over me such an awful determination that, if there was anything in the country, it should go; the thing should move — such an awful determination to win and succeed in accomplishing something. I had a very good horse, which I immediately traded off to get a poorer horse, and money enough to pay my debts on the circuit where I had lived, so that there need be no feeling of lack of confidence in a Methodist preacher."

The only place they could secure in which to live, was one room with a very small bedroom connected with it, access to which was gained solely by going through the living room of the people who owned the house. Into this place they moved with Ernest, their first child, who was born

40

while his father was at conference. They dwelt in these quarters for several months. The young preacher told his brethren that, as there was no money in the country, anything that they brought for quarterage, from chips to saw mills, would be very acceptable. Most of the quarterage was paid in wheat and dressed hogs. The young folks had a large bin filled with wheat, and were given such vegetables as the country produced.

In the midst of the year, a preacher by the name of J. H. Early, was driven out of Missouri by the Ku Klux, as were most of the preachers of the Methodist Episcopal church at that time. In those days, Missouri was too hot a place for Methodist preachers of what they called the "Church North." Brother Early had a span of small horses and a light wagon, in which he had escaped from Missouri. As he had to earn a living, Doctor Bresee suggested to him that they hire eighty acres of prairie land in that vicinity which had been broken up by the plow, the idea being that Bresee would furnish the wheat, and Early could use his team to cultivate the land. As a result of this agricultural enterprise, which was fairly successful, young Bresee was able to sell his wheat and get a little money. He determined that he would not get in debt again, and in order to assist him in carrying out this resolve, he bought a pair of little mules, and broke them.

I remember talking to Doctor Bresee about these mules a short time before his death, and the mention of the little animals provoked a smile, and awakened pleasant memories. On a prior occasion he described the mules as follows: "They made the gayest little team that I ever saw. They were just two rabbits in their get-up and travel. I put a tongue in my old buggy, and there was sleighing all winter, the finest sleighing I ever saw. I got me a little sleigh in some way, and used to drive those mules. They were the greatest team I ever drove. If I wanted to go five or six miles, they would run with all their might. One fellow said 'that preacher Bresee would drive the Devil to death,' and I

41

suggested to him that I would undertake the job, if he would hitch him up. One of those mules was the wildest, ugliest animal that almost ever lived. I found out afterward that a man could hardly go in the barn yard where he was. After I bought him, they put him in the barn, got a rope around his neck and tied him up in the stall. When I came home, Brother Butin, who owned the stable, and in whose house we lived, came running in all out of breath, saying, 'Brother Bresee, that animal you got down there will kick the roof off the barn.' He said that I would have to do something with him. I went out, and, sure enough, he was kicking the furthest for his size of any animal I ever saw. I picked up a little trace chain, and as he kicked so, I struck him with this trace chain two or three times — a very small, fine chain it was — and scared him almost to death. I never had any trouble with him after that, except what would arise from his fear of me. I would come home and unharness that mule, or harness him, the darkest night. The little mules served me nicely for a time. A man took a fancy to them, and wanted to trade me out of them; so for those mules and the little buggy I had and the harness, I got a big, five-year-old horse, a new, two-horse harness and another buggy, not quite as good as the one I let him have, and fifty dollars. Out of that outfit, I got me a splendid pair of horses, a fine team and a new harness — nice brass-plated harness — and kept the same buggy. So that year I had a good living, paid my debts, and went to conference with just as fine a team as you would see anywhere."

That year at Galesburg was a great crisis in the life of young Bresee. It tested his mental caliber, and brought to the surface and into action qualities which might otherwise *A Great* have lain dormant for years. Of this time in his *Crisis* life he says: "In regard to this awful impulse which was upon me that things should go, I do not know whether it was so much a matter of inspiration of the Spirit, or whether it came out of my deep indignation at the kind of appointment I had received. It may not have been intensely spiritual or religious. I can hardly define it, but it was an awful feeling of determination that things should go. I have sometimes said that it reminded me of the fellow who met the bear, and began to pray. He finally told the Lord that if he would n't help him, not to help the bear, and he would see one of the biggest fights that ever happened. I had that kind of feeling. It should go, anyhow; it should go; live or die, it should go. I thought that the Lord would help me, but if He did not help me, it should go any way. I did not put it in that way, but that was about the spirit of it. I was in desperation."

On the first Sunday of his work in that circuit, he announced that in two weeks he would begin a protracted meeting at one of his six appointments, and pledged the *Revival* people to such support as he could obtain from them. This meeting began in October and lasted *Methods* until spring, the revival services extending over the six appointments. The young circuit rider preached the best he could. He visited the people, who were interested and came in such numbers that they filled the large schoolhouses, where the meetings were held. After preaching, Brother Bresee would give the invitation for seekers to come to the altar, and if they did not respond, he would go out among the people. As soon as he had induced some one to admit the need of salvation, and kneel down, he would jump on a bench, and call to the members of the church to gather round, thus turning the back of the place of meeting into an altar. In this and every other possible way, he charged the Enemy, and recklessly threw himself into the conflict. As a result, to use his own words, "The Lord gave him the country." He once remarked to me of this period of his life: "That charge did me more good than any I ever had. It broke me up, and broke through the chrysalis that was about me, and in some way taught me and impressed me that desperation, earnestness, intensity, would win, God helping, in doing God's work."

That year he took one hundred and forty people into the

church, and the revival fire burned from one end of the circuit to the other. In the spring, he bought a comfortable parsonage, and moved into it with his family. At the expiration of the year, he desired to remain, but the Presiding Elder sent him to Des Moines. He had won his spurs that year. It was the biggest thing in the District. He and Sister Bresee had many dear friends there, who were greatly grieved that they did not stay.

CHAPTER IV.

In the autumn of 1862, Brother and Sister Bresee began
their work in the pastorate of one of the two Methodist
Episcopal churches in Des Moines. It was in the eastern
part of the city, and was in the Iowa Con-
First Pastorate ference, the dividing line between that con-
in Des Moines ference and what was then known as the
Southwestern Iowa Conference, was the
Des Moines river, which then as now divided the city into
two parts. At that time the population of Des Moines was
not more than 6,000.

The church was in a very bad condition. The building
had been erected entirely with borrowed money. The former
pastor who had arranged for the building of the church,
had secured a loan of the money and given the church's note
for the indebtedness, to be paid in gold coin with interest
at ten per cent. At this period, gold had so enhanced in
value that it was worth two and a half times as much as
paper money. This, of course, greatly augmented the debt
of the church, which was on the verge of dissolution. But
there were a few good, earnest people there. Brother Bresee had learned the lesson of desperation, and he at once
began to drive on the Enemy. The Lord gave them a revival which lasted all the year. During his pastorate of two
years, the church was rebuilt and arrangements made to
compromise on favorable terms with the holder of the indebtedness, who offered to accept a sum equal in value to the
property of the church.

Among the first services held in the new church was the
Watch Night meeting. During those two years in Des

45

Moines, the Lord had given Brother Bresee almost a constant tide of salvaion — no very great outbreak at any one time — but a state of revival, which gradually strengthened the church, and put it in a comparatively strong condition in every way.

During their stay in Des Moines, a beautiful little girl, their second child, was born to Brother and Sister Bresee. They named her Lily, and, as will appear later, she died in her infancy. Among those who were especially *Birth of* helpful to Brother Bresee during his pastorate in *Lily* Des Moines, was Mr. James Wright, the Secretary of State. He was an unusually faithful, earnest, and efficient worker, and as Sunday school superintendent rendered valuable services. During the rebuilding of the church, Mr. Wright secured the use of the state house for the Sunday school, which was very large.

During their residence in Des Moines, the church grew and flourished, and Brother and Sister Bresee were well provided for, lived comfortably and rejoiced in the Lord.

In the meantime, the financial condition of the *Improved* country had greatly improved. Large amounts *Financial* of paper currency had been issued by the gov- *Conditions* ernment and were in general circulation. The purchase of cavalry horses on a large scale seemed to be the first noticeable agency in making times better, and shortly after that the soldiers began to send money home. As a result of these and other things, prices went up and money was abundant. Although the currency was inflated, it performed all the functions of money, and times rapidly improved.

In the latter part of the year 1864, and a little preceding the session of the conference, Brother and Sister Bresee went to New York on a visit, taking with them their two little children. While in New York, the baby's illness detained them beyond the session of the Annual Conference. Shortly before this, the General Conference had changed the time of possible pastoral service from two to three years. Brother Bresee was very much opposed to this change, and for that reason, declined to serve the third year at Des Moines, although urged to do so by his church.

Upon his return to Iowa, he learned that he had been appointed as Presiding Elder of the Winterset District, where as soon as possible, he removed with his family and

Appointed Presiding Elder

remained for two years. The district was a very large one, embracing about seven counties, and extending from near Des Moines to the Missouri river. It was before the days of railroads and telegraphs, and the district spread widely over the great prairies. There were frequently long distances between the settlements, and Brother Bresee sometimes had to drive thirty miles between habitations. He traveled with a pair of ponies and a buggy.

These trips gave him exceptional opportunities for reading, study and thought, and many times he would read all day as he drove across the prairies. During those two years,

Reading and Study

he read the "History of the United States," by Bancroft; Motley's "United Netherlands," "The Rise of the Dutch Republic," and many other books. He held great quarterly meetings throughout the district. People came long distances, staying over Saturday and Sunday, and they had salvation and blessing. Brother Bresee preached frequently, and did evangelistic work as well, holding meetings for the brethren on their charges and pushing the battle. His health became impaired under the strain, but he kept at work just as hard as ever. Whenever he could, he took Mrs. Bresee with him on his long trips over the district, which took from two to four weeks.

On one of those trips, they went to Lewis, Cass county, where Brother Bresee was helping in a meeting, and their little girl, Lily, became sick and died. Although the people were mostly strangers, they were very kind, raising money to help the sorrowing parents, and doing everything possible for their comfort. One of the sisters of the church accompanied them on the long eighty-mile drive to Des Moines, where the parents and sister of Brother Bresee resided. Taking with them the body of their precious little one, they left Lewis in the afternoon, spent the night at the house of a friend, and reached Des Moines late the next night. Little Lily died on the 7th of May, at the age of fifteen months, leaving Brother and Sister Bresee with their eldest son Ernest, who at that time was a very delicate boy. In December of the same year, 1865, Phineas W., the second son of Brother and Sister Bresee, was born.

The year 1866, was the centennial of Methodism, and was celebrated all over the United States. There was a great flame of enthusiasm throughout the Winterset District, and largely attended meetings were held in groves and churches, celebrating *The Centennial* the anniversary of the coming of Philip *of Methodism* Embury and Barbara Heck to New York, and the beginning of the work of Methodism in the United States.

It was in the autumn of that year that Brother Bresee finished his work as Presiding Elder. He persuaded Bishop Ames that it was not best for him to continue longer on the district, as he was overtaxed physically. This condition was largely due to the irregularities in the way of diet, which he was compelled to undergo. At the close of the evening meetings, he frequently had to go several miles to a place of entertainment, and after arriving there was compelled to wait until supper was prepared. After eating a late meal, he would snatch a few hours sleep, get up before daylight, and eat breakfast by candle light. Then would come the early morning prayermeeting, the lovefeast at 9 o'clock, and the preaching at 10:30. After the regular morning service, the sacrament of the Lord's Supper was held, and the meeting generally would not close until after two o'clock in the afternoon. Under these circumstances, Brother Bresee had no appetite for breakfast, was feeling faint when the time came for him to preach, and later on when dinner was finally ready, would be almost too weak to eat. Still later in the day, out-of-door meetings were held in the grove, and the preaching there seemed greatly beyond his strength.

At the conference in 1866, a very pathetic incident occurred. Arrangements had been made there, as at all the other conferences, for a great anniversary of Methodism, and Dr. U. P. Golliday had been selected to preach the anniversary sermon. He was a man of considerable eloquence and ability, and was a cousin of Dr. Jos. H. Trimble, who, it seems, had the distinction of being the first man in this country who had graduated from a distinctively Methodist college and subsequently entered the Methodist ministry. His father was Governor Trimble, of Ohio. Joseph H. Trimble was present at this conference, and between his family and that of Dr. Golliday, there had grown up in the past a wide separation, which had much to do with Dr. Golliday's embarrasment on that occasion. A great crowd had gathered, and Dr. Golliday took for his text: "A handful of corn in the top of the mountains shaketh like Lebanon," etc. He spoke perhaps a dozen or twenty sentences, and stopped. It seemed that everything was blank to him. He began at the beginning, and came right up to the same place and stopped. The congregation sang a verse, and he commenced once more, but when he reached the same point he again stopped. It was impossible for him to proceed, and putting his face down on the Bible, he wept bitterly. His inability to remember even the outline of the sermon he had prepared, was the more remarkable from the fact that he was an exceedingly fluent speaker, and the possessor of an unusually large vocabulary. Some one suggested that Dr. Trimble go on with the service. He did so, and made an off-hand address on the "Rise and History of Methodism."

During all the time that Brother Bresee was Presiding Elder of the Winterset District, he was passing through an

A Pathetic Incident

awful experience along the line of doubt. To use his own
words: "I had a big load of carnality on hand
A Peculiar always, but it had taken the form of anger,
Temptation and pride, and worldly ambition. At last,
however, it took the form of doubt. It seemed
as though I doubted everything. I thought it was intellectual, and undertook to answer it. I thought that probably I had gone into the ministry so early in life, that I had
never answered the great questions of being, and of God,
and of destiny and sin and the atonement, and I undertook
to answer these great questions. I studied hard to so
answer them as to settle the problems which filled my mind
with doubt. Over and over again, I suppose a thousand
times, I built and rebuilt the system of faith, and laid the
foundation of revelation, the atonement, the new birth,
destiny, and all that, and tried to assure myself of their
truth. I would build a pyramid, and walk about it and
say: 'It is so. I know it is so. It is in accord with revelation. It is in accord with my intuitions. It is in accord
with history and human experience. It is so, and I do not
question it.' And I would not get through the assertions of
my certainty, before the Devil or something else, would say,
'Suppose it is n't so, after all?' And my doubts would not
be any nearer settled than they were before."

In the fall of 1866, Brother and Sister Bresee went to
Chariton, the county seat of Lucas county. It was a pretty
little city of about 3,000 inhabitants. The Methodist church
was the strong church of the town, having a
Appointed good congregation, with some wealth, and a
to considerable degree of worldliness. Brother
Chariton Bresee, in narrating this chapter in his career,
says that he kept about a quarter of the congregation angry at him all the time, but not the same quarter, as they took turns. He did this by preaching to them
about their worldliness and needs, and, to put it in his
words, "They seemed peculiarly adapted to not liking it
very well." One dear sister said, "He will never get me

50

mad," and the very next Sunday she went home feeling very much offended. He preached to them one morning on their idolatry, and told them that they were worshiping the world, and were without God. At the classmeeting which followed this service, the local preacher, who had been a traveling preacher, but was broken down in health, said that it was very difficult for him to have things properly adjusted; that whatever he did, he did with all his might; and when he went to college, he studied with all his might; and when he preached, he preached with all his might; and now that he was a farmer he farmed with all his might. He concluded his remarks by saying: "If I don't get to heaven, I will be the worst disappointed fellow you ever saw."

Winter came on and they were in the midst of a protracted meeting, but the terrible doubt which tortured Brother Bresee during his Presiding Eldership, continued to plague him. To again quote his words: *Is Sanctified* "There came one of those awful, snowy, windy nights, such as blow across the Western plains occasionally, with the thermometer twenty degrees below zero. Not many were out to church that night. I tried to preach a little, the best I could. I tried to rally the people to the altar, the few that were there, and went back to the stove, and tried to get somebody to the Lord. I did not find any one. I turned toward the altar; in some way it seemed to me that this was my time, and I threw myself down across the altar and began to pray for myself. I had come to the point where I seemingly could not go on. My religion did not meet my needs. It seemed as though I could not continue to preach with this awful question of doubt on me, and I prayed and cried to the Lord. I was ignorant of my own condition. I did not understand in reference to carnality. I did not understand in reference to the provisions of the atonement. I neither knew what was the matter with me, nor what would help me. But, in my ignorance, the Lord helped me, drew me and impelled me, and, as I cried to Him that night, He seemed to open heaven

51

on me, and gave me, as I believe, the baptism with the Holy Ghost, though I did not know either what I needed, or what I prayed for. But it not only took away my tendencies to worldliness, anger and pride, but it also removed the doubt. For the first time, I apprehended that the conditions of doubt were moral instead of intellectual, and that doubt was a part of carnality that could only be removed as the other works of the flesh are removed."

Under the ministry of Brother Bresee, the work at Chariton was fairly prosperous. The Lord gave him more grace, liberty and blessing in every way. He held a good revival meeting with some fruits. It seemed, however, as if there was always a fuss in reference to something. The folks were stirred up about tobacco, or worldliness, or something else. But many friends rallied around them. They met with good success, and the church grew and prospered. As Dr. Bresee put it, "Nobody got sanctified but myself, and I did not know anything about it." There was an uplift of spirituality, and one or two seemed to enter into the experience of full salvation. But, as Brother Bresee preached a more spiritual gospel, there was more antagonism.

The two years pastorate at Chariton was a trying time. When the Bresees went there, they found no proper conditions for a minister's family. As there was no parsonage, they moved into a part of a house, where they *Hardships* had the use of one room and a little bedroom, which had been changed into a kitchen. A young woman of the family, lived in the other room, taught music, and played the piano to the point of distraction. The members of the family, however, were fine people and the mother, Mrs. Mitchell, was a mother in Israel. Her son was a Methodist preacher, who in 1912, was still living in Northwestern Iowa. His name was Bennett Mitchell, and he was then Presiding Elder of the district in which Chariton was located. Often the mother and her daughters would take care of the baby while Mrs. Bresee went to church at night. The room occupied by the Bresees was their bedroom, study, dining room, parlor and everything but the kitchen. They were compelled to make beds on the floor.

Shortly before leaving Chariton, in the autumn of 1868, their daughter, Bertha, was born. At the beginning of their second year in this place, they secured a cottage with four rooms, where they lived very comfortably, so far *Bertha* as house room was concerned, but they were *Is Born* greatly tried financially, and as Doctor Bresee expressed it: "There never was a time when we had as much difficulty in getting along, and getting something to eat, as during our second year there. I do not know how or why it was, but there was not anything in the market, and we did not have money to get along with. We left the charge in debt. We did n't have butter, meat, or the ordinary things. We fared very hard indeed. I do not know that we went hungry, but we lived in the most frugal way. We were like old Brother Thayer, who said that he did n't know that the Lord had allowed him to go hungry, but he had allowed him sometimes to have a most excellent appetite."

CHAPTER V.

At the conference in the autumn of 1868, Brother and Sister Bresee were sent to their former church at Des Moines. It was a very good charge. They had left it in a prosperous condition four years before.

Sanctification This second pastorate was of two years
of Mrs. Wright duration. During the first year of his pastorate in Des Moines, Brother Bresee called a 9 o'clock morning meeting, which continued for a number of days. At one of these meetings, Mrs. E. M. Wright, a very quiet little woman, the wife of the deputy Secretary of Stat, suddenly entered into the experience of full salvation, and, without any warning, fell over in her seat. She had been seeking holiness for some time, and the Lord wonderfully sanctified her. Brother Bresee, without realizing it, had been preaching holiness to the best of his ability. Mrs. Wright had a very remarkable experience, and an unction, power, victory and transformation, surpassing that of any other person that Dr. Bresee ever knew. She wrote her experience and her pastor sent it to Mrs. Phoebe Palmer to be published in the "Guide to Holiness." Mr. Wright took the creeping paralysis and got worse and worse through the long, long months and years. He had two children, and came to know much poverty, losing his position and also his salary as deputy Secretary of State, under his brother. Through all the bitter trials that came to her, Sister Wright never flagged or faltered, and always had victory and glory. There were several others sanctified at the same series of meetings. Otherwise, this pastorate was not very eventful. Towards the end of the two years spent at Des Moines, Brother and Sister Bresee again visited New York.

In the fall of 1870, largely as a result of arrangements

54

made by Rev. Joseph Knotts, the Presiding Elder of the Council Bluffs District, Brother Bresee was appointed to
Appointed to Council Bluffs the Broadway church in Council Bluffs. Knotts was a comparatively young man, a West Virginian, who had come to Iowa in early life. He was in Des Moines at the time of Brother Bresee's first appointment there, and they came to be warm friends.

The pastorate at Council Bluffs was an eventful one and lasted three years. The church building was new, well appointed and commodious. It had been built a few years previously under the pastorate of Rev. Knotts. Afterward difficulties had arisen and the church became heavily embarrassed with debt.

The Council Bluffs District was a very difficult field. It was steeped with Mormonism. The Mormons upon their departure from Nauvoo, Ill., stopped at Council Bluffs, where
The Mormons they established their headquarters. Rev. William Simpson, the first Presiding Elder of Brother Bresee, was sent to Council Bluffs as a missionary, while the Mormons were there, and the conflict between him and them became rather severe. On one occasion they invited him to preach in their temple. He accepted the invitation, and took for his text, "The Frogs at Armageddon." He said that Armageddon meant simply a pleasant gathering; that Council Bluffs was Armageddon, and that the frogs were a very apt type of the Mormons. In the first place, frogs were very fond of water. That was pre-eminently true of the Mormons. They baptized every time they sinned, and thought that they thus washed away their sins. The frogs were also covered with a slimy covering. This represented the doctrines of the Mormons. He then undertook to show how slimy they were. In the next place, he said frogs made a specialty of croaking, which was emphatically true of the Mormons. Frogs also possessed a peculiar ability in the way of swelling. He had heard of one in Aesop's Fables that had tried to swell to be as big as

an ox. This also was true of the Mormons. In the next place, frogs when they became numerous grew very troublesome, and down in Egypt there got to be too many of them. This, he said, was especially true of the Mormons. He then took up their history at Nauvoo and the difficulties that they had fomented. He concluded by showing how troublesome they were in a general way.

As a result of this discourse, the Mormons anathematized Simpson, and placed him under their curse. He was a large, powerful man, and when he shook his head, it was like a lion shaking his mane. He told those Mormons and the world at large that he was resting under a Mormon curse, and that ,if anything happened to him, or his family, or his property, he would hold the Mormons responsible for it. They finally removed the curse from him. Subsequently two of his children died. He made the coffins himself, dug their graves with his own hands, and conducted their funeral services.

Council Bluffs was laid in Mormonism. The city was cursed with whiskey, gambling, and debauchery. This condition of affairs was due not only to Mormonism, but to the fact that Council Bluffs was in early days on the extreme western frontier of civilization, and was the outfitting place for the multitudes who crossed the plains.

Where the old Broadway church stood, and where the Broadway Methodist Episcopal church still stands, was once the old Ocean Wave saloon. This groggery had the reputation of being the worst place between the Atlantic and Pacific oceans.

Church life in Council Bluffs was always difficult to maintain and propagate. The congregations of all the churches were comparatively small, and wickedness and worldliness were in the ascendency. Nevertheless, during the pastorate of Brother Bresee, the congregation grew, the church prospered, and there was a good tide of salvation. Several persons were sanctified during this pastorate.

During his ministerial labors in Council Bluffs, and at

the conference of 1871, Brother Bresee was elected to the General Conference, which was held in Brooklyn, N. Y., in

Elected to General Conference the spring of 1872. It was in 1871, that his third son and fifth child, Paul Horace Bresee, was born. Dr. Bresee was accompanied on his trip to the General Conference by Sister Bresee and Brother Knotts, who had also been elected a delegate. They went first to West Virginia, Brother Knotts' old home, and spent a few delightful days amidst scenes which were full of reminders of the great conflict. The fields were yet desolate from the war, and the fences had not been restored in the areas where the two armies had destroyed everything. A cousin of Brother Knotts named Harry Kincaid, lived in West Virginia, and the party stopped at his house. Soon afterward, a boy was born in the Kincaid family, and they named him Bresee.

Dr. Bresee was one of the youngest — if not the youngest — members of the General Conference. He did not take a prominent part in its proceedings, but in a private, quiet way managed to accomplish some things. He had more to do than any one else with the matter of securing action of the General Conference directing the residence of one of the bishops should be at Council Bluffs. But the chairman of the committee that had that matter in hand reported Council Bluffs or Omaha, and although this report was made without proper authority, the proponents of Council Bluffs, could never get it changed. Doctor Bresee also rendered effective service in bringing about the election of Bishop Gilbert Haven, one of the eight bishops who were elected at that General Conference. He was a very brilliant man and a radical Abolitionist. In consequence he was unpopular, especially with the South and the border country. Brother Bresee secured for him the Iowa delegation and some others, without which he could not have been elected, as the vote was close and the opposition strong.

Upon his return to Council Bluffs, Brother Bresee made

a strenuous effort to wipe out the debt on the church, but did not succeed in fully paying it. It was in Council Bluffs, on the 6th of August, 1872, that Melvin Arthur, his fourth and youngest son, was born.

CHAPTER VI.

In 1873, Brother Bresee was sent to Red Oak. This
town was in a comparatively new part of the state, and had
a population of not more than 2,500. It was the commercial
center of a very fertile country which was
Appointed developing rapidly. All the churches were
to Red Oak numerically weak, and the church buildings
were correspondingly small. The members of
the Methodist church were very earnest in their desire for
Doctor Bresee's appointment, and sent a delegation to the
conference for the purpose of bringing it about. The leader
of this delegation was Brother Crandall, an able, insistent
man, who was largely influential in securing Brother Bresee's appointment. He had some wealth, and was a leading
member of the church. He assured Brother Bresee at the
conference that he would be well cared for. This promise
was kept. The church rented a good commodious place of
residence, and made proper financial provision for the new
pastor. Under these auspices he began the work, commencing with $1,200 a year and a house, the rent of which
was about $300 annually. This compensation was the equiv-
alent of what Dr. Bresee had received in Council Bluffs.

Soon after his removal to Red Oak, his only sister died.
She was a resident of Council Bluffs, and her parents lived
with her. After her death, the father and mother of Dr.
Bresee came to live with him, as they were get-
Death of ting old, and could not live alone. They con-
His Sister tinued with his family from that time until
their death in California.

Early in October, Doctor Bresee undertook to hold what
he called a Home Campmeeting for ten days. He invited his

ministerial brethren from adjoining charges to help in the meeting, but they failed to respond. Thus *His First* unaided, he went through the ten days' meet- *Home* ing with comparatively little success, and at *Campmeeting* its close, announced that the meeting would be continued indefinitely. At that time the religious life of the city was at a low ebb, and this was true of the Methodist church, as well as of all the other churches. After the meeting had been in progress for perhaps two weeks, some of the Sunday school children came to the altar.

The work gradually spread among the people, and more and more the interest grew. Dr. Bresee carried on the meeting until the first of March, without any *A Great* assistance other than that of a few, casual visit- *Revival* ing ministers, of whom there were probably not more than half a dozen during the entire period. That was before the day of evangelism. But the revival took hold of the families, and the leading men of the town came under its influence. Merchants, lawyers, editors, and contractors, with their families and employees, were converted, and outcasts and drunkards also gave their hearts to God. At the close of the meeting not less than three hundred persons had been saved. All classes were represented. As soon as men of means and influence were converted, they would begin to pray for the salvation of their employees, and would not rest until it was accomplished. Thus the work went on in a wonderful way. Dr. Bresee considered that it was the mightiest revival ever held in Western Iowa. The number of converts was greater than the seating capacity of the church could accommodate. The revival revolutionized the city, and turned the tide of everything towards Methodism.

Immediately after the revival, arrangements were commenced for the erection of a new church, which was not completed until the end of Dr. Bresee's three years' pastorate. It was a large and expensive church for that country and that time. It cost $25,000, which would be the equivalent of more than $100,000 now. The members of the church were at first skeptical as to the possibility of its erection, and a great deal of special work and preaching on the subject was required in order to arouse the attention and enthusiasm of the public.

These conditions led Dr. Bresee to say that one of the great necessities of carrying on the work of the Lord, was a large, commodious place of worship, and that people who would not do what they could to accomplish this purpose, and who refused to work in harmony with those who had it in hand, would not be received in full connection into the church. He had just taken in a large number of young converts on probation, according to the Methodist custom. This was made the occasion for an article in the newspaper at Red Oak, to the effect that they had a new ritual at the Methodist church; that the first article was, "Do you believe in Bresee?" the second article was, "Do you believe in the early completion of the new Methodist church?" The third was, "Will you do all in your power to accomplish that result?" The article went on to state that, if they answered those questions satisfactorily, Crandall would arise and say that Bresee could write their names in the Book of Life.

During these great revival services, Dr. Bresee preached short sermons. He held meetings at which they planned the work somewhat, and covenanted together to co-operate in it. During part of this protracted meeting, if not all of it, it was arranged that after Dr. Bresee had preached, he was to sit down, whereupon the people would immediately begin to sing one of the old hymns; that he would then go out into the congregation, and that all of those who had covenanted with him would also go among the people and reap for the altar. It was understood that they would thus work and get all the seekers they could and then they would rally at the altar in the old, Methodist fashion, and pray with and for the penitents until they got through. During this period, Dr. Bresee had very little time for the preparation of sermons, so that most of his preaching was improvised and of a hortatory character. The campaign was not systematic or carefully planned. They went on, not knowing how long to continue, and the work was done measurably by individual labor. Men would be converted, and then go after their friends, employees, and families, until they would bring them to the altar and get them saved.

The revival aroused such general attention and interest, that many people could not find room in the building. They would come long before the hour of service, and crowd around the door. One night Mrs. Bresee was detained by some family cares and came a little later than usual. The crowd was all around the door, extending out into the street, and they said nobody could get in. One fellow swore that he could get in; that he never saw a place so crowded that he could not force his way through. He no sooner said this, than he crowded through the people, reached the door, pushed it open, and got in.

Such a gospel campaign as this, is sure to arouse more or less opposition. One night some rowdies were disturbing the meeting. Dr. Bresee was dwelling for a moment on the objects of worship of different people. He *Rowdies* said that some people worshipped them-*Nonplussed* selves, whereupon the rowdies made so much noise that he stopped and told them that he would sit down a moment, and, if they had anything to say, to get up and say it to the whole congregation, after which they would have quiet and he could go on with the service. One tall, lanky fellow, arose and said: "I was just saying that that is us; that is me; I worship myself." By the time he got that far, his ideas ran out, and he sat down; but one of the papers of the town took it up and told how this fellow, giving his name, stood up like a kangaroo on his hind legs, and said he worshipped himself. The paper continued to ridicule the poor fellow until he fled from the town.

As an illustration of the zeal and fervor of some of the men of that church, William Clark might be mentioned. He lived about three miles in the country, and scarcely missed a meeting in all those months. Fre-

William Clarke quently during the winter it was so cold that he would not bring his horses and leave them standing outside, but came afoot so as to be there and help push the battle. He was a most effective and blessed man of God.

One day in the afternoon meeting they were planning for the night campaign. Dr. Bresee explained the *modus operandi* to be followed, as heretofore stated, and further said that all those who were pledged thus to do, would not require any special notice from him, but would carry out the plans spontaneously so far as movement was concerned. Among those present was one old brother, a man of some prominence, but rather uncultured and peculiar. The next day, when they came to discuss the matter, he arose and said: "Last night when Brother Bresee asked those that would arise at once and go back and try to find somebody that they could bring to the altar, I rose up. I had right smart faith that I was a-lyin', but I was not. I went. The Lord blessed me." The success of the meeting from the human side, was the result of continual perseverance. Of course, there entered into it much of prayer and sacrifice, but stubborn perseverance, and determination to do God's work, were the predominating elements, under God, in accomplishing such glorious results.

During his second year in Red Oak, Dr. Bresee was largely occupied in conserving the results of the great revival. That summer, the Presbyterian pastor, whose church building was larger than the Methodist church, was compelled to be absent from the city, and his people, instead of seeking a supply, invited the Methodists to occupy their church, stating that they would work with them. The Methodists accepted the invitation, and Dr. Bresee preached during the summer in the Presbyterian church, both congregations worshiping there together.

During the third year of his pastorate in Red Oak, the church occupied the basement of the new building, which afforded much larger facilities than the old structure, although the audience room was not yet completed. This year was also very blessed in the way of revival influences, and the salvation of souls. In those days the revival meetings were held exclusively in the winter, as they had not learned to expect salvation all the year round. Quite a number were converted, among them some men that made good, substantial members of the church.

While at Red Oak, Dr. Bresee dedicated several other churches, and on each occasion he was away over Sunday. His church was so strong and full of life, that it could push the work during the absence of its pastor. Some local preacher would preach, and the meeting would go on with good results.

On one of these occasions, Susan, the youngest child of Brother and Sister Bresee, was born. Brother Bresee agreed to dedicate a church, but was compelled to wait at home until the birth of his little daughter, after which he went and dedicated the church, arriving at his destination on Sunday morning.

Among other things accomplished at Red Oak was the building of a good parsonage adjoining the new church building, where the pastor and his family lived in comfort. The entire three years at Red Oak was a time of great blessing and power. At the close of this period the Annual Conference was held in the new church building. In those days Red Oak was the second church in importance in the Conference. A large majority of the most influential people in the city were converted and added to the church. Some of them are still alive.

The editor of one of the papers was saved during that great meeting. On the occasion of one of Dr. Bresee's last visits to Denver, he called on this editor and his family, as they had taken up their residence in that city. One of the editor's sons, who is an attorney there, and formerly held the position of Prosecuting Attorney, heard that Dr. Bresee was in town. He, with their other boys, was converted in the Red Oak revival, and he came clear across the city of Denver to see Dr. Bresee. While in Denver Brother Bresee held the meeting at the Nazarene church, during which this young man helped the church to raise some money. He announced a plate offering, and asked those who would give a dollar apiece to hold up one finger, those who would give two dollars, to hold up two fingers, and those who would give five dollars, to hold up all five fingers. The editor's son was there, held up both hands, and gave ten dollars.

The leading merchants in Red Oak were converted. One had a very large store, and bought considerable quantities of goods. As a result of his solicitation, all the merchants from whom he bought goods in Chicago and New York, gave subscriptions to the Red Oak church. Red Oak has been a first-class appointment ever since that great, historic revival.

Dr. Bresee in conversation with me, deplored the fact that at that time he did not know how to preach holiness, and had not learned how to lead seekers into the experience. While a few of the converts at Red Oak may have obtained full salvation, there was nothing definite along the line of holiness. The work consisted of taking the people from all classes of worldly society and getting them converted, and in that regard Dr. Bresee stated that the meeting surpassed any other revival campaign in which he had ever participated.

CHAPTER VII.

At the session of the Annual Conference, held at Red Oak, in the autumn of 1876, Bishop Foster presided. A very sad thing occurred at this session. The year previous, when the Annual Conference was held at Indianola, a ballot was taken for the election of delegates to the General Conference, and a member of the Conference stuffed the ballot box in his own favor. The tellers, in counting the votes, detected that there were more votes cast than there were voters, and reported that some inaccuracies in the vote would necessitate the taking of another ballot. This was ordered taken, and the tellers, being very watchful, discovered the culprit, as he repeated his former fraudulent conduct. His character was immediately arrested, and he was put on trial under the most intense excitement. He was not given a charge at Indianola, although his trial was not completed until the following Annual Conference at Red Oak, when he was tried before a special commission, and found guilty. The trial commission brought in its report late in the Conference session, and at a late hour of the night. The great church was packed with people. Intense interest in the matter had been aroused, and when the report was read, stating that the accused was found guilty, and expelled from the church, his wife became hysterical, and began to cry and scream so that she could be heard a block or two away from the church. She was taken from the church and carried home, and all the way to her house, the streets were filled with her cries. In the solemn stillness that fell upon the great audience after she was gone, Bishop

66

Foster said, speaking tenderly of her, that it was not to be wondered at, for sin was an awful thing.

The Presiding Elder of the district in which Red Oak was situated, was detained from the Conference by sickness, so at the invitation of Bishop Foster, Dr. Bresee acted in his place. The Bishop was determined to appoint Dr. Bresee as Presiding Elder of the Council Bluffs district, but to this he made the most strenuous objection, as he never felt called to the Presiding Eldership, as he did to the pastorate. It seemed, however, that his objections would be overruled, and that he would be appointed to the Presiding Eldership, but late in the session, a special committee of influential men came from Clarinda, with the object of securing Dr. Bresee's appointment to that church. Bishop Foster yielded to the solicitations of these men, and in conversing personally with Dr. Bresee, informed him that they had put him down for Clarinda.

Appointed to Clarinda

Clarinda was a beautiful town, not more than fifteen or twenty miles distant from Red Oak, and was the county seat of Page county. It was a city of about the same size as Red Oak, and the Methodist church there was a remarkable one in regard to its personnel. Among its members were a number of brilliant and cultured families, and some men of considerable wealth.

William P. Hepburn, a member of the United States house of representatives for so many years, belonged to this church, and William McPherrin, a brilliant lawyer, was a member. Bro. McPherrin died of tuberculosis many years afterward, at the residence of Dr. Bresee in Los Angeles, leaving a wife and several children, who were still living in that city in 1912.

William P. Hepburn

Brother and Sister Bresee remained in Clarinda three years. There was nothing peculiar or striking about the pastorate. No especially great revival occurred, but there was good, steady growth, and a fair degree of success. The pastoral salary was $1,500 a year. Upon the arrival of Dr. Bresee in the city, his brethren proposed that he should not say anything about money, or have anything to do with finances, but should merely draw his salary monthly from the bank. He complied with the request for the first year, after which he found that it was necessary for the pastor to devote some attention to the finances of the church, not on his own account, but for the good of the work. He never had any trouble about his support in the Clarinda church.

The Methodist Episcopal church at Clarinda was characterized by great singing ability. It was said to have the best choir, the best double quartet, and the finest chorus in the state of Iowa. Great musical conventions were held in the city, and the Methodist church was always in the forefront of these gatherings. While it is possible that these musical accomplishments did not hinder the work, it is certainly true that they did not help it to any great extent along spiritual lines.

A Musical Church

At Clarinda Dr. Bresee began to introduce the modern gospel songs which he had used so effectively at Red Oak. Among the first of these books was that issued by Phillips. It was a song book with choruses which were sung with great power at Red Oak. These Brother Bresee used at Clarinda, but not in the regular services. The people were grand singers and sang the old hymns in a delightful manner. The only peculiarity that characterized their singing in the church at Clarinda, was manifested at the prayer-meeting in this wise: After a season of prayer, and just as the people were rising, they would begin to hunt a hymn, and the pianist would commence to get ready. In a little while they would announce the number, and would commence to sing. This little peculiarity was objectionable to Dr. Bresee, as tending to cut off the whole tide of spiritual life, and he met the situation in a way that was characteristic of the man. As soon as he rose from his knees he would begin to sing a hymn. He was incapable of striking the

68

tune, but he would do his best, and Mrs. Bresee, or some other good singer, would take up the tune, and they would carry it along. Dr. Bresee stated that he considered it quite probable that this method of beginning a hymn was somewhat humiliating to the people, for he noticed that in a very short time they learned to sing without hesitation or preparation at the end of a season of prayer.

At the Annual Conference in the autumn of 1879, with the full consent of Dr. Bresee, and in accordance with the desire of the Presiding Elder, the former went to Creston, a railroad town, which was becoming a place *Appointed* of considerable importance. All the church- *to* es there were weak, but the Methodist church *Creston* was especially so. Upon the arrival of Dr. Bresee and his family at Creston, on a rainy day, nobody came to meet them. After stopping at the hotel one day, they cleaned the parsonage, had their things brought in, and began the work. The church was very small, and Dr. Bresee suggested to a few of the brethren that they had not any place in which to accomplish anything; and that the church would not hold enough people to bring about real success. The brethren looked very serious, and said that they would be greatly pleased if the church could be fairly filled.

Brother Bresee started the work with his usual earnestness and zeal in the cause of the Lord. As a result, the people came, and God began to pour out His spirit, and crowd the little place clear out to the sidewalk. Later on, they accomplished the wonderful feat of making the little church wider than it was long. They put two sides on it, and spread it out so that it would seat a fairly good sized audience. The revival for the first time attracted the railway men, who made rather a unique congregation. They would remain until the time came for them to get on their engines, when they would leave the church. If somebody whom they did not like got up to preach, or if they were not especially interested in the preacher, they would rise in a body and go out.

When Dr. Bresee commenced his work, the church was poor, owed money in all directions, and had no credit. He made it his business, however, to search out the different creditors of the church and pay their bills, sometimes with his own funds, for at that time he had an income from sources entirely disconnected with his pastorate. So little confidence had men who held the notes and other obligations of the church, that they could scarcely be induced to look up the matter and ascertain the amount of the indebtedness. On one occasion Dr. Bresee called on a man who held one of the church's notes, but he did not remember how much it amounted to. He was utterly indifferent in regard to the matter, and wanted to know what Dr. Bresee's object was in inquiring about it. When informed that the debt would be paid, he was very much pleased, and soon found the note, which was promptly paid in full.

As time went on the church was still further enlarged, so as to seat four hundred people. Brother Bresee's pastorate at Creston lasted two years.

In the fall of 1881, at the earnest request of the Broadway church, at Council Bluffs, Dr. Bresee again became its pastor, and remained there for one year. The work went on quietly but steadily, and there were conversions and a fair degree of prosperity.

Council Bulffs   At the close of the year quite a number of the members of the Broadway church, and some leading citizens who did not belong to any church, combined together and asked that Dr. Bresee be appointed to a new work in the southwestern and newer part of the city, the object being to build up a large, central church. After Brother Bresee left for Conference, these people held a meeting, and put in definite written form their desire or request. This recommendation or petition was brought to the Conference by Brother Knotts, one of the men who planned to enter into the new arrangement, and by his arguments and persuasions, Dr. Bresee was induced to undertake the work.

The understanding was that he was not to begin regular preaching services immediately, but was to secure a suitable lot and to proceed as fast as possible with the erection of a church building. Early in 1882, a very desirable corner was obtained, the financial arrangements being made by Brother Knotts and Judge Wright. When this was accomplished, Dr. Bresee deemed it wise to begin a service in that part of the city, without waiting for the erection of the church building; so he rented an old theater, where he held regular services.

During the winter of 1881-82, a tremendous storm, accompanied by a cloud-burst, swept over Council Bluffs. It filled the little stream that ran through the city to overflowing, and caused immense damage, especially in the portion of the city where Dr. Bresee and his friends were planning to carry on their work. In fact, the loss caused by the storm was so great, that they concluded that it would be impracticable to continue the enterprise.

In the meantime some pressure had been brought to bear upon Dr. Bresee to induce him to go to California, and upon the abandonment of the new church enterprise in Council

Attention Directed to California Bluffs, he was led to give more serious consideration than he would otherwise have done, to the suggestion that he make California his future home.

Outside conditions entered so largely into this matter, as to require somewhat detailed explanation in another chapter.

CHAPTER VIII.

During Brother Bresee's first pastorate at the Broadway church, in Council Bluffs, Rev. Joseph Knotts, although in his middle manhood, had become superannuated by reason of ill health. Subsequently he engaged in various business enterprises, one of which was the publication of a religious paper, called "The Inland Advocate," of which for a time Dr. Bresee was editor. Brother Knotts, although his lungs were so affected that he could not preach, owned a book-store, and other interests. He was a man of intense activity, and could not resign himself to idleness.

About this time the large hotel building in which his principal store was located, was destroyed by fire, and his business ruined. In trying to save some of his property from the fire, his bronchial difficulty was much aggravated.

Thus thrown out of business, and more broken in health, he began to canvass the situation, and seek for some financial opening. With this in view, he went to Washington City, and spent the winter in studying the political and business conditions, not only of this country, but of the entire American continent. For this comprehensive and analytical investigation, he was well qualified, as he possessed rare mental and moral endowments. Persistent, courageous, magnetic, sagacious, and intimately acquainted with all the influences that affect the heart and move the will, he was a great leader of men. He was resourceful, daring, and could bring things to pass. Like all dominating, masterful men, he had initiative and executive ability in a rare degree.

In his moral and spiritual attainments he also far surpassed the average man. An earnest Christian, his heart beat in sympathy with all that was good and noble. He was stubbornly loyal to his friends. Those whom he trusted could rely upon his standing by them to the very end. Being a strong preacher, he had held good appointments, and was a member of the same General Conference, to which Dr. Bresee was elected in 1872. I deem it important to give this pen portrait of the man, in view of the fact that he and the subject of this biography were so closely associated during a long term of years.

During Mr. Knotts' stay in Washington, he concluded that Mexico, the resources of which were beginning to attract attention, offered him the best opportunities. He did not form any definite plans, however, until he had carefully canvassed its great mineral and agricultural possibilities.

Having influential friends at the national capital, he was appointed American Consul to the state of Chihuahua, after which he returned to Council Bluffs, and made his preparations to start for Mexico, with the idea of being on the alert for exceptionally good investments and business openings.

On the eve of his departure, Dr. Bresee told him that, if he found anything especially promising, he would join him in it. Although Dr. Bresee was not wealthy, he could command some means, and felt that, in *They Engage* view of his large family, it would be de-*in Business* sirable to make some profitable invest-*Enterprises* ments.

Together. Within a few months, Knotts got in touch with some of the richest men in Chihuahua, and through them secured options on several great mining properties. At the same time he entered into arrangements with prominent capitalists in the United States to furnish the funds required for the development of mineral properties.

Probably the richest and greatest of these was the old, historical mine at Parral. This was really a group of mines, embracing the Prieta, Tajo, and other celebrated mineral deposits. These had yielded immense quantities of bullion, especially silver, as can be seen by reading the data concerning them in the Encyclopedia Brittanica. But, having been worked down to where the water seeped into the mines to such an extent that the ore could no longer be carried out in sacks by peons, they were abandoned, with the exception of a little work on the upper levels.

Knotts, returning to Iowa at this juncture, perfected a permanent organization, made up largely of leading capitalists in Iowa and Illinois. The company lost no time in sending men and machinery into Mexico, rehabilitating the mines, erecting reduction works, and commencing work on the lower levels. The water was pumped out, the mines were cleaned and re-equipped, and everything pertaining to them placed in first-class condition.

Dr. Bresee put what money he had into this property, and afterward, with Brother Knotts and numerous financiers of Illinois, Iowa, Wisconsin, and Indiana, became interested in other large mines in different parts of Mexico. Among these were the Mapimi, an iron mountain, in Durango, and Dry Mountain, in Chihuahua. A company was specially formed to purchase the Mapimi, which was literally a mountain of iron, and probably the greatest deposit of iron in the world. In some places the native iron was so pure that a horse-shoe could be hammered out of it. Since then the Mapimi property has produced millions of dollars worth of ore.

The organization was perfected at Chicago, and among those present and participating were Jay Cooke, Judge Helfenstein, and other capitalists of national reputation.The combination brought about by Knotts was a very strong one, but it was premature. There were no railroads in that part of Mexico, and no demand for iron.

The men who were associated in these Knotts' enterprises were bankers, capitalists, wholesale merchants, and manufacturers. Of this epoch in his career, Dr. Bresee says: "We would go to Chicago, hire a large room in a hotel for our meetings, spend a week together, and have a great time. They were fine men, not large capitalists, in the sense that the term is used now, for that was before the day of multi-

74

millionaires. They belonged to what I regard as the finest class of men in the country; men to whom the people entrusted their interests, and who proved themselves worthy of such trust. There was nothing mean or little about them, and they did not scheme and maneuver to cheat those who confided in them, out of their money. They liked to make money, but were magnificent losers. If things went well, they were glad. If they went ill, they would put in more money, and plan for success. But Brother Knotts was easily the dominant personality in all our meetings. He was resourceful, and his associates trusted him, and would do what he said.

"He depended on me to help him somewhat. I was in close touch with him, and familiar with his enterprises. I could set them forth clearly, and with some degree of force. It was thoroughly understood that Brother Knotts and I were out and out religious men; and, in fact, most of the men with whom we were associated were also religious. They were not all, however, religious in accordance with our idea. Among our number was a wholesale liquor man, of Decatur, Illinois. He was a ruling elder in the Lutheran church. He was a native of Germany, and a great-brained, great-hearted man. It had never occurred to him that liquor-selling, conducted on a large scale as a wholesaler, was not as legitimate as selling corn, or anything else. At one time he and I went to Denver and Leadville, for the purpose of securing a metallurgist, and buying an outfit of machinery. That man was thoroughly honest, but he was unenlightened on the liquor question.

"While I had some stock in all the Knotts' companies, and was a director in several of them, my investments were largely in the Parral properties, and the ruin that came to them fell heavily upon me. Soon after the beginning of operations in the old Prieta mine, at Parral, the explosion of a blast caused a subterranean river of water to pour into the mine, and the workmen, leaving the tools and machinery behind, barely escaped with their lives. A good deal of money was spent in the effort to clear the mine of water, but the undertaking was too great for our financial strength. That property was capitalized at $500,000, and the stock was considerably above par; but, for all practical purposes, it was destroyed in an hour.

"This made it so that my other investments no more than met my liabilities, and I was left without either money or property. I felt some degree of embarrassment at the thought of remaining in a country where

End of His Financial Career

I was supposed to be wealthy, when, in fact, I was very poor. Hence, I deemed it best to take a transfer to some distant Conference. I formed the firm conviction at that time that I would never more attempt to make money, but would give the remainder of my life, whatever it might be, to the direct preaching of the Word of God. During all this time I had not neglected my ministerial labors, but had devoted my spare time and energy to business. I began to engage in these enterprises when at Red Oak, and continued in them for nearly ten years."

CHAPTER IX.

For a time Dr. Bresee gave serious consideration to the
advisability of removing to San Antonio, Texas, as he had
friends there who desired him to accept the pastorate of
the Methodist Episcopal church in that city. But he found
that the South was still very much prejudiced against
what they called "The Methodist Church North," and he
concluded that it was sufficiently difficult to fight the world,
the flesh, and the Devil, without also fighting prejudice.

Much pressure was brought to bear upon him to remove
to Los Angeles, California. His friend, Knotts, had visited
Southern California once or twice, on his way to Mexico,
going from Los Angeles to El Paso, instead of taking the
more direct route from Denver. He was very much
pleased with Los Angeles and its vicinity, and urged Dr.
Bresee to take a pastorate there.

Mr. H. C. Sigler, formerly a banker at Osceola, Iowa,
but at this time a resident of Los Angeles, was a warm
friend of the Bresee family. He also urged Dr. Bresee to
come to California. He prepared the way
H. C. Sigler by securing from the Presiding Elder a
special invitation to unite with the Southern California Conference of the M. E. church. Hardly
knowing what course to take, Dr. Bresee wrote to Bishop
Simpson, with whom his relations were quite friendly, and
the Bishop replied that, if he needed climatic conditions
for himself or family, Los Angeles would be a desirable
place, but, otherwise, he did not so consider it. He stated
that Southern California was a new country, and that there
was not much there in the way of churches; that the First
church in Los Angeles, was the only strong church in the

77

Conference; and that the time was not ripe to make the change. Bishop Simpson had not visited Los Angeles for three years, but Bishop Hurst had presided quite recently at the Southern California Conference, and was charmed with the country. Dr. Bresee called on Bishop Hurst, who advised him to transfer to Los Angeles, and said that he himself would be glad to have any little church around the corner in Southern California. He further stated that, if he had known that Dr. Bresee contemplated going to California, he would gladly have appointed him to the First Methodist Episcopal church in Oakland.

As a result of all that he had been able to learn, Dr. Bresee felt drawn to Los Angeles, but the financial problem seemed very formidable. His family consisted of his parents, six children, and a nephew, besides himself and wife, and the cost of transportation would be large. In discussing the matter with his friend Knotts, Dr. Bresee finally said that it would cost a thousand dollars; that he had no money, and that he had better accept one of the three or four invitations to churches in Iowa, and do the best he could. Although Knotts himself had lost heavily, and was much embarrassed by adverse financial conditions, he authorized Dr. Bresee to draw a check on him for whatever money he needed to make the trip. This generous offer was accepted to the extent of a thousand dollars, and Brother Bresee and family started for Los Angeles in August, 1883.

At that time he had only a general invitation from the Presiding Elder. In the First church at Los Angeles, there were a few of his friends, but he had not been called by the church. In view of the necessity of economizing in every possible way, Dr. Bresee *Starts for Los Angeles* consulted with the general ticket agent of the Union Pacific Railroad at Omaha, who was a friend of his, and the latter sent over a car to Council Bluffs, for the exclusive use of the Bresee family. They fitted up the car with beds, curtains, etc., and arranged for a comfortable camping trip on the way across the continent. A few friends who also wanted to go to California, were permitted to ride in the same car. Among these were two teachers for the Indian school.

To use Dr. Bresee's own words: "The trip was in every way full of interest and picturesqueness. Sometimes our car was hitched to the express train; sometimes to a freight train, and sometimes it was sidetracked. Occasionally we were left over two or three hours in some village, and that gave us fine opportunities for observation and pleasure.

"One very sad incident occurred. We were hitched to an emigrant train, and a lady from Germany was making the trip, with several little children. Her husband had come to America in advance, had secured employment *A Sad* at San Francisco, and saved money enough for *Incident* her and the children to join him there. The little mother was greatly distressed because one of her children had sickened and died on the train. She was without money. I went through the train and took up a collection for her. When we reached a small city, I purchased a coffin for the child and was going to bury it, but the authorities would not allow me to do so, unless I secured a death certificate from one of the local physicians. I scarce knew what to do. The mother was not in condition to be taken off the train with her family, and left in that place. Finally, in conversation with the railroad men, they proposed to haul our train outside of the city limits, and that they would help us to bury the child. We followed their suggestion. The workmen dug a grave in the sand beside the tracks, and the occupants of the train gathered around. I conducted a little funeral service, and made arrangements with the sheriff of the county that, if the father sent for the child, he would disinter the remains and send them to San Francisco. I never heard anything more about the family."

Eight days were required for the journey from Council Bluffs to Los Angeles, where Dr. Bresee and family arrived on Saturday afternoon, August 26, 1883. They were met at the depot by Mr. H. C. Sigler, who, by their request, had secured a furnished house for them, and placed it in readiness for their occupancy. Like Paul of old, they went to their own hired house, where they were comfortably situated. On the following Sunday morning, they attended the First Methodist church, located on Fort street (now Broadway), between Third and Fourth. They were a little late, and found the pastor awaiting them in the study, where he had given Brother Sigler directions to bring them. Hurriedly ushering him into the pulpit, the pastor stated that Dr. Bresee was to preach, which he did, and in a manner that was highly acceptable to the members of the church, as events later showed.

The remainder of that week was spent resting and looking about the city and its surroundings. The next Sunday morning Dr. Bresee preached for the Rev. A. M. Hough, pastor of the recently organized University Methodist Episcopal church, which held its services in the second story of the small building where the University of Southern California had just begun its work. Brother Hough had been the pastor of Dr. Bresee in his childhood.

That week the Southern California Conference convened in the First church, Bishop Warren presiding. Dr. Bresee's transfer from Bishop Simpson was presented, and he was placed on the list of Conference preachers, which was a very small body. When the Conference was over, and the appointments read, Dr. Bresee's name appeared as pastor of the First Methodist Episcopal church.

Appointed to Old Fort Street Methodist Episco-_pal Church

Los Angeles at that time only claimed a population of about twenty thousand, and the First church for a city of that size, was a very strong organization, having between three and four hundred members. It was distinguished for the character of its personnel and family and social life, and contained within its membership much deep and earnest piety. There were those in it who were determined to put

80

it on a basis of fashionable church life, and there were also those who were intensely spiritual.

In due time the Bresee family found themselves ensconced in the parsonage, which was a cottage on Broadway, between Fourth and Fifth. They remained in this church three years, with steady and growing success throughout that period.

Dr. Bresee here found for the first time in his ministry, a class of fully sanctified people. They were clear, sound, substantial, evangelical, and were earnestly and intelligently, although rather quietly, pushing the work of full salvation. Dr. Bresee says of these people: "I instinctively in spirit allied myself with them, and, while they must have known that I was not in the clear enjoyment of the blessing, they seemed to appreciate whatever efforts I could and did make, in assisting them in the work of holiness. They were very kind and gentle. They doubtless prayed much for me, but they did not pray at me, and they stood close by me, and sustained me in every way throughout my ministry. The spiritual life of the church continually increased, and there was a good degree of blessing on my ministry, the church rapidly growing in every way."

In the second year of this pastorate, through the instrumentality of the leading holiness members of the First church, and other holiness people in Los Angeles, arrangements were made for Doctors Mac Donald and Watson to come to the Pacific coast, and hold a few meetings. They held services in the First church for a period of three weeks. Dr. Bresee stated to me that, while the meeting was a good one, it did not seem to him as at all remarkable. A number of persons were sanctified, and there were some conversions, but, while there was no special, outspoken opposition, the work of holiness seemed peculiarly unpopular, and was exceedingly difficult. Nevertheless, in this meeting good progress was made.

The MacDonald and Watson Meeting

81

Dr. Bresee thus characterized this crisis in his career: "I passed through this meeting in general accord with both the teaching and spirit of the brethren, and did what I could to help push the work of holiness. However, I *A Great* did not come to any special realization of my *Crisis* own lack and need. But it was not very long after the meeting before I began to be awakened to the deep necessities of my own heart. This realization grew more and more intense, until my heart cry began to go out to God for the mighty grace that was adequate to all my needs.

"At this time there came to me in answer to prayer, a very striking experience. I had been for some time in almost constant prayer, and crying to God for something that would meet my needs, not clearly realizing what they were, or how they could be met. I sat alone in the parsonage, in the cool of evening, in the front parlor near the door. The door being opened, I looked up into the azure in earnest prayer, while the shades of evening gathered about. As I waited and waited, and continued in prayer, looking up, it seemed to me as if from the azure there came a meteor, an indescribable ball of condensed light, descending rapidly toward me. As I gazed upon it, it was soon within a few score feet, when I seemed distinctly to hear a voice saying, as my face was upturned towards it: 'Swallow it; swallow it,' and in an instant it fell upon my lips and face. I attempted to obey the injunction. It seemed to me, however, that I swallowed only a little of it, although it felt like fire on my lips, and the burning sensation did not leave them for several days. While all of this of itself would be nothing, there came with it into my heart and being, a transformed condition of life and blessing and unction and glory, which I had never known before. I felt that my need was supplied. I was always very reticent in reference to my own personal experience. I have never gotten over it, and I have said very little relative to this; but there came into my ministry a new element of spiritual life and power.

People began to come into the blessing of full salvation; there were more persons converted; and the last year of my ministry in that church was more consecutively successful, being crowned by an almost constant revival. When the third year came to a close, the church had been nearly doubled in membership, and in every way built up."

CHAPTER X.

When Dr. Bresee began his ministry in Los Angeles, he found a great deal of conflict in reference to the holiness question. There had recently been somewhat of a holiness

The Holiness Movement in Southern California
work in the church and city, which had resulted in the organization of a holiness mission not far from the First church, which was the beginning of the so-called holiness churches in Southern California.

A few members of the First church had gone to this mission, and considerable opposition had been aroused. To again quote from Dr. Bresee: "This had been soothed away, and my ministry here did not arouse any conflict on the subject of holiness, my preaching probably not being sufficiently definite in its doctrinal aspects to especially arouse opposition, it being given more to a deeper spirituality through the incoming of the Holy Spirit. At that time I did not preach the second work of grace very definitely. I preached it, but did not give it such emphasis as called out opposition, or as led so many people into the experience as otherwise would probably have been the case. While I had not a very wide popularity in the city at the end of the three years, I did have a popularity and love in the First church and among the people generally, which was almost, if not altogether, universal. At the end of my third year, there would have been but one voice in reference to the desirability of my ministry, if I could have remained longer. At that time there seemed to be a unanimous acclaim of devotion to me. During the next four years this condition changed radically.

"During my pastorate in the First church, my ministry was in the transition state. The reason for this was that my preaching had not the definite element to arouse opposition, and I had a strong hold on the people on account of my personality. I carried them with me generally, with much prayer and deep piety. If I had known more when I came to this coast, and had had experience and sense, I could have swept the whole of Methodism into holiness. It was not set against it enough to prevent me from putting my hands on everything in Methodism in Southern California, and drawing it into holiness; but I did not know enough. I neither had the experience nor the general ministerial wisdom to do it. I am very sorry.

"What leading men there were, had been aroused more or less by this holiness work and movement, and, coming to the First church as I did, with the influence that the position gave, these men came to me to talk about this subject more or less, or in conversation opened their hearts to me, to a greater or less extent. Here I saw M. M. Bovard, the president of the University of Southern California, and he talked over the matter very earnestly with me. If I had been in the experience, and had had wisdom enough, I could have led him into the blessing, and thus impressed the whole of Methodism in Southern California; but I did not; and yet, I was preaching holiness."

At the meeting of the Annual Conference in 1886, Dr. Bresee was appointed to the First Methodist Episcopal church in Pasadena, which at that time was a new town. A

Appointed to Pasadena

few years before it had been a sheep ranch. A handful of men from Indiana, came and purchased a large tract of land there, and looking around to find some beautiful descriptive name, called it "Pasadena," which means "The Crown of the Valleys." They laid it off by making streets and avenues some half a mile apart, and setting out small, scattered orchards of both deciduous and citrus fruits. For some time it did not become much of a town, although a few houses were built on the tract; but along in the 80's there began to be quite a center of small buildings at Colorado and Fair Oaks. Then, under the touch of the boom which was on Southern California, it began to grow rapidly, and sprang into a village and city almost as if it had been under the influence of Aladdin's lamp, as described in the fairy tales.

This cluster of buildings in 1886, was only a very small hamlet in the midst of the Pasadena tract, but it was already under the impulse of the rising tide of immigration and prosperity. A little prior to this, a small Methodist church had been erected on Orange Grove avenue, about two miles from what seemed to be the central point of the village, when it began to take form; and only a short time before this little church had been removed into the nucleus or cluster of buildings. There were about one hundred and thirty members.

When Dr. Bresee was asked what he was going to do at Pasadena, he replied that, by the grace of God, he would make a fire that would reach heaven. At that time the membership of the church was considerably scattered, and the tide of religious life was not high. During the summer of 1886 the church had had union services with the other little churches around about. At the beginning of Dr. Bresee's pastorate, a new structure had been commenced on Colorado street, where the Methodist Episcopal church now stands. This building was then under way, and was completed the following winter.

About Christmas the congregation moved into the building in an unfinished condition, and it was dedicated in the spring of 1887, by Bishop Fowler.

Some weeks after Dr. Bresee's arrival in Pasadena, he began a protracted meeting. Already there were many men employed in the building of houses, and he and his workers would hold meetings at the corner of Fair Oaks and Colorado streets, only a short distance from the church. They would first sing two or three hymns. This would gather a crowd of men, and after prayer, as soon as he arose from his knees, Dr. Bresee would announce that they were to have a service in the church nearby, and invite them to come. Then he and his little company would sing a hymn and march to the church as rapidly as possible. The crowd would follow and fill the auditorium. During this meeting there were forty conversions, and but one woman among them. The converts were men, gathered together and brought into the church as a result of the brief meetings held on the street. From that time on for four years, there was a constant tide of salvation.

A number of special meetings were held, conducted by the holiness evangelists, William Mac Donald, J. A. Wood, and others. The work grew and prospered, however, not so much *Some Special Meetings* because of special meetings, as by reason of the constant means of grace. It was a great inflowing tide of spiritual life, power, and salvation.

The Tabernacle at Pasadena The new church was finished and dedicated, but the crowds that gathered were so great, and so overtaxed the capacity of the building, that a tabernacle was constructed adjoining it, at a cost of $10,000, which had a seating capacity of 2,000.

During those four years Dr. Bresee took into the church, either by letter or on probation, a thousand persons. Throughout that period, although not all the membership *A Constant Revival* was in the enjoyment of sanctification, the church was on the high tide of spiritual life, glory, and full salvation.

It was while in Pasadena, that the first great Christmas love feast was held under the leadership of Dr. Bresee. At that first Christmas love feast, the new church was crowded, and it was a season of marvelous power and glory, never to be forgotten by those who were present. The songs of victory and shouts of triumph and holy joy, went up to heaven. These Christmas love feasts have been a characteristic of the holiness movement in Southern California ever since that time, and until the Christmas following his death, in 1915, Dr. Bresee conducted all these glorious meetings.

It was during Dr. Bresee's pastorate that the great prohibition movement began in California, as a result of which Pasadena became a prohibition city, and I think, the first

The Prohibition Campaign

in the state. The fight was a very hotly contested one, and after the adoption of prohibition, the matter of the right of a city of that class to have such a law, was carried to the supreme court, which decided in favor of the law. Dr. Bresee took a very prominent part in that conflict, so much so, indeed, as to draw the fire of the enemy upon himself. The opponents of prohibition were so aroused that they burned him in effigy, and attacked him in the most vituperative manner in the public press of the city.

The term of ministerial office in the Methodist church, was lengthened from three to five years while Dr. Bresee was pastor of the First church in Pasadena, and, as a result

Reasons for Leaving Pasadena

of this change, he remained four years. At the end of the fourth year, opposition of some strength had developed against the preaching and work of holiness, and a few of the members, who were influential because of their wealth and standing, opposed Dr. Bresee, and objected to his return to the charge, because of his favorable attitude toward holiness. This was to him a new experience, as up to that time, he had never met with any opposition to his return to a charge. For this reason he was more sensitive in regard to the matter than he otherwise would have been, and, although the opposition was confined to not more than half a dozen persons all told, he declined to return. He felt that he could not work advantageously in a church where some of the members were antagonistic to the gospel that he preached. He subsequently came to see that this was a faulty judgment and a great error. Many good men who were then members of the Pasadena church, realized that he was making a serious mistake, and some of them wrote to him at the Conference, saying that, if he intended to make that the criterion of his future action, he had better lower the standard of his preaching. Both the Bishop and the Presiding Elder proposed his return for a fifth year, contingent upon his consent, but he declined. He left a large and flourishing church, as intensely spiritual and triumphant as any of which he had ever been pastor.

CHAPTER XI.

When it became known that Dr. Bresee was not going back to Pasadena, the official board of Asbury Methodist Episcopal church, Los Angeles, invited him to that church.

Appointed to Asbury Church Los Angeles

He accepted the invitation, subject to appointment by the Bishop, and was sent there in the autumn of 1890. The church was not in a flourishing condition, and its members had hopes and expectations that Dr. Bresee would be enabled to bring it forward to success. But, notwithstanding this expectation, many of them agreed together that they would not accept full salvation.

A short time after the beginning of the new Conference year, a brief meeting of about two weeks

A Great Tide of Salvation

duration was held in Asbury church, at which Dr. Mac Donald and Dr. Wood assisted Brother Bresee. The Lord very graciously poured out His Spirit, and on the afternoon of the second Sabbath of the meeting, many persons were at the altar, and at a subsequent meeting one of the leading members of the official board cried to God for full salvation. Admidst tears and prayers, he looked up, and seeing some of the brethren of the official board standing by, exclaimed: "Brethren, you can't depend on me any longer." God wonderfully sanctified him, and all, or nearly all, the members of the board came into the experience of sanctification. A goodly number of persons were converted, and there was a great tide of victory.

In the midst of one of the protracted meetings held in

Asbury church during this period, Amanda Smith, the noted colored evangelist, came to Los Angeles. She helped at the meetings for a few days. Dr. Bresee gives the following eloquent description of this mighty woman of God: "She preached one Sabbath afternoon, as I never heard her preach before, and as I have rarely ever heard anybody preach, in strains of holy eloquence and unction, almost equal to Bishop Simpson in the zenith of his power and sacred oratory. The Lord opened heaven on the people in mighty tides of glory."

Amanda Smith

Among those who were sanctified, was a young preacher who was still in one of the Conferences. He was so overwhelmed by the mighty baptism which came upon him, that for days he was confined to his bed, and about all he could do was to lift up his hands and exclaim: "The Lord God of Elijah." He did not get over it for a long time. The last I heard of him he still claimed to be sanctified. Pearl Sigler, another young preacher, was also sanctified at this meeting. He joined the Southern California Methodist Episcopal Conference, and maintained and preached the experience up to the time of his death in Kansas City.

During the year of Dr. Bresee's ministry at Asbury church, he was absent nine weeks attending national campmeetings in the eastern states and middle west, and the tide of salvation in Asbury had received such marvelous impulse by the outpouring of the Spirit, that it went right along throughout his absence, without any diminution in the downpour of victory and glory.

Dr. Bresee desired and expected to return to Asbury church the second year, and was invited to do so by the church, but Bishop Mallalieu, against his earnest protests, appointed him as Presiding Elder of the Los Angeles District. Brother Bresee put forth every effort that was possible to avoid having this appointment thrust upon him, but he was unsuccessful.

The Los Angeles District was a large and influential District, embracing many churches, and was the very heart of Southern California. Dr. Bresee says of this *Appointed* time: "The importance of this year of service *Presiding* can scarcely be over-estimated in my *Elder* life, because of so many things entering into it, which were finally influential in determining the course of my career in the work of holiness, and the future great Nazarene movement."

Soon after the Conference, Dr. Bresee called together the ministers, and as many laymen as practicable, in a public convention for the consideration of the work, and the best means to employ in carrying it on to success. In his address to the convention he said that they were aware that he was on the District at the point of the bayonet; that he had done everything possible to prevent his appointment; that, if he were simply to be an officer of the church, going about holding quarterly Conferences, and asking the question: "Are there any complaints?" "Are there any appeals, etc?" he would resign the Presiding Eldership. But on the other hand, if they would arrange to push the work of real spiritual life and salvation, he would throw himself into it, and do his very best.

After considerable discussion, it was resolved by those present at this meeting, that Dr. Bresee should go around the District, during the first three months of the year, and organize the work. Then he should take *Conducts a* the next three months for evangelistic ser- *Holiness* vices, securing such men as he desired to *Campaign* assist him, and going to the churches where he and his assistants might be invited. A strong committee of twelve laymen was appointed to stand behind him, and help him carry on the work.

In conformity with the action taken at this convention, Dr. Bresee secured the help of the Rev. William Mac Donald, the Rev. A. J. Wood, and the Rev. Dr. Cobb, for three months of evangelistic services. Several invitations were received in advance, the first being North Pasadena, where the first meeting was held, and upon which the Lord peculiarly placed His seal. The pastor, Rev. C. A. Bunker, spent a whole night in prayer, seeking the blessing of a clean heart. In the morning, with one hand upon the open Bible, where he had been reading the promises of God, and the other upon the open Methodist hymn book — this hand resting upon some full salvation hymns of Charles Wesley — God marvelously baptized him with the Holy Ghost and fire, transforming his whole being, and making him, at least for a time, a flaming herald of holiness.

After holding a few meetings in the order of their invitation, Dr. Bresee and his helpers were invited to First Methodist Episcopal church at Los Angeles. The pastor, who had recently been transferred from the Pittsburg Conference, did not himself desire the meeting, but was urged by Bishop Mallalieu to secure the help of Dr. Bresee and his assistants for evangelistic efforts. Not feeling at liberty to ignore the earnest request of the Bishop, the pastor went one day to the meeting, which was being held in Vincent church, in Los Angeles, and told Dr. Bresee, that, if they were going to get the three thousand souls which were to be converted in this Conference, as expected by Bishop Mallalieu, it would be necessary to get a goodly number of them in the First church, and they had better arrange and hold a meeting there. This invitation was most gladly accepted, and arrangements were made to hold a meeting at the earliest possible moment. This revival was one of marvelous power.

The pastor and a number of the influential official members, were intensely antagonistic to the spirit of the revival, by reason of their hostility to the work of full salvation. The meeting had gone on only a few days, when there occurred a service of such unusual power and unearthly glory, as to be really epochal. It was in the afternoon. Dr. Bresee had preached only a short sermon, which was followed by a testimony meeting, upon which the heavens were so opened, and the Spirit of the Lord was so poured out in Pentecostal glory and majesty, as to be almost overwhelming. Such a manifestation of the divine presence is rarely witnessed. It seemed to come upon the people like a tornado from the sky, sweeping everything before it. To use Dr. Bresee's own words: "It would move with the roar and thunder of a cyclone, and then would become as quiet and still as death. Then in a little while it would burst out anew in almost unthinkable and indescribable manifestations of the real Shekinah glory. So great was this manifestation, that even the opponents of holiness seemed overwhelmed and confounded."

The next morning, at the early meeting, when there were probably not more than forty or fifty persons present, Dr. Bresee said: "Let us begin this meeting at the altar," and immediately the people gathered for earnest prayer. After a somewhat prolonged season of prayer, when the house had become filled with worshipers, he said: "There has been much questioning in reference to this great doctrine of entire sanctification as a second work of grace. I am going to prove it, and I will do so this morning in such a way, and so fully, that it never can be questioned by any of these people any more. I will not prove it as a theory, or as a doctrine, but as a fact — a fact and experience known in consciousness, the most clear and satisfactory method of knowledge. I now ask the men and women who know this in their consciousness, to testify in reference to this matter."

About half a dozen of the leading members of the church arose, one after another, and slowly and deliberately testified to the fact of their conversion, their clear experience of the pardon of their sins, and of the manifest grace of God unto them; of their subsequent realization of the need of a further work of grace in their hearts, and how they sought and obtained the cleansing of their hearts from all sin, and the fulness of the indwelling Spirit of God. These testimonies were not only very clear and definite, but were given under great unction. After about half an hour spent in this way, Dr. Bresee said: "I have proved by these witnesses the fact of the experience of entire sanctification as a second work of grace. The testimony of these witnesses would hang any man in Los Angeles, and they have clearly testified that they know by this best method of knowledge, their own consciousness, that this is a fact. If there is anybody here who doubts their testimony, or doubts the fact that they have witnessed it, I want him to say so, for I will prove it this morning so that no one present can ever question it again. Now, if there are any here who doubt in reference to this matter of the second work of grace in a human soul, let them stand up, and I will prove it to them so that they will never doubt it again. No one arose, and he then said: "You accept it then, as a truth. You believe these witnesses, and you believe that men and women are sanctified as a second, definite work of grace." Then he said: "You had better seek it."

At this point, the pastor of the church sprang to his feet in the pulpit, and was followed to the altar by a large number of the members. The revival broke out with such depth and power, that the meeting had to be continued a week longer than had been planned.

Just at the close of this meeting, Bishop Fowler, resident at San Francisco, having heard of the character of the preaching and services, came to Los Angeles with the avowed purpose of wiring Bishop Mallalieu and having Dr. Bresee removed from the District. Bishop Fowler had little sympathy with the Wesleyan doctrine of entire sanctification, and was currently reported to have said that it was an intellectual idiosyncrasy. But, for some reason, he did not carry out his purpose, and Dr. Bresee was undisturbed in the Presiding Eldership.

The work of holiness continued to spread more and more during the year, at the close of which a great holiness camp-meeting was held at Long Beach. Dr. Fowler, for many years president of the National Holiness Association, and

Dr. McLaughlin, were present, and conducted the meeting — this being their first visit to the Pacific Coast. At this meeting the conflict was very fierce, several of the leading ministers of the District being earnestly opposed to the teaching and work. The brethren in charge acquitted themselves well in both preaching and altar services, and there was a great tide of spiritual life and divine manifestation.

I will give the account of this Conference in Dr. Bresee's own words: "In 1892, the annual Conference was held in San Diego, and was presided over by Bishop Vincent, whose chief mission seemingly was to see *The Annual* to it that there was a new Presiding Elder *Conference* for the Los Angeles District. The year pre- *of 1892* vious, at the annual Conference, it had been ordered that an evangelistic service be held at the seat of the next Conference, for a few days preceding its session, with the object of promoting the devotion and spirituality of the Conference, and with the thought that the Conference itself might be a great season of spiritual victory. A committee, of which I was chairman, was appointed to take charge of these meetings. Previous to the Conference session it was arranged that these services should begin about a week before the sitting of the Conference. For this purpose, at the appointed time, I went to San Diego, being the only one of the committee who was present for the preceding services. I held the meeting for several days and nights, and there was a very precious outpouring of the spirit of God upon the people.

"When the time for the opening of the Conference arrived, there was no further arrangement or provision for the carrying on of the services, it being evident that the Presiding Bishop did not so desire."

CHAPTER XII.

"Bishop Vincent had little difficulty in arranging for my removal from the District, as my desire to withdraw from the Presiding Eldership was as strong as his wish to remove

Appointed to Simpson Methodist Episcopal Church
me could possibly have been. His method of accomplishing that result, however, showed his determination in the matter.

"As he was calling over the appointments, and came to some which were more or less uncertain, he called out Simpson church, and said: 'Dr. Bresee, who is to go to Simpson church?' I replied: 'I do not know. It is possible they may be compelled to have a transfer.' He then said: 'Why don't you go there yourself?' I answered that I had told the committee which had approached me in reference to the matter, that, if it were thought best by the Presiding Bishop for me to go there, I would serve them to the best of my ability. He said: 'What are your initials?' I said 'P. F,' and he wrote down: 'To Simpson church.'

"His attitude toward holiness was clearly brought out in the cabinet in connection with some other matters bearing on the appointments. As the names of the preachers

Bishop Vincent's Opposition to Holiness
were called or referred to, that of Rev. T. E. Robinson was mentioned, and the Bishop said, meditatively: 'Robinson, Robinson. Is he that holiness crank?' I remarked: 'Brother Robinson preaches holiness, but is a very sane, safe, and able man.' When it was proposed to send another brother, a young man, the Bishop said again, thoughtfully: 'There is a lay-

97

man up there, a holiness man, who I am afraid will spoil that young man, if I send him there' — indicating the fact that the men who preached or professed holiness in the Conference were marked men, and evidently not marked for favor. When the appointments of the Conference were read, I was appointed to Simpson church, Los Angeles, California."

This was a comparatively new church, with a fine auditorium, but a rather small congregation. The enterprise had been launched a few years previous, and the church built with the hope of making a great and popular organization. A heavy church indebtedness, however, and other adverse conditions, had worked against the accomplishment of these hopes.

Dr. Bresee entered upon the pastorate of this church with a feeling of satisfaction at being relieved from the work of the District, and with the hope that he might be able to help bring about what seemed to be a great possibility.

When the year was half spent, he was convinced of the futility of his hopes.

The heavy debt was almost crushing, and after much consultation and some effort, it was seen to be impracticable to provide for it.

There were very few in the church who were willing to accept the deeper things of God, and such consecration and faith as were required to enable them to enter into the glory and power of the Pentecost. It was not much *Obstacles* past the middle of the year when Dr. Bresee *to* quietly notified the official members that, *Success* while he would do the best he could to the end of the year, he could not remain longer. He advised them, as they were not far removed from the First church, to either make some arrangement for coalition with it, or to sell the property, pay the debt, and move out further into the residence portion of the city, where their possibilities might be enhanced. The year, as a whole, was not very satisfactory.

The annual Conference in the autumn of 1893, was held by Bishop Andrews, and Dr. Bresee was appointed to Boyle Heights Methodist Episcopal church, in Los Angeles. He entered upon that field of labor with alacrity, rejoicing to be free from the embarrassment of an indebtedness on the Simpson church, which amounted nearly to bankruptcy. The Boyle Heights church was not encumbered by any special indebtedness. It had been very difficult, however, to meet the running expenses of the church Money had been borrowed, and the resources of the future had been used and pledged for the purpose of securing money to meet the expenses at the close of the church year.

Appointed to Boyle Heights

During the pastorate of Dr. Bresee the congregations were built up, the membership increased, the spiritual life of the church quickened, and the whole year, while not characterized by any great revival, was a good one. There was a constant upward trend in the general Christian experience, as well as in the church life and work. The finances also were well provided for, so that at the end of the year, money was left in the treasury to be used during the next year.

I deem it best to quote from Dr. Bresee as to the circumstances and motives which actuated him in withdrawing from the church of which he had so long been an honored member: "It had been my long cherished desire to have a place in the heart of the city, which could be made a center of holy fire, and where the gospel could be preached to the poor. In the early part of this year (1894), such an opportunity presented itself. Persons into whose hands had come as a trust, an amount of money sufficient to open a work of this kind, came to me with proposals to enter upon such an enterprise. They desired me to co-operate with them in securing a proper location, putting up suitable buildings, and conducting a work of such magni-

Conditions Preceding Dr. Bresee's Withdrawal from the M. E. Church

99

tude as might be sufficient to accomplish the results that we all so ardently desired. The conditions of this enterprise were such that, if it was entered upon, it must necessarily be undenominational. At first, the matter was scarcely entertained, but the proposal being repeated and pressed, thought and much prayer were given to it, and finally the conclusion was reached that this was a providential way to accomplish the object which had been sought. Agreements were entered into, arrangements made, property purchased, in the heart of the city, a block erected, which contained a large auditorium and other rooms for services and for rent.

"At the end of the conference year this building had been completed, and was ready for dedication. The dedicatory services were held and the work entered upon, the second Sabbath after the opening of the new year. All this necessitated unforseen courses of action. I had supposed that it would be possible for me to carry on this undertaking in connection with the Conference of which I was a member, as the law of the church made such a course possible. I supposed that, at any rate, I could take a supernumerary relation to the Conference, still remain a member thereof, and at the same time do this much needed mission work, even though it was undenominational. Through my Presiding Elder, I formally and in writing, asked the Bishop and Cabinet, if it was thought desirable and practicable to arrange for me to do this work by regular appointment; but, if this was found unadvisable, for my Presiding Elder to ask of the Conference on my behalf, a supernumerary relation. I am not informed whether the former proposition was ever seriously discussed, but I was advised that it was impracticable. Hence, my Presiding Elder, in executive session of the Conference, asked for me a supernumerary relation. After continued discussion, in which my course was strongly deprecated, the request was refused. In this discussion I had taken no further part than to reply to some questions asked me by the Presiding Bishop, as to the methods which I purposed to pursue.

CHAPTER XIII.

"The action of the Conference placed me in a position where I could not remain one of its members and go on with the work for which I had arranged, without transgressing the law of the church. So, after a night of prayer and thought, I told my Presiding Elder that he might ask for me a location. This he did, and it was granted without apparent reluctance.

Is Forced to Withdraw from the Conference

It seemed as though the Conference felt that it was relieving itself of the responsibility of this great question, when in fact, it was assuming it in a far more vital way.

"I was now out of the Conference. I had been a member of an annual Conference from the time of my boyhood, having united with the Iowa Annual Conference when I was 18 years of age. I had thus held my membership for a period of 37 years. I scarcely knew any other home relationship in the church than the annual conference, and when I laid it down that day, it seemed to me that I laid down everything pertaining to the church which I had so loved and labored for. My heart was full of almost unbearable sadness. The night was spent in much prayer, and with many tears.

"In the morning when I arose and went into the sitting room, I took up my Bible, and asked the Lord to give me some message from its sacred pages which would comfort and strengthen me. It had not been my custom to look for random readings in the Bible, having been taught to search the Word of God for His truths and teachings; however, I asked God to guide me at once to a helpful portion. I opened the Bible to the 66th chapter of Isaiah, and the 5th verse, which I read, and which was applied to my heart greatly to my comfort and peace. That verse is as follows: 'Hear the word of the Lord, ye that tremble at his word; Your brethren that hated you, that cast you out for my name's sake, said, Let the Lord be glorified: but He shall appear to your joy, and they shall be ashamed.' "

As has been already stated, the Peniel Mission building was dedicated on the second Sabbath after the annual Conference. The intermediate Sabbath was spent at Redlands, in the Methodist church, in a great all-day service, conducted by Dr. Bresee, at which about seventy-five persons were at the altar, seeking the Lord, most of them for entire sanctification. In connection with this service, arrangements were made for Rev. Joseph H. Smith to hold a meeting in Redlands in the not distant future, finally resulting in his removal to that city, where he resided for a number of years.

The new building, which was situated on Main street, between Second and Third streets in Los Angeles, was dedicated with large audiences and great blessing. The enterprise was entered upon with good prospects of ultimate success. The work, which was conducted in connection with the persons with whom arrangements had previously been made, was earnestly pushed. Three regular services were held on Sunday, besides Sunday school and prayermeeting. There were meetings every night in the week. In addition to these regular services, special meetings were conducted, especially two great meetings of three weeks each, one led by Rev. Joseph H. Smith, and the other by Dr. Carradine. At these revival services large numbers of people went to the altar. The entire year was one of marked success and victory. A training school for Christian workers was organized and carried on throughout the year, and there seemed very large possibilities opening up before this mission enterprise.

I will close the description of Dr. Bresee's connection with the Peniel Mission in his own words: "In the summer of the year I went East to be gone two or three months, and to assist at a number of the national campmeetings. While in the East, I was informed by my coajutors of their unwillingness to go forward with me in the work. As to their course, and the treatment accorded me by them, which made it seem necessary for me to withdraw myself finally from this work, I prefer to draw a veil."

This brings us to the year 1895. Doctor Bresee was now without a place in the Conference, and apparently without opportunity for service, but immediately a new door was opened for him. Many of the peo-

Events Preceding the ple who had gathered about him
Organization of the in the mission hall, rallied around
Church of the Nazarene him, and after considerable
consultation and prayer, a hall
was provided at 317 South Main street, where, with glad hearts and great rejoicing, the people gathered to worship God and "push the battle." This was on the first Sunday of October, 1895. Fortunately the little notice which was sent out among the friends, apprising them of this meeting, and its time and place, was preserved. The notice is as follows:

NOTICE OF FIRST MEETING.

DEAR FRIENDS: Los Angeles, Cal., Oct., 1895.

Permit us to inform you that Rev. P. F. Bresee, D. D., will preach next Sabbath, October 6th, at 11 a. m., in the hall at 317 South Main street, Los Angeles, Cal., instead of at Peniel Hall as heretofore.

There will be a special holiness meeting at the same place at 3 p. m., conducted by Rev. J. A. Wood, D. D.

Rev. J. P. Widney, LL. D. will preach at 7:30 p. m.

We are also very glad to be able to announce to you that Drs. Widney and Bresee have arranged to associate themselves, together with such Christian people as may desire to join with them to carry on Christian work, especially evangelistic and city mission work, and the spreading of the doctrine and experience of Christian holiness.

We cordially invite you to the opening services of this work next Sabbath, October 6, 1895, at 317 S. Main street, Los Angeles, Cal.

Committee.

There came into the work at this time what seemed a providential agent in the person of Dr. J. P. Widney, who brought with him a good degree of influence, giving much cheer and hope. I will let Dr. Bresee him-
Rev. Dr. self characterize his old time friend and
J. P. Widney associate, Dr. Widney: "He was a member of the Southern California Conference of the Methodist Episcopal church, and a noble, cultured Christian gentleman. His life had been largely given to his profession as a physician, until some years previously he had founded and organized a medical college, of which he became dean. He was afterwards elected to the presidency of the Southern California University, because of which relation, he had united with the annual Conference. He was a man of ripe scholarship, and earnest Christian life. He at once entered heartily with me into the work of organization and evangelism. His training and teaching were such as not to adapt him in all respects to the various features of such a work as had been undertaken, and after about four years, he withdrew from the Church of the Nazarene, and returned to the Methodist Episcopal church, taking up the regular work of the ministry in that church."

On the third Sabbath of October, 1895, the work of organization heretofore referred to, was begun. At the morning service eighty-six men and women stood together and plight-
ed to God and each other their fidelity
The First in the organization and carrying on of
Church of the the work of the Church of the Nazarene,
Nazarene with the declared purpose of preaching holiness, and carrying the gospel to the poor. The numbers were added to, so that during that day one hundred were enrolled, and the list of charter members being kept open for a few days, the organization was finally consummated with 135 charter members.

The songs of praise and shouts of triumph in this hall were distasteful to its irreligious owners, and before the first month expired, they, with such kindness as was possible indicated that while they did not desire to put the little company to any inocnvenience, they did wish them, as soon as convenient, to vacate the hall. Another larger and more commodious hall was secured on North Main street, near the junction of Spring and Main, the first service in which was held on Thanksgiving day, 1895. Here a larger audience could be accommodated, and the place was filled with earnest worshipers. The First Church of the Nazarene held its meetings in this hall until the early spring of 1896, when, on account of the necessity of remodeling the interior of the building, it became necessary to seek another meeting place.

It was a very serious question as to where the church could find a home. The city was thoroughly traversed and a vain effort was made to secure a large store building, or some hall where an audience *Conditions Necessitating* might be accommodated and *the Erection of* the work go on. The renting *the Tabernacle* of a theatre for Sunday services was contemplated, but the expense seemed too great. There was much prayer in reference to the matter, and no little solicitude.

CHAPTER XIV.

"I Have Given Myself to You" — The Old Tabernacle an
Attraction to Tourists — Victory Day — Dr. Bresee's
Description of the Christmas Love Feast — Early
Evangelistic Services — Some Prominent
Members of the Church —
Colonel Duncan

Just at this period, as Dr. Bresee was riding one day down
Grand avenue in his buggy, he came upon a church building in process of erection, which was large and commodious.

"I Have Given Myself to You" A number of churches had been erected in the southwestern part of the city, and he was surprised to see this church and the progress that had been made in its construction. Stopping his horse for a moment, his heart almost sank within him as he realized that there was no place to be found for him and his people, when so much provision was being made for various other congregations. Involuntarily, as he closed his eyes, he cried out to God, saying: "Oh, Lord, there is plenty of money seemingly for great churches out in this part of the city, I would that Thou wouldst give me some money to make a place for the Church of the Naza-rene." Immediately as though a voice from heaven, there were uttered in his very consciousness the words: "I have given Myself to you." Dr. Bresee exclaimed: "Thank Thee, Lord, that is enough. I would rather have Thee than all else, and with Thee we have all things." Immediately it was impressed upon him and upon others, that they should lease a lot and build a temporary building. As a result, a lot on Los Angeles street, between 5th and 6th, was leased, and, as the people were poor, and it seemed impossible to raise the money, a personal loan was made of about $800, the note being signed by the leading members of the church. This amount was sufficient to purchase the boards and shingles for the temporary building, the work on which was done largely by the members themselves, a few of whom were carpenters.

106

It was a happy day when the corner stone of the new building was laid, or rather, the corner nail was driven.

The Old Tabernacle A great spike was brought to be driven into the appropriate place, and each member of the church in turn took the hammer and helped to drive it home. This was done in the midst of prayers, testimonies, and songs of praise. The spike was afterward extracted from the building and was kept by Brother Shaw for many years, and is now in the archives of the Nazarene University.

This building was simply a board structure with sides and roof, but in the mild climate of Southern California, it was sufficiently comfortable. It would seat about 400 people. In a little time it was found inadequate to accommodate the congregation, and its enlargement was determined upon. Here was commenced the unique method of money-raising which was the habit of Dr. Bresee, and which he advocated from that time on. This was as follows: After telling the people the needs, and joining with them in prayer for the Lord to enable them to bring such offerings as were in accordance with His purpose, the congregation was asked to stand for a moment. Then as the members sang and shouted, they brought their offerings and laid them on the table at the altar. On this occasion they asked the Lord to enable them to bring $300 and lay it on the table. When the money was counted, however, it was discovered that $400 had been brought. This amount was sufficient to buy the boards and shingles with which to put up an addition to the building. In this plain, unpretentious, and yet comparatively commodious place, the congregation worshiped for about seven years.

This building, little more than a great barn, enters into the history of the Nazarene movement, and becomes one of the sacred places, full of hallowed memories. In connection with it, we can not but recognize the Divine providence which began more and more to be made manifest with reference to the work. Truly the plan of God could be seen in the fact that this place, so unpromising in all outward things, should be made a center, or point of converging conditions, for multitudes. Here it was that the outgoing of great tides of spiritual life and influence began to mark more clearly the Divine call that entered into this work. It could not be more evident that the very place of beginning was arranged with Divine wisdom.

Los Angeles was one of the eyes of the world. To it people came from every part of the land, and from other lands. Many of them began to get in touch with the fire that burned and glowed in this tabernacle. They felt the impulse of the constant tides of blessing and salvation, and the touch of Divine power. Many of them came into the glorious experience of full salvation, and carried the sacred fire back to the lands from whence they had come, thus blazing the way for the work of full salvation.

During these years there was a constant and sweeping revival, and God gave mighty victory in the sanctification of believers and conversion of the unsaved. People were drawn to the services by curiosity, as well as the ordinary impulses which move people to places of worship. It seemed to be not only a new, but a somewhat strange thing, to have a center of fire in the city, where the people triumphed in the power of the gospel, and men and women were being saved from week to week throughout the year. The triumphant songs and mighty shouts of salvation were heard around about, sometimes to the displeasure, and sometimes to the joy of the people. It came to be in some sense one of the sights to be seen by strangers in the city.

This was illustrated by a scene like the following: A company of tourists one day, leaving the city for their eastern homes, were overjoyed to tell what they had seen in Los Angeles, and one of them asked: "Did you go to the Church of the Nazarene?" The other answered "No, we heard about it, and intended to go, but in some way were hindered." The first rejoined: "Well, you ought to have gone.

You never saw anything like it. The people sang and shouted and stood up and said they were sanctified, and it was the greatest thing you ever saw."

On one occasion a gentleman secured a bus and driver to show him the sights of the city. Among other places, he was taken to the Church of the Nazarene. Stopping before a place which looked more like a great barn than anything else, the driver opened the door of the bus and said: "This is the Church of the Nazarene." The stranger alighted, looked at it for sometime, and then asked: "Is that all?" No, it was not all. It was the least part. To use the words of Dr. Bresee: "It was the fire that burned within that gilded its boards with glory, and made them shimmer and shine with the glistening light of heaven. When the multitude is gathered together and there are hundreds of one mind and heart, and the Holy Ghost descends in His plenitude and power, that place is garnished with a beauty and glory in comparison with which all the adornings of Solomon's temple would be barrenness. Every board shines with the jeweled beauty of the walls of the New Jerusalem. What are carved marble, and overlayings of gold, and trimmings of silver; what are arches and turrets and spires; what are the formations of art, and even the triumphs of human genius, in comparison with the beauty of the Lord, and the glory of the Divine presence? This board tabernacle to us is far more beautiful than the most costly marble temple that was ever reared. Here we have seen the Lord. Here in a marvelous way He has been pleased to manifest His power to save. Here He has revealed His glory. It has seemed as if this was the very place of which John wrote when he said: 'And I saw as it were, a sea of glass mingled with fire; and they that had gotten the victory over the beast, and over his image, and over his mark, and over the number of his name, stand on the sea of glass, having the harps of God. And they sing the song of Moses the servant of God, and of the Lamb, saying, Great and marvelous are thy works, Lord God almighty, just and true

109

are thy ways, thou king of saints.' We do not ask for, we do not desire costly churches. We do desire the power and glory of the manifest divine presence. We rejoice in Him. In this board tabernacle the poor are made rich, the sorrowing to rejoice. Heaven greets and fills our souls."

Before taking up in detail the early years of the Church of the Nazarene, in Los Angeles, which constituted a distinct and remarkable era in the Nazarene movement, I shall give Dr. Bresee's own account of some of the most prominent of his coworkers, and some of the most notable events of that glorious epoch.

He summed these up as "Great Events in the Old Tabernacle," and described them in the following order.

"On the first Sunday in May, 1900, at one of the gatherings in the old tabernacle, God so opened the windows of heaven and deluged our souls with unspeakable glory, that, when the waves had passed by a little, and it was possible to say something, I said: 'This is Victory Day. This first Sunday of May, we will henceforth celebrate as Victory Day. We will put 'Victory' up over our altar.' That is the reason you see it there now. In some sense we have celebrated that day on the first Sabbath of May in each of the intervening years.

Victory Day

"In the beginning of the work, the First Church became the repository of certain streams of blessing which had already started, among which was the Christmas love feast. The first of these love feasts was held by me in the First Methodist Episcopal church, at Pasadena, in 1887. I felt strangely impelled at that time to announce and hold a love feast. On Christmas morning, to the surprise of everybody, the house was filled with people. Already in this church the holiness work had become predominant, and this meeting was a gathering to some extent of the holiness forces of Southern California. Among these were the Rev. J. N. Marsh and his wife, both of whom were most saintly and marvelously anointed people. Brother

The Christmas Love Feast

110

Marsh used to be strongly overcome by the Spirit of God. His presence and testimony were a great benediction. The Lord very particularly used him to manifest His own presence and glory. Often the overwhelming anointings that came upon him were greater than his physical strength could bear, and when the meetings were over, it was necessary to remove him to the parsonage and put him to bed, where it would be hours before he would be strong enough to be taken home.

"Sister Marsh was a woman, not only of rare ability, but of singular unction. I have never known or even heard of any other woman who had the anointing that rested upon her. In prayer, testimony and praise it seemed as though the holy fire glowed and burned in all her being and utterances. On that Christmas day, as the meeting advanced, and the testimonies were being given, she arose in the middle of the church and stood and testified and praised God with outstretched hands and burning hallelujahs, that have never been forgotten. The echo of them seems never to die in the memory of anybody that heard. The outpouring of the Holy Spirit was so great and mighty, that probably it had never been equaled in the church in Southern California up to that time. Hence, it was generally felt that the Christmas love feast must be an abiding institution. There were two more held in Pasadena during my pastorate, and then the love feast came to Los Angeles and was celebrated one year in Asbury Methodist Episcopal church, the second year in the First Methodist Episcopal church. During the two following years it was held successively at Simpson Methodist Episcopal church, and Boyle Heights Methodist Episcopal church, after which it found a resting place, like Noah's dove, in the Church of the Nazarene.

"I brought Dr. Mac Donald and Dr. Watson from the East to do evangelistic work, and they were the first holiness evangelists that had ever been brought to this part of the country. I did this when I was in the First Methodist Episcopal church in Los Angesles. Later when I went into Peniel

111

Hall, I brought Joseph Smith and Dr. Carradine to Southern California for evangelistic services. After we came into the Church of the Nazarene, Dr. C. J. Fowler held our first evangelistic meeting, lasting three weeks. Afterward we had H. C. Morrison, Bud Robinson, and Will Huff, who also conducted a great meeting; and at the time of the General Conference of the Methodist Episcopal church, Dr. C. J. Fowler took charge of another very successful meeting in our church. Associated with Dr. Fowler in that meeting were Bud Robinson, H. C. Morrison, and Brother and Sister Harris. At the time that we went to the new building on the corner of 6th and Wall street, a great evangelistic meeting was in progress, conducted by Rev. C. E. Cornell, the present pastor of our First church. Long before that, in the early days of the church, we had Brother Kent as an evangelist. At other times we held meetings conducted by Rev. J. T. Hatfield, Rev. C. W. Ruth, Rev. L. Milton Williams, Rev. Jeff Rogers, Mrs. Rose Potter Crist, Rev. Seth C. Rees, and Rev. I. G. Martin.

"I had for assistant pastors Brothers Ruth, LaFontaine, Whitcomb and Walker.

"Among the first to join our church, was Brother Howland. He was sanctified early in life. By occupation he was a paper manufacturer, in New York, and was a man of such spirituality that he attracted general *Prominent* attention. Leading men in the Methodist *Members of* church at Troy, New York, got him to *Our Church* come to that city, putting up money and building large paper mills for him, and it was through his influence that the famous Troy Praying Band was organized, of which Brother Hillman was the renowned leader. Brother Howland was one of the founders of Ocean Park campmeeting. He was a man of peculiar faith, devotion, and fidelity to God, beautiful in his life and experience, and always foremost in his testimony to the power of the sanctifying blood of Jesus Christ. He was a great sufferer from internal cancer for a number of years.

He longed to depart, and sent for me at one time to pray for him that the Lord would take him home. After talking with him, when I began to pray, I was led to ask the Lord to spare him, and Brother Howland thought that I did not fulfill the mission for which he sent for me. He was somewhat restored, however, and lived a number of years after that incident. He was a man of marked personal appearance, and great religious power.

"One of the men that came into the Nazarene work at the very beginning, was Dr. Whistler. He was a remarkable man, a physician. He lived at El Monte at the time of the Civil War, and was among the first earnest Union men in that section. It is said that many efforts were made to kill him, and but for the fidelity of an old dog which belonged to him, he would probably have been killed. Soon after that he came to Los Angeles, and was an earnest apostle of holiness here all through the years. Although a man of some peculiarities, he had great intensity of spirit, and was well known as a real advocate and witness of full salvation. His funeral was a very marked occasion. It seemed almost impossible to have a formal service. The Spirit of the Lord was so poured out that the people arose and testified to the power of God's grace and salvation. The sweeps of victory and glory that came down were so wonderful that many said, among them Rev. Dr. Cantine, who was present, that they never saw anything like it.

"Another of those who entered heartily into the movement from the beginning, was C. E. McKee, who had been sanctified in the very incipiency of the holiness movement in Southern California, about 1880. Because of his attendance at holiness meetings, he, with several others, had their letters of dismissal sent to them by the church of which he was a member. He threw himself with all his vigor into the Nazarene movement, and was for many years a leader of the Young People's Society. He bore the brunt of the battle. He is very gifted as a leader of devotional meetings, and as a worker at the altar.

113

"Among the firm, devoted and unyielding laborers in this work from the beginning, were Brother and Sister Ely, of Pasadena. Brother Ely was wonderfully converted at the Methodist church in Pasadena, early in my pastorate. He soon after came into the experience of entire sanctification. He and Sister Ely became connected with the Nazarene work at the very beginning, and brought into it all the devotion, intensity and fidelity which it is possible for anybody to bring to a cause. Brother Ely got under conviction, while out of doors, listening to my sermon, and had a very peculiar experience in his conversion. When he came forward to the altar for sanctification, he fell over on his back, and as he lay there, almost shouted himself to death. He has been shouting, and shouting loud, ever since. Sister Ely has been matron of the young ladies ever since the organization of the Nazarene University.

"Mrs. Baldwin and Mrs. Knott, two sisters, were Kentucky women of distinguished ability. Their early life was given to society and worldliness. Although members of the Methodist church for many years, they were not converted. As a result of the holiness movement in Southern California, they were brought under conviction and marvelously saved. Soon afterward they were very clearly and definitely sanctified, and at any sacrifice, they threw themselves into the Nazarene movement. Mrs. Baldwin became one of the founders and teachers of the Bible College, and wrote quite extensively for the Nazarene Messenger. Her personal influence and religious and social power were a great help to the movement in its incipiency and early life. Probably no one blazed the impress of his intellectual force and spiritual power more on the early work of the Church of the Nazarene than she.

"Mrs. Lucy P. Knott early became the leader of a somewhat noted movement among the young women, which led her into the wider field of a minister among us. In the early years of her work she became pastor of what was known as the Mateo Street mission, which was soon organized into a church, and afterward came to be known as the Compton Avenue church. This has been one of the most successful churches of our denomination. It is now known as Emmanuel church. Sister Knott has been especially interested in the missionary work, both home and foreign, and her influence, together with the large offerings which her church has made, have been felt in many lands. As a preacher and leader in the church, she has shown peculiar ability. The Lord has greatly blessed her work, giving her a constant tide of salvation among all classes, from little children to old people. She has always enjoyed the hearty co-operation of her husband, Judge W. S. Knott, who entered our movement with her, and thoroughly sympathizes with her in her work, himself preaching and teaching as occasion offers. Recently her son, James Proctor Knott, has been associated with her in the pastorate of the church, and the conduct of a very successful parish school, which she opened and conducts in conjunction with the church.

"This work attracted to itself a great variety of personalities. A peculiar illustration of this was the case of Colonel Duncan. When he came in contact with the Nazarene movement, he was a man of mature life, had *Colonel* regarded himself always as an Episcopalian, *Duncan* and had much prominence in business and political circles, being a man of considerable wealth and many business enterprises. He was a Southerner, and closely identified with the War of the Rebellion. He was a friend of Jefferson Davis, the president of the Confederacy, and when it was impossible to secure proper paper for the making of the Confederate money, Colonel Duncan engaged successfully in the manufacture of paper for that purpose. Being in Europe during part of the Civil war, and the Southern Confederacy not having representatives in the papal states, the pope gave him a passport to the papal states, which he retained and which I saw. It bore the signatures of the pope and his cardinals. Brother Duncan was brought to our church by his friend, Mrs. Willard. As a result, he professed conversion and united with the church. He became one of its first benefactors in arranging for and helping provide for the securing of a permanent home for the work."

CHAPTER XV.

During the first two years of the life and work of the Church of the Nazarene, in Los Angeles, it had no regular paper. Occasionally a little leaflet was published, containing a few items of church news, but, unfor-
The tunately, only one of these, so far as I know,
Church has been preserved. It was not until January,
Paper 1898, that the regular publication of a church paper was commenced. It was called "The Nazarene," and was a four-page paper, with three broad columns on each page, the size of the pages being about ten inches in width by fifteen inches in length. It was published monthly in different forms, Dr. Bresee and Dr. J. P. Widney being the editors. In August, 1898, it was changed to an eight-page paper, with two columns to each page, the pages being about eight inches wide and twelve inches long. The place of publication was 526 South Los Angeles street, and the subscription price fifty cents per year. Dr. Bresee became the sole editor of the paper, in October, 1898, Dr. Widney at that time withdrawing from the Church of the Nazarene. In July, 1899, the paper was changed to an eight-page weekly, with Dr. Bresee as the editor, and J. P. Coleman and E. H. Catterlin, as the associate editors.

In the issue of July, 1898, I find the following appeal, under the heading "Our Church Paper":

"We would urge upon our people a more general subscription to our church paper, THE NAZARENE. The paper is published with a double object; first, that our people may know regularly the condition and the progress of our own work, and have in their homes a publication devoted to the spread of Christian holiness here in our city; and second, that the paper with this information may be carried by our

117

workers into the homes of the people whom we are trying to reach and lead to God. It is true there are many papers devoted to kindred topics that are published over the land, but they can not do the local work here any more than the great New York dailies or weeklies could do the local work of Los Angeles, or take the place of our home paper.

"The Nazarene, at first published occasionally and irregularly, as the needs of the work seemed to demand, is now issued as a monthly. Fifteen hundred copies of each issue have been circulated and put into the homes of the people in the parts of the city where our work chiefly lies. A portion goes to our struggling churches elsewhere. Only eternity will reveal the good done and the souls that have been touched and influenced. While many of our people are subscribers to the paper, we need two hundred new names to put it upon a self supporting basis. The subscription price is fifty cents a year. The Rev. J. P. Coleman contributes his time as business agent. Subscriptions made to him will be promptly attended to. The editors receive no compensation for their time and labor. It is for the Lord.

Brethren, Sisters, subscribe promptly."

In the issue of October, 1898, the following appears: "Heretofore we have published The Nazarene, first to the subscribers, and then for gratuitous distribution, as a method of advertising the work, and as a *"The* tract, using it as a means of securing the *Nazarene"* attendance of those who otherwise might not know of our church and work, and are not attendants upon church services anywhere. From henceforth it will be published for the subscribers. We have enlarged the amount of matter, and generally improved the paper. The subscription price will still be fifty cents a year. Those subscribing now will get the paper the rest of this year and next year at the same rate. We hope just as many of our friends as possible will subscribe for the paper. And those who are now subscribers will renew their subscriptions, and that those who have not paid for the current year will do

118

so. The paper needs the money from each subscriber. Most have paid, but some have not. Let our friends roll up a magnificent list for next year. Not only take it yourself, but get others to do so. Subscriptions need not necessarily be paid in advance. The paper will need money all through the year."

It was not until the year 1900 that the name of the paper was changed from "The Nazarene," to "The Nazarene Messenger," which title it retained until after the General

The Nazarene Messenger
Assembly, which met in 1911, when it was consolidated with the HERALD OF HOLINESS, and ceased to exist under its former name.

During the nearly fourteen years which elapsed from the beginning of the publication of "The Nazarene," until the inauguration of the "Herald of Holiness," Dr. Bresee did

Dr. Bresee As an Editor
a prodigious amount of editorial work. Although most of this labor was done under pressure, many of the articles written by Dr. Bresee are religious classics, which, if properly gathered together and classified, would make several extremely valuable and interesting volumns.

Much of the data contained in the following pages has been collated from the files of "The Nazarene Messenger," which at first from month to month, and later from week to week, faithfully recorded the progress of the work in the parent church, the rapid extension of the movement; the incoming of new workers; the triumphant death of many of the older members of the church; the great evangelistic services which are held from time to time; the missionary activities of the church; the organization of new churches in different parts of the country; the establishment of a Bible College, which later became the Nazarene University; the various Assemblies which were held from year to year; the articles of faith adopted by the young church; the journeys undertaken by Dr. Bresee in the upbuilding and extension of the work; and finally the mighty tides of spiritual power, glory, and salvation which rolled on year after year, sweeping many thousands of souls into the kingdom of God, and the cleansing fountain of Jesus' blood.

Doubtless no period in the history of the Church of the Nazarene has been more important than the two years and two months which elapsed between the organization of the First Church in Los Angeles, and the publication of the first number of "The Nazarene." I recognize the importance of devoting as much attention as possible to this crucial epoch in the life of Dr. Bresee. In doing so, the only data at my command is the shorthand diary which I have kept for more than twenty-seven years.

The Formative Period

Excerpts From Diary

I had a very voluminous correspondence with Dr. Bresee during this period, but all his letters were destroyed in the great San Francisco fire of 1906, and my replies in connection with the work in Berkeley throw little light upon what was going on in Los Angeles. In my diary of Oct. 15, 1895, I find the following: "I have just returned from Dr. Bresee's. During a conversation which lasted several hours, he told me just how it was that he left Peniel Hall. * * * Dr. Bresee and Dr. Widney have started what will be a new church. The Doctor has been driven to it, and regards it as the will of the Lord that he should do this." On October 23, 1895, I attended the prayermeeting at the Church of the Nazarene, and said: "There was a great spiritual power there, and I was blessed. One man sought salvation, and I hope found it before he left." On Sunday, October 27th, I state: "Dr. Bresee preached a grand sermon from Luke 7:25, 'Whom went ye out for to see?' He brought out several entirely new thoughts."

I made another trip to Los Angeles with the Supreme Court, in April, 1896, and on the 19th called at Dr. Bresee's residence on San Julian street, and went with him and his daughter, Sue, to the church on Los Angeles street near 5th. I noted in my diary as follows: "It is a rough frame structure, 65 by 45, which cost $900, and will seat six hundred people. They got in it last Sunday. It was filled this morning, and there was a good meeting tonight. The address was by Dr. Widney." The following are other quotations from my diary:

"On April 20th, I called on Dr. Bresee again, and we talked over the new church enterprise, the principles of primitive Christianity, and the best way of getting God's people organized along Christian lines."

"On April 21st I attended the holiness meeting. There were seventy or eighty there, and it was a splendid service. Several came to the altar seeking salvation and sanctification. The message was by Brother Marsh, and the power of the Holy Ghost was with him."

"On Wednesday, April 22d, there were at least 120 at the prayer meeting. I gave a Bible reading, and a lady who sought pardon as a backslider, came to the altar, believed that her sins were forgiven, and made a complete consecration to God." I made another trip to Los Angeles in October, 1896, and under date of October 18th, I find the following entry in my diary: "I walked to where Dr. Bresee formerly lived, and found that he had moved. I then went to the church building, on Los Angeles street, between 5th and 6th, and got there just as the meeting closed. It had been a wonderful manifestation of the power and presence of God. Dr. Bresee took me in his buggy to his residence on 11th street, and I ate supper with them and went to the meeting with him and his wife and mother. I led in prayer. It was a grand meeting. No one was saved, but the invitation was extended cordially, and I tried to get one young man to come forward, but he was stubborn and rude. It is just a year since the church was organized, and 350 members have been taken into it, nearly all of whom are still there. Souls have been saved and sanctified right along. They have had to extend the building, and make it twenty-five feet longer. It will hold eight hundred people. It is truly a wonderful work, and I do not think that there is anything that will compare with it in the United States."

Under date of October 19, 1896, I find the following entry in my diary: "Dr. Bresee called for me about 6:15 p. m., and five minutes later we started. We drove first to the residence of Brother McKee, in East Los Angeles, where he joined us, and we went to South Pasadena. It was the residence of Brother and Sister Helm, two of the grandest old saints it has ever been my good fortune to meet. There were about thirty present, and we had a glorious prayer-meeting. Nearly all gave stirring holiness testimonies. Dr. Bresee led and prayed with his usual earnestness, unction, and vigor, and I read the Word and spoke for a few minutes. Among the testimonies that did me the most good were those of Brother and Sister Helm, Brother McKee, Brother Ely, and a Scotch lady, whose name I did not catch. I gave my testimony." Under date of Tuesday, October 20, 1896, I find the following in my diary: "This afternoon I went to the Church of the Nazarene. Dr. Bresee led the altar service, and one young lady came out brightly for sanctification."

On Wednesday, October 21, 1896, I attended the prayer-meeting. There were from 130 to 140 present, and it was a grand meeting.

I remember well the trip to South Pasadena with Dr. Bresee, on the evening of October 19, 1896, for it was on that occasion that I told him how much I would like to have a Church of the Nazarene in Berkeley. He replied that, if I meant business, and would become the pastor of the church, he would come up there at any time and hold a ten-days' meeting, for the express purpose of organizing a Church of the Nazarene. I told him that I would do so, but asked for time in which to pray over the matter, so that I might be plainly led as to just when to take the important step.

On November 7, 1896, I wrote a letter to Dr. Bresee, in which I stated that, after more than a year of prayerful consideration, I had determined to withdraw from the Methodist Episcopal church, and to do what I could to help organize a church on the lines of primitive Christianity. I said that I had announced my decision to Dr. Bentley, my pastor, who had given me my church letter. Among other things contained in this letter, was the following: "I think perhaps that the best time for you to come would be early in January. I will work it up in every possible way, and we will have a glorious time, and good results. It shook me up considerably to take this step, but I am overjoyed since I took it. Hallelujah to Jesus!"

Early in January of 1897, Dr. Bresee went to Berkeley, a Church of the Nazarene was organized, of which I became the pastor; and the center of holy fire then established in that place, has been maintained there ever since. Dr. Bresee's account of this will be given in another chapter.

Organization of Other Churches

In the following April, he made a trip to Oakland, and organized the Church of the Nazarene there, of which Brother W. E. Shepard became pastor. During the year 1897, Dr. Widney made two trips to the northern part of California, and conducted meetings in Oakland and Berkeley. Dr. Bresee had arranged to visit San Francisco and vicinity in the latter part of that year, but an attack of pneumonia prevented him, and Dr. Widney went in his stead.

A society, which later became a Church of the Nazarene, was formed in Elysian Heights, Los Angeles, in the latter part of 1897, the Rev. J. H. McIntyre being the first pastor. About the same time, a church was organized in South Pasadena, of which the Rev. Mr. Clark was pastor.

During all this period the work of God went gloriously forward in the mother church in Los Angeles. Multitudes of souls were saved, and vast numbers of believers were sanctified wholly.

When the First Church was holding its meetings at 208 North Main street, shortly after the beginning of the work, an undated paper or pamphlet was issued by the church. It bore the heading "Church of the Nazarene." In this little

sheet I find the following words of triumph by Dr. Bresee:
"The holy benediction and hallowed joy which come in such
fulness, seem almost a marvel in these days. The voice of
prayers and hallelujahs trembling on the lips; the shouts of
those who conquer, are no infrequent things in the Church
of the Nazarene. Evangelical faith brings pentecostal
glory. The presence of the Lord is often so manifest as we
are gathered together, that not only do our hearts burn
within us, but our tongues are tuned to praise, and triumphant hallelujahs fill the house — to Jesus be all the glory."

This brings us down to the beginning of the year 1898,
and from that time on, I have been able to obtain much
valuable data from "The Nazarene," "The Nazarene Messenger," and still later from the HERALD OF HOLINESS.

CHAPTER XVI.

A Review of the First Two Years — Salvation of the Aged
— A Month of Victory — A Significant Incident — The
Praying Meeting — The Holiness Meeting — The
Young People — Company E — The Brother-
hood of St. Stephen — The Sabbath Ser-
vices — A Pen Picture of the Early
Church of the Nazarene

In the issue of "The Nazarene," of January, 1898, Dr.
Bresee thus summarizes what God had wrought up to that
time: "It is now somewhat more than two years since,

*A Review
of the First
Two Years*
under a peculiar yet unmistakable call of
God, the Nazarenes, putting the old things
behind them, went out to follow in the foot-
steps of Him whose name they bear — to
bring comfort to the sorrowing, help to the
downcast, a message of help to the broken-hearted, and to
carry the gospel of peace to lives burdened with sin. They
went out as a feeble band to a new and untried field of labor,
taking as their especial work the neglected quarters of our
city — yet soon finding that there are hungry hearts and
neglected lives in homes that the world does not call poor,
and so the work has broadened out beyond the field originally selected, until now they feel that the call is to go where-
ever lives are burdened with sin, and hearts crying out,
'What shall I do to be saved?' Surely the seal of Divine
approval has been upon the work. From the first day in that
hall upon Main street, a revival fire has kept burning that
has spread and broadened, until now the Nazarenes are
organized, and have their places of worship, on Los Angeles
street, in Elysian Heights, in East Los Angeles; in South
Pasadena; and in Berkeley and Oakland. Only the lack of
available leaders has delayed the opening of the work at
other points from which a call has come."

Attention is called in the same issue to the number of
conversions among people of advanced years. In Oakland,
a lady of seventy-five gave herself to the Lord, and found

125

peace during the June meeting. In the December meeting, her husband, who was in his eighty-second year, was also saved. He said in his testimony: "I have been looking for fifteen years to find a Church of the Nazarene." In a meeting at South Pasadena, a man in his ninetieth year gave himself to God. In the parent church, in Los Angeles, there were many conversions of persons between the ages of sixty and seventy years. And all these marvelous cases occurred prior to 1898.

How the work prospered in those days, is indicated by the following paragraph, in the issue of March, 1898: "The past month has been one of especial blessing. At the close

A Month of Victory of every month we feel that we have more to praise God for than ever before. It has been one blessed tide of salvation all through the month. Nearly every service is crowned with the salvation of souls and the sanctification of believers. Last Sabbath — the last Sabbath of the month — was a day of special victory. We have never seen the church so crowded, morning and evening, and a large meeting in the afternoon. And each service full of blessing. There were eighteen at the altar during the day. More and more may Jesus see of the travail of His soul and be satisfied. Glory to His Name!"

The far-reaching nature of the influences that radiated from the old tabernacle, is shown by the following incident which occurred in the early part of 1898: Three ladies and

A Significant Incident their two babies left Los Angeles one evening for their home in Butte, Montana. They had been in Southern California but a short time, but the three women had all been converted and sanctified, and during their stay among the Nazarenes had dedicated their little ones to God. A few of the brethren and sisters accompanied them to the Arcade depot, and as the train started, they all sang: "There will be no more parting when Jesus comes." Dr. Bresee

126

closed his account of this scene as follows: "What so sweet on the evening air as a song of Christian triumph, and what hope so blessed in the parting hour as being together forever with the Lord!"

During the early years of the church, the prayermeeting was indescribable in its glory and power. It was invariably crowned and characterized by the manifested Divine presence. The attendance was very large, and great *The* numbers sought and found salvation and heart *Prayer* purity at this meeting. I will try to convey *Meeting* some slight impression of this mighty gathering of the saints by narrating a few typical instances. At the prayermeeting on June 1, 1898, there were songs of victory, prayers for many special cases, and testimonies triumphant and pointed. The altar was filled with seekers for purity and pardon. Nearly all swept into the kingdom, and there were shouts of rejoicing.

In August, 1898, Dr. Bresee thus spoke of the prayermeeting: "The mid-week meeting held on Wednesday night, continues the great and blessed gateway to heaven which it so long has been. We are thankful to see such a multitude at it; but the way to increase the number that are saved, is to formally invite and secure by our influence the attendance of the people to this means of grace. Many have no idea what a live, glorious prayer and testimony meeting is. They think that religion is a thing to be endured. To get them to this meeting would be a revelation to them."

The evening of Wednesday, September 13, 1899, was a time of peculiar heart-searching and crying to God. The Lord's people felt that new anointing with fresh fire was an imperative necessity, and with strong cries and tears they went deeper down, until tides of heavenly strength and glory came into their souls. Several were converted and sanctified.

At the prayermeeting on August 25, 1900, there were at

127

least three hundred persons present, and there was a great
tide of blessing.

Without giving the dates of other prayermeetings, except
on very special occasions, I will merely note some of the
salient features of these marvelous mid-week services. They
were times of refreshing from the presence of the Lord,
with much of Divine glory, and many seekers for pardon
and purity. Early in 1901, I find the following record:
"The Wednesday night, mid-week prayermeeting this week
was one of peculiar interest and power. About three hundred were present. The prayers, the faith, the testimonies
were strong and full of triumph. Several seekers were at
the altar, and the Lord was in the midst to save. The bugle
blasts of victory never gave a more certain sound in the
Church of the Nazarene than in these days. Glory to Jesus!"
On another Wednesday evening, five were converted and
two sanctified.

The holiness meeting, on Tuesday afternoon, has been
maintained and made much of ever since the organization of
the Church of the Nazarene. It has certainly been a season
of wonderful blessing and salvation. Dr.
The Bresee spoke of this meeting, early in 1898
Holiness as follows: The Tuesday holiness meetings are
Meeting seasons of profit and blessing. They are especially along the line of the second blessing,
and the experiences in the land of Canaan. There have been
no evil reports. The fruits are luscious, the milk and honey
good, the springs and wells of water abundant. It is a goodly land. We love to sing: 'I am living in Canaan now.'
There is a good attendance, and many souls have found the
fulness of the blessing of the gospel at these meetings. Indeed, it is a rare service when some hungry soul does not
plunge into 'the fountain of blessing so sweet.' Let our
people make a great specialty of this meeting, and always
find some one to bring with them to it."

In August, 1898, Dr. Bresee said: "The holiness meetings

were never better. Clear teaching, definite testimony, and some getting into the cleansing fountain. This meeting seems more deeply rooted in the hearts of the people than ever. Its utility and blessings are very great. We urge upon all who can to make it the one week-day afternoon meeting which they specially provide for, bringing with them those whom they hope to interest in full salvation."

On another occasion he says: "I wish that special emphasis may be laid upon the Tuesday meeting. It is at 2:30 p. m., and is known as the week-day holiness meeting. It is an accusation that with us every meeting is a holiness meeting. We do not deny it. We are trying all the time to help somebody into the glorious mystery, which eye hath not seen, nor ear heard, neither hath entered into the heart of man, but which the Holy Ghost reveals unto us in these days. We trust that we may ever abide so close to the cleansing fountain that we may constantly be pushing needy souls into the purifying tide. But this Tuesday meeting stands somewhat by itself. It is on a week day. The attendance of those who can be secured at no other time can be arranged for at that hour. It has peculiar opportunities and possibilities for teaching and testimony, for the deepening of experience, and leading people into the blessing. It can reach its highest success only by the most enthusiastic efforts of all the lovers of holiness. Many attend, but conscientious effort could largely increase it. Let us by our faith and enthusiasm make it the great rallying point of Southern California."

In December, 1898, Dr. Bresee said of the holiness meeting: "At some of the meetings the power of God has been displayed in a wonderful manner. On the second Tuesday of the month, Rev. Thomas Fluck, of the Free Methodist church, was present, and gave a heart-searching message from Luke 5 : 5: 'Nevertheless, at thy word, I will let down the net.' The Holy Spirit was manifest in such power that great grace was upon the people. Souls were converted and sanctified, and gave testimony to their new-found joy and victory. On the fourth Tuesday, Dr. Campbell, of the Rock River Conference of the Methodist Episcopal church, was present, and gave a message of peculiar sweetness and power, consisting largely of his own experience. Precious testimonies and an altar service with salvation followed. On the fifth Tuesday, Rev. J. E. Langen, pastor of the holiness church in Pasadena, read and expounded Zachariah 4 : 2, 3. A precious testimony meeting and altar service followed, and one soul was happily converted. Both the attendance and the spiritual power of the meetings have greatly increased during the month."

In the early days of the work of the Church of the Nazarene, the Young Man's Band was organized, and about the same time the young women of the church came largely under the leadership of Sister Lucy P. Knott. *The Young People* The two organizations held separate meetings, but from the begininng there were regular young people's services. Later on the Brotherhood of St. Stephen was formed to take the place of the former organization of young men. Miss Emma Stine was for some time its faithful and efficient leader. At a subsequent period the young people of the church were brought into the Young People's Society, which took the place of both the other organizations.

On July 1, 1898, the young men had charge of the Sunday evening service. The house was packed. The Lord was present in power to awaken, and Brother C. E. McKee, who led, was at his best.

The Young People's Meeting was held on Friday evening, and all, whether old or young, were urged to attend and take part. At this meeting there were prayers, songs, testimonies, a short message from the Word. All enjoyed the greatest liberty, and those who preferred to sing their testimony, were perfectly free to do so. Salvation was a characteristic of the service, and there were very many cases of triumphant conversion and sanctification.

Company E, an organization of girls and young women, was originally a part of what was called "The Buttonhole Brigade." Practically the entire working membership of the church was divided into companies, each *Company* of which took for its name a letter of the *E* alphabet. The idea was to promote individual work on the part of the people, but as time went on, the organization gradually ceased to have any real existence, with the exception of the company led by Mrs. Lucy P. Knott. With great fervor and rare executive ability, this anointed woman labored for the salvation of the girls and young women, and marshalled them into a compact, enthusiastic body, vibrant with holy life and power. It always retained the name of Company E, and grew into a membership of more than one hundred. Its members were full of fire and zeal for the salvation of other girls. They were imbued with the true missionary spirit, and their holy activities were manifold.

In August, 1898, Dr. Bresee thus spoke of this company: "The work among the young ladies goes steadily on, largely through the agency of Company E. It is one of the sights that makes the heart rejoice, to see such a multitude of saved and sanctified young women, praying and laboring to bring other young women to Christ."

The night service on July 4, 1899—one of the most glorious days in the history of the church, and of which I will speak more particularly in another place — was conducted by the members of Company E, about fifty of whom were on the platform. They gave their testimonies and sang their songs of rejoicing and praise. It was marvelous to see and hear these young women. They had found something infinitely better than the world could give, were happy in Jesus' love, and only intent on leading others to the Master. At the close of this unique service, Mrs. Knott gave an earnest invitation, and one man was very blessedly converted.

The Brotherhood of St. Stephen was also an effective organization, and the heroic young men of its membership were veritable firebrands for God. Under the able leadership of Brother R. E. Shaw, who succeeded Sister Stine on her departure for Seattle, a mighty work was accomplished. Brother Shaw, while not a charter member of the church, came to it at a very early period in its life, and was greatly used of God for many years, not only as the director of the young men, but as the superintendent of the Sunday school, and leader of the choir. Much of thrilling interest might be told of this company of Spirit-filled young men, but I will confine myself to a single instance, which may be regarded as typical of their work. One Tuesday evening in May, 1901, they held their regular weekly service at the Plaza, and had great victory. A sister who was with them, sang a song in Spanish, and a Mexican who had been converted the previous Sabbath, gave a clear testimony of the power of God to save. Then Brother Shaw, standing in the open air, and in the heart of the Spanish or Mexican business section of the city, earnestly urged seekers to come to the fountain of Jesus' blood. While he was exhorting, a bright young man who had stood directly in front of the band of workers during the whole meeting, knelt on the ground, and the Lord's children knelt around him and engaged in fervent prayer. He soon wept his way to Calvary, and with shining face told the people what God had done for his soul, at the same time exhorting them to do as he had done. There were many earnest prayers and songs during the altar service, and, as the meeting progressed, the crowd of interested spectators grew larger, and it was evident that the Holy Spirit was moving on the hearts of men.

The Sabbath services consisted of a young people's prayer

Brotherhood of St. Stephen

meeting at 8:30 a. m., followed by the Sunday school at
9:45 a. m. Then, as now, there were four other great services, viz., a preaching service at 11 a. m., a great
The testimony meeting in the afternoon, the young
Sabbath people's meeting at 6 p. m., and a rousing evan-
Services gelistic service at 7:30 p. m. These meetings
were all very largely attended, and were characterized by unctuous and fiery preaching, deeply spiritual
and fervent prayer, much burden for souls, great tides of
salvation, and waves of holy joy and divine glory.

In April, 1899, I spent some little time in Los Angeles,
and wrote the following description of the Nazarene work
as it was carried on at that time: "My twentieth semi-
annual trip to Los Angeles was
A Pen Picture blessedly spent in communion with
of the Early Church the Lord's people, and aggressive
of the Nazarene work under the direction of Dr.
Bresee. In spite of the smallpox,
which broke out during the winter in the immediate vicinity
of the church on Los Angeles street; in spite of the dry
season and hard times, and consequent removal of many of
the workers to other localities; in spite of many other opposing forces, which may be briefly summarized as the resis-
tance of the world, the flesh and the Devil, the work of the
Church of the Nazarene in Los Angeles and thereabouts
goes grandly on.

"I was much impressed with the depth of love for sinners
which animated the people, and the burden for souls which
the Lord had put upon them. In the Wednesday night
prayermeeting, April 19th, this was especially apparent,
and, as a result of the spirit of prayer which there prevailed,
God manifested himself in a solemnity and awfulness which
can not be described. I can not better epitomize the character of the meetings which I attended at the church on
Los Angeles street, than by saying that mothers wept for
their unsaved children, and implored the saints of God to

133

pray importunately for their salvation; wives besought the prayerful interest of fellow Christians for the conversion of their husbands; friends requested that friends be earnestly remembered at the throne of grace; prayers for the sick and dying were asked with great depth of feeling; women with tears streaming from their eyes, told of what God had shown them of the sin, suffering, and misery all around them, all of which might be removed and alleviated by the precious blood of Jesus; men whose appearance showed the intensity of their struggle for the merest necessaries of life, proclaimed exultantly the saving and sanctifying power of Christ, and almost danced for joy; young girls narrated in joyous accents the sweet story of their salvation; colored sisters sang with power and pathos the quaint hymns of their people; colored brothers told with touching eloquence of how Jesus brought peace and rapture to their souls; Dr. Bresee preached with shining face and kindling eye, amidst fervent choruses of hallelujahs and amens, the mighty power of God to save now and to the uttermost, every soul who sought Him in sincerity; the place resounded until the very rafters shook with the songs of salvation; seekers came to the altar in quest of pardon and the baptism with the Holy Ghost and fire; and all around were the tokens that God was in the place, and that it was the very gate of heaven. One dear brother, dying with consumption, came there for the express purpose of getting saved. He said that he gave himself completely to God, and it is quite likely that ere this he has passed through the pearly portals, and is now amidst the throng of the redeemed who sing so rapturously around the throne of God and the Lamb.

"I felt while I was in Los Angeles, that the Church of the Nazarene was on the very eve of greater victory than it had ever known. This was what the people were praying for, and what I feel confident they will receive. There as here, Satan is entrenched in most of the families of the church, and there, as here, only a mighty outpouring of the

Spirit of Him who holds the universe in his hand, will suffice to drive the enemy from these entrenchments.

"As I drove with Dr. Bresee to the Mateo street charge, where Sister Hagg and Brother and Sister Snelling and others are working so faithfully; as I accompanied him to South Pasadena, and joined in the work for a few moments with Brother Clark, Brother and Sister McReynolds, and the brethren there; as I rode out to Elysian Heights with Dr. Bresee and Brother Sisson, and preached to the people and saw the evidences of the harvest which had already resulted from the faithful labors of Brother and Sister McIntyre, Brother and Sister Jaynes, and their fellow laborers; as I went with Brother Bresee and Sisters Knott and Baldwin, to Jefferson street, and there in a little cabin joined hands with Brother and Sister Allison and their blessed work among the children and families of that neighborhood, and listened to the happy testimonies of salvation — I was more than ever impressed with the fact that God is using the Church of the Nazarene in Southern California to carry the gospel among the plain people, and to permeate with the highest and most victorious type of Christian life and experience whole neighborhoods which heretofore have known hardly anything of the Savior's love. The glorious work in Los Angeles, and the encouraging signs in Berkeley and Oakland, cause me to thank God, and believe that greater power and victory than we have ever seen or known are just ahead."

CHAPTER XVII.

On Easter Sunday, 1898, there were great congregations, mighty outpourings of the Holy Spirit, and many souls saved and sanctified. Dr. Bresee said that he never realized more the resurrection power of the Lord.

Notable Sabbaths at the First Church

Sunday, May 29, 1898, and the following Monday were devoted to the celebration of the anniversary of the Pentecost. The services on the Sabbath were peculiarly precious, and the outpouring of the Spirit in the morning was so blessed that songs of praise and shouts of victory burst out in the midst of the preaching of the Word, in such a way as to make it at times impossible for Dr. Bresee to go on with his sermon. The all-day meeting on Monday, which was really a continuation of the Sabbath services, was a scene never to be forgotten. At times the waves of glory were such that amid the shouting and singing and dancing one could easily recognize what it was that made the outside world think that the disciples were drunk. Seekers got into the fountain of cleansing and souls were converted. In reporting this occasion, Dr. Bresee said: "We rejoice that we live in the abiding Pentecost; that there is more to follow; that the infinite ocean never runs dry; that the waters of divine love and power grow deeper and wider, and to our taste become sweeter and more all-absorbing."

During the Sabbath services in August, 1898, there were very large congregations, the place was filled with the presence and power of God; the anointing on the saints so thrilled their souls that they shouted with gladness; and

136

there were many precious trophies of the Savior's dying love and resurrection power. Dr. Bresee said that these rescued ones were stars in the Redeemer's diadem, and harbingers of further triumphs, for, though the uplook was always good, and God's promises were continually filling the heavens with light, a succession of victories brought them down where more eyes could see them, and so he prayed and looked for still greater tides of salvation.

Of the September services Dr. Bresee was able to truthfully say: "The meetings have seemed to have a depth and sweetness which we have not before experienced. Fresh oil has been poured upon the heads and hearts of believers. Exceeding great joy has been the experience of many. Shouts of victory have been heard in almost every meeting, and sometimes the waves have rolled very high. Souls have also found the way of life, and there has been joy among the angels of God, as well as among the blood-washed company down here."

During the home campmeeting in October, 1898, the anointings with the Holy Spirit, and the tides of blessing and victory were at times very marvelous. The 6th of October was a red-letter day in the experience of *Red-Letter* many souls. As the people were engaged in *Days* prayer, there came upon them such a spirit of prayer that many began to pour out their hearts to God in all parts of the house, and there rolled over the assemblage such tides of glory and power that several lost their strength. Little was done during the rest of the service but to wait and praise, while such a sacred wave and heavenly glory filled the place as to be beyond all power of portrayal.

October 23d of the same year was another day of Pentecostal glory, and the waves of divine life and love which flowed over and through God's people, were a real fulfillment of the promise, "I will pour you out a blessing that there shall not be room enough to receive it."

Easter Sunday, 1899, was a glorious day. The congregations were large, and resurrection power was in the midst. The Easter song by Miss Clemmie Gay, and the song 'Sighting the Golden Gate,' by Brother Ledford, were both full of unction and the Spirit, and brought tears to many eyes and shouts of victory to many lips. Dr. Bresee preached mightily, and salvation flowed like a river.

On July 4, 1899, there was a great all-day meeting. In the afternoon, during a general testimony service, as persons from other localities, a number of Christian veterans, and some new converts, were called upon to testify, the people could no longer be restrained from rising and proclaiming the power of the blood. A scene ensued which it is impossible to describe. The Holy Ghost fell upon the people in Pentecostal fashion, and probably fifty persons were on their feet at once praising God. The old patriarchs, with streaming eyes, rushed into each other's arms, giving glory to Jesus, the young converts waved their palms of victory, many shouted, and all gave themselves up to the mighty tide of glory and power. Two souls were marvelously sanctified to God.

September 3, 1899, was a notable day at the First church, which was crowded with glad worshipers. Dr. Bresee preached morning and night, and Rev. W. E. Shepard in the afternoon. Nine were baptized, eight persons sought pardon or purity, and six were received into the church, in addition to eight who had come in during the preceding week. The waves of power and blessing which swept over the congregation were most glorious. People wept and shouted in holy triumph, and salvation flowed in mighty tides. Many testified that it was the best day of their lives, and Dr. Bresee expressed the opinion that it was the best day the church had ever seen.

The home campmeeting in 1899, closed on the last Sabbath of October, and it was the last and greatest day of the feast. In the morning more people were crowded within

138

the tabernacle than ever before, and at night many were unable to get in. The streets seemed filled with people who desired entrance. Dr. Bresee, before preaching in the morning, briefly reviewed the history of the Church of the Nazarene, and stated that during the four years of its life, 916 persons had been received into its membership in Southern California, exclusive of Redlands. Among other things he said: "Many who are at a distance, turn their faces with prayer and love toward this place, and those who have gone up on high love it with such an intensity that, if it be the will of God, they will hover over this scene today, unperceived amid the throng, and join in the joy and victory of this hour." He preached from Psalm 102 : 13. At the close of the sermon, Brother and Sister Helm, two aged saints, gave their testimony in glowing and triumphant words, and six were received into the church. Hundreds partook of the sacramental service in the afternoon. Jesus presided and fed His people with His own life. Testimonies followed, and it was near nightfall when, their hearts all aglow with holy love and joy, the people dispersed. Brother Shepard preached in the evening, the Spirit wrought mightily, and five seekers were blessed. Dr. Bresee recorded this as one of the best days he ever saw, and humbly and gratefully gave thanks to God for it.

On the afternoon of Sunday, December 21, 1899, the sacramental service was a season of remarkable blessing. There was a deep, mighty tide of spiritual power. The invisible verities seemed nearer and more all-controlling than visible things. The presence of God was singularly manifest throughout the day, not only in refreshing and anointing the saints, but in saving and sanctifying souls.

Of the Christmas services on December 28, 1899, Dr. Bresee said: "We have never known a time when all the fountains of love seemed so wide open. All the services were crowned with the presence and blessing of the King of Glory."

139

The love feast on Christmas morning was a remarkable service. After a few introductory words by Dr. Bresee, he was presented with a fine overcoat, and Mrs. Bresee was remembered in the gift of a beautiful purse, with its contents of money. The tears began to flow, and when the pastor thanked his people for the tokens of their appreciation, there was hardly a dry eye in the audience. Five, who were present at the first of these love feasts eleven years before, gave glowing testimonies. Among these was Brother Marsh, who sang and shouted the praises of God. Then the great tidal waves of testimony, song and victorious hallelujahs began to roll. Dr. Bresee said that it was one of the great gala days of his life. As the testimonies began to multiply, two spoke at once, then three, then four, until at last the mighty throng of joyous worshippers rose to their feet, and in a voice like many waters burst forth in one loud, happy acclaim, "Glory to God in the highest!" If the transition of the great day had suddenly burst upon that glad multitude, they would have joined without embarrassment in the singing of the new song.

The Friday night meeting on April 27, 1900, was a memorable occasion. The divine presence was manifested in a marvelous manner, and the saints were overwhelmed with the blessedness of the power of God. Wave after wave of glory swept over the people, until all seemed filled with heavenly awe and rapture. There was a sinking down into the fathomless, boundless ocean of divine love.

In a preceding chapter I have given a brief description by Dr. Bresee of this notable day, which I shall here supplement with extracts from the Nazarene Messenger, of May 24, 1900. In the morning Dr. Bresee spoke of

Victory Day the victory that is won before the throne, in answer to the abiding faith of God's holy people. In the afternoon the mighty manifestations of the presence of God are thus described: "We have seldom witnessed such a time of glory. After the opening of the service and prayer for special cases, Dr. Gregory addressed the meeting for a few minutes in a very interesting way, in the interest of the Boys' Home, at Artesia. Then came most heart-searching and triumphant testimonies. The glory of God fell upon the people in an indescribable way. Who can tell the mighty power of the fountains of life which thus burst forth? The holy fire and mighty triumph of that hour can never be forgotten by any one who had the privilege of being present. It seemed a repetition of the scene in the upper chamber. The word that stood out with glorious emphasis amidst the shouts and tears, was 'Victory' — 'Victory.' Thank God for such an hour on earth. It tells a little of the possibilities of heaven."

July 4, 1900, was one of the great days in the old tabernacle. Although Dr. Bresee was present and really took charge of all the services, he did not preach. The messages were given by Dr. Bowers in the morning, Rev. C. B. Eby in the afternoon, and Rev. Thomas Fluck in the evening. There were altar services following each sermon, and during the day twelve seekers pressed their way forward, some of whom were gloriously saved. Conspicuous among the seekers was Brother Lewis, who was marvelously sanctified, transformed, and raised up as one of the most glowing witnesses of holiness that I have ever known. In the evening the young boys filled the platform, and gave their testimonies preceding the sermon. Mrs. A. P. Baldwin, leader of the Boys' Praying Band, sat on the platform with them, and spoke briefly of the work among the boys. Brother and Sister Leslie F. Gay sang with great spiritual power.

The progress of the church in the month of July, 1900, is thus summarized in the Nazarene Messenger: "The month has been a memorable one in the annals of the Church of the Nazarene. From the all-day meeting on the 4th, there has been a great tide of blessing. Many souls have been saved and sanctified. But the last Sabbath was the

141

crowning day of all. It was the greatest day, taken as a whole, that the church has ever seen. The Sabbath school opened with impressive services, many of the children leading in earnest prayers. The house was crowded at the eleven o'clock service. Many of the saints had been led out in special prayer for the morning service. Heaven seemed open from the beginning. There were songs of triumph, prayer, and a few testimonies. Dr. Bresee preached in the morning, taking for his text St. John 6 : 21: 'And immediately the ship was at the land whither they went.' The tide kept rising, and when the sermon was perhaps three-quarters through, there came such a cloud-burst of glory falling all over the congregation, that the preacher could not be heard, and he cleared the way for seekers to come to the altar. Before the meeting was over, there were three or four altar services in different parts of the church, and souls swept into the kingdom. The afternoon service was led by Brother C. E. McKee. Brother Clark preached a short but blessed sermon from the prayer of Jesus: 'Sanctify them through Thy truth. Thy word is truth.' There were many testimonies. In the evening Dr. Bresee preached on Hell. The altar was filled with seekers, and the Lord was present to save."

It seemed as if this mighty, pentecostal outpouring of the Holy Ghost was in some sense preparatory for the severe trial which was soon to come upon the church, and which even at this time was so close at hand that the people all unconsciously were in the shadow of it. But God knew what was going to happen, and graciously reinforced and undergirded his saints, so that when the blow fell they would not yield to discouragement. I refer to the terrible accident which befell Dr. Bresee and those who were with him in his carriage, as he was driving home from the prayer-meeting, on the evening of August 8, 1900. A full account of this tragic event appears in the next chapter.

CHAPTER XVIII.

On the evening of August 8, 1900, Dr. Bresee, and those who were with him in his carriage, met with a terrible accident, which caused the death of one of the party. The following is taken from the report of the disaster written by Brother W. S. Knott, who is one of the charter members of the Church of the Nazarene, and a prominent attorney of Los Angeles:

A Narrow Escape From Death

"On Wednesday night, August 8th, a carriage containing Dr. P. F. Bresee, Mrs. M. J. Willard, Mrs. L. L. Ernest, Mrs. Ada Bresee, and Mary Robinette, while crossing Hill street a short distance south of Pico street, in Los Angeles city, was run into by a Traction electric car, and crushed to fragments. Mrs. Willard was almost instantly killed, Dr. Bresee was seriously injured, Mrs. Ada Bresee sustained a fracture of the collar bone, which, though not dangerous, caused her much suffering, and both Mrs. Ernest and Miss Mary Robinette were painfully bruised.

"Dr. Bresee, who was driving, started the horse rapidly across the street, but before the carriage could clear the track, the car bore down upon them with fearful velocity, and crashed into the carriage with the dreadful results stated.

"Dr. Bresee was cautious and careful, and the sad calamity was the result of the recklessness of those in charge of the car.

"The Young People's meeting Friday night was largely devoted to earnest supplications to God for his speedy restoration to health." Brother Knott concluded his report as follows:

"When we last saw our dear Sister Willard in life, she had just been kneeling at the altar with an unsaved young woman, praying with her, and pointing her to the Christ who died for her, and she was then listening to the young woman testify to the glorious fact that the Lord had pardoned her sins. Not more than twenty minutes after this, Sister Willard had passed through the pearly gates, and cast her crown at Jesus' feet."

A page of the issue of the Nazarene Messenger, of August 16, 1900, is devoted to the memory of Sister Willard, who was born in Philadelphia, Pa., March 19, 1829. She was an honored member of the Church *Mrs. Mary J. Willard* Board of the First Church of the Nazarene, a deaconess of that church, and a most earnest and efficient teacher in the Sunday school. She was also a member of the Board of Publication of the Nazarene Messenger. In labor she was more abundant, and her works do follow her. Mrs. Alice P. Baldwin, the sister of Mrs. W. S. Knott, signed a beautiful tribute to the deceased, in which she said, among many other things: "She was a woman of faith; she was a woman of deepest humility; she was a woman of joy; she was a woman of song. God had given her pre-eminently the gift of song. Surely if ever one sang and made melody in her heart unto the Lord, it was she. Those of us who heard them, will never forget the songs she sang to the sick and dying, especially that sweet refrain, 'Lie low, dear heart, at Jesus' feet.' "

In the issue of "The Nazarene," of September 14, 1899, there appears a very interesting article written by Sister Willard, and headed "My Experience." She states that. *The Experience* although she had Christian parents, her *of Mrs. Willard* youth was a careless one. Having a voice of some sweetness and compass, she was much interested in opera music, and enjoyed the praise and flattery which her singing received. Her mother continued to pray for her, and to plead with her. As a result of serious sickness, she was converted, and joined the Episcopal church, in Louisville, Ky. On account of her husband's ill health and business losses, they came to California. She was sanctified in 1892, through the ministry of Dr. Bresee, and secured the witness of the Spirit that the work was done. In 1895 she became a member of the Church of the Nazarene. Putting it in her own language, she said: "What a blessing it has been to me; the teaching from Dr. Bresee and others; the loving hearts in Christ; the manifestations of the Holy Spirit. Surely God is in this place, and this is the very gate to heaven! I want to thank Him for all that He has done for me. He has drawn me with loving kindness, and with tender mercies does He keep me day by day, cleansed in His blood, and made ready for the glory of His coming."

Two or three years before his death, and speaking solely from memory, Dr. Bresee gave the following account of the tragic event:

"In the summer of 1900, a very serious accident occurred, which well nigh terminated my career. At *Dr. Bresee's* the close of the Wednesday evening prayer-*Account of* meeting, August 8th, on our return home, *the Accident* we had taken into the carriage some friends, to bring them to their residences. The occupants of the buggy, in addition to myself, were my daughter-in-law, Mrs. Ada Bresee, Mrs. L. L. Ernest, Mrs. Willard and her niece, Miss Robinette. On our way through what was then comparatively the suburban part of the city, it became necessary for us to cross the street car line at a place where, at that time, the night cars ran at great speed. A rapidly-moving car struck our carriage, hurling the horse, the vehicle, and the people in it more than forty feet. The speed was so great that the car itself could not be stopped for fully a block. The carriage was entirely demolished, and Mrs. Willard was instantly killed.

145

I was picked up in an unconscious state, not regaining consciousness for two or three days. Mrs. Dr. Paul Bresee, my daughter-in-law, had her shoulder fractured, and was otherwise badly bruised. Mrs. Ernest and Miss Robinette were also badly hurt, although the latter was more slightly injured than any of the others. I was carried into a nearby house and laid on a bed, the ambulance took Mrs. Paul Bresee to the hospital, and Mrs. Ernest and Miss Robinette were able to minister to the others. The alarm, however, was immediately given, and Dr. F. A. Seymour, an old friend of mine, whose residence was in the immediate vicinity, came directly to my side, took charge of me, and summoned my son, Dr. Paul Bresee, who was also a physician. Shortly afterward I was removed to my home, and in three or four days I began to ask about conditions, and it was thought best for Dr. Seymour to tell the facts. In the meantime, Mrs. Willard had been buried; so he told me of her death and burial, and where and how I was. It was some five or six weeks before I was able to be about.

"When I got out, I was hardly recognized by my friends. My hair had turned white, and I was emaciated and an old man in appearance. My daughter-in-law was confined to the hospital for several weeks, and for some years was greatly weakened in her physical constitution, but finally recovered fair health. A naturally strong constitution, and great care, enabled me to rally and secure a fair degree of physical vigor and health for the years that have followed.

"Mrs. Willard was brought into the experience of full salvation under my ministry, was a woman of strong personality, and beautiful Christian life."

It was not until September 10th, that Dr. Bresee was able to be present at any of the services. His return is thus chronicled in the Nazarene Messenger: "Sabbath was a wonderful day at the Church of the Nazarene. A large audience assembled in the morning, and from the very beginning, the Holy Spirit was present in great power and glory. While the preliminary services were being conducted, the audience was electrified by the appearance of the pastor, Dr. Bresee, after an enforced absence of several weeks. The congregation stood and sang the long-meter Doxology, and sang it again and again, while tears filled the eyes of hundreds, and many shouted aloud. Brother Clark, of Pasadena, led in prayer. The services were conducted by Dr. Bowers, who called upon Dr. Bresee to say a few words to the people, which he did, greatly to their joy and comfort. A little time was given to testimony, and so wonderful was the manifestation of the Spirit, that it was difficult to close that feature of the meeting."

On October 2, 1900, Dr. Bresee resumed his public ministry. His sermon in the morning was full of the old-time vigor and fire, and brought joy to many hearts. His text was Galatians 2 : 20. He spoke of Sister Willard, Sister Dean, and Brother Hazard, all of whom had been called to their heavenly home since he last preached.

Much of interest and profit might be said of the noble men and women who by their fervent prayers, holy lives, and self-sacrificing labors, contributed to the success of the young church, and were translated before *How the* it grew into a mighty movement. But the *Nazarenes* limits of such a work as this make it im- *Died* possible to do more than merely mention a few of the Christian heroes whose faithful co-operation enabled Dr. Bresee to carry the banner of holiness through so many glorious victories. They passed to their reward, and doubtless gave their beloved pastor a joyous reception when he entered the Eastern Gate.

Mrs. A. Neil, a beloved member of the blood-washed company, was suddenly lifted into the glory of the holiest of all, on August 2, 1898. Apparently in her usual health, she went to spend the afternoon with a friend, Sister Hill. As the time drew near for her return home, they bowed together in prayer. With especial earnestness she prayed for

147

each one of her family by name, pleading for their salvation. And then, without a struggle, she ceased to pray and ceased to live at the same moment, for God took her. From her knees, from her pleading lips, her soul went up to God. It seemed like a translation — one moment a pleader on earth, and the next with the ten thousand harpers before the throne. She was led to Jesus and into the fulness of His love, about two years before, at the altars of the Church of the Nazarene, from whence she was borne by loving hearts on August 4th, the funeral services being simple and triumphant.

This patriarchal hero, one of the large company of elderly people who formed the vanguard of the Church of the Nazarene, died on August 28, 1898, at the age of eighty-one. He was constant in his attendance

Silas McClure upon the means of grace, loved the altars of God, and rejoiced in the gospel of Christ, and the testimonies of the redeemed, in which he gladly took part. As Dr. Bresee was about to bid him good-by one day, when he could speak only with difficulty, he said: "Peace, peace, peace." His last words were: "Praise the Lord!"

Gardner Howland was born in New York, Aug. 1, 1817, and died in Los Angeles, Jan. 4, 1899. In his youth he became a paper manufacturer. He was converted in his early manhood, and four years after, through

Gardner Howland hearing the testimony of a young girl, was led to seek and find the blessing of entire sanctification. Strange, overruling providence led him to sell his mills, and go to Troy, New York, where he erected mills, and carried on the manufacture of paper. In that city he led many into the experience of full salvation. He was a member of the famous Troy Praying Band, which was used of God to lead thousands to Jesus. In the spring of 1847, on account of broken health, he and his son,

William, came to California by way of Panama. He afterward brought his family to the Southern part of the state. Brother Howland was a man full of faith and the Holy Ghost. Just before his death he said: "In my early life I was very much afraid of death; it was a torment to me, but when I was converted, that fear was somewhat broken, and when God sanctified me wholly, the fear of death was all taken away, and I have had complete victory over death for more than fifty years. I challenge death to his worst." His dying message was: "Preach holiness; preach it as a definite second work of grace. It has done everything for me. It cleansed my heart. Jesus came in to dwell. It has been Christ in me, the hope of glory. If we have this, we need no further blessing. We are dead unto sin. We need die no more. We are alive unto God. We have the power of an endless life. It is all done through holiness, received as a second definite work of grace. Preach it; urge people into it." Dr. Bresee said of this prince in Israel: "His dying chamber was a place of great glory. I have never felt nearer heaven than in receiving his dying benediction." Brother Howland came into the Church of the Nazarene soon after its organization. I knew him personally, and shall never forget the peculiar unction, sweetness, and likeness to Christ, which made his very presence as ointment poured forth.

This grand old veteran of the cross was born in North Carolina, in 1826, came to California about 1874, and settled in Los Angeles. He was converted when a child, and came into the experience of sanctification in 1881, in the very beginning of the work of holiness in Southern California. He *Robert Marley* was a charter member of the Church of the Nazarene. Though in ill health, he seldom missed the Sabbath morning service. It was no strange thing for him to rise in the midst of the sermon and sing:

149

"I would rather be the least of them, who are the Lord's
    alone,
"Than wear a royal diadem, and sit upon a throne."

Dr. Bresee paid this tribute to him: "We shall hear his
shouts of victory and songs of triumph no more here; but
we doubt not that he has gone where the songs he loved
are sung with sweeter cadence, and the shouts are like
mighty thunder and the sound of many waters. He died
January 11, 1899, conscious to the last, and triumphant to
the end."

Dr. Whistler was born in Virginia, in 1817, practiced
medicine in Philadelphia, and lived in Arkansas for ten
years. He left the South because of slavery, and came to
California in 1852, settling in El
Dr. Michael   Monte, where he lived until 1873,
Everley Whistler when he removed to Los Angeles, and
there resided until his death in April,
1900. He was converted at the age of eighteen, and was a
devout and earnest Christian. When Rev. Adam Bland,
the pioneer Methodist missionary, came to Southern California in 1853, he found a home at Brother Whistler's house,
and soon afterward, the first campmeeting in that section
of the state, was held at El Monte. A little later, largely
through his influence, the first Pentecostal church was built
in that town. While traveling along the highway near El
Monte, in 1881, he was enabled to trust God that then and
there the blood of Jesus Christ cleansed him from all sin.
As he arose to tesify that night, the baptism with the Holy
Ghost fell upon him. Dr. Bresee conducted the funeral
services at the Church of the Nazarene, assisted by several
other clergymen.

Among other members of the church who were called
home to God during the first few years of its history, and
who left bright and triumphant testimonies behind them,
were the following: William W. Herbst, Miss Clara Morris, Mrs. Charlotte A. Langdon, Mrs. Phoebe M. Kinnie,

Charles Hazard, J. W. Miller, George W. Penneman, Miss Mabel Louise Mott, Dr. W. M. Johnson, Mrs. Sarah V. Bartlett, Mrs. Virginia Hayworth, Norman Ingraham, and Miss Lillian Emma Moore.

In many cases Christians not members of the church, were sanctified at its altars, and were only permitted for a brief period to bear testimony to the glorious experience of full salvation. Among these was Mrs. Elizabeth Hightower, who died May 31, 1901. She was converted in early life, but knew not the joy of a heart made whiter than snow by the blood of the Lamb. At the Tuesday Holiness Meeting, a few days before her death, she was a seeker for sanctification, and was gloriously baptized by the Holy Spirit. At a meeting on the following Thursday, she gave sweet testimony to the sanctifying grace of God in her heart, and went home to fall asleep in Jesus the next day.

In later chapters I will add somewhat to the illustrious list of those who were associated with Dr. Bresee in the great battle for souls, and who from time to time passed to their eternal reward.

CHAPTER XIX.

The first Council of the Church of the Nazarene was held at the tabernacle on Los Angeles street, on April 18, 1898. It was composed of ministers, official members, and others especially interested in the work. Dr. Bresee called the meeting to order, and *Early* made a brief address, sketching some of *Legislation of* the peculiar providences which led to the *the Church* organization of the church, the blessings which crowned it, the precious fellowship and holy love which had prevailed, and the open doors through which hungry souls beckoned them to enter. He then called Dr. Widney to the chair, and the latter spoke of the history and prospects of the church. Rev. E. A. Girvin and Rev. M. Clark reported respectively as to the progress of the churches of which they were the pastors, in Berkeley and South Pasadena. Rev. J. H. McIntyre, pastor of the church at Elysian Heights, Los Angeles, told of the glorious work of God under his ministry. Brother and Sister McIntyre were among the earliest sheaves gathered into the garner of the Lord through the instrumentality of the young church. About two years before, when passing the doors of the tabernable, they were led to stop and listen. They heard earnest words and shouts of victory. They felt that those within had something which they needed and did not possess. They entered, were converted, sanctified, and anointed to tell the old-new story of redeeming love. When Brother McIntyre finished his report, Brother C. E. McKee spoke of the Buttonhole Brigade, Sister Lucy P. Knott told of the work among young women, carried on by Company E. Then short addresses were made by Brothers Coleman, Allison, and others, after which the character of the meeting changed into a general love feast, wherein the Holy Spirit was manifested, and all were blessed.

On October 14th and 18th, 1898, a delegated meeting of all the churches of the Church of the Nazarene, was held in the tabernacle on Los Angeles street. The principle object of this meeting was to prepare a man-
The First   ual for the church, which would more fully
Manual   represent it than the articles and general rules which had previously been adopted and published. Some other business was transacted, chief of which was the acceptance of the resignation of the two General Superintendents. It was felt that the article in the constitution, giving to the General Superintendents a life tenure of office, required modification. As it was a personal matter, beginning and ending in the then incumbents, it was unanimously thought best for them to resign. A law was then passed making the term of the office one year. Good progress was made with the manual, but it was not completed at that time.

The first meeting known as an "Assembly" of the Church of the Nazarene, met in the tabernacle on Los Angeles street, October 16, 1899. After a very blessed season of prayer, Dr. Bresee called the meeting to order, Broth-
The First   er W. S. Knott, the secretary of the delegated
Assembly   meeting held a year before, called the roll, and thirty-three delegates responded, of whom eleven were ministerial and twenty-two were lay delegates. Dr. Bresee, the General Superintendent, who had been re-elected a year previous, made a brief statement in reference to the work, and considerable time was profitably spent in hearing and considering reports from the various localities in which local churches were organized. A committee of seven was appointed to report on the best method of incorporating the "Nazarene" into the framework of the

153

church, and Dr. Bresee was unanimously re-elected as General Superintendent for another year.

The third annual Assembly of the Church of the Nazarene, was held at the old tabernacle on Los Angeles street, on October 16, 1900. Dr. Bresee presided, and a half hour was spent in prayer, after which there was *A Notable* preaching, followed by a testimony meeting *Assembly* and an altar service. On the following day the Assembly reconvened, and there was a time of great spiritual refreshing at the sacrament of the Lord's supper. An interesting report was presented from the Board of Directors of the Nazarene Publishing Company. Dr. Bresee reported as pastor of the First Church, that since its organization, 933 persons had been received into membership, of whom thirty-one had died, and fifty-six had been dismissed by letter or otherwise, leaving a membership of 846, which included the congregations at Elysian Heights and Mateo street, Los Angeles, and the charge at South Pasadena. Mrs. Lucy P. Knott and Mrs. Alice P. Baldwin made very interesting reports of the work of Company E, and the Boys' Band, respectively, and Miss Emma Stine (now Mrs. Colburn), told of the progress of the Brotherhood of St. Stephen. There were reports from Elysian Heights, Mateo street, South Pasadena, Cucamonga, Redlands, Berkeley, and Oakland. Brother Shaw, Superintendent of the Sabbath school of the First church, stated that three-fourths of the scholars in the school were converted. A commission on church building and work was appointed, consisting of Dr. Bresee, Col. B. Duncan, W. S. Knott, C. E. McKee, and C. H. Edwards. This action was taken in view of the need of a larger and more commodious building for the First church, and with the object also of helping other churches in the denomination. Dr. Bresee was again unanimously chosen as General Superintendent for another year.

Although Dr. Bresee spent most of his time in Los Angeles and its immediate vicinity during the early life of the Church of the Nazarene, he did some traveling in the interests of the work. In 1897, he organized *Missionary* churches in Berkeley and Oakland, and in *Efforts of* February of the following year, in company *Dr. Bresee* with Brother Moncton, he again visited those cities, and held rousing evangelistic services in both churches, greatly strengthening and augmenting their membership. At a meeting conducted by him in West Berkeley, a woman gave herself to God, and her husband became so greatly angered that he threatened to commit suicide, and absented himself from home for several days. During this trip the saints were blessed and edified, and a goodly number sought the Lord for pardon and sanctification.

Dr. Bresee gives the following interesting account of this trip: "Thursday, June 23, 1898, when the train pulled out of the Arcade depot, Los Angeles, I had found my seat in a Pullman sleeper. My first feeling *The Work in* was rest and prayer. I had been so con- *Berkeley* stantly at work day and night for so many weeks that to sit down my full weight, and lay my head back on the cushions and rest, seemed sweet and restful. The next morning at eight o'clock, I was in the office of our dear Brother Girvin, at the supreme court. He reports for that court, as Paul made tents, so that he may preach the blessed gospel of Jesus. That night I preached at Oakland. Sabbath was a day, not only full of labors, but of blessings as well. I began the day at Berkeley, attending and addressing the Sabbath school, then preaching at eleven o'clock to a good congregation. Our church at Berkeley is doing excellently well under the able, enthusiastic and judicious leadership of Brother Girvin. The church and congregation are steadily growing. It is a perennial fountain of spiritual life and power. A goodly number of efficient men and women are now gathered within its folds. Full salvation is clearly taught and testified to, and people are pressed into the experience. The services, like those of the church in Los Angeles, are full of enthusiasm and power. The red hot amens and shouts of victory come from triumphant hearts. They make much of street meetings, and in every way crowd the battle. It has been nearly a year and a half since this work was begun under what seemed the most unpromising conditions. The one great fact was that God had here raised up a man, and anointed him to preach the gospel in its fulness and power. A little band of heroes answered to the call. Some have not been faithful, and some have gone hence. Mostly they have been true to the divine call; and others have been raised up, and the work has steadily advanced. This little church is an oasis in a desert. Here is the State University, with its higher criticism. Here are churches peculiarly dead, and without salvation. But here is a place where the waters of life flow. Brother Girvin and his fellow workers are as happy and triumphant a band as can be found. I especially enjoyed the showers of blessing Sabbath morning. Seven persons united with the church."

On the evening of Sunday, June 26, 1898, Dr. Bresee preached at the Oakland church one of the greatest and most forceful sermons that I had ever heard from his lips up to that time. His theme was: "I am sure

Dr. Bresee in Oakland that when I come, I shall come in the fulness of the blessing of the gospel of Christ." The burning, earnest message was graciously owned by the Lord, and it came with great power and glory to the hearts of all present. In its presentation of mighty truths, heretofore unrecognized by the people of God, its grasp of the great underlying principles of this dispensation, its exposition of the gospel of full salvation, or the baptism of the Holy Ghost and fire as the great distinguishing characteristic of this age, and its vivid picture of Paul as a man who had the "blessing" in all its glorious fulness, the sermon which Dr. Bresee preached that night took high rank in homiletical literature.

In August, 1899, Dr. Bresee made a short trip to Springfield, Illinois, where he took a leading part in the annual campmeeting of the Illinois Holiness Association. In his account of this meeting, he speaks of several *A Trip to* brethren whom he met, most of whom after-*Illinois* ward united with the Church of the Nazarene. Among these were Rev. L. B. Kent, the president of the Association; Rev. J. B. Creighton, then of Missouri; and Rev. N. B. Warrington. In his report, Brother Bresee stated that Brother Creighton preached twice with great effectiveness; that Brother Warrington was regarded as the Abraham of the campmeeting, and was one of the honored fathers of the holiness work; and that Brother Kent was one of the oldest preachers of the Word, and expounder of the doctrine and experience of holiness, that he had ever had the pleasure of hearing.

In September, 1901, Dr. Bresee started for Seattle, accompanied by Brother C. E. McKee, and Brother and Sister A. F. McReynolds. He held a ten days' Pentecostal meeting in that city. In speaking of this *A Meeting* meeting he said: "There were some peculiar-*in Seattle* ly striking cases. A gentleman was sanctified who had come twenty-five miles to attend the meeting. A friend of his, a member of our church in Los Angeles, had written him to be sure to come. He came, testified to his sonship in Jesus, and when the opportunity was given, came at once to the altar, earnestly opened his heart and mouth in prayer, and received the baptism of the Holy Ghost, which cleanses and fills. He went on his way rejoicing. I have been permitted to meet a number of old friends, among them Rev. H. D. Brown and wife and sister. He is pastor of Battery Street Methodist Episcopal church. I had the pleasure of giving him a license to preach when we were both comparatively boys. He is much the friend of the Church of the Nazarene. His wife and sister are both eminent Christian workers. The last day of the meeting was one of power and great blessing. There were twenty-five seekers at the altar, many of whom were either converted or sanctified. During the eight days, there were sixty seekers. One of the hopeful things about the work has been the fire of full salvation kindled among the Swedes in the Swedish Methodist Episcopal church. Seattle greatly needs a strong, vigorous Church of the Nazarene, under able leadership, to push the cause of holiness in this and adjoining states. We trust that this may soon be."

Dr. Bresee thus describes the scenery in the Siskiyou mountains: "We were at an altitude of a little more than four thousand feet. Below us were the tops of tall pine trees. On the right and left were the for- *A Poetical* ests of pine and fir. Mountains and hills *Description* spread out before us, and rising again, mountain on mountain, as far as the sight could extend — varigated forests, green and deeper green, with here and there hillsides of russet gold. Over all were the silver clouds, darker here, and there, the sun shining through the rift, while spread over mountain and valley was a most beautiful rainbow, crowning nature's greatest beauty with heavenly glory. It told us of the mountains of God, with the rainbow round about the throne."

As the years went swiftly by, Dr. Bresee made many journeys in the interest of the great work that God had called him to. These will be referred to in chronological order in subsequent chapters.

An account of the early period of the Church of the Nazarene, and Dr. Bresee's fellow laborers in the kingdom of God, would not be complete without at least a brief sketch of Brother J. H. Crowell, who was even then a veteran in the army of the Lord. At one of the Tuesday afternoon holiness meetings, in November, 1900, he spoke of his experience, which was one of the most thrilling in all

158

the glorious annals of Christian martyrs and heroes. He was converted at the age of sixteen, and soon afterward shipped on a sailing vessel, with a crew of twelve, he being the only Christian on board. Previously he had promised his mother that he would meet her three times a day at the throne of grace. To accomplish this, he would go below, where, feeling that his prayers were not satisfactory unless they were audible, he always prayed aloud. This brought terrible persecution upon him from the sailors. They tried to compel him to desist from praying, but he would pray. They danced and sang around him while he was engaged in his devotions, but he would pray. They threw pieces of wood at him and bruised him, and poured buckets of water upon him, but could not extinguish the fire in his soul. Then they tied him to the mast, and laid thirty-nine stripes upon his back, the marks of which he carries today, although now more than ninety years of age. But still he prayed. Finally, they tied a rope around his body and threw him overboard. He struggled and swam as best he could, but when he would take hold of the side of the ship to climb up, they would push him off with a long pole. At last his strength gave way, and, supposing that they really meant to kill him, he made a final effort, and called to the sailors: "Send my bundle of clothes to my mother, and tell her that I died for Jesus." He then sank into the deep, but his persecutors pulled him out, and up on the deck. He was almost dead, but their long-continued efforts resulted in his resuscitation. Conviction then began to seize those sailors. Before night two of them were gloriously converted, and while they were praying down below with the young martyr, the others thought that the two were again persecuting him, and called upon them to desist, saying that he had been tormented enough. In less than a week every one on board the vessel, including the captain, was blessedly saved.

In a little while the ship put into a port near Cape Cod,

because of an approaching storm. Other vessels gathered there, to the number of nearly three hundred. The heroic boy had been conducting religious services every Sunday. Unknown to him, when the vessels were lying at anchor, the captain sent word around that on the next Sunday, services would be held on his ship, and that a boy would give his experience of how he had been persecuted and nearly killed for Jesus' sake. While the boy was down below preparing something to say in the meeting as usual, the sailors began to come on board. They filled the ship's deck, climbed into the rigging, crowded every available space, and also sat in boats all around the vessel. When the young preacher came on deck, this was the sight that met his startled gaze. The crew formed a ring around him. They sang, and he prayed, after which he took for his text: "Except ye repent, ye shall all likewise perish." The Holy Ghost began to work, and after giving an earnest message, the anointed lad invited all who wanted to be prayed for, to so manifest. From every direction the sailors responded and asked for prayer. The work of grace broke out, and salvation flowed, until it was estimated that there were one hundred conversions that afternoon. This was the beginning of a glorious revival in the assembled fleet. Men continued to seek and find Christ, and while the ships lay in the harbor, word kept coming to young Crowell that on such and such a vessel a meeting had been held and some one saved.

The foregoing is only one of almost innumerable interesting and thrilling events which formed part of the life history of Dr. Bresee's associates in the early work of the Church of the Nazarene, but the limits of this volume will not permit their narration.

CHAPTER XX.

In this chapter I shall try to give some dim outline of the scope and characteristics of the labor performed by Dr. Bresee in connection with the church paper of which he was the chief editor for so many years. In the issue of the "Nazarene" for October, 1898, he thus discusses the ever-present question of the money required to carry on the work of God:

Early Editorial Activity

"The needs of the work in so many ways are necessarily considerable. The question is often asked, 'How will you get the money necessary to carry it on?' We believe that the work is of God, that we are called simply to co-operate with Him, and that He is not hard up. We believe that He has the means at His disposal for His work, and that He will put it into the minds and hearts of His servants. With this faith we went to this work. We went with the conviction that there should be no assessments or subscriptions; that there should be no outside methods of raising money, no begging, nothing that would discriminate between those who were possessed of this world's goods and those who were not; that there should be no financial classifications or barriers in the way of the poorest to feel as much at home as the richest. We were convinced that houses of worship should be plain and cheap, to save from financial burdens, and that everything should say welcome to the poor. We went feeling that food and clothing and shelter were the open doors to the hearts of the unsaved poor, and that through these doors we could bear to them the life of God. We went in poverty, to give ourselves — and what God might give us — determined to forego provision for the future and old age, in order to see the salvation of God while we were yet here. God has not disappointed us. While we would be glad to do much more, yet hundreds of dollars have gone to the poor, with loving ministry of every kind, and with it a way has been opened up to the hearts of men and women, that has been unutterable joy. The gospel comes to a multitude without money and without price, and the poorest of the poor are entitled to a front seat at the Church of the Nazarene, the only condition being that they come early enough to get there. In the midst of it all, let each of us ask what will the Lord enable me to do, that there may be meat in the house of the Lord? He allows His loving ones to be His almoners, supremely blest in being permitted to be workers with Him. We do not give merely a tenth — 'our all is on the altar.' "

In the issue of the "Nazarene" of September, 1898, Dr. Bresee says: "Preceded by providential leadings that could not well be misunderstood, we stood face to face with the problem of going forth from old rela-

Dr. Bresee Reviews the First Three Years tionships to a work into which the Spirit led. It was as little of our seeking as the call of Abram from the land of Uz was his seeking. The way before us seemed just as indefinite. But it was to be a way in which He would lead us. A few things were clear. It was to the utmost freedom and liberty to preach a full salvation, and to lead seekers into the blessed experience. It was to be where this work would be so intense and radical that none who were opposed to it would come, to be obstacles in the way, and to defeat the work. It was to seek the conversion of the unsaved by the way of the Pentecost, believing what Jesus said, that when the Holy Ghost is come, he will convince the world of sin and righteousness and judgment. It was to seek especially the poor, to preach the gospel to them, entering every door of ministry through which we could come and bring the good tidings of eternal life. We did not then know, and we do not now know, what it will grow

162

to. We are not anxious about final results, but to do the service day by day, which we may be permitted to do under His leadership. That day three years ago, we stood in the little hall on Main street, a little company, neither looking backward nor forward, simply looking up. Many doubtless thought that the outlook was poor, but the little company who waited that day, felt that the uplook was good, and there was the light of the Divine Presence on their pathway which has never been withdrawn, and which has never grown dim. The words spoken to Joshua have been verified to us: The doors have been opened, the difficulties have been removed, a highway has been cast up, and there has been one continued song of victory. Workers have come from every direction, and have been also raised up from the stones round about. Singers and players upon instruments, and those who can proclaim the truth of God, have been raised up under the blessed inspiration of the Holy Spirit. Souls have been converted and sanctified from week to week, without cessation, for 156 weeks.

"It pays to follow the Lord fully. It pays in our own souls. It pays in the work that He calls us to do. The way He leads sometimes seems to human wisdom the way of foolishness. But God's ways are not our ways. They are so much higher and their orbits so different, that they seem to us sometimes to be erratic. But those who follow where God leads, have no need that sympathy should be squandered upon them. These have been the three most blessed years we have ever known. The manifest Divine Presence, the open heavens, the sweeping glory of salvation, have far more than made up for all else. A few weeks ago I sat with a wife beside her dying husband. They had both come into this work through much opposition. As we sat and communed together, the wife said: 'We have never for a moment regretted that we went into the Church of the Nazarene.' I have yet to hear of one of that little company that went forth that day — about as many as were in that other upper chamber — who has ever regretted it. They went forth, not to churchanity, but to spread scriptural holiness over these lands, and their hearts have glowed and burned, not only with joy and victory, but with thanksgiving and praise."

These words are among the noblest that have ever been uttered in the English language, and for their simplicity, charm and lofty sentiment, deserve a place beside the greatest expressions of Shakespeare, Bunyan, Wesley, and our own martyred Lincoln.

In the issue of the church paper of February, 1899, Dr. Bresee says: "I am deeply interested in the work of God everywhere. But I am absorbed with the battle which God gives me to fight. My eyes are fixed on the *Some* particular fortifications of the Enemy which *Memorable* God has given me to storm and carry. While *Utterances* I am interested in the whole army and the outcome at every point, I am overwhelmingly absorbed in the work of the particular division He has placed me in, that it bear that blood-stained banner on to victory. If I am so much interested in the general battle that I allow the banner of my division to be trailed in the dust, or allow defeat to come to that department of the service, I am of no value to the army, and, in spite of my general interest, am virtually a deserter or traitor. In answer to earnest prayer, God will put every one in a place where He most needs him, and where He can most glorify Him. Then there is one thing to do, and that is to see that the division where he is placed, pushes on to victory. These are days when there are more or less of those who belong no where, who run here and there, wherever they hear the loudest firing. They are somewhat interested, but they are not absorbed. They are not the people who make circumstances and conditions, and bring things to pass. One soldier is worth a battalion of such. God calls us to the rank and file; to the forward march; to the personal encounter;

to the wresting of victory out of the hands of the enemy. It is possible to have such a general interest as to be good for nothing. God calls us to stand in our lot, to be good for something. And He will enable every faithful one who seeketh not his own in any sense, but the things which are Jesus Christ's, to be a conquering hero in the place where He has put him, and to say at last: 'I have fought a good fight.' "

In the same issue, Dr. Bresee says: "I would that every one might feel that those who are won to Jesus Christ are won generally by personal influence; that, if people are now reached, it must be by the effort of some *Personal* anointed soul, who can get close enough to *Influence* them to take such a hold upon them that he can draw them to Calvary. In this way every one is to be a missionary. We have a center glowing with celestial heat, where, when we bring souls, we are sure there will be burning words and melting testimonies and triumphant songs, and where there will be many to unite their faith and efforts with ours to bring them to Christ. You can find some family that does not go to the house of the Lord, or some soul that is far away, and you can compass the getting of them there. You can introduce them to other workers; you can pray for the awakening Spirit to come upon them; at a proper moment you can urge them to the altars of God, or kneel with them in their seats; you can hold on to them and see them safe in the fold. Let us not tarry; the time is too short; the King's business requires haste. Nothing but the indwelling Christ will give the soul-passion and power we need. Open wide the door, and He will come in and fill you with the Holy Ghost, and to win souls will be the passion of your being."

In "*The Nazarene*," September 21, 1899, Dr. Bresee wrote, under the head, "Unction."

"This is a strange word, but no other will quite express it. It is a word full of mystery, also full of meaning. It is that peculiarity of human speech which manifests forth the presence of the Holy Ghost. It is the power of God in human utterance. It is the promised power in testimony and ministry that was to come when the Holy Ghost fell upon us. It may be impossible to describe it, but every one recognizes it when it is present. It is that, without which attempts at preaching and testimony are vain. Nothing reaches the soul of men through human agency in conviction, either for pardon or purity, without it. Without it all our efforts are sounding brass and tinkling cymbals. The presentation of truth is nothing without this divine presence, which lifts Godward, which awakens, impels and saves. We must have it. We do well to stop all machinery and cry to God — well, to do nothing else until into our souls comes this personal fountain of life to pour Himself through us to His glory. We must have unction; it is the sword that pierces between soul and spirit; the hammer that breaks the hearts of men, and leads them unto the cross; the word that stirs up believers and impels and leads them on until the cleansing blood, and the power of the Holy Ghost brings them to the fullness of the stature of Christ. O, brethren of the ministry, we must have it. Let us never preach another sermon without knowing that God is speaking through us to men. O, brothers, sisters everywhere, it is your enduement of power; you must receive it fresh, by the breath of God, or you are nothing. That you once had power, that you sometimes feel a moving within your soul, will not do; nothing but hallowed streams of divine power through your souls will do. Rivers of water will flow out of your hearts by the Holy Spirit. Gaze upon Jesus, call upon Jesus, live unto Jesus, until the consuming fire which He gives burns through you, as the fire burned in the bush at Horeb. Ask — ask largely; believe — believe obstinately; receive — receive unto overflowing fulness, that thy soul, thy joy, thy ministry may be full."

In the issue of "*The Nazarene*," of December 13, 1900,

Dr. Bresee wrote the following weighty words: "The work has its difficulties. The world, the flesh, and the Devil are against us; and some difficulties more or less peculiar beset our pathway.

Difficulties of the Work

"A new movement, especially if it is successful, gathers to itself some elements which become a hindrance. They come to it for place and opportunity, and possibly for help which they have been unable to get in other places. They soon necessarily find their place and level, as they have done before — and always will, and they become dissatisfied and disintegrating forces. We have been fortunate in having so few of these, but have not been entirely exempt from them.

"A new fire always draws some who are watching for any comfortable place to warm themselves. These soon discover that there is the promise of a fire somewhere else, and they try to stampede the people to it; we have had a few of these.

"Fanatics of almost every kind expect a new movement to embrace their particular fad; and when they find that it is the same old gospel, made hot by the fire of the Divine Presence, which is fatal to all fanaticism, they rise up to declare that here there is no special message, and betake themselves to more congenial climes; we have had some of these.

"There are those attracted to a new movement, into whose heart it was never born. When the sun is risen, when there is the call for the peculiar devotion, and sacrifice, and heroism, which such a work demands; to bear, and to suffer for it, they sell out. The results of Solomon's method of discovery, as to which was the real mother of the child, by proposing to cut it in two; with the result that the one who had not borne it was willing to sacrifice it, are still seen. Those who have not borne the work with the pains of motherhood, are willing it should perish, if they are not especially served by it. We have not been entirely exempt from these.

167

" 'God is our strength.' The abiding, indwelling Holy Spirit gives power for conflict and conquest. He puts in human souls the strength, and courage, and fidelity, and hope, and love which mean victory. God has raised up human souls above all self-seeking; above all ambition or seeking for worldly gain or place, far above seeking for entertainment — even religious entertainment. God has raised up men and women of fidelity, true to God, and their fellow workers, and all men, those whom God has trusted, and men could trust, who have not been a disappointment to heaven and earth. They have stood in their places, and with steadfast gaze and finished faith, have held fast their testimony, without wavering, and have shone as lights in the world. The presence of such men and women, who could not be turned aside or held back, being filled with the fulness of God, has made it possible for God to work.

"The day is full of blessing and hope. The great Captain of our salvation leads the battle. The victory is sure. We are led, not to experiment, but to assured triumph."

These are words which we will all do well to take to our hearts.

CHAPTER XXI.

As the work grew, the old tabernacle became more and more inadequate, and the need of a larger place of worship began to be keenly realized. Dr. Bresee thus described the situation:

A New Church Building   "It began to be felt that greater permanency ought to be given to the local work, in Los Angeles, by the securing of property and the building of a suitable home church. One morning, as I was about to commence preaching, Colonel Blanton Duncan arose, and asked if he might be permitted to say a word. I assented, and he said that in the olden times, when there were special answers to prayer, it was customary that some thank-offering be made; that two or three weeks previous he had asked the church to pray for his wife, who was very ill, and that there had been such manifest answers to the prayers of the church in her behalf, that it seemed appropriate to him to make a thanksgiving offering. He said that he thought the time had come when we should secure for ourselves lots, and begin the building of a permanent church home. Hence, he desired, as a thank offering for the blessing of God thus received, to make a gift for that purpose, to be the beginning of a church building fund. He then handed me a bank bond for $500. Some other friends added smaller offerings, until the fund amounted to about $1,000. A committee was then appointed to try and find a suitable location."

The thought which the brethren had in mind when choosing the location of the old tabernacle, was still maintained. In Dr. Bresee's words: "We felt that the location should

169

not be far removed; that we should be not distant from the center of the city; that we should be toward the poorer people, and within reach by car lines of the whole city. The ground was carefully canvassed within what seemed to be the proper radius for a site, and no suitable place was found. Brother McKee, being one of the committee, met Brother Jaynes, whose residence had long been situated on the corner of Wall and Sixth streets, and told him that in his opinion, he, Brother Jaynes, had held that corner, and paid taxes on it all these years, for the use of the Church of the Nazarene; that he felt the force of the provision that whatever your feet press shall be yours; and that he had gone around the property in the name of the Lord, claiming it for our work. Brother Jaynes replied that it was not for sale, but that, if the church needed it, and would appoint a competent committee to estimate its value, the church should have the property at the price thus fixed. This proposition was acted upon, a competent committee appointed, the valuation fixed at $7,500, the property purchased at that price, and the $1,000 which had been secured for the building fund, paid on account of the purchase price."

To again use Dr. Bresee's words: "It was then agreed that an offering should be made toward the purchase of the lot. A time was fixed two or three weeks in advance, notice was given, much prayer was made, and *An* one Sabbath after the morning sermon, the *Offering* people were requested to stand and sing and *Taken* praise God and bring their offerings and lay them on the altar. With great rejoicing and shouting, they responded, and, when the offering was counted, it was found that they had brought $2,800.

"After about six months, it was determined to make a further offering. The people again poured out their hearts to God, and again after the Sunday morning sermon, they stood, and with shouts of praise, brought their offerings, and laid them on the altar as before. This offering aggregated $3,100, which amount with some little further gathering, enabled the church to pay in full for the lots. It was a question whether we should wait and recuperate from the exhaustion of the offerings which had been made, or whether we should try to find some way to proceed at once to the erection of the much needed building. It was thought that a building such as would be necessary, could be built for $20,000."

Dr. Bresee continued his narrative as follows: "I then suggested to the Board that we proceed to build at once; that we borrow $10,000 on a mortgage covering the land and the building which should be erected *The* upon it; and that I should ask the people *Thousand* to give $10,000 more during the erection *Golden Eagles* of the building. This plan was carried out. The loan was made, and the enterprise entered upon. I immediately advised the people of the necessity of raising the $10,000, and asked them to bring me a thousand golden eagles. I told them that I would make my vest pocket an eagle's nest; that every ten dollars should be an eagle, every five dollars a wing, every dollar a quill, and every fraction of a dollar a feather, until the thousand eagles were gathered."

Dr. Bresee thus describes this important event: "In due season the building was begun, and on Saturday afternoon, October 18, 1902, the foundation having been put in, and the basement walls erected, the corner *The* stone was laid. It was then suggested that *Laying of the* eagles made their nests in the rocks, and *Corner Stone* that the corner stone would make an appropriate nest. Appropriate addresses were given, an opportunity was offered for homing the eagles, and the people came forward and laid $2,100 in the corner stone.

"It was soon discovered, however, that on account of the fire limits, it would be impossible for us to build of wood,

171

and that to construct the building of bricks, stone and iron, would cost twice the amount anticipated. This almost discouraged the brethren, but providential encouragement was given, and it was resolved, that, notwithstanding the greater cost, we would go forward with the enterprise. The house was completed, at least so far as the audience and Sunday school rooms were concerned, and arrangements were made for its dedication."

This is Dr. Bresee's description of this great, historic march: "A great march was planned from the old tabernacle to the new church. This was carried out on Friday night, March 20, 1903. The chairs and *The March From* other furniture had been taken out of *the Old to the* the old tabernacle, and into its empty *New Building* shell as many of the people crowded as could gain access. They sang 'Hallelujah, Amen, and prayed and praised God. Then, led by drums and other musical instruments, they marched to the new church. The occasion drew together a vast concourse of people, estimated to have been at least ten thousand in number. When we had entered the new building, and it was packed from top to bottom, at least 2,500 persons being in it, the great crowds on Sixth and Wall streets did not seem to be diminished. In fact both of these streets were packed with people. Brother C. E. Cornell, the lay evangelist, who years afterward became the pastor of the First church, preached that night, as he happened to be conducting an evangelistic service at that time."

I can not do better than to give Dr. Bresee's brief but vivid account of this memorable occasion:

"On Sunday morning, March 22, 1903, the house was packed from top to bottom. Before the dedicatory sermon could be preached, a man hurried to the altar, seeking the Lord, and prayed through to victory, after which I preached a short sermon. The great altar was filled with tables, and arrangements were made for the people to make their offerings toward the building of the church. Plans had been carefully arranged for the people to march by the altar from the body of the audience room and the galleries, men being stationed to hasten their march as much as possible. Songs of triumph were sung, and the people marched. Shouts of victory went up to heaven, as they marched as rapidly as they possibly could. Nearly an hour was taken up with the marching of the multitude. It was a time of great blessing and victory. When the offerings of the day were counted, it was found that $10,300 had been laid upon the altar, which was in addition to about $4,600 that had previously found its way to the eagle's nest. That day was crowned with wondrous triumph, and marked an epoch in the history of the church, which entered upon larger and grander possibilities.

"This new building became the great center of the work for a number of years, a kind of cathedral of the church at large, and for several years during which I was permitted to preach and carry on the pastorate, the blessing of God was upon it, multitudes of persons were saved and sanctified, and the work spread throughout this part of the country."

During his pastorate of the First Church of the Nazarene, Dr. Bresee's labors were so manifold and difficult, that it became necessary for him to have an assistant pastor, not only to help him in the immediate duties and responsibilities of the First Church, but to aid in the conduct of the church paper, and in the administration of the Bible College, which was brought into being very providentially in the early period of the church's history. Fortunately I have in my possession Dr. Bresse's account of all these matters, and I am sure that I can do no better than to quote his words in reference to them:

"Long prior to the erection and dedication of the new church, it had been necessary to have assistance in the pastorate. Providentially, Rev. C. W. Ruth was invited to hold a series of meetings in the late summer or early autumn of 1901. These meetings proved so successful, and his ministry was so blessed to the people, he was called as associate pastor, which call he accepted, and at once removed from Indianapolis to Los Angeles, and entered upon his duties. He labored here enthusiastically and successfully for about a year and a half, doing excellent service, both as a pastor and as a preacher. He conducted the more evangelistic meetings, and preached nearly every Sunday night. Throughout this period, and as long as I was in the pastorate of the First church, I preached regularly Sunday mornings, unless the multiplying duties of the church at large demanded my presence elsewhere. While the pastorate gave opportunity for the manifestation of the spirit of evangelism, it scarcely saved Brother Ruth from the trend of continued evangelistic service, and he felt impelled to move on in the old field, and take up the evangelistic work which had so long absorbed him. His personality, preaching and pastoral work, left a deep, abiding impress upon the church, and gave him a large place in the hearts of the people belonging to, or associated with, the church in Los Angeles.

"In March, 1904, Rev. C. V. LaFontaine, pastor of one of the Methodist churches in Chicago, taking a short vacation to Southern California, with his wife, for the benefit of her health, became acquainted with our church, which acquaintance led to his being called to be the associate pastor of the First church. This position he occupied for about three years. His ability as a preacher, together with his scholarship, made him a very efficient and able associate. Toward the latter part of his pastorate, he occupied the office of District Superintendent of the Southern California District, the duties of which position he discharged in conjunction with those of pastor.

"In the spring of 1908, Rev. A. L. Whitcomb, president of a Free Methodist college, at Greenville, Illinois, a man of ripe culture and fine preaching ability, accepted a call, and became associate pastor of the First church, but he remained only a few months.

"Immediately after Brother Whitcomb's pastorate, Rev. J. W. Goodwin, who was already District Superintendent of the Southern California District, accepted a call to the associate pastorate of the First church, and continued as such until the meeting of the District Assembly, in 1910, a period of more than a year and a half.

"Rev. E. F. Walker, after a pastorate in the First church, in Pasadena, accepted a call to the associate pastorship of the First church in Los Angeles, early in 1911, with the understanding that he was to be largely responsible for the pulpit and pastoral work of the church, because of the fact that I was engaged most of the time in the work of the General Superintendency. Dr. Walker is a preacher of great ability, especially as an expository and theological expounder of the Word, and probably as a preacher of holiness from that standpoint, he is unexcelled. He did good and effective service, and after serving the church a year, he again entered the evangelistic field.

"I was convinced that no one could be secured as an associate, or as an assistant pastor, who would do the work as well as if he were the fully responsible pastor of the people, and that it would be for the best interests of the church and all concerned, for me to resign the pastorate, not only on that account, but for the added reason that my duties as General Superintendent, President of the University, and in other capacities, were so exacting as to require all my time. The brethren of the First church urged me to remain as pastor emeritus, but I felt that it was for the best interests of the church for me to be entirely separate from it, and to thus open up for the new pastor the broadest possibilities.

"For these reasons, I tendered my resignation, which was accepted with great reluctance by the brethren, and Rev. C. E. Cornell, who had been for more than five years pastor

175

of the First church, in Chicago, Illinois, where he had met with great success, was called to the First church, in Los Angeles. He accepted the call, and began his pastorate here in April, 1911."

At this point, it will be in order to give Dr. Bresee's brief resume of the origin and growth of the Publishing House of the church, which has now become a great institution, as follows:

The Publishing Interests "At the very beginning of the work some method had to be devised for communicating with the people through the medium of printed matter. Our principles had to be set forth and proclaimed, and some evangelizing agencies inaugurated. Immediately, and without any reference to future plans, a paper called 'The Nazarene' was printed, scattered broadcast, and sent to parties who might be interested in the work. Only a little time elapsed before a successor to this issue became a necessity, and another issue was printed. Soon it was made a regular monthly paper, and after a time it was changed into a weekly. Still later its name was changed to 'The Nazarene Messenger,' and under that title it was continued for many years. This paper was an earnest advocate of the great, central doctrine for which we stood, entire sanctification. It also stood strongly for organized holiness, so as to make the work efficient and permanent. It became the organ of the movement, throbbed with its life, told of its advances, and thus chronicled with great fidelity the early history of the church.

"While the chief burden of editing this paper naturally fell upon me, the brethren rallied around me, and rendered efficient service. Among those who were especially helpful in this regard were Mrs. Alice P. Baldwin, Mrs. Lucy P. Knott, Brother W. A. Powers, Rev. J. P. Coleman, Rev. C. A. Snelling, Brother Earl D. Hinchman, Rev. W. E. Shepard, Mrs. Annie T. Armour, Rev. F. E. Hill, Rev. E. A.

Girvin, and others. Later on, Rev. C. W. Ruth, Rev. Robert Pierce, Rev. C. V. La Fontaine, Rev. C. E. Cornell, and Rev. P. G. Linaweaver, rendered very valuable services as contributors to the paper.

"Around the Nazarene Messenger gradually gathered the nucleus of a publishing house. Among the early and efficient agencies connected with this work, was Mrs. L. L. Ernest, who, gifted with excellent business qualifications, took charge of its affairs. It was in the day of small things, and, while we had to have a competent person, it was impossible to give proper remuneration for such service. She, being a deaconess in the church, was taken into our family, that she might have a home while she did this work. During this time a printing office was established, and considerable job work done, together with the publishing of the paper and other religious literature. The work became so heavy, that on April 13, 1905, Rev. C. J. Kinne was secured as business manager. He entered the work at large sacrifice, leaving a place where he was receiving a good salary, and accepting in his new position not more than one-half of what he had previously earned. The business was gradually enlarged, and the publication of Sunday school literature was begun in 1907. This was continued until the General Assembly, at Nashville, in 1911, when a Board of Publication was appointed for the church, and the publishing interests were turned over to that Board. The Nazarene Messenger and Sunday school literature were absorbed in the church's general publishing interests, and the HERALD OF HOLINESS became the official organ of the church."

CHAPTER XXII.

I will necessarily devote considerable space to the University in subsequent chapters, but in this connection, I deem it appropriate to give Dr. Bresee's own account of the origin and growth of that institution.

The Bible College and University "The need of special educational help for young men and women who were called specifically to this work, became apparent. Men and women were coming from other churches and taking part in the battle; but among the young people who were converted and brought into the church were those whom God called into pastoral, missionary and evangelical work, and who needed further training for efficient service. In the providence of God, some property was offered which would make the beginning of a Bible College a possibility. Because of the many duties which already devolved upon me, I was slow to take up this department of work. Encouraged, however, by Brother Ruth, the matter was taken up and adjusted, and arrangements made for the opening of the school, which took place in the autumn of 1902, thus preparing the way for the final incorporation of the institution known as the Nazarene University and Deets Pacific Bible College. This school was carried on under my general supervision, Miss Leora Maris being principal for several years. After a time it was found necessary to add another department, and an academy was opened under the principalship of Miss Cora Snyder. This was carried on until the latter part of 1910. Among those who taught in this school up to that time were Rev. C. W. Ruth, Rev. Isaiah Reed, Rev. A. L. Whitcomb, Rev. C. V. La Fontaine, Mrs. Alice P. Baldwin, Mrs. Lily D. Bothwell, Brother Leslie F. Gay, Miss Bessie Wood, Mrs.

Annie T. Armour, Rev. B. E. Sherwin, Rev. P. E. Ryland, Dr. F. A. Seymour, Miss E. J. Kellogg, and Mrs. A. F. McReynolds.

"In 1909, Rev. W. W. Danner was called to be principal of the institution, and served for one year. This school did excellent service, and turned out some young men and women who have made their mark in Christian work in the church.

"It was during this period that Brother Jackson Deets, of Upland, became much interested in the college, and felt that larger opportunities were a necessity to its growth; that we must have a place for better and more commodious buildings. For this purpose he gave the institution $30,000, with which a campus of about nine acres was bought. It was a beautiful location, between Los Angeles and Hollywood.

"Toward the latter part of 1908, a very serious matter occurred, which threatened the life of the Bible College, and serious injury to the church. Through a misunderstanding, a schism took place, which carried with it some of the teachers of the Bible College and many members of the First church, who seceded from the church, and organized an independent mission. But through the good providence of God, the church was sheltered from ultimate serious harm, and the matter was overruled to the larger outcome and service of the college. A complete change was made in the personnel of the teaching corps of the Bible College Department, and it was at this time that Rev. W. W. Danner became principal, or dean, and a new force of teachers was appointed.

"But the great result of this upheaval was to change the plan of the location of the school, and greatly to enhance its scope. This led to the purchase of the magnificent tract of land in the city of Pasadena, since known as the University Park Tract, of 134 acres, at a price of $165,000. The campus purchased in Los Angeles previously, was sold for

$25,000, and the money invested in this new enterprise. Fifty acres of this was set aside for a University campus, and the remainder was platted as a park and subdivided into residence lots, the proceeds of which were to complete the payment on the property, and make such improvements as were possible.

"This was a very great undertaking, involving the expenditure of a very large sum of money. Streets had to be opened and paved, gutters made, sidewalks laid, and temporary buildings put up for the housing of the school, such as dormitories, dining-hall, etc. It was possible, fortunately, to utilize the old palatial mansion as an administration building. Street cars, also, had to be brought through the tract, for which it was necessary to raise a bonus of $22,000, of which amount the University was compelled to pay about $5,000.

"After the removal to the new site, which took place in 1910, the school was opened with enlarged facilities, consisting of a College of Liberal Arts, an Academy, and a Bible College, together with departments of music, oratory, and other things essential to such an institution. I remained president of the school, but the teaching force was under the control of Rev. H. Orton Wiley, who was elected as Dean of the College of Liberal Arts, and vice president of the institution. Miss Cora Snyder retained her position as principal of the Academy, and Brother Wiley also became dean of the Bible College. A good faculty was secured from different parts of the country, and the first year was a great advance over all the preceding years in both the number of assistants and the work accomplished."

In subsequent chapters I will describe the growth of the University, and tell something of the great service rendered it by Dr. Bresee, who to the last, prayed mightily and labored indefatigably in its behalf.

I shall later take up the missionary activities of the church, especially as they gathered around, and were connected with Dr. Bresee, but it will be in order at this stage of the narrative, to give his own account of the inception of the organized work of missions in the Church of the Nazarene.

The Mission-
ary Interests

"This movement was of itself essentially a missionary one. The people who were in it in the beginning had to go out under the stars, and commence at the foundation of things, to go into the desert, and make a new type of religious life and polity. Hence, necessarily they were absorbed in getting a roof over their own heads for a place of worship, and the sustaining of men to push the work at home. This, in fact, all through these years, has necessarily absorbed largely the possibilities of the church. Everywhere it was new; everywhere there was strong opposition; usually there was poverty; and it was all that the infant church could do to get the people saved and sanctified, organize them into association together, get a place for them to worship and carry on the ordinances of religion, and make of themselves centers of fire to push the work of holiness. Nevertheless, as is always the case, while a great degree of force must be expended in Jerusalem and Judah, there are spirits that long for the wider sweeps of the world beyond; so from the beginning there were those that yearned for the possibilities of preaching the gospel to those that were without.

"Early in the movement, work was begun in Los Angeles, among the Spanish-speaking people, who, though they were Roman Catholics, were neglected on account of their poverty, and were as really pagan as though they lived in Africa or China. Among the early trophies of the work of full salvation here, was Sister A. F. McReynolds, who, immediately after her sanctification, began to study the Spanish language, under the impulse of a call to labor among these Spanish or Mexican people. She soon afterward left her secular work, being in the employment of a railroad, and entered upon her missionary activities. The church made some provision for her and her fellow workers, establishing a mission in the heart of Los Angeles, and carrying on the work in various other portions of the city, and of Southern California, reaching out beyond as far as El Paso, Texas. A Spanish school was organized in Los Angeles, which has been carried on for several years, with a fair degree of success, a goodly number of persons having been saved and sanctified through the agency of this mission.

"It has been a difficult task because of the migratory habits of most of the class of Spanish people whom it has been possible for us to reach. They have mostly been laborers on the railroads, and while here, they would be in one place for a time, and soon would be changed and gone away. Hence, it was difficult to keep track of them, and thus the work was rendered very hard."

Dr. Bresee gives the following interesting and vivid portrayal of the singular manner in which the Church of the Nazarene was led to take an active part in the redemption of India:

The Work "In 1906, through a very strange and mys-
in India terious providence, the mission work was
    opened up at Calcutta, India. Some years before that time, a high-caste woman of India, Mrs. Banarjee, whose relation was such as to bring her into great sympathy with the child widows of that country, had been led to begin a work among them in a small way, she herself having been, like most of the girls in that heathen land, married in her babyhood, and compelled to live with her mother-in-law from an early age. She became a child mother, and was sent with her two children to the jungle to be destroyed by the wild beasts, according to the custom of the country, but in a marvelous manner she escaped with her little ones. Falling in with pilgrims on their way to the sacred river Ganges, she went with them. As a result, she finally came in touch with some Christian people, through whose instrumentality she was converted. Soon afterward she interested herself actively in the rescue of those who were sufferers like herself.

"In the early nineties she came to the United States with some American ladies, and in her endeavor to secure some funds to help in the conduct of the enterprise which was so near her heart, she succeeded in interesting some Christian women in Portland, Oregon. Among these was Mrs. E. G. Eaton. Having secured from them quite a sum of money, she returned to India, and established in Calcutta what was known as the 'Hope School.' It was really an asylum and mission for child widows, where they could be taught and led to the Savior.

"In 1906 Mrs. Banarjee returned to this country to secure further assistance. The ladies at Portland again undertook to assist her, and some arrangements were made to raise money. It was thought wise to seek a wider field, and San Francisco was chosen. At the time of the great earthquake, in April, 1906, Mrs. Banarjee and Mrs. Eaton were on their way to San Francisco, accompanied by a young gentleman named Biswas, a preacher, who had graduated from a Baptist university in India."

At this time some of the most singular providences occurred, which are narrated by Dr. Bresee as follows: "They learned that the city was destroyed, that the ruins were being consumed by fire, and that the *Some* inhabitants were fleeing by the trainload *Remarkable* in every direction. In their earnest, agoniz- *Providences* ing prayers for succor and guidance, the Lord seemed to speak to Mrs. Eaton, and say to her: 'Go to Dr. Bresee, in Los Angeles, and he will help you.' She said: 'I do n't know Dr. Bresee. He does n't know me. He does n't know anything about these folks or conditions. It does not seem opportune for me to go to him.' But again the voice said: 'Go to Dr. Bresee, and he will help you.' She replied: 'I have n't the money to go. Thou wilt have to send me money, if I go.' In a little time a woman came in, and saying that the Lord had sent her, put in Mrs. Eaton's hand some gold pieces. She had never seen this woman before, and has never seen her since. With this

183

money she bought their tickets, and they came to Los Angeles, arriving late in the afternoon. Mrs. Eaton asked the matron at the depot to call me up and say that some missionaries from India were there, and wanted to find my house. I replied that I did not know anything about them, but after a little conversation over the telephone, I asked the matron to put them on the car and send them up. They were delayed in coming, getting the wrong car, but, just as Mrs. Bresee and I had started for the prayermeeting, we met them. We knew by the Indian dress of Mrs. Banarjee who they were, and so when we made sure of their identity, and learned that they were tired and hungry, Mrs. Bresee decided to go with them to our residence, get them supper and put them to bed, while I continued on my way to church. The next morning they told me their strange history, and opened up before me the work that they had in mind. It seemed a very inopportune time, as the earthquake sufferers were being shipped into Los Angeles by trainloads. We had taken a large offering for them the Sunday night previous, amounting to $1,200, and had turned our church building into a receiving station, putting up many beds in the Sunday school department, the idea being to receive them, and pass them along to such places of a more permanent character as might be provided. The city was full of refugees, and the offerings of our people were seemingly exhausted. But, after talking over the matter with them, I decided to call together our Mission Board.

"The Board of Missions was then largely a local board. The church had not extended very far, and the members of the board resided, with few exceptions, in Los Angeles. I laid the matter before them, and the statements from Mrs. Eaton and Mrs. Banarjee were repeated and considered. The board prayerfully and thoughtfully went over the conditions and possibilities of the work, and finally agreed that, if Mrs. Banarjee saw fit to put her rescue enterprise and herself in the bosom of our church, that we would take the responsibility of carrying it on. This was done. On the Sabbath a public statement was made, Mrs. Banarjee, Mr. Biswas, and Mrs. Eaton were received into the church, and at the evening service an offering of $1,200 was made toward this new missionary undertaking. We marched around and placed it on the table.

"Arrangements were made for the visiting of our churches in different parts of the country, and the Rev. Charles V. La Fontaine and his wife accompanied Mrs. Banarjee and Mr. Biswas to the north and east, holding meetings and taking offerings at Chicago, Spokane, Berkeley, and other places. Much enthusiasm was aroused, and a considerable sum raised for the work.

"Some time later Mrs. Eaton, who had kept in constant touch with the Hope School and Mission, in Calcutta, and had given much of her time to the securing of funds for the support of the child widows of India, was induced to visit that country in the interests of the mission, as she was regarded as its American mother.

"Shortly before the arrival of Sister Eaton at the mission in Calcutta, a marvelous Pentecost came upon the school, giving it great power and victory. The needs were such, that while there she saw clearly that a home *A Pentecost* should be secured for the school, which *in Calcutta* would give us larger facilities. Much prayer was made by the school itself and others during her stay there, for God to open up the work. The Lord gave her what she deemed a promise in these words: 'She hath considered a field and purchased it,' and the girls in their prayers and shouts of victory said that they would call the place 'Hallelujah Village.'

"On the return of Sister Eaton to the United States, she began to tell the church of the great need and possibilities of the mission, and money commenced to come in for its use. Finally a day was set apart as Hallelujah Day, when the Sunday schools were asked to make contributions through the whole connection. Five thousand dollars was thus raised, which was devoted to the purchase of a beautiful

185

plot of ground in one of the suburbs of the city of Calcutta. It was about seven acres in area, and with this little tract were included buildings, fruit trees, artificial lakes, and oher things which had been provided for institutional work.

"While these events were transpiring, Mrs. Banarjee had overworked herself, and in 1912, was in such a condition that a vacation was absolutely necessary. It was suggested to her that she should visit Denmark, which would give her not only a sea voyage, but a change of climate and scenery.

"Strange providences awaited her. No sooner had she arrived in Copenhagen than she was thrown into the company of a wealthy gentleman whose daughter was preparing for missionary work in India, and who was much interested in her recital of her experiences. He took her to his own palatial home, and opened up ways and places for her to meet and address the people, who at once became quite enthusiastic, and gave her liberal offerings, and while she was there made her much at home among them.

"Mr. V. C. Jaques, a business man, of Los Angeles, and a member of the Emmanuel Pentecostal Church of the Nazarene of that city, became deeply absorbed in the mission at Calcutta. In fact, it was so much on his heart that he sold out his business, and thus provided for his own support, so that he might devote his energies to the conduct of the business matters connected with the mission, and at the same time do all that he could for the salvation of souls. He soon became an efficient and valuable agent in the management of the mission.

"When the eastern and western branches of the church united, the eastern branch had missions in Western India, and at Cape Verde, where a number of missionaries are employed.

"Later, when the Holiness Church of Christ, an organization in the South, united with us, its missions in Mexico, Japan, Africa, and elsewhere, became part of our foreign work."

CHAPTER XXIII.

Dr. Bresee thus expressed himself in regard to this important subject: "In the organization of the church it was undertaken to make it neither Episcopalian, nor Congregational nor Presbyterian, but a mingling *The General* of all of these polities, bringing in *Superintendency* much of Congregationalism, some such centralization as is given by presbyteries and synods, and sufficient general superintendency to bind the whole together and make it effective, with such limitations of power as would preserve the efficiency without the dangers. Thus came what is known as the superintendency of the church.

"In the beginning the work of superintendency in the Church of the Nazarene naturally centered in me; and, taking charge of the First church as pastor, I began as providential openings developed, to attend to the work of further organization. When our organization had assumed sufficient proportions to become a District, I for the time, attended to the duties of District Superintendent. As other Districts were organized, District Superintendents were elected, and I took charge of the General Superintendency up to the time of the union of the Church of the Nazarene with the Eastern churches. When this was consummated, two General Superintendents were elected, Rev. H. F. Reynolds, of New England, and myself.

"During this time special emphasis was given to the heroism essential to those who were to be a part of and workers in this movement. There was no effort to proselyte from other churches. Ministers and laymen who turned toward us were carefully warned of the great difficulties and hard-

187

ships of the work. Over and over again they were told, when they asked what kind of openings there were, that we had nothing to offer but what Garabaldi offered to the Italians who might come to his standard, hunger, thirst, nakedness, death, and liberty.

"After the union of the churches of the East, West, North and South, the country was divided into Districts. District Superintendents were elected, and the whole was supervised by three General Superintendents, who were elected at the General Assembly held at Nashville, Tennesse, in October, 1911. The duties devolving upon these General Superintendents demanded wide travel, both to the annual District Assemblies, and for the purpose of doing such other work as naturally came within the scope of the Superintendency. The general interests of the church had to be conserved, churches dedicated, conventions held, and the work presented and represented at campmeetings, and such other great gatherings as might be necessary for the furtherance of the movement.

"Without any realization of the work itself, or what was to be done, provision was made by a strange providence in the foundation of the very first church for a General Superintendency, this evidently being a divine indication of what was to come. For the first year the work was confined to the mother church in Los Angeles, and such outlying places as were immediately contributory to it.

"In October, 1896, there came a very providential opening to begin work in Berkeley, California. E. A. Girvin, a local preacher in the Methodist Episcopal church, was a resident of that city, and his duties as phonographic reporter of the supreme court of the state of California, frequently brought him to Los Angeles. He had become acquainted with our work, and was much impressed with the necessity of a similar work in Berkeley. He was a man of earnest spirit and good ability, and an effective worker for the kingdom of the Lord Jesus. He had come into the experience of sanctification some years before, and his great desire to see the doctrine and experience of holiness carried forward, seemed to be largely hindered by the conditions of the church in Berkeley to which he belonged.

"Being in Los Angeles attending a session of the Supreme Court, he went with me one night to South Pasadena, to attend a cottage meeting at that place. On the way we discussed the possibility of an opening of the work of the Church of the Nazarene, in Berkeley. Brother Girvin said: 'Doctor, we ought to have a Church of the Nazarene in Berkeley.' I replied: 'I will go there and hold a ten days' meeting for the purpose of organizing a church in that city, if you will become the pastor.' He immediately answered: 'I will do it.' A definite time was fixed, the first part of January, 1897, at which time I went there, and we held a ten days' meeting. This meeting was remarkable in several respects. It was the first effort to establish new centers of fire outside of the First church, in connection with this work. It grew out of the desire of Brother Girvin to have a place where the revival fire could burn continually, and the work of salvation go on constantly — a place where people could be invited to hear the gospel of full salvation. By reason of the fact that he was so well known in Berkeley, San Francisco, and other places about San Francisco Bay, the meeting, although held by a hitherto unknown people, aroused very general attention. The dailies of the Bay cities gave it special prominence, and thus without our solicitation, advertised it very widely. They went so far as to interview both of us, and print our photographs."

Dr. Bresee's narrative continues: "Quite a commodious hall had been secured, and with the aid of the advertising, a very fair hearing was had. Considerable opposition was at once manifested, especially *A Providential Helper* on the part of the churches. A number of persons were converted, some sanctified wholly, and at the end of ten days a church was organized with eighteen members, Brother Girvin being elected pastor. This proved to be the begin-

189

ning and center of a constantly increasing and widening work, which has since extended to various cities about the bay, and in the central part of California. An interesting feature of this meeting at Berkeley, was the providential sending in of laborers. One of these was the Rev. George Egleston, who lived in Oakland, and was a local preacher, in the Methodist Episcopal church. I do not know whether he had seen the articles in the papers or not, but he came the very first day of the meeting, and told me that he had had a strange, marvelous vision; that in a dream he saw a train of cars flying through the sky toward Berkeley, with the name 'Church of the Nazarene' written all over it, and that he felt so peculiarly moved by it that he had come to hunt up the meeting. He proved to be a most valuable helper, without whom it would have seemed almost impossible to have held the services. Brother Girvin, on account of his official duties, was compelled to be absent from the day meetings, and there was no one residing in Berkeley, who was available to assist in the singing and services, but Brother Egleston supplied this want, led in song, was gifted in prayer, and assisted in every department of the service. He was of inestimable value in the work, and was in constant attendance until the close of the meeting, becoming one of the charter members of the young church, and being for a time its associate pastor. Not long afterward he was called to his heavenly home, and several years later, his daughter, Miss Marjorie, was married to Mr. W. H. Girvin, the eldest son of Brother E. A. Girvin."

The narrative of Dr. Bresee continues as follows: "In April, 1897, I held a meeting in Oakland, as a number of persons in that city desired the organization of a Church of the Nazarene. The meetings, which *Extension of* were held in a large hall, were well at- *the Work* tended, and there was considerable power and blessing. Quite a number of persons were converted and sanctified, and a church was organized with fifty members. The Rev. W. E. Shepard, who with his wife enrolled among the charter members, was elected pastor. A permanent hall was rented and furnished, and regular church services were instituted, with a promising outlook.

"Classes were soon organized at Mateo street and Elysian Heights, in Los Angeles, and also at South Pasadena, at each of which a church was built.

"In January, 1904, the Church of the Nazarene had extended its labors to the following additional places: Vernon, a suburb of Los Angeles, Pasadena, Cal., Ocean Park, Cal., Cucamonga, Cal., Schiller, Texas, Spokane, Wash., Boise, Idaho, Salt Lake City, Utah, Garfield, Wash., Omaha, Neb., and Maples Mills, Ill."

The First Church of Chicago, Ill., was organized by Dr. Bresee personally, in August, 1904, and the circumstances connected with this memorable epoch in the religious life of that city will be set forth somewhat fully in a subsequent chapter. Speaking of the rapid progress of the church, Dr. Bresee said: "Churches were organized in different parts of the West, until in 1906 there were about forty-five distinct local churches. Districts had been organized in Southern California, San Francisco, the Northwest, and in the region of which Chicago is the center. During this time I *Rapid Growth of the Movement* traveled through the western part of the nation, and visited various cities, organizing churches and supervising the work, at the same time retaining my position as pastor of the First church, in Los Angeles, having as previously stated, associate pastors.

"After the union of the churches, my field of labor rapidly extended, and I spent several months of every year in organizing and holding District Assemblies. In this capacity I have held Assemblies in the Washington, New York, New England and Pittsburgh Districts. I have presided over Assemblies on the Pacific coast and in the middle states several times, and also in the South. On one occasion I visited Canada, holding a meeting and organizing a church at

Victoria, meeting the brethren at Vancouver, holding a District Assembly at Calgary, and assisting in a campmeeting in connection therewith. The District of which this was the center had been organized the year previous by Rev. H. D. Brown, who had been appointed missionary superintendent to that country. In conjunction with him I held a week's meeting. I then went to Washington, where I held a campmeeting at Spokane, and a District Convention at Walla Walla. From there I went to North Dakota, and held the Dakota District Assembly. Thence I journeyed to Iowa, by way of St. Paul, Minn., and held the Iowa District Assembly. From there I went to Louisville, Ky., where I held the Kentucky Assembly. Next I held the Chicago Central District Assembly, at Chicago, going from there to Tennessee, where I presided at the Clarksville Assembly. Leaving there, I visited Nashville and Birmingham on my way to Mississippi, where I held the Assembly of that District. While at Clarksville, I preached two nights. Going to Little Rock, I preached at night, hurried on to another city, and held the Arkansas District Assembly. Thence I turned my face westward toward my home in Los Angeles, which I reached after having traveled about eight thousand miles, and preached 120 sermons. I presided at eight District Assemblies, and held a number of campmeetings and conventions."

Having given this brief synopsis, which I committed to paper as the words fell from the lips of Dr. Bresee some three years before his death, I will now turn back a little, and take up the events in his busy and useful life somewhat in their chronological order, beginning with the year 1903, and immediately subsequent to the dedication of the First church in Los Angeles.

At the time of the march from the old tabernacle into the new one, and for a few days thereafter, Brother C. E. Cornell, at that time a lay evangelist, conducted a series of revival services in the First church. During these meetings, which closed on March 30, 1903, there were two hundred seekers at the altar, and a great tide of salvation.

On March 31st, immediately following Brother Cornell's meeting, a great twelve-day campaign began in the First church, led by the Rev. C. J. Fowler president of the National Holiness Association, Rev. Bud Robinson, Rev. Will Huff, and Mr. and Mrs. Harris, the gospel singers. Although almost incessant rains interfered very much with the attendance at these great meetings, there was much salvation, and the service closed on Sunday, with twenty-two definite seekers, and a mighty manifestation of the presence and power of God.

From this time on, the relations between Dr. Bresee and the Rev. Bud Robinson, became closer, and a few years afterward the latter united with the Pentecostal Church of the Nazarene. I can not better describe
Bud Robinson   him than in the words of Dr. Bresee: "He is a marvelous exhibition of what the grace of God can do for a man. The ignorance, suffering, and sorrow of his early life can scarce be conceived, but the wonderful transforming power which can so lift up and make new and glorious, is far beyond the grasp of human thought. It is love, measureless love, and grace, boundless grace, which do these 'greater works.' The conditions from which he has been taken, and the abounding grace, make possible his unique personality. His other gifts are peculiar, so that when you hear him with his unpremeditated humor and spiritual pathos, you feel that he is a mixture of elements made up of Mark Twain and the Apostle Paul, but all these elements filled with the Spirit of our Lord. We glorify the grace of God in him, and believe that this grace manifest in him will lift up many that others could not reach. Only those who have heard Rev. Bud Robinson, have any idea of this gentle, earnest personality, with genius to see and say things, with native humor and pathos, which the Holy Spirit uses to utter the truth — much of which is in exact Scripture phraseology — to reach the hearts of men. The people greatly enjoy hearing him, but more than that,

hearts open to him as flowers open to sunshine, and he is enabled to lead them in the way of life."

On April 30, 1903, Dr. Bresee began a series of meetings in the Berkeley church, and on May 3d, he dedicated the new church, and took up a large table offering. I gave my impressions of the occasion, and of the ministry of Dr. Bresee as follows:

Dedication of the Church in Berkeley

"I can not find words to tell what a blessing to our little band was the coming of this bold hero of the cross; this battle-scarred warrior in the army of Jesus. Truly, the Lord was never more manifest in Brother Bresee's work and ministry than during the last few days. As he stood in our little tabernacle before crowded audiences, and proclaimed the dispensational message with a tongue of fire, the Holy Ghost put the seal of the divine approval upon him, and the people trembled before the onrushing, dynamic power of the message of full salvation. As I sat and watched this faithful preacher of holiness, and thought of how unstintedly during the years that are gone, he had poured his life, and energy, and sympathy, and thought, and talent into the glorious work to which Jesus called him when a boy, as I felt the glow of his fervor, and the tenderness of his love for Christ and humanity, I found myself transported in thought to other days, and could scarce refrain from imagining that I was listening, not to a preacher of the twentieth century, with its materialism, higher criticism, and worldly ecclesiasticism, but to Wesley, or Whitefield, or Luther, or Melancthon, or Finney, or Caughey, or Redfield, or Maxwell. Thank God for a man who preaches the old-time religion with the old-time zeal and power, and touches of the divine glory! Over and over again Dr. Bresee, my dear comrade in the war against sin, emphasized the truth that our business was to keep heaven open, and to bring the holy fire down from the skies. May the Lord help us all to remember these great, cardinal principles of the holy warfare and the holy victory. His visit was an

194

inspiration to us, and God used him to encourage our hearts, and renew our resolve to push the battle of holiness."

In view of the fact that this faithful brother was so long and so prominently associated with Dr. Bresee for so many years, and that the Lord called them to their heavenly home about the same time, I deem

Rev. W. C. Wilson it fitting to quote from an editorial by Dr. Bresee, in the Nazarene Messenger, of October 1, 1903, as follows:

"Rev. W. C. Wilson, of Hanson, Ky., whose name, together with those of his family, appear in this issue of the Messenger as having been received into the Church of the Nazarene, has been a minister, doing evangelistic service in the Methodist church, South. He was expelled from that church for holding a meeting in the Baptist church in the city in which he lived, which was blest of God in the salvation of souls. He had the consent of the pastor of his own church to hold the meeting. The presiding elder brought a committee with him and held a trial, and, as Brother Wilson refused to sign an instrument saying that he was sorry, and would agree not to repeat the action which gave rise to the trial, as he felt that he had not broken any law,,though two of the committeemen withdrew, unwilling to have further relation to the matter, he was found guilty and excluded from the ministry and membership of the Methodist Episcopal Church, South. We are indebted to the Pentecostal Herald for a full statement of the facts. We are glad to receive a man of that moral fiber and backbone into the Church of the Nazarene. He will probably be able to push the work in that country. He says: 'I think I can organize a church in the county seat of this (Hopkins) county, and later could organize a small class here. I think it best to begin at Madisonville, the county seat, and then the work at other points, as the Lord directs. The holiness people, or a large percentage of them, are anxious for a way out of church oppression. I am well known to many of the holiness evangelists and people in this and other states. I am in the regular evangelistic work all the time, have plenty of work, and am happy in the field. Pray for us.'" Not long after this time Brother Wilson removed with his family to Southern California. He will be mentioned frequently in later chapters of this work.

On Sunday, October 18, 1903, the eighth anniversary of the organization of the Church of the Nazarene, was celebrated at the First church, in Los Angeles. Dr. Bresee preached in the morning from Psalm 2 : 8.

A Great Anniversary Service There was blessed victory and salvation throughout the services of the day. It was my privilege to be present and to take part, and under the heading "Anniversary Meditations," I thus wrote:

"It did my soul good to be present at the First church last Sunday, and take part in the celebration of the eighth year of its life. As I looked around and saw the spacious edifice which God has given us, and the great multitudes of devout and joyous worshipers, and heard the hearty amens and glad hallelujahs on every hand, I felt like exclaiming as did one of old, 'What hath God wrought!'

"As Dr. Bresee stood on the platform — a gray-haired, venerable man — and eloquently, fervently and thoughtfully proclaimed the story of salvation, that old, old story, which is ever new, my mind went back to fourteen years ago, when I heard him preach the same blessed gospel in the First Methodist church in Pasadena, to a great congregation, when, with hair as black as the raven's wing, and in the full vigor of middle age, he held high the standard of holiness. I saw him as one year later he led the saints of God in Asbury Methodist Episcopal church, Los Angeles, in their fight against sin. I went with him in my memory as in the position of presiding elder he organized a great holiness campaign, and pressed the battle victoriously throughout the length and breadth of his District. I was with him once more in Simpson tabernacle, as he preached the glad tidings of the great salvation in such a way as to make the children of the King shout for joy. I went with him to Boyle Heights Methodist Episcopal church, and joined with him in the glorious conflict against the world, the flesh and the Devil. I was by his side once again in Peniel mission. I was with him when, in following the divine guidance, he was constrained to tear himself away from his conference, from the church in whose ministry he had spent two score years of consecrated effort, from a thousand tender associations and almost hallowed ties, and when, like Abraham of old, he went forth not knowing whither God would lead him. I was with him in the Peniel mission, and was one of the throngs of worshipers who crowded its hall, and knelt at its altars, and listened with rapt attention to the glowing messages which came from his anointed lips. I was with him when he was persecuted and driven from the mission. I was with him on that fateful epoch-making day, eight years ago, when, with that little band of heroes whose deeds are now historic, he organized the First Church of the Nazarene. Again in that hired hall on Main street, I saw their shining faces, heard their triumphant testimonies, and joined in their shouts of praise. Through the mystic corridors of my memory they lived and moved once again, and prominent among them were many of those warriors of the cross who have been promoted from the church militant to the church triumphant, whose places in the serried ranks of the army of Jesus have been filled by the young recruits who have enlisted in such great numbers in the Nazarene division of the grand army of heaven. I was with him and them again during the years of hallowed service and holy victory in the old tabernacle, on Los Angeles street, that birthplace of thousands of souls, that trysting place for the followers of Jesus, from whose doors troops and battalions of Christian soldiers have marched forth bearing weapons of spiritual warfare, and pressing the battle to the ends of the earth. I was with him three years ago when he was brought so close to the boundaries of the holy city, that for weeks, as he lay on a bed of pain, its pearly gates seemed constantly to flutter in their readiness to open and give his ransomed soul entrance into the habitations of glory.

"As I sat there in the midst of that blessed anniversary service, these and other scenes of the past renewed and repeated themselves, and lived again in the chambers of my memory, and I was glad and wept for joy, and rejoiced in the consciousness that I had played a humble part in the great events which made the Church of the Nazarene a possibility, brought it into being, and with God's blessing made it what it is today.

"As I sat there and hung on the words which fell from the lips of our beloved leader, and felt their pathos, and united with those around me in making the place resound with hallelujahs, I realized that the influences, human and divine, which had united during the past eight years in making our church what it was, would grow, not only in power and intensity during the next eight years, but in the scope and extent of their operations; that much of our work thus far had been done beneath the surface, in the way of making the foundations deep and strong; but that in the future the Nazarene movement — for it is a movement, and a great movement — would grow and extend in geometrical ratio; that now its character and identity and distinctive peculiarities were fixed and pronounced, and ready to be projected and transmitted to the four quarters of the earth.

"As I sat there and thought of these things, I was more thankful than ever before that nearly seven years ago we started a Church of the Nazarene in Berkeley, the second of the name in the world; that ever since then we had kept on with the work through good report and bad report, maintaining a place where the holy fire burned perpetually, and where souls by the scores had been saved and sanctified wholly; and that now, after much persecution, and many trials and disappointments, our work there was more firmly rooted and prosperous than ever before."

CHAPTER XXIV.

In a previous chapter I have given a brief account of the
first few annual Assemblies of the church. It would be a
delight to tell of every one of these gatherings, but the space
at my command is not sufficient to warrant my
Eighth doing so. They grew larger and more impor-
Annual tant from year to year, and were participated
Assembly in by greater numbers of delegates. The Assembly of 1903 was a memorable one. The
work had progressed more rapidly during the preceding
year than during any other equal period in the history of
the movement, and in looking over the reports of the different sessions, the names appear of new workers, who were
destined to play an important part in the future activities
of the church.

The address, written by Dr. Bresee, is a very able one,
covering every department of the work of the church, and
being of great historical value. In it, among other things,
he says:

The Address of "In bringing you this report, and ren-
the General dering to you in some sense an account
Superintendent of the stewardship entrusted to me by
you, I can but express my gratitude to
God for the possibilities of labor which have come, for the
fellowship of the heroic souls with whom I have been permitted to be associated, and especially for the victories He
has given us. Chief among these are:

"That the fires of the Pentecost in which this church was
born have not grown dim. That the sanctification of be
lievers through the baptism with the Holy Ghost by our

199

risen Lord, giving power to witness for Him, has not ceased. That the conviction of sinners by the Holy Spirit and their conversion to God, still goes on among us.

"There prevails among us everywhere the deep conviction that the dispensational truth is that Jesus Christ baptizes with the Holy Ghost, cleansing, filling, and empowering, and that when He thus comes, He convinces of sin, of righteousness, and of judgment; and that the conflict with the powers of darkness is brought on, to the glory of our conquering Christ. The result is that our people live, mostly, in the Pentecostal glory, and souls are continually added to the company of the redeemed and bloodwashed.

"While we have never sought to push this work as an ecclesiasticism, and our lack of funds — going forth as we have, more especially to the poorer people — has been such *New Fields* as to preclude our entering many doors which otherwise would have been opened to us, and securing agencies which might otherwise have been employed, nevertheless, we have joyfully entered such doors as have been clearly opened and our entrance made possible, using such agencies as in the providence of God have been by Him raised up. During the year the work has been opened up at Ocean Park, where a vigorous class has been organized, and under the pastoral care of the Rev. Thomas Fluck, promises well for Jesus Christ.

"Several months ago work was so successfully opened at Salt Lake City by the Rev. I. G. Martin, that at a subsequent meeting held by the Rev. C. W. Ruth, a Church of the Nazarene was organized, and has been vigorously pushing the battle.

"At Boise, Idaho, a proposition to turn over to us a church and parsonage property, led to Rev. R. Pierce being sent to that field, and the organization of our work there, of which Brother Pierce is pastor.

"At Omaha, Neb., the Rev. J. A. Dooley and wife had for some time been carrying on an independent work to push

200

the cause of holiness in that great center. It came to be the desire both of them and of the entire church to unite with the Church of the Nazarene, which transfer was made.

"Brother and Sister Dooley felt called some time since to go to Minneapolis, Minn., to open the work there, and the church at Omaha is for a little time without a pastor, but seems to be in a vigorous and hopeful condition. I hope soon to visit them and arrange for the continued prosecution of the work there, in accord with the desire and faith of the heroic band who hold the fort.

"At Maples Mills, Ill., Rev. J. A. Smith, of Pekin, Ill., has recently organized a very promising Church of the Nazarene, of which the Rev. William McFarland has been constituted pastor.

"Openings for the church are multiplying; hungry hearts longing for the gospel of full salvation call us. People who see the need of organized church life, to hold and build up in holiness those who are brought to the *Openings for* fountain of cleansing, and to press the *the Church of* new-born souls to the standing-ground of *the Nazarene* perfect love, in many places beckon us to come. The felt insufficiency of holiness evangelists — compelled to turn the results of their work over to the tender mercies of the careless or opposed to the work, to die — look to us and wait for us to supply, or help to supply, this great need. I am impressed that God wants us to occupy, to strongly occupy, the great centers. A great holiness fire should be kindled, and be fed and propagated through simple but efficient organizations in these great centers, which would soon shine out into the cities, villages and country round about. I feel assured that God will speedily answer our prayer in raising up the proper agencies, and supplying sufficient funds for this work. Our Christ can and will raise up the heroes to accomplish this planting of the work.

"A very great work lies before us. A work which can not

201

be forecast or provided for by human wisdom, or accomplished by human power.

"It becometh us to lie low at the
A Very Great Work feet of Jesus; to be ready to suffer
for Him; to possess our souls in
patience; to be filled with love toward each other and to all men; to be deeply conscious of the call of God to this work. Only those who see the great providences of God in this work, and are so deeply conscious that he has called them to it, that they can do no other way than, with every force of faith and work, push the cause of God through the channel to which they are called — only such — will be of the greatest value in a work beset by so many difficulties as this to which we are called.

"Again thanking God for the way He has led us, for the abundant blessings bestowed, for the faith and heroism He has breathed into the people of the Church of the Nazarene, and for all the victories won, and especially for what He is going to do for us: let us pray that the greatest wisdom may be upon our deliberations, and that the meekness and gentleness of Jesus may be in all our hearts."

A mere list of the committees and their members, will be illuminating. They are as follows:

State of the Church: B. H. KENNEDY, MRS. D. WALLACE,
MRS. EBERT, STEWART NOBLE, J. H.
The Committees CROWELL.

Prohibition: DR. S. BOWERS, C. W. RAYMOND, MRS. LILY BOTHWELL, C. H. EDWARDS, G. L. SHEPARDSON.

Sunday School: R. E. SHAW, MRS. PAUL BRESEE, V. J. JACQUES, H. N. ELLIOTT, MRS. HAGUE.

Missions: L. F. GAY, MRS. A. T. ARMOUR, C. W. RUTH, MRS. D. WALLACE.

Publishing House: W. P. TRUMBOWER, C. E. MCKEE, R. PIERCE, MRS. D. WALLACE, MRS. PAUL BRESEE.

Press Committee: LUCY P. KNOTT, J. P. COLEMAN, LILY BOTHWELL, C. W. RUTH, DR. S. BOWERS.

Young People: R. E. SHAW, MRS. L. P. KNOTT, MRS. D. WALLACE, ROSIE TAIT, MRS. F. A. LAW.

Educational: MISS LEORA MARIS, MRS. LILY BOTHWELL, B. E. SHERWIN, J. C. ANDREWS, C. W. BENTON.

Revision of Manual: R. PIERCE, J. P. COLEMAN, C. W. RUTH, W. S. KNOTT, LESLIE F. GAY, DR. P. F. BRESEE.

Deaconess: MRS. M. BISBEE, MRS. H. C. SEVIER, FRED HOWLAND, R. P. LAWSON, MRS. HORTON.

Resolutions: J. P. COLEMAN, T. A. ASBRIDGE, DR. S. BOWERS, H. A. IRISH, S. P. SMOTT.

Church Extension: GEO. NEWTON, F. G. WOODWARD, MRS. ELY, W. H. SLACK, MRS. ROBERT YOUNG.

Rev. Mrs. De Lance Wallace, pastor of the First Church of the Nazarene, at Spokane, Wash., read an interesting report, stating that the church held its services in a rented hall; that there were 175 members; that *The Church at Spokane* there was a promising class of twenty at Garfield; and that God was giving tnem blessed victory in the work.

The roll-call of the Assembly disclosed a total membership of ninety, most of whom seem to have been present. The Rev. R. Pierce was elected secretary, and Rev. C. W. Raymond assistant secretary. Dr. Bresee was re-elected as General Superintendent, and Rev. E. A. Girvin was appointed historian, and requested to write the history of the Church of the Nazarene up to that time.

During the progress of the Assembly a great home camp-meeting was conducted by the Rev. C. W. Ruth, assisted by Rev. Isaiah Reid, Rev. S. S. Chafe, Mrs. De Lance Wallace, Rev. George Newton, Rev. R. Pierce, and others. The glory of God was present throughout these great services, and some two hundred seekers knelt at the altar, most of whom claimed either pardon or purity.

Rev. Isaiah Reid, of Iowa, thus describes this great meeting, in the Nazarene Messenger, of December 10, 1903:

"It is a great inspiration to face a congregation of from one thousand five hundred to two thousand, where one feels that the expctation and the joy is to hear, not only about the 'common salvation,' but that uncommon measure of it involved in full salvation. An anti-holiness preacher who perchance might have found himself in this pulpit to preach, would find himself unable 'to go on without pro-ceedin,' as the colored man explained when he found him-self unable to introduce the subject he had in mind. With such countenances before him, such a regiment of eyes look-ing him full in the face, and such an atmosphere around him, anti-holiness insinuations, even in his words, would paralyze his tongue, and the ringing chorus of 'No! No! No!' confuse his thought world. Imagine him in such a tidal wave as struck us the last Thursday night of the meet-ing. The very building seemed surcharged with the divine presence. The songs took fire at once. The melody was grand, but the thought in the words was like fire in the dry grass on a prairie on a windy evening. When there was prayer, it was in pentecostal measure. The season of song surpassed the former. The organ was more melodious. The piano keys danced to the holy music, and the chorus of four horns was actually needed to give fuller tone and additional noise to the voluminous chorus of human voices. The even-ing thankoffering went in as an actual part of the service. Then we sang again. When the hymn was ended, some of it had to be sung again, for the praise spirit was not yet satisfied. When one song ended, some one in the congrega-tion would strike up some other chorus. When this was done, another in another part of the house would do the same. At last the shouts drowned the songs. The hands went up of their own accord till they looked like a miniature forest. Then each tree in the forest waved with a white hankerchief. It was like the noise of many waters. Brother Ruth had arisen to try to preach. He could not. Once he got to where he thought he could read the text, but again the shouts broke out, and the strong cedars of Lebanon bent again and again from the mighty wind from the skies. The altar began to fill up. The rest of the evening was all

204

taken up with altar work. Few will ever forget that mighty cyclone of divine power."

Shortly after the Assembly, Dr. Bresee, accompanied by Brother and Sister Earl Hinchman, and Brother C. E. McKee, went to Omaha, Neb., where they held a ten days' meeting, and greatly strengthened and *Trip to Omaha* encouraged the church in that city. Dr. Bresee, in writing about the meeting, said:

"We found here a heroic band of Nazarenes, about thirty in number. They have held the fort and earnestly pushed the battle without a pastor since the removal of Rev. J. A. Dooley, two or three months ago, to Minneapolis, Minn. They have been much helped by Rev. J. R. Lindsey, of Council Bluffs, who has now united with us here, and will do all in his power to push the work. He is spoken of as an able and efficient preacher, but is in business in Council Bluffs, and can not give his whole time to the work. However, he, with the others who have united from Council Bluffs — among whom is Brother Ogden, who leads the singing — are a great help. There have been a goodly number of seekers, both for pardon and entire sanctification, and some seasons of great victory, as they came through shouting the praise of Jesus. Perhaps the greatest blessing of the meeting was in the melting of the saints into sweet and blessed unity, and the pouring upon them of new enduements of love and power. They are enthusiastic Nazarenes, and are anxious to learn, and catch the tread and step of the personality of this movement of which they rejoice to be a part. We received into the church thirty-six, making sixty-six members, which gives them a good start.

"Omaha is a great center, one of the strategic gateway cities in which it means so much to have the Church of the Nazarene firmly planted. The need is very great for a heaven-inspired and anointed work of holiness, free from fanaticism, and unhindered by side issues, a work which continually leads people into the cleansing fountain, and thus makes way for the conviction and conversion of souls by the present and manifest Holy Spirit. An organized work, which cares for those saved and sanctified, leading them forth into ways of strength and usefulness, thus saving them from the repression and overthrow which so often come to them by their being relegated to dead churches from the barren desert wastes to which fanaticism and side-tracks lead.

"Brother C. E. McKee, who so generously came with me, has been — as he always is — in the thickest of the fight, preaching, exhorting, singing, leading souls to the altar, and helping them through. I do not see how we could have gotten along without him.

"We spent part of a day at Council Bluffs. I was for several years, and at two different times, pastor of Broadway church, in that city, transferring from there to California. A little gathering was planned by Brother and Sister Arthur, and Brother and Sister Orcutt, at the home of Brother Arthur — of some of the old friends who were here so long ago. So we had the opportunity of seeing, talking, and praying with them. We will soon all be there. 'What a meeting that will be.'

"We go to Salt Lake City for a few days, to Boise, Idaho, for a few more, and then will hasten home. 'There is no place like home,' but having Jesus with us, all places are blessed.

"One of the things which has greatly helped in the work, inspiring confidence, and strengthening the hands of the workers, has been the number of persons resident here, who have been in attendance upon the Church of the Nazarene in Los Angeles, some having spent some time there. Having been greatly blessed through its agency, they bear uniform testimony to the manifest presence of God and His blessing upon the work, and their longing that it might be repeated in this city."

Dr. Bresee wrote of his visit to the church in Boise, as follows:

"The city itself nestles almost in the lap of the mountains on the northeast. It has some beautiful streets, and nice public and private buildings, and seems *The Church in* enterprising and prosperous, with much *Boise, Idaho* improvement and many new houses.

"We arrived here on Tuesday afternoon, December 8, 1903, for the purpose of holding a few days meeting in the Church of the Nazarene. We found a pleasant home at the parsonage, with Rev. R. Pierce and family. The meeting opened on Tuesday evening, with a good audience. The program has been meetings afternoon and night, with an all day meeting on the Sabbath. The services have been well attended; some souls have been converted, and some sanctified wholly. The Church of the Nazarene has a nice location in the northern part of the city, on the corner of Eastman and Twelfth streets. A neat, tasty church is built on the corner, and there is a good parsonage on Eastman street, all in excellent repair, and presenting an attractive appearance.

"The property was built under the supervision of the Quakers, and the work carried on by them until they proposed to turn it over to us, some months ago. It is probably worth from $2,500 to $3,500, with an indebtedness of $700. Rev. R. Pierce was appointed to arrange the transfer, and organize a Church of the Nazarene, which he did, and at the desire of the brethren, became the pastor.

"The little church is putting on the swing and victory which characterize and give such strong personality to the Church of the Nazarene and its work. It is something of a transition from Quakerism to the ways of the Church of the Nazarene, but, having the Spirit, they soon catch the step and rhythm.

The attendance upon the meetings was somewhat hindered by the stoppage of all electric cars, caused by the failure of power resulting from a break in the water ditch, which turned the city into darkness and stopped all cars.

"During the latter days there was also snow and rain,

which added to the obstacles in the way. But the Lord over-rules all things to the advancement of His work, as His people trust Him, and so, doubtless, with these conditions, the foundations could be built up with the greatest certainty.

"Brother and Sister Deem, who are and have been friends of ours for years past, and who were largely instrumental in the turning over of this plant with its work to us, were almost constantly at the meetings, though they live five miles away in the country. Brother Deem is the Sunday school superintendent, Sister Deem teaches the primary department, and they have a very promising school.

"Brother and Sister Pierce have been faithfully laboring to create a center of fire where the people might come and be saved, and built up in holiness. The churches — from what I could learn from some of their members — are peculiarly dead, filled with worldliness and worldly ends, while salvation is almost, if not altogether, an unknown thing.

"There are some hungry hearts, but the strength and prejudice of churchanity cause people to prefer old forms, and to draw nourishment from the breasts of a dead mother, rather than to find life and power by uniting heart to heart, getting heaven open, and making a place of Pentecostal fire and life and power.

"How long will the hungry souls who long for holiness, and who see that without it they not only can not enter heaven, but that no advance can be made in the Lord's work, continue to perpetuate this folly?

"What is any ecclesiasticism to an immortal soul, when that ecclesiasticism has determined to put from it the holiness of God, and the work of grace by which it is secured, and the conditions by which it is maintained, and when will holiness people and those who desire the blessing, see that they must join hands, and push the battle irrespective of old affiliations, as God leads?"

CHAPTER XXV.

This is the title of a very notable editorial by Dr. Bresee in the Nazarene Messenger, under date of January 7, 1904. It is as follows:

The Way of Victory "We are pressed by several correspondents for words in reference to the way of success in winning souls to Jesus. It is a subject the theory of which has as little value of itself as almost any that we can consider; and yet, if we are earnestly seeking to know the Lord's way in the matter, surely He has not withheld the light. He has not sent us to do a work without making possible for us to know how to secure the end for which He sends us. He has evidently sent us forth with encouragement as to success. We are the bearers of His message to men, and He has declared that it should not return void, but that it should prosper in the thing whereto He has sent it. And Jesus said in reference to our going, that all power is His, and that He will be with us always. These and similar statements encourage us to expect that something will be accomplished through our ministry. The voice which comes to us from various sources is, sometimes, almost a bitter cry from human hearts to know why only barrenness is round about them. If God blesses some, and souls are saved in some places, why are they so left to struggle on without any tangible results, so far as soul-saving is concerned? In a given case, it might be difficult to answer, and give the prescription for the removal of the difficulty, at least without close examination of conditions, and clear knowledge of all the facts.

"But there are certain general truths which will help any earnest, honest soul to discover what the difficulties are,

209

and to know what would be the remedy, whether he is able to apply it or not.

"We live in the dispensation when Jesus Christ baptizes believers with the Holy Ghost, and when the conviction of sinners, and the empowering of believers to carry on the work of Jesus Christ in the world, depends upon their having become subjects of this baptism.

"Not only is the church's effective testimony to Jesus Christ shut up to the unction of this baptism, but it is when He has come in that sinners are to be convinced. The general absence of conviction, is clearly the result of the absence of the Holy Ghost in the hearts of professedly Christian believers.

"The effort to get men saved is evidently not to be manward, but God-ward. All human effort to awaken sinners, is as ineffective as to preach to a graveyard. If the power of God can not be prayed down from heaven, the task is hopeless. But it is not the power for this conviction that is to be primarily sought, but the incoming of the Holy Spirit into our hearts to do for us what He did for the disciples on the day of Pentecost, 'purifying our hearts by faith.' And when the Holy Ghost has come and finds His basis of operations, He will surely do what Jesus has promised, that is, He shall convince of sin. All other methods or ways are evidently humanly devised plans and methods, and whatever they accomplish in the way of social or club life, they will fail of doing the divine work of salvation. Praying in the Holy Ghost, preaching and testifying in the power of the Holy Ghost, are God's way of doing His work, and can not be defeated by environments or conditions. What every cluster of people must have, whether small or large, what every individual heart must have, is the baptism of Jesus with the Holy Ghost. 'Then shall I teach transgressors thy ways, and sinners shall be converted unto thee.' "

In the issue of the Nazarene Messenger of March 3, 1904, there appears an editorial by Dr. Bresee, on the subject of Reliability, which is characteristic of the man. It is as

210

follows: "The Lord lays great and emphatic stress on the abiding qualities. The roots of a tree are supposed to be as long, taken as a whole, and to carry as much material, as the trunk and limbs. It is their fixedness and strength which gives stability to the tree, and enables it to sway in the tempest and stand erect when the storm is past. We say of a man, 'he has the root of the matter in him.' In other words, he is not easily moved. Depth of conviction, of inwrought Christian principle, have been wept and prayed into the deepest depths of his being, and then the new birth, and Christian life, give him love and fidelity for and to God and man.

"The Christian graces mingle and crystalize in reliability, so that men can trust us — invest their confidence in us, without the possibility of being betrayed. All words, all expression, all forms of speech, all forms of worship — be it the quiet of ritualism, or the ranting of a fanatic — are but outer things, and have value, or are an excrescence, according to the reliability of the underlying life that continually pours its waters into the viaducts of human society. There are men who, like Mount Shasta, are there, crowned with whiteness every day of their years. You can depend upon them when the sun rises and when it sets, when the storms sweep the earth, and when the sunshine kisses it. If the grace of God has not so had its way in our hearts as to create reliability, all our words and songs and shouts are a mere pretense, deceiving some, possibly, but duping ourselves most of all.

"One of the saddest sights, is to see a self-duped Pharisee raking the earth and the tombs to find people to condemn, that he or she may stand on the pyramid of skulls, and manifest what soon appears in its hideousness — themselves.

"But reliability, first pure then peaceable, thinking upon the things that are pure and peaceable, and of good report, with eyes fixed upon Him who comes to save men and women, changed into His image, and made conformable unto His death, standing to help men to Him; so like Him that

211

we are the same yesterday, today, and, by His grace, for ever — is to be of real value to this world. Not pretense, but reliability.

" 'Surely the Captain may depend on me,
" 'Though but an armor-bearer I may be.'

"And if the captain, then the whole company as well."

Early in March, 1904, Dr. Bresee, accompanied by Rev. C. V. La Fontaine, Brother C. E. McKee, and Sisters Sevier and Ernest, went to Cucamonga, where Rev. S. S. Chafe was conducting a Nazarene mission, and held a very successful all-day meeting, conducting a service the same evening at Uplands, four miles distant. The hall at Cucamonga was full of people. Dr. Bresee preached, Brother La Fontaine exhorted, and testimonies were given to the truth as witnesses had found it in their experience of the cleansing blood. There were seekers and salvation at each service. The work at both of these places was reported to be in a flourishing condition. The strong tide of opposition had largely passed by, and the people were getting hungry for the salvation of God. As a result of this feast of fat things, the people were greatly encouraged.

All-Day Meeting at Cucamonga

In this period of his life, and in fact, during all the years of his mighty ministry, Dr. Bresee gave out many rich nuggets of divine truth. One of these of very peculiar beauty, I find in a short editorial in the Nazarene Messenger of March 24, 1904.

Touches of Glory

"There is a company of white-robed worshipers in some country, those who 'have washed their robes, and made them white in the blood of the Lamb.' Some of them surely are in this world, for we are told that, 'If we walk in the light, we have fellowship one with another, and the blood of Jesus Christ, His Son, cleanseth us from all sin.' That is in reference to the present time, and David prayed, 'Wash me and I shall be whiter than snow.'

"Some of the blood-washed, some who wear the white robes, are surely in this world. We find it said of them, 'Therefore, are they before the throne.' The only thing that separates us from God is sin. When that is taken away, and the soul is made thoroughly clean in the blood of the Lamb, that soul is before the throne. He has access to God, he abides in His presence, and is filled with His love.

" 'They serve Him day and night in His temple.' They never pass out of the holy precincts of worship and devotion. Songs are upon their lips, and hallelujahs are in their hearts.

"The days are full of triumph, and the nights are filled with praise. 'And He that sitteth upon the throne shall dwell among them.' The indwelling divine presence in a holy heart is very peculiar and glorious. It is the unspeakable fact of which we speak with almost bated breath, and with unutterable awe, knowing that none can tell of the sweet tones and heavenly words, and touches of glory that come to the consciousness of him in whom He dwells. But they know the sweet satisfaction of the state of which it is said: 'They shall hunger no more, neither thirst any more; for the Lamb which is in the midst of the throne shall feed them, and lead them unto living fountains of waters, and God shall wipe all tears from their eyes.' "

In May, 1904, the National Holiness Convention was held in the First Church of the Nazarene, Los Angeles, the services extending throughout the entire month. The meetings were conducted by Rev. C. J. Fowler, *National* president of the National Holiness Association, *Holiness* tion, Rev. H. C. Morrison, of Kentucky, *Convention* editor of the "Pentecostal Herald," Rev. Bud Robinson, and Revs. J. M. and M. J. Harris, the two last named having charge of the singing. Dr. Bresee, in announcing this great meeting said: "Continuous prayer is being offered, and we ask for the saints everywhere to unite with us in supplication for a most marvelous outpouring of the blessed Holy Spirit. The time is

213

opportune — many strangers will be in Los Angeles, as there were in Jerusalem on that historic Pentecost. Many will have come purposely for the meeting. A real Pentecost will reach in hallowed blessings and holy power to the ends of the earth — the sound of its dashing waves of glory will be heard in every land, and many will tell in the different languages of this babbling earth, with fresh and enlarged unction, the story of redemption. A new movement, so much better than ecclesiastical, and so much wider than merely social or intellectual, may be inaugurated by the Spirit of God. God is anxious to give a new tide of life, to reinforce whatever there may be of spirituality on the earth. Great tides of holy life and power from heaven, sweeping many to Calvary, and into the cleansing fountain, are not accidental, but come in answer to faithful prayer to God. Our meeting of the conditions, and then asking in humble, obedient faith, is sure to be crowned with the abounding glory from Him who said, 'Ask and ye shall receive.' We are expecting that our Heavenly Father will open upon us the windows of heaven, and pour us out a blessing that there will not be room to receive it. The great blessings of the past would encourage us; but the promises of God abide, sure and steadfast."

The General Conference of the Methodist Episcopal church was held in Los Angeles at the same time, drawing to the city a multitude of people from all over the world.

God answered the prayers of His people, and during the month of the Holiness Convention, mighty tides of salvation flowed from the throne and more than five hundred persons came to the cleansing fountain and gave victorious testimonies of the saving and sanctifying power of the Lord.

In the midst of the convention, Rev. H. C. Morrison wrote as follows:

"I am at this writing, engaged with Dr. Fowler, Bud Robinson, and others, with Dr. Bresee, the pastor, at the

Church of the Nazarene, in Los Angeles, Cal., in a Pentecostal Convention. It was my privilege to labor in revival work with this congregation some five years ago. The growth and general progress of this church since that time is something remarkable. The organization of this church grew out of the strong opposition to the doctrine and experience of entire sanctification. The church was organized eight and one-half years ago. There were only about one hundred charter members, but in these few years the membership has grown to something more than sixteen hundred members. I doubt if there is another congregation in the United States, in a city with the population of Los Angeles, with so large a membership as this. Several other churches of this same denomination, have sprung up in other parts of the country, and thousands of souls have been converted or sanctified at the altars of this church, who have been members of other churches.

"Los Angeles has tens of thousands of visitors from the outside world every year. Many of this transient multitude come to the altars of this church, are saved, and go out to the ends of the earth to tell of the cleansing power of Christ's precious blood.

"One of the excellent effects of this church, is that its existence has a gracious spiritual effect upon the entire community. A church and a congregation like this, make other churches more tolerant in their attitude toward full salvation from sin. I think that this feature of the good effect of this church amounts to more than any one suspects. That we can be provoked to love and good works, there is no doubt, and you may be certain that this great company of Nazarenes, working with diligence and joy in this city, has not had a tendency to produce lethargy and stagnation in other churches. It also stands here as a suggestion to the ecclesiasticisms of the land, that the God of this universe is not shut up to any one place or people, but that when occasion requires, He can raise up for Himself a people who will preach, without fear or apology, the full atonement that there is in the Savior's blood.

"This congregation has recently built a great tabernacle, with ample Sabbath school rooms and a great auditorium with seating capacity for two thousand people, and great multitudes of people come to hear the gospel.

"Only last night (May the eighth) with the General Conference in session, and distinguished preachers filling the pulpits all over the city, this vast auditorium was packed from altar, aisle and gallery, and many were forward seeking the Lord. Meanwhile, three other small churches of this same denomination in other parts of the city were crowded with worshipers, and many souls were saved. Our convention has now been going forward for eight days, and more than one hundred souls have been to the altar, most of them finding pardon or purity. Dr. Bresee, its pastor, while yet strong, and full of vigor and activity, has very wisely secured the assistance of Rev. C. V. La Fontaine as copastor. Brother La Fontaine is a fine combination of physical, mental and spiritual strength. He has served a number of large congregations in the Methodist Episcopal church, and combines excellent qualifications of head and heart for the great field in which he has come to work. May the Lord anoint him from on high for this important task.

"Dr. Fowler is preaching with his usual force and clearness, pressing the battle with untiring zeal; and Brother Bud is preaching the Word with marvelous simplicity and power. He is indeed a miracle of grace. Think of a man who only a few years ago did not know the alphabet, and now he quotes *verbatim* one-sixth of the Bible, Old Testament and New, without looking on the Book.

"The ingenuity and pathos with which he illustrates the sublimest truths with the simplest objects in every day life, is remarkable, often amusing, but always with effectiveness.

"May the peace and power of the Holy Ghost abide with all those of whom I write. Amen."

In the latter part of July, 1904, Dr. Bresee started for Chicago, Illinois, his first stopping place being at Howard, Kansas, of which he thus spoke:

An Eastern Trip "Howard is the county seat of Elk county. This is a beautiful country, the prairie more rolling than western Kansas, with streams and groves — native timber along the streams, and groves which have sprung up under the hand of cultivation. The soil is good, and the people seem prosperous.

"This year the heavy and continuous rains have affected the crops, but they are recuperating under the genial sunshine.

"The Nazarenes are having a campmeeting two and one-half miles southwest of Howard, which is the occasion of my visit to these parts. Some three years ago, the Rev. Herbert Buffum held a very successful meeting in connection with the Methodist church at Moline, a town nine miles south of Howard. In connection with these meetings he organized a County Holiness Association. This was thought to be a necessity, because of the attitude of the churches toward the holiness work. The work was greatly hindered by this hostility — the new pastor at Moline so opposing the work that the results of the great meeting there were almost lost.

"A few months ago Brother Buffum held another meeting at Howard, when the people who composed the County Holiness Association desired him to organize them into a Church of the Nazarene, which he did, there being forty-one members. These were scattered in different parts of the county, but having a very good church building at Howard.

"It is these people who have arranged and are holding this campmeeting. It is held in a beautiful grove, and the presence of the Lord is manifest. When the church here

217

was organized, Rev. H. J. Starkey, of Salt Lake City, was invited to become its pastor, and accepted, arriving with his wife about a month ago. He has already taken up four preaching places, viz: Howard, Moline, Elk Falls, and Highlands, and this is thought to be an open door and an inviting field for our church, in which to spread Scriptural holiness."

Dr. Bresee thus describes this meeting:

"It fell to the lot of the writer to do most of the preaching, the pastor, Rev. H. J. Starkey, and Rev. J. R. Maybury, of Chase, Kansas, each preaching once, and helping to push the battle. There is here an excellent band of workers, real Nazarenes. They have the holy zeal, anointing, and victory of the Home Church, and the Nazarenes generally. They pray and sing, testify and shout in such a way as to cause one to feel at home — in heavenly places — at once. There were a number of things that seemed disadvantageous to the meeting, all of which I believe to have been overruled, and most of which were made advantageous. It was far from town and could be reached by very few people without conveyances. This, of course, would curtail attendance. The season has been very wet, so much so that crops are expected to be exceptionally poor, and the rain having recently ceased so that work could be done, workers were demanded at the work. It was regarded as a Nazarene meeting, and this did not appeal to the church people very largely, there being in this country much prejudice against the holiness work, and such organized efforts as the Church of the Nazarene represents, in particular.

The Meeting at Howard, Kansas

"But the people came in carriages and wagons from the different parts of the county, and God wrought — souls were saved and sanctified, and the saints were greatly edified. One of the peculiar excellencies of the meeting has been the advance made by those who had already entered into the experience of full salvation. They seemed to eat and drink the Word, and lie down in green pastures beside

218

still waters, and rejoice with exceeding joy. Prejudice melted away, and the people received the Word, to sow it again in all the country and towns round about. I have rarely seen a meeting that seemed to me to promise so much for future victories. Some devoted warriors united with the Church of the Nazarene, and the older heroes declared that it was to them the best campmeeting they ever saw. Once each Sabbath the table was set at the altar, and the people came and laid their glad offerings upon it, which fully provided for the expenses of the meeting. Just as the last afternoon service was closing, a heavy storm burst upon us — thunder and lightning and torrents of rain — making any further services for the day an impossibility; so amidst the tempest, the people sang and praised God, and brought the very precious meeting to a close."

CHAPTER XXVI.

Prior to reaching Chicago, Dr. Bresee set forth the considerations bearing upon the organization of the Nazarene work in that city, as follows:

The Chicago Work "At the urgent invitation of a large number of holiness people in Chicago, who are desirous of a real holiness church, that is clean, clear, definite, and full of Holy Ghost power, the General Superintendent of the Church of the Nazarene is now on his way to Chicago.

"Chicago is a great city, the possibilities for a great work are large, and it is the object of this article to enlist every follower of Jesus that is in the blessing of entire sanctification to pray more than earnestly for the marvelous presence and power of God to be displayed, that the work of organizing a Church of the Nazarene may be accompanied with an open heaven, sending down the flood-tides of glory. Chicago needs a good, strong holiness church, and with the stalwart men and women who are behind the invitation and the movement, it is sure to be an epoch for religious people to have a Church of the Nazarene come into their midst.

"There are hundreds of clear, definite holiness people there who want a home. The old Wesleyan doctrine of holiness as a second, definite work of grace, is not acceptable to hundreds of churches and preachers, who are substituting suppression or repression, or 'get-it-all-at-conversion' for the old time-honored preaching of Jesus, St. Paul, St. John, and Wesley, that entire sanctification is a second, definite work of grace in the heart of a regenerated child of God.

"The great national conventions for the promotion of holiness, are always seasons of great spiritual blessing, and hundreds of people come into the experience of full salvation, but there are very few places, comparatively speaking, where they can find a spiritual home, where a clear, strong testimony to perfect love, or entire sanctification, is accepted, or where the holiness people are welcomed. They will be found mostly in the missions or some smaller churches that are struggling for existence, who are glad to welcome the holiness folks, for they have the fire that keeps things from freezing up, and they have the fulness of blessing that keeps things from drying up. Much of the work of the holiness conventions is lost for the want of being taken care of. It is providential that the Church of the Nazarene is thus to be organized. It has a bright future.

"We ask all holiness people to bear this important work up before the throne, that God may marvelously show forth his power."

Before going to Chicago, Dr. Bresee held several other meetings in Illinois, the first of which was at Maple Mills. I can not do better than to describe this meeting in his own graphic words:

Maple Mills "I arrived on the campground here on
Campmeeting Thursday afternoon, August 4, 1904, the meeting beginning that night. There are a number of tents — twenty-one — besides the tabernacle in which the meeting is held. We are in a nice grove, surrounded by a well cultivated and rich farming country. The towns in the immediate neighborhood are small hamlets, although there are some towns of several thousand people a few miles away, among which are Lewiston, the county seat, and further away the larger city of Canton; but this is strictly a farming country. The night services from the beginning have been well attended; the services during the day have been thus far made up mostly of those tenting on the grounds. The Sabbath services throughout the day brought all those that could be accommodated. The grounds are quite distant from the railroad, and seem to one unacquainted with the ways of getting here, to be rather inaccessible to people from a distance.

"One lady residing at Rockford, Ill., who takes the Nazarene Messenger, and who was hungering and thirsting for full salvation, left her home on Saturday, and was so delayed that she did not arrive until Sunday. She came into the meeting Monday morning, and at once arose and told of her hunger and thirst, and that she had come to seek the blessing. While she spoke, the heavens opened upon her, and with great joy and holy triumph she was able to tell of the sanctifying power of the blood of Jesus.

"I have with me here as special workers in the meeting, Rev. B. W. Golden, an evangelist from Bagley, Iowa, who is a member of the Society of Friends, thoroughly Wesleyan in his preaching, and an experienced and able worker; also Mrs. Rose Potter Crist, from Topeka, Kansas, a lady of excellent ability as a leader of song, and as a general worker, especially at the altar.

"This meeting, like that which I held in Kansas, has been largely made up of country people. I am led to think that, while the city has its difficult questions in reference to reaching the people, especially the young people, with the gospel, that the country districts are not without their own problems relative to the same matters, which must be studied from their own standpoint. For a long time I have been so far removed from them, that I do not suppose I have compassed them, but I can not help seeing something of the conditions.

"Their social life, together with its entertainments and amusements, seems to be quite different from what they are in the city. They come together from considerable distances, and getting acquainted and associating together, they seem to come more under each other's influence, to have less individuality and independence, and to be more gregarious, to move more as a flock, than the young people of the city, at least of the Western cities with which I am more especially familiar. I am not discussing the excellencies of either class, but these conditions make the country class, as it seems to me, more difficult to reach, in that it is almost impossible to get one segregated from the common influence of the flock, and to persuade him to come out from among his fellows and seek the Lord — as all must — on his own hook. When a revival occurs in a particular District, and a break is made, and some influential person goes, the flock follows. Few of them, however, get any real experience, and others soon drift away to the worldly flock, which seems always at once to reorganize. To secure and hold a spiritually anointed company of young people in the country, who shall be continually influencing and drawing the other young people in the way of life, seems to me as necessary, and even more difficult, than in the city.

"Some have been saved and sanctified, and we are looking for great victory."

In his letter to the Nazarene Messenger, of August 25th, Dr. Bresee gives the following vivid report of the closing days of the campmeeting at Maple Mills:

A Tide of Salvation "The campmeeting closed last night, having lasted ten days. The preaching was done by Rev. B. W. Golden, especially secured for this meeting, and the writer. The singing was led by Mrs. Rose Potter Crist, of Topeka, Kansas, who is one of the very best leaders in campmeeting singing, both from the platform and at the altar, with whom it has been my privilege to be associated. When the altar call is made, she goes to the altar, and prays and sings the seekers to the bosom of Jesus. She has the blessing, and knows how to help others in. She was reinforced by the coming of Sisters Jennie L. Reeves, and Mattie I. Barnes, from Iowa, singers and evangelists, who labor in connection with Brother Golden. They were to help him in a meeting at Canton, Ill., at the close of this meeting, and came on thus early to have a little part with us. They are effective, singing the gospel in the spirit, and with power.

"Though the grounds are so located that a meeting held here must be largely a local one, yet there was a good attendance, at night usually taxing the accommodations, and on Sabbath many more than could get under or near the tabernacle.

"The meeting deepened and widened in spirituality and power, and the last day was one that the people in attendance are not likely to forget or get over.

"After the forenoon sermon, the altar was filled with earnest seekers, the fire fell in great glory, all of them were swept to Calvary, and the saints rejoiced. In the afternoon the sacrament of the Lord's supper was had, when the multitudes were hushed with sacred awe, and the children of the Lord ate and drank, and praised Him.

"An address was then made (by Dr. Bresee) on the privileges of Christian fellowship and co-operation, especially the duty and privilege which is now upon us of creating centers of fire wherever it is possible, where people can be constantly brought to Jesus, and believers find the Pentecostal fire.

"Opportunities were then given to persons who might desire to unite with the Church of the Nazarene. At this point, Rev. B. W. Golden asked to say a few words. He spoke of his own church relations in the past, and told how for some time the Lord had been impressing upon him the great need of a church home for the holiness people, where they would be free from the peculiar hindrances and petty persecutions which destroyed the spiritual life of so many of those who were led into the experience, and which so largely prevented the advancement of the work. He said that for some time he had been led to think that the Church of the Nazarene was such a home and such an advantageous place for pushing the work; that he had become so thoroughly convinced of this fact, together with his fellow workers, who like himself had been brought to this meeting through a series of special providences, that, after much prayer and many tears before the Lord, they and he had fully made up their minds — believing that they were led of the Holy Ghost — to unite with this church; and that they would do what was possible for them in the way of opening its doors of privilege to others, and reinforcing the great work of establishing, as well as spreading, scriptural holiness over these lands. Having thus spoken, he with the Misses Reeves and Barnes, took their place with quite a number of others — eighteen in all — and were received into the church amid the joyous welcome of many hearts.

"At night Brother Golden preached, an altar service was held, a season of precious thanksgiving had, and amid handshaking and praises to our risen Lord, with songs of expectant hope that when the mists are rolled away, there would be reunions at the Eastern Gate, the campmeeting closed."

After leaving Maple Mills, Dr. Bresee spent a little time at Peoria, where there was a small Nazarene mission conducted by Brother and Sister Southey, at 705 Main street.

Peoria He held four services for them, three at night and one in the afternoon. The hall was full at each service, there were hungry hearts, and several were clearly sanctified. At the last meeting five united with the church. Rev. J. W. Gibbs, who had assisted him at Maple Mills, helped also at Peoria. Dr. Bresee concludes his account of this meeting as follows:

"One of the pleasantest things of my trip occurred here in the coming of Sister Funk from Bloomington, to meet me and enjoy another real Nazarene service. She is greatly anointed of the Lord, and spoke with much unction and power. She is a real Nazarene, and is praying for the coming of our church to Bloomington. I said to her: 'I see that you wear the Nazarene badge.' She replied: 'O yes, our dear Sister Baldwin pinned that on the day that I united with the church in Los Angeles, and it has been the sweetest gift, and the fountain of the most blessings of any present I ever received.' Thank the Lord for such representatives of the work scattered over the land.

"Another very happy occurrence in connection with the meeting here, was the providential stopping of Sister Coffin, who was on her way home from the campmeeting at Maple

Mills, where she had been gloriously sanctified. Having to change cars here, she was wrongly directed by a railroad man, and took the wrong train. So the best they could do was to send her back, and when our company arrived — waiting a little for a street car — she came in. As the railroad company proposed to give her an extended ticket, she concluded to stay to the meetings, to which she was a great blessing. How true it is that all things work together for good to those who love God."

Writing from Lake Bluff, Dr. Bresee said:

"Lake Bluff is a suburb of Chicago on the Northwestern railroad. It is very rural and pleasant, the summer residence of quite a number of people. Here *A Day at Lake Bluff* is a Deaconess Rest Home of the Rock River Conference of the Methodist Episcopal church, where these workers, when worn and weary, find a place to rest and recuperate. Here a friend — Mrs. N. C. Radford, a deaconess much engaged in evangelistic work — resides. She was converted under our ministry years ago, and urged us to a day of rest and a visit. It was a pleasant day, and in the evening at their request, I told them of the Church of the Nazarene, and the peculiar, providential leadings in its formation and up-building.

"All people who wish well to the cause of Christ, are deeply interested in every movement which brings souls to Jesus, and believers into the cleansing fountain. These friends were especially interested in the emphasis laid upon the dispensational truth, that Jesus baptizes with the Holy Ghost. There are very hungry hearts everywhere, but the surroundings and force of gravity make it so difficult to retain that definite faith and testimony necessary for the maintenance of the experience. We prayed together, and I went on my way to Chicago."

Dr. Bresee continues his narrative:

"I arrived in Chicago Saturday morning, and was met at the depot by Prof. J. W. Akers, who had hurried home from

Yours Very Truly
P F Breese

Yours very truly
Mrs P F Breese

P. F. BRESEE AT EIGHTEEN

DOCTOR AND MRS. P. F. BRESEE
AT TIME OF MARRIAGE IN 1860

M. E. CHURCH, RED OAK, IOWA, 1874

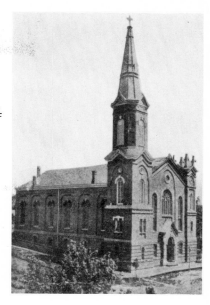

DOCTOR AND MRS. BRESEE,
1868, CHARITON, IOWA

DOCTOR BRESEE, 1878

FIRST TABERNACLE ON
LOS ANGELES STREET, LOS ANGELES

INTERIOR OF FIRST TABERNACLE

PHINEAS W. BRESEE   ERNEST H. BRESEE   PAUL H. BRESEE   MELVIN A. BRESEE
JOHN TYLER PARKER   MRS. DR. P. F. BRESEE   PHINEAS P. BRESEE   MRS. PHINEAS P. BRESEE   DR. P. F. BRESEE   FRED R. CROWLEY
SON-IN-LAW   SUSAN E. BRESEE   MRS. PHINEAS W. BRESEE   MRS. BERTHA BRESEE PARKER   NEPHEW
                    J. TYLER PARKER

FAMILY GROUP, 1893

PACIFIC BIBLE COLLEGE, LOS ANGELES

NAZARENE TABERNACLE, SIXTH AND WALL STREETS, LOS ANGELES

J. C. BEARSE   C. E. CORNELL   JOHN NORBERRY   W. H. HOOPLE   H. D. BROWN   E. E. ANGELL   T. H. AGNEW

C. V. LA FONTAINE   H. B. HOSLEY   J. H. NORRIS   P. F. BRESEE   JOHN N. SHORT   C. W. RUTH   L. B. KENT   E. A. GIRVIN

LEGISLATIVE COMMISSION, CHICAGO, 1907

ADMINISTRATION BUILDING,
NAZARENE UNIVERSITY

DOCTOR BRESEE IN HIS STUDY

DE LANCE WALLACE   E. A. GIRVIN   J. N. SHORT   H. G. TRUMBAUER
     H. F. REYNOLDS   P. F. BRESEE   E. F. WALKER

GENERAL SUPERINTENDENTS AND JUDICIARY COMMITTEE, NASHVILLE, 1911

an educational meeting, in Boston, to be here at the opening of the meeting. He conducted me to the hotel, where I am being entertained. Later in the day several of the brethren called to talk over plans for the meeting. They are full of expectancy for great things, and especially that the Lord will establish here an organization whereby the holiness work can be subserved and cared for, and from which as a center the work can be spread abroad."

"This is the Sabbath, the first day of the meeting, a day of considerable heat, but a propitious day, full of promise for the work. A large tent is pitched on Lexington avenue, near Sixty-third street. It is the same tent used at the Pullman campmeeting. It is nicely seated and well arranged.

A Propitious Day

"At nine a. m. a goodly number of the saints gathered for prayer and praise. At 10 : 30 the tent was well filled, and at the close of the sermon four persons presented themselves as seekers, and God heard and blest.

"In the afternoon the tent was packed, and at the close of the sermon eleven persons came to the altar, the fire fell, most of them were blest, and the saints rejoiced.

"At night a terrific rain storm made the meeting impracticable.

"There is a strong band of people here who mean business in pushing organized holiness work. They are conservative but aggressive, and thoroughly Pauline in theology and experience. We believe that their organization will mean much to this work. There are many open doors, and God will raise up agencies. The time is doubtless near for a great onward move."

In the issue of the Nazarene Messenger of September 8th, Dr. Bresee writes very graphically of the continuance of the meeting in Chicago, as follows:

"The second Sabbath of our meeting here is just past, and I am thankful to be able to report victory.

"I was invited by representative holiness people to come

227

here and hold a meeting, with the end in view of organizing a Church of the Nazarene. They were convinced that the work of securing the sanctification of believers, and the conversion of sinners, together with the caring for them and building them up in holiness afterward, was not being as efficiently subserved as it should be. What is known as the interdenominational work through associations, was being, perhaps, as well conducted as it could be; but its elements of weakness are necessarily so great that it lacks, and must lack, any great degree of abiding efficiency. In the first place, 'interdenominational work' is a misnomer. A few persons belonging to different churches, having come into the experience of 'perfect love,' have combined to hold special meetings for the promotion of this experience — with which their churches have no sympathy, and with which they have nothing to do — and put themselves in a position where their church places in them no trust, and has with them no co-operation. Hence, they find that they can not trust the churches to do the work that they are trying to do. The fact that these ostracized people are of different denominations, does not make their work — despised and rejected as it is by the churches — interdenominational; and to call it such is at least misleading. Real interdenominational holiness work is at present an impossibility, and denominational work of this kind in any effectual way, in what we call the 'old churches,' is equally impracticable. To attempt to do an outside work of holiness, and to turn over the newly born and Holy Ghost-baptized souls to the enemies of the work, is not unlike turning over the 'Innocents' to the sword of Herod. These people here had grown sick of such conditions, and desired a church home where the gospel of holiness could be preached without let or hindrance, and where the people thus housed and protected from the destroyer, could be built up and led out into the richer and deeper glory of the fulness of God.

"The proposed meeting opened in a large tent on Lexington avenue, between Sixty-second and Sixty-third streets,

Sabbath, August 21st. I have already written of the first day of blessing and salvation. The meetings have run steadily on, with services each week-day at 2:30 and 7:30 p. m., the usual weekly all-day meeting being given over to us for Friday, when Rev. L. A. Townsend preached in the forenoon and at night with great acceptability. With the exception of one sermon preached by the Rev. Mr. Marsh, of the Free Methodist church, of Evanston, the preaching has devolved upon myself; but we are expecting help for the rest of the meeting.

"The meeting culminated yesterday (Sabbath), August 28th. An old-fashioned lovefeast was held at 9 a. m., and as the people partook of the bread and water — tokens of love for each other — the fire of heavenly love burned in their hearts, and the place was filled with glory. There was a good morning and evening service, with a goodly number seeking the Lord. But the great interest centered in the afternoon service.

"I had been asked to speak on the providential rise and guidance of the Church of the Nazarene, which I did, and then gave opportunity for those who felt called to unite together to form a Church of the Nazarene, to come and stand on and around the platform. A large and anointed company of people came, and crowded the platform and about it. They came, old and young, with tears of joy, and shouts of holy triumph, whom I received, on confession of their faith, into the Church of the Nazarene.

"I think that no such scene has been witnessed since the company stood together in that hall at 317 South Main street, Los Angeles, now nearly nine years ago. Indeed, in many respects, it was much like it. It did not have the solemn awe of an entirely unknown way, which was upon us then, for the way has now been at least 'blazed out,' but there was much the same sense of leaving all behind them — not careful of the way by which they came out — the same full yielding of themselves to the divine guidance; the same unyielding faith and holy victory. Strange as it may seem, there was the same number in the afternoon — eighty-six people on and about the platform, who joined hands for the work of Jesus Christ. At night the opportunity was again given, and enough united to make it a full hundred. This was the exact number in Los Angeles at first, and just about, if not the exact number, for the day. They are an earnest, devoted class of people. A prominent minister who was present at that service, and who was for the first time in this meeting, said to me: 'There are on that platform some of the best holiness people in this city.'

"We believe that this means much for the work of Christian holiness, not only locally, but for the whole country. A great holiness church in Chicago, on a good, clean basis of loving brotherhood, to stretch out its hands to help in every way, will mean untellable things. We are praying that this work may not only repeat the work done by the First church, in Los Angeles, but be as much greater as Chicago is a greater city, and as it is surrounded by greater cities and towns, and thus open up the work in its vastness. God calls us to great faith and great expectancy from Him. He doeth the work, and we are permitted to be 'workers together with Him.' Let the whole church pray for a great Pentecost upon the church in Chicago.

"Among those who united here were some ministers, of whom were Rev. L. A. Townsend, Rev. F. G. Bingley, Rev. Herbert Hunt, and Rev. E. A. Burlison."

In the issue of the Nazarene Messenger of September 15th, Dr. Bresee gives his closing account of the organization of the church in Chicago. It is as follows:

Blessed Outpourings "I was invited by representative holiness people of Chicago, to hold a meeting there at my earliest convenience, for the purpose of organizing a Church of the Nazarene in that city. After a careful examination they believed that the Church of the Nazarene best represented the Pauline-Wesleyan doctrine in reference to entire sanctification, free from cant and fanaticism, and in its polity the most simple and effective of anything of which they knew. This, together with the blessings of heaven which have rested upon it, led them to seek organization with it.

"Accordingly, I began the meeting with them August 21st, and have continued with them two weeks, including three Sabbaths. The result has been a very blessed outpouring of the Holy Spirit, and a goodly number of people have been converted and sanctified wholly. Indeed at almost every service souls have swept their way to Calvary. There were an unusual number of what we sometimes call special cases. They came from almost every branch of the church, seeking holiness.

"We organized a Church of the Nazarene, with 155 charter members, representative people, a picked company, as royal a set of men and women as were ever brought together. A peculiarity of the Church of the Nazarene, seems to be the kind of people who are attracted to it, or rather are gathered together to push the work of holiness through it. They have been from the beginning 'the salt of the earth.' There were among these six ministers, of whom — as yet unreported — are Rev. L. B. Kent, the famous old veteran of the holiness work in this country, so well known and so dearly loved; and Rev. Frank A. Doty, the president of the Young Men's National Holiness League. Some of the men entering this work have a providential history behind them, which has led them to this work, which if written would read like a new 'Exodus.'

"The Church Board was properly organized, and they invited Rev. I. G. Martin to the pastorate for the ensuing year, he accepting the call, and cancelling all engagements, that he might give himself immediately and entirely to the work. Brother Martin has held several series of meetings with them, is greatly beloved by them, and has had much to do in bringing things about. He enters upon one of the greatest fields of labor that it is ever the lot of man to enter.

"The church is negotiating for the purchase of what will be — at least for the time — the central place of operation, and which is a fine, well-located property. It has on it a church building, which will do for temporary purposes. It is expected, and already planned, to open missions in different ·parts of the city. The hand beckons them to many open doors.

"I believe that this has been and is — for it still goes on — one of the very greatest meetings ever held, holding in its bosom the vastest possibilities. It is in the midst of one of the world's greatest centers, and opportunities are boundless. Cities and towns — a great multitude — cluster about it. Hungry hearts from all about, who have been asking bread and getting a stone, are calling for the creation of centers of fire in their midst, and God is raising up agencies. As He has so miraculously raised up and guided the Church of the Nazarene in the past, and has now opened this great door, He will fill it with advancing hosts. Those whom He has called are following the conqueror from Bozra. He will lead them in His triumphant way, 'mighty to save.'

"Sabbath, September 3d, was a very great day. From 9 to 10:30 a. m., there was a prayer and testimony meeting of great power, led by Professor Akers. Then, after a short sermon, the sacrament of the Lord's Supper was celebrated, and souls sought the Lord. At 2:30 p. m., after song and prayer, the people, with joy and praises, came and laid their offerings on the table for the expenses of the meeting. Opportunity was then given for persons who desired to unite with the church to come forward. It was a beautiful and inspiring sight to see half a hundred men and women stand in double and treble rows about the altar, and plight their faith to God and the church. After preaching, a goodly number came as seekers, and were blest.

"At night there was another great meeting, with preaching of the Word, and seeking the way of life. Monday being a holiday (Labor Day), an all-day meeting was held. I was present at the forenoon and afternoon services, which were seasons of much power and salvation. Brother C. W. Ruth was with us a day, and preached once with great

232

power. He came from Indiana between his campmeetings, for this little time with us, which was greatly appreciated. Sister Johnson was also here much of the meeting, coming from Michigan; also Sister Croft, who is now resident in Chicago, and who will be for the time identified with the church here.

"With prayers and adieus, I turn my face toward the Western sea."

CHAPTER XXVII.

Echoes From the Chicago Meeting — The Ninth Anniver-
sary — The Ninth General Assembly — General Super-
intendent's Report — A Chinese Mission — The
Pressure of Fanaticism — Progress of the
Church — The Superintendency — The
Greatness of the Work — Other Pro-
ceedings of the Assembly — The
Home Campmeeting

Among those who united with the church at Chicago as
charter members, were Rev. F. C. Bingley, a converted Jew,
and his estimable wife. Rev. L. A. Townsend, a minister
Echoes From the *Chicago Meeting* of the Congregational church, preached
several times, and united with the
church. He was a brilliant man, who
some time before was gloriously sancti-
fied in his pulpit, and lay quite a while under the mighty
power of God. Rev. E. A. Burlison and wife also enrolled
their names; and Brother and Sister E. I. Ames, well known
in California, for several years officers in the Salvation
Army, and at that time residents of Chicago, also belonged
to the happy company who were charter members of the
Chicago church.

One Methodist minister was sanctified in the meetings.
He had attended regularly, and at last came to the altar.
He prayed through to glorious victory, and went home to
his own people and told them the wonderful things that
God had done for him. He was about to be transferred to
one of the Dakotas, and promised to be true and definite
as to holiness.

An elderly Presbyterian minister was also swept into the
fountain of Jesus' blood. While Dr. Bresee was dwelling
upon the inheritance to which we come, and quoting the
words, "We are come unto the spirits of just men made
perfect," as having reference to the perfection of justified
men through the blood of Jesus by the baptism with the
Holy Ghost, this Presbyterian minister asked how about
Paul's declaration in the epistle to the Philipians that he

234

was not perfect. When shown that the writer of the epistle spoke of resurrection perfection, immediately afterward proceeding to declare his present Christian perfection, the minister asked what John meant when he said: "If we say we have no sin, we deceive ourselves." He was shown that this referred to any man who said he did not need sanctification after he had been converted, and after a few more questions, he came to the altar, and by faith entered into the promised inheritance.

On Sunday, October 16, 1904, the ninth anniversary of the organization of the Church of the Nazarene, was observed at the First church, in Los Angeles. In the morning Brother and Sister Leslie F. Gay sang a song of triumph, after which Dr. Bresee spoke of the "Providential rise and work of the Church of the Nazarene." He called attention to the special preparation for this movement through the years which preceded it, to the circumstances that led necessarily to the withdrawal by himself and others from previous church relationship, and later, the organization of the church. He referred to the special purpose to go to the poorer people, and preach full salvation from sin. He emphasized the peculiar guidance of the hand of God, in making provision for the church, its place of worship and other needs; and of the constant Pentecost which had come from the skies. He told of the organization and growth of the work elsewhere, and the blessed spirit that pervaded it. He closed by appealing to the saints for the highest devotion and heroism in following the Lord fully in this great work.

The Ninth Anniversary

Previously these gatherings had been known as "Annual Assemblies," and it was not until November 2, 1904, that what was called a "General Assembly" was held. The Assembly convened on that date at the First Church of the Nazarene, in Los Angeles. The calling of the roll disclosed that there were ninety-nine accredited delegates.

Ninth General Assembly

235

PHINEAS F. BRESEE

Dr. Bresee, who presided, read a very able and interesting report, in which, among other things, he said:

"I greet you again with unspeakable thanksgiving to God who has so mercifully *General Superintendent's Report* spared our lives, and so lovingly breathed the inspiration of His Spirit upon our faith and hope and love, enabling us to see this day, and look into each other's faces, and out upon the work to which He has called us, 'in the fulness of the blessing of Christ.'

"We come from fields of conflict and victory. We have not been without tribulation and persecution and suffering; but we rejoice that in all conditions our Christ causeth us to triumph. We praise God that we have proved again the sufficiency of His grace, and the greatness of His power to usward, and that the God of all grace, who hath called us unto His eternal glory by Christ Jesus, is stablishing, strengthening, settling us. To Him be glory and dominion for ever and ever amen. We rejoice that, as in the days of the early church, though 'there are many adversaries, yet also that the Lord hath set before us an open door.' The attacks of the adversary upon this work, to which the Lord has called us, and our brethren, have been greater this year than any previous year, but amid it all God has vindicated His own cause. Through the grace of God, by the power of the Holy Ghost, our cords have been lengthened and our stakes strengthened. While we have continued the same general course which we have followed in the past years, of opening new work only where it seemed clearly providential to do so, and agencies were raised up to carry it forward, deeming it worse than useless to plant unless the work could be cared for, still there has been a good advance. A promising church has been organized at Vernon, in this city, which has just completed a new church building. A Spanish mission has also been opened in this city, which has already been the means of much good — the report of Sister Mc-Reynolds in reference to which you will be glad to hear.

236

Through her anointed ministry a goodly number have been saved and sanctified. This is a very faithful and promising field, cultivated largely by our devoted missionary, Sister McReynolds, and materially aided by our Brother Trumbower. But this work must be better housed and more amply provided for."

"There has also been opened up a Chinese mission in Chinatown, of this city, where a commodious building has been erected on leased ground, and Rev. Ko Chow, assisted by a band of devoted workers, has *A Chinese Mission* begun what promises to be a very successful mission among these people. Rev. Ko Chow is a man of experience, with gifts and graces, and has an efficient corps of helpers. This is a field where Holy Ghost baptized laborers are not only needed, but where they find as we believe, a rich harvest for the Master's garner."

"While we believe that most of our churches will be found to have maintained their ground, and to have made very satisfactory advance in the real elements of strength, we have found that testings of the work, *The pressure* which prove what is wood, hay, and stub- *of Fanaticism* ble, sometimes in a work like this, lessen numbers, while at the same time they strengthen the work and prepare the way for greater victories. It often occurs in a new movement, that hobbyists, cranks, and fanatics — more or less—come to it for the purpose of advancing their own peculiar notions; and when they find that this is the embodiment of the old gospel of salvation to the uttermost, without side tracks, they usually disembark at the first station, to the great relief of the crew and through passengers. It seems to be a necessity that most of our churches from time to time be subject to this ordeal. We are grateful that hitherto so little harm has been done to the work. The pressure from fanaticism on the outside has been especially brought to bear upon some of our churches during the last year, but that it has been allowed to harm us so little, either in spirit or the wrecking of so few souls, is a matter of thanksgiving. While most of the churches have done well, the work in some parts has notably advanced.

"This is true especially in Illinois, where, in the city of Chicago, a most prosperous work has been opened, which already has a good membership and a very promising outlook. Church property has been

Progress of the Church   purchased, an additional mission has opened, and many souls have already been gathered to the cross. We believe that the successful opening of the work in that great center, means for this organized work of holiness very great things.

"Work has also been successfully opened at Canton, Ill., under the leadership of Rev. W. B. Golden, who has charge of the contiguous work in Fulton county. The work in Canton has been peculiarly successful, and seems to me, from the reports, to be very promising.

"A class has also been organized in Oakland, Cal., which is as yet allied with the church at Berkeley, but is anxious to put on the strength and maturity of an individual church.

"Advance has been made in other places, notably in Eastern Washington, which will doubtless appear in the reports. I had hoped to have visited that country again during the year, but have not been able to do so. I trust, however, that the General Superintendent may be able to do so in the not distant future. The churches generally have earnestly and vigorously pushed the work of full salvation to which we are called. While it has been a year of severe conflict, yet the churches have held manfully on their way, and I believe the reports will show substantial progress. In answer to the prayers of His people, God has poured out His Spirit, and continuously souls have been saved and sanctified at the altars of the Church of the Nazarene, wherever she has gone."

After speaking of the progress made by the publishing

interests, and the Pacific Bible College, Dr. Bresee tells something of his own labors, as follows:

"As to my own time and *The Superintendency* strength and possibilities of labor, I am thankful to say that while my time has been necessarily largely devoted to the pastoral work of the First church of this city, together with editorial work on the paper, and teaching in the Bible College, yet through the forbearance and generosity of this First church I have been able to make two quite extensive trips, one to the East as far as Omaha, Neb., and north as far as Boise, Idaho, taking in Salt Lake City, Utah; and the other as far south as Southern Kansas, and as far east as Chicago. The first was made possible by the providing by the church here the services of Rev. C. W. Ruth, who very efficiently labored during my absence. I was accompanied and greatly assisted in my work by Brother C. E. McKee, of this city, who generously took the time, and bore his own expense in this extended trip. The other was made possible by the good fortune of the church here in securing the services of Rev. C. V. La Fontaine as my associate pastor. These two trips took me nearly four months of the year, most of the expense of which, outside of traveling expenses, was borne by the First church here, in itself a considerable contribution to the general work.

"It is more and more evident that God has called us to a great work, and that He is leading us forth as the way is prepared — and as we are prepared — toward its accomplishment. The growth and development *The Greatness* of all life that is to be abiding, is at first *of the Work* slow. A gourd may spring up in a night, but not so an oak. In a marvelous manner God prepared the way for this work, and in no less marvelous way has He brought it on. Slowly but surely it has taken root, and begun to spread its life abroad. The evidences of divine guidance and overruling providences, have been beyond questioning, and the constant glory of

239

the pillar of cloud by day, and the burning, shining light by night, upon its dwelling places and Assemblies, has been a marvel and joy. Converted and sanctified souls are its crowning and rejoicing. Let us walk carefully before Him. Let us have but one desire and aim — that He shall lead us all the way. Let us have but one passion — to glorify Jesus Christ. Ready to be counted as the offscouring of the earth, only so that the glory of the Lord shall go forth as brightness. Denominational success is not our aim, but that souls may be saved and sanctified. To this end we not only have suffered, but are ready to continue to suffer, the loss of all things. There is not among us, and we trust that there never will be, either honor or preferment, other than that of toil and burden-bearing. We have heard the Master call, and we are here to say again, 'Where He leads, we will follow.' "

The Committee on Orders recommended that the credentials of the following brethren be recognized, and that they be recognized and approved as elders in the Church of the Nazarene: Charles V. La Fontaine, *Other Proceedings* L. B. Kent, Penrose G. Lineweaver, *of the Assembly* Robert L. Vickers, Nathan P. Steves, Mrs. S. E. Taylor, and W. B. Golden. The Committee also recommended that Herbert J. Starkey, Herbert Buffum, Mrs. Lillie Buffum, J. H. McIntyre, S. B. Rhodes, and C. J. Kinne be elected to elder's orders. The report of the committee was adopted.

Dr. Bresee was unanimously re-elected General Superintendent for the ensuing year. The business of the Assembly was carefully attended to, and the anointings of holy love rested both upon the delegates and the gathered multitudes. Few who were present at the opening exercises will ever forget the faith and victory which filled the hearts of the delegates and others present. A continuous heavenly benediction rested upon the Assembly all the way through, ready to burst out in holy triumph at any time.

The Home Campmeeting, which continued from Novem-

ber 4th to November 13th, inclusive, was conducted by Rev.
H. C. Morrison, and was held in the First Church of the
Nazarene, Los Angeles. The attendance
The Home   was large and Brother Morrison preached
Campmeeting   with great power and unction. The altar
was often filled with seekers, and nearly
two hundred sought for pardon and entire sanctification.
There were seasons of great power, when the Spirit of God
swept through the assembled multitudes, making earth
like heaven. The meeting was cumulative in power and victory to the end. The Bible readings in the forenoon meetings were given by Rev. L. B. Kent, of Jacksonville, Ill.,
were greatly enjoyed and were food for the soul. The whole
spiritual life of the Church of the Nazarene in Southern
California was deepened and widened, the cords lengthened
and the stakes strengthened.

CHAPTER XXVIII.

Toward the end of November, 1904, Dr. Bresee, accompanied by Brother C. E. McKee, his companion in so many journeys, started for Spokane, Washington. The following interesting report of the trip *A Trip to the Northwest* was written by Dr. Bresee, and published in the Nazarene Messenger, of December 15th:

"From Tuesday night, November 29th, to the Saturday morning following, was taken in traveling from Los Angeles to Spokane. At Sacramento, as it was Wednesday evening, we thought to look in on one of the prayermeetings, and say 'Amen' with the gathered worshipers. Knowing only the location of the Sixth Street Methodist Episcopal church, we went thither, and found that Rev. H. C. Morrison and Rev. Joseph H. Smith had been holding a ten days' meeting, and that, while Brother Morrison had preached his last sermon the night before, and left the city during the day, Brother Smith was still there, and was to preach and hold the closing meeting of the series that night. We had no sooner entered the church and slipped into a seat near the door, than we found Brother and Sister Davis and their daughter, of the First Church of the Nazarene, of Los Angeles. They were in the seat just in front of us, and were as much surprised to see us as we were to see them. Dr. Case, the pastor, whom we have known in other days, coming back to where we were, did everything he could to welcome us and help us to enjoy the service. Brother Smith preached from the 51st Psalm, and there were several seekers at the altar.

"At Sacramento we spent the hours in conference with friends, mostly in reference to the ripeness of the conditions for the Church of the Nazarene in that city. There seemed to be a deep feeling of the need of a church, which would be out and out for full salvation, and at the same time free from fanaticism and side issues. Capable and anointed leadership seemed to them the great desideratum. We are to see them further on our return, and, if possible, hold a few days meetings with them.

"We overtook our dear Brother Kent here in Spokane. He had preceded us, and had been holding meetings for our people for a week. On every hand there were good reports. He had edified and helped the church, and souls had been daily added to the Lord.

"Brother McKee and myself joined the advancing hosts in the Saturday night service, which was a blessed meeting, with salvation; and the Sabbath was a great day of victory and power. At the services on Saturday night and during the Sabbath, some twenty-five seekers have been at the altar.

"The work here seems in a very satisfactory condition, and there are continued blessing and salvation. The hall which our people use is surrounded by saloons, and is opposite the great Cour-delene Theater, where every night preceding the performance, pictures are thrown upon the walls of the buildings to attract the people, and great multitudes gather, in the midst of whom our people hold their outdoor meetings, and many are gathered in. Like all mission work of this kind, many are transient, but the seed is widely sown, and some brings forth fruit that abides. The work here is reaching family life more than ever before. There are in the church here a fine class of workers, especially among the young people.

"The hall was packed and the people standing last (Sabbath) night, and the Holy Spirit was manifestly present in great power. The weather as we have found it thus far in the Northwest, is pleasant, crisp and energizing."

In the issue of the Nazarene Messenger of December 22d, Dr. Bresee continues his narrative as follows:

"Spokane is a beautiful city of about 65,000 people. One of the greatest attractions, as *A Life Saving Station* well as sources of prosperity, is the magnificent falls in the Spokane river at this point, which is utilized for power to drive machinery for flouring and lumber mills, electric plants, etc.

"There are fine blocks lining the streets, good systems of street railways, and all of the appliances and conveniences of a modern city. Like all the cities that we have seen in this great Northwest, it is greatly cursed by the saloon, and, as a result, there is much drunkenness. How this liquor blight everywhere is turning strength into weakness, and beauty to ashes; yet it is licensed by the people, who share the spoils of its robbery of the poor, and who are thus guilty of its crimes. When will the American people learn righteousness and wisdom?

"But the Church of the Nazarene has a life-saving station in the darkest place in the city — in a block almost literally filled on its four sides with saloons and places of wickedness. Here a few heroic souls started a mission about five years ago, opposed by the church of which they were members, because it took them from the work of the central church, whose energy was spent largely in other directions than in getting people saved.

"About three years ago they determined to organize a Church of the Nazarene, in which they found sympathy and co-operation in this mission work, so much needed, and upon which they had already entered. They organized the church in the midst of much opposition and misrepresentation from those with whom they had previously associated. But the blessing of the Lord has been greatly upon the work, and He has made it a lighthouse, not only for this part of the city, but for this whole Northwest.

"They have a large hall on the lower floor, with entrances from two streets, where every night and all day on Sunday the blessed work is pushed. Street meetings, preaching of the Word, testimony and song, are continually present.

While Sister Wallace is the efficient pastor, Brother Wallace is conspicuously effective in almost every department of the work, and there is a noble and enthusiastic band of workers, who sing and pray and shout, and bring people to Calvary, and to the cleansing fountain, in truly Nazarene fashion.

"They are especially blest with a most excellent band of young people. They have a good Company E of young women, and a Brotherhood of St. Stephen of young men, and they are capable and ready to take the work at every point and carry it forward. Some of them have been rescued from the sad conditions which environ the church.

"Here it is that for nine days we have been permitted to join in the battle. We are glad to be able to say that it has been constant blessing and victory. About one hundred souls have bowed at the altar as seekers, and many have been blessed, converted, and sanctified.

"On last Sabbath, seventeen united with the church, among whom were four ministers of the gospel: Brothers Brown, Spangler, Lee, and Franklin. It was an impressive sight, as these veteran ministers stood among men and women, to give themselves anew to the work of God in pushing the doctrine and experience of Christian holiness. On the last night the hall was packed with people, the altar filled with seekers, and the very air was filled with holy triumph.

"On Thursday and again on Saturday there were gatherings of our people from various places to consult together in reference to the work in this great Northwest. After full consideration, they unanimously requested the General Superintendent to form an Assembly District, to be constituted of Washington, Oregon, Montana, and Idaho, and to appoint a District Superintendent to oversee and push the work, especially in the many fields which are asking for our help. An executive committee was appointed to advise and co-operate with the District Superintendent."

"In accord with such request the District has been constituted, and Rev. H. D. Brown, of Seattle, has been appointed District Superintendent. We believe that mighty

The Northwestern District victory awaits the Church of the Nazarene in this great Northwest. Many people are hungry for the old gospel of power.

"Brother Kent has been with us, and has delighted and edified the people. He will stay yet one more day, when he will leave for Chicago, and then for his home at Jacksonville, Ill. His trip to California to attend the General Assembly, and his return through the Northwest, has been thoroughly appreciated by the multitudes who have heard the Word from his lips.

"Brother C. E. McKee, whom I am so fortunate as to have for my traveling companion and helper in this trip, has rendered invaluable service. We go from here to Garfield, for a two days' meeting, and from there to Seattle.

"There being a loud call from Kalispel, Montana, Rev. I. H. Dear has been appointed there, and he goes there at once, to prospect and open the work in that locality."

Dr. Bresee, in his report of the opening of the Nazarene work in Garfield, Wash., says among other things:

"We took the train Monday morning at Spokane, and

The Work in Garfield about ten were at Garfield. It had been arranged that we should have meetings that afternoon and evening, and then an all-day meeting on Tuesday. There is a little band of Nazarenes here, but seventeen in all, including the pastor and his wife — as undaunted and self-sacrificing as any warriors that ever faced the enemy. The pastor, Rev. G. L. Carr, was converted but fourteen months ago, and yielding himself fully to the Lord, found His sanctifying grace, heard His call, and said, 'Here am I, send me.' The little church here needed a heroic leader, and called him, and he left for the work. He says that he 'has the best job in Washington,' and, if heroic, self-sacrificing labor is the measure of the excellence of a job, it seems that his estimate is not far from the truth. He and his devoted wife seem given to sacrifice or labor, as the Master may direct. God will surely bless their devotion, and give them His own presence, which means all things.

"Our people have purchased a building, which was erected for a business house, and have it nicely fitted up and seated. It will easily accommodate two hundred people. Here we held five services, three of them in the day time, and two at night. The pastor of the Baptist church was with us at every service, and the Methodist and Cumberland Presbyterian ministers were present once each. The day meetings were not large, but sweet and refreshing. Both nights the house was crowded with people, who gave attention to the Word, but were unmoved. There were but three seekers at the altar, and the multitude seemed fully set in their determination to 'not have this Man to rule them.' I have rarely seen a people so determinedly set against salvation. I made such inquiry as I could, as to the causes which might lead, in this so-called Christian land, to such conditions. I found that there had been great opposition to holiness; that it had come from almost every quarter, until the young people, of whom the congregation were largely composed, had come to feel that to have anything to do with it, would be a disgrace. They had been led to despise the whole matter.

"The rejection of holiness by the churches in any community, leads to the hardening and ruin of that community. Its more and more general rejection by the churches in this country, bodes great evil."

Dr. Bresee thus recounts his trip to the city of Seattle:

"On Wednesday night, December 21, 1904, after an enthusiastic meeting at the mission of the Church of the Nazarene at Spokane, we boarded the train *Conditions in Seattle* for Seattle, where we arrived on Thursday, at 2 p. m. The ride along the river and over the mountains for more than 400 miles, is full of interest.

247

"Arriving at Seattle, we were met by Rev. H. D. Brown, who conducted us to his pleasant home, at 1636 Fifth avenue, West. Arrangements had been made by the Western Washington Holiness Association for us to preach Thursday and Friday evenings, at the Battery Street Methodist Episcopal church, where we had large audiences, and a good tide of salvation.

"We concluded to tarry at Seattle, and take a partial day of rest, as we had been preaching from once to three times a day since coming to the Northwest."

Dr. Bresee gives the following vivid description of a service which he attended Sunday morning, at Seattle:

"Sabbatic rest includes the attendance upon public worship, if possible. So, as there *A Disappointing Service* was no Church of the Nazarene in Seattle, we determined to go to the First Methodist Episcopal church, where we understood that a noted doctor of divinity was the pastor. We found a church of fair size, well filled with people; I should judge from five to six hundred. There was a gossamer vail of ceremonies — readings, anthem, prayer, ritual, etc., according to the printed program, until we came to the place for the sermon, when the Reverend Doctor arose and quoted: 'Inasmuch as ye have done it unto the least of these, my brethren, ye have done it unto me.' He said that you get the good will of a mother by noticing her child, and that was the principle involved here, we pleased the Lord the same way. He revamped the little story of the shoemaker to whom the Lord was to come, but came in the person of some needy ones. He said that next Sabbath they would pile flour and potatoes and clothes for the poor on the altars — he hoped higher than the pulpit. He took the offering, had a little duet, and closed. There was no sermon, no message, no gospel: a real fiasco. We had come because it was a church, a Methodist church, hoping at least for a little bread, and did not get even a stone. We got nothing. To say that we were disappointed would express it mildly.

Indeed, we left the church after this poor little perform-ance, praying earnestly to be kept from utter disgust. An intelligent gentleman, a member of this church, told me afterward that he thought the people liked that kind of a thing. We were reminded again of Mr. Lincoln's saying, that 'If you like that kind of a thing, that is the kind of a thing you like.' This gentleman also said that 'This min-ister, in his public performances, is a Socialistic Unitarian, though probably, if asked, he would maintain his belief in the atonement.' There was nothing in this few minutes' of talk, but what a heathen might accept and still be a heathen.

"How thankful we were for the privilege of a church where the dispensational blessing of the baptism with the Holy Ghost is clearly proclaimed, and where hearts burn with holy fervor and triumph; where men and women are led to Calvary, and into the cleansing fountain; and where the shouts of the redeemed fill the place. A pile of potatoes and flour is well enough, but we question whether the adver-tisement of it should take the place of the gospel message on Sabbath morning, or whether its place is the altar of God, or, being there, it is a token of the near approach of the Pentecost. Let the poor be fed and clothed, let us pour out of our substance for this purpose; but let us keep heav-en open, that they may receive the unspeakable gift of His love, in the transforming power of the Holy Ghost.

"In the afternoon a few friends gathered at the residence of Brother Brown, desiring that we tell them a little of the work of the Church of the Nazarene. All joined in thanks-giving for the way God has led in this precious work. The beginning of the organization of a class has been made, several names having been given by those desiring to enter upon the work. It is the expectation that a place will be secured — probably built — at once, and a suitable leader secured for this great city, and this Northwest, and the battle pushed to victory. As of old, 'A great and effectual door is opened, and there are many adversaries'; but faith sees only the door opened by God's hand, and knows only His call to go forward."

Dr. Bresee stopped at Tacoma. He said of his visit to this city: "We had the pleasure of meeting Professor and Mrs. Grumbling, friends of other years. He has charge of the Department of Science in the Univer-

At Tacoma. sity of the Puget Sound, a Methodist institution. We were guests of the Rev. L. F. Tuttle, who is much interested in the work of the Church of the Nazarene, and had come to Seattle to meet us, and arrange for a meeting in Tacoma. He is supplying as pastor of one of the Methodist churches here; but he is large and broad enough to be interested in and thankful for the real service of God, wherever and by whomever carried on.

"We had the privilege of preaching at night to a good audience, in a hall engaged for the purpose, and of seeing several seek and enter into the blessing of full salvation. When the altar service was over, they asked us to give them some account of the work of the Church of the Nazarene, and, seating themselves, listened attentively for an hour, while I told them of the blessings and providential leading, and a little of the victory God has given. Some of them had known something of the work, but seemed delighted to hear more about it. From the expressions of interest and desire, it seemed as if it only needed a little time and proper presentation, to auspiciously open the work in this city. Indeed, the hearts of many hungry people in every city turn anxiously toward it. May we be able to meet the demands of the hour."

Dr. Bresee gave the following interesting narrative of his visit to Portland: "It is a little more than half a day's ride through beautiful scenery and the crossing of great rivers, from Tacoma to Portland. We were

A Visit met at the depot by the Rev. L. C. Elliott and
to Portland Mrs. Whitesides, who had made arrangements for our entertainment, and for the holding of meetings, though several friends had joined

them in the invitation to us to tarry, if possible, for a few days, and hold some meetings. We found it practicable to stay but two nights, and had thus but three services, one in the afternoon. They were all well attended, a good interest was manifest, and some seekers were at each service. The last night, by special request, we spent the hour in telling them about the rise and progress of the work among us. There seems to be a good opportunity for the establishment of the work here.

"Portland is Oregon's chief city, and seems to be rapidly growing, and developing in all those things which make a great city. There are some large churches here, besides some smaller ones; some missions, some fanaticism, together with all of those isms which are likely to be found in a western city, especially along this coast, where things seem to flow as into a whirlpool, and, finding no further outlet, go round and round.

"We were no sooner through our first meeting than we were accosted by a group of people, first by way of questioning, and then assaulted by their notions, as to church organization, in which they did not believe, and in reference to fine clothes and ornaments, and as to whether we believed in feet washing. We modestly tried to tell them that we really believed in feet washing. We confessed and denied not that we sometimes practiced it to the extent of washing our own. Our clothes seemed to us to be themselves our defence along that line; and we averred that we highly prized the relation which we have with our brethren and sisters in church fellowship. They attacked us on the score of secret societies, and I had to confess that I was a member of two societies, one in some sense a secret society, it being somewhat exclusive, and composed of only my wife and myself; but that the other was open to all good people, it being the Church of the Nazarene. I learned that they call themselves 'The Olive Branch,' but they did not seem to me to be waving it conspicuously. I understand that they regard themselves as saints; but I could not help advising them that henceforth, if they could find it possible, it would seem to me to be well for them to attend more exclusively to their own business. One of the elements of fanaticism seems often to be a feeling of necessity for those thus affected to impose their own notions about social and economic things and methods upon everybody, and to regard everybody as heathen who does not exactly think and do according to their shibboleth.

"We found here some true and heroic souls, who are bearing aloft the banner of holiness, and they would heartily welcome the advent of the Church of the Nazarene among them."

By the beginning of the new year, 1905, Dr. Bresee, after having spent a profitable Sabbath at Berkeley and Oakland on his way south, found himself once more in the midst of his activities as pastor of the First Church at Los Angeles.

CHAPTER XXIX

In the issue of the *Nazarene Messenger* of December 22, 1904, I find the following account, written by myself, of the heavenly influences prevailing in the First Church of the Nazarene at Chicago: "It took me several *Spiritual* hours on December 10th to find the location *Warmth* of our church in Chicago. Having found it, *and Power* I went to the church on Sunday morning, December 11th, and was much pleased with the building, situation, and entire neighborhood. There was a heavy snowstorm all day, but the attendance was good at all the services, and it was my blessed privilege in the morning to preach to probably two hundred and fifty people. As soon as I entered the building I felt the spiritual warmth and power which, thank God, characterize the meetings of the Nazarenes everywhere. I heard the hearty Amens! and the fervent Hallelujahs! and immediately I felt perfectly at home, and my whole being thrilled with holy joy. Brother Martin, who had just returned from a few days' campaign in Ohio, pressed me into service, and I gave the message from the fifteenth chapter of St. John. The dear saints held me up in their arms of faith and love, and carried me through with their prayers and shouts of victory. God greatly blessed my soul. Brother and Sister Berry insisted on taking me to their home for lunch, and the dear brethren were all so kind and cordial that I felt happier than I had on any other Sunday since leaving my home in California. May the dear Lord bless them more and more.

"I was greatly impressed with the character and quality of our membership in Chicago. There are two hundred and fifteen members, and they are just the kind of men and women that began the Nazarene work in Los Angeles—not religious tramps, fanatics, or comeouters; but clean, conservative, sensible, well-balanced Christians, most of whom have enjoyed the experience of holiness for years. ' They are ripe in the experience, know what it is to endure persecution, are capable of discriminating between the true and the false, the real and the sham, and keenly appreciate the privilege of having a place where the fire of God burns continually, and where holiness has not only the right of way, but is kept primarily in the forefront of every service. Praise the Lord!

"The glorious work is spreading in this vast and mighty city. Full salvation is preached in four Nazarene missions, and within eighteen months there will probably be not less than twelve Churches of the Nazarene and missions in this great strategic center of population and commerce.

"Brother Berry led the afternoon meeting, and Brother Martin, the pastor, preached with power and unction in the evening. During the day twenty-two seekers found their way to the altar, and most of them pressed through to victory.

"The atmosphere of the church was simply heavenly. Happy smiles, holy laughter, tears of joy, shouts of praise, songs of victory, glad clapping of hands, fervent, effectual prayers, preaching with the Holy Ghost sent down from heaven, and testimonies with the exultant ring of full salvation in them — these and countless other manifestations of the presence of the Holy Ghost in the midst of His people, characterized all the services of a day which I shall never forget."

Sometimes persons were very remarkably directed by the Spirit of God to associate themselves with the Church of the Nazarene. This was especially the case with Mrs. Lily D. Bothwell, for many years a member of the First Church in Los Angeles, and now belonging to the Pentecostal Church of the Nazarene in Pomona, California. In the issue of the

Nazarene Messenger of January 5, 1905, she makes the following interesting statement:

"When the Church of the Nazarene was organized at Berkeley, I was very much interested in reading an account of it, and also of the founding of the church at Los Angeles, of which I had never before heard. My interest was at once awakened in what seemed to be an extraordinary moving of the Lord through this new channel. After this when meeting persons from Los Angeles, my first thought was, 'They will know something of the Church of the Nazarene there,' and I never failed to make inquiries about it.

"Thoughts of this church were continually in my mind and I began praying God's blessing upon it. For more than two years, every night at worship, I prayed for this people, and I would see in vision God's care over the church, and the light of His glory shining upon it. How my heart would warm and glow as I prayed! Something of the glory of the church rested upon me, and made me one with a people who did not know me, but whom I knew in the Holy Ghost.

"When I came to Los Angeles in June, 1900, I went to the old tabernacle on Los Angeles street, and found my heart's church home. There, with the shadows of the pepper trees glinting across the threshold, and Dr. Bresee at the door greeting the people with a warm handclasp, the Lord said to me, 'Here is thy home.' I knew it then — I know it still. There abides in my heart praise and thanksgiving for the riches of His grace; for grace so freely poured out upon this people; for the great salvation with which He hath visited us; for blessings and for trials — the latter to make tried and strong 'a peculiar people zealous of good works.' Thanks be to God for the future to which He calls us. Praise and honor and glory to the Lamb for the cleansing Blood, enabling us to keep in the middle of the road — God's highway of holiness — avoiding fanaticism on the one hand and lukewarmness on the other.

Glory to our conquering Christ, who leads us on to victory through the power of the Holy Ghost."

Writing under date of March, 1905, Brother E. I. Ames, then a member of the First Church in Chicago, gives the following vivid picture of an afternoon service there:

A Japanese Preacher "The 2:30 meeting was a mighty season of song and testimony. I will try to give a few color touches of that glorious spiritual harmony on which our souls feasted. Oh, hallelujah! Such singing! We have rarely heard it equaled, and never surpassed. Brother Stewart was on his feet several times, but gave way to others until he could hold in no longer. Then, in his intense and positive manner, he testified to a week of the greatest trials of his life, but crowned with victory and perfect peace. He declared that he was never more self-possessed, and that it was possible to have a heart on fire, and a head as cool as an icebox. Brother J. F. Tanigochi, the Japanese preacher, gave an earnest testimony, after which Brother Van Habson jumped to his feet and said that, while on a farm near the Pullman camp last year he was told that the Polish people had been stealing things from his farm. Hearing a noise in the woods one day, he went out, thinking that it might be a thief, and found Brother Tanigochi praying. He said to himself, 'Are n't you ashamed of yourself to think you have n't prayed for twelve years?' He got so under conviction that Tanigochi was enabled to lead him to Christ. Brother Tanigochi was called upon in the evening to give his experience, which he did, interspersed with the reading of several chapters in Romans, in his intense and inimitable way. It was wonderful to hear how the Lord had dug him out of heathenism. He tried for years to get peace through the teaching of Confucius, praying and fasting night and day for a week at a time. He would spend long seasons in this way on the tops of high mountains, trying to find that for which his soul for years had hungered. He finally was converted in Ozaka, under the teaching of a native missionary, and four

256

years later, in Tokyo, during a great revival, he was filled with the Holy Spirit."

In June, 1905, Dr. Bresee again turned his face to the great Northwest. He spent some little time at Ashland, Oregon. He thus describes the Nazarene work as he found it at that place: "This place, like Jeru-
Another Trip salem, is 'beautiful for situation,' with
to the Northwest the mountains round about. In the midst of the spurs of the great Siskiyou mountains, its scenery is unsurpassed — the mountain sides, clothed in verdure and forests, green, bronze, golden, with snowcaps in the distance and streams of crystal beauty, fresh and cool, and, to complete the picture, a city of nearly five thousand people, nestling like a jewel on the bosom of beauty.

"Here the Church of the Nazarene has found its way, and hence this pilgrimage hitherto also. We arrived Friday evening, June 9th. The pastor, Brother S. B. Rhoads, also Mrs. Stoner, met us at the depot, giving us hearty welcome. We were soon in pleasant quarters, as the guests of Sister Stoner. It was the planting here of this precious family of Nazarenes that has brought forth the harvest which is being gathered. They have been faithful and definite in their faith and testimony, and the God of holiness has been faithful to them. Not without difficulty and temptations, not without some of the manifestations of the spirit of persecution have these heroic souls seen the victories which have already been won. There are now more than fifty members in this young church, many of whom have recently been brought into the kingdom. They have the real spirit — the enthusiasm, holy joy, and heavenly triumph — which belongs to this Pentecostal work. A delightful Sabbath school filled the hall on Sunday morning. We were with them at eight services — three on the Sabbath, three week-day nights, and two week-day afternoons. There was good attendance and much blessing."

Dr. Bresee then speaks of the prejudice and opposition

to the work of holiness in Ashland as elsewhere, and continues: "In these few meetings there were some conversions, some souls were sanctified, nine persons united with the church, and there are more to follow.

"One of the marked features here is the joy and triumph of their singing. A band of anointed singers, conducted by Miss Pearl Stoner, made up mostly of young soldiers, led the people in the most triumphant service of *Joy and* song that we have heard. It is worth a trip here *Triumph* to hear and join in these shouts of victory. And yet it seems very difficult, if not impossible, to reach and move the people to Calvary and the cleansing fountain, in any large numbers. One here and one there — mostly handpicked — seems all that it is as yet possible to reach. Here, as in most places, there seems on the part of professing Christian people, little recognition of the need of holiness, and little conviction of sin on the part of sinners. They alike listen to the Word, seem in some sense to have an intellectual appreciation of it, but no deep feeling of the need of salvation. There is such a sad absence all through the country of the Holy Ghost convincing of sin, of righteousness, and of judgment.

"It seems very clear that the general neglect of, or opposition to, His definite work and indwelling in the human soul, has so grieved the Holy Spirit that there is little awakening. Where holiness, by the baptism with the Holy Spirit, is definitely preached, there is so much of contempt poured upon the work by the professed church that people who come and hear, often seem to feel that they are more than justified in ignoring all appeals, both by the truth and the Spirit, to yield to God. The holiness work is a hard battle, but it is the Lord's, and He will lead us on. He does not leave us without fruit, but men are perishing, and we pray for a thousandfold of salvation and life."

Dr. Bresee reached Portland, Oregon, on June 14th, Sister Whitesides meeting him at the depot. He preached at the all-day meeting of the Holiness Association there, and had the pleasure of meeting Sister Martha Curry, the well-known holiness evangelist, who prior to this had preached at the First Church in Los Angeles, and had held a successful meeting at the Church of the Nazarene in Ontario, California.

Dr. Bresee arrived in Seattle on June 16th, where he was met by Brother and Sister H. D. Brown and Sister Colburn. While in the city, he held a series of meetings in a tabernacle, which had been pitched on James street, *Labors* near the City Hall. He was assisted by Mrs. *in Seattle* DeLance Wallace, of Spokane, and Dr. Kent, of Jacksonville, Ill. The meetings were well attended and lasted ten days. Through some misunderstanding, the services which began in the tent and continued there for several days, were concluded in the Battery Street Methodist church, of which Rev. H. D. Brown had formerly been the pastor. At the afternoon service on the closing Sunday of the meeting, a band of men and women, who felt called to the work of the Church of the Nazarene, stood around the altar, took each other by the hands, and looked up to heaven for strength to carry on the work. On Monday evening the band was organized into a class, and Brother J. R. Amon was appointed leader by Brother Brown, the District Superintendent, and was heartily approved by the class. Dr. Bresee concludes his description of the situation of the work in Seattle in the following words:

"We know of nothing since the days of the Reformation, and the early days of Methodism in England, more heroic than the position of this little band, desperate in their loyalty to conviction of the call of God. God will make them the seed of the kingdom, and though considerably scattered, they will multiply — may it be a hundredfold." While in Seattle, Dr. Bresee made his home with Brother and Sister Brown, who are richly endued with the grace of hospitality.

The Northwest District Assembly met at Spokane, July 4, 1905, and was in session two days. There was a good attendance of delegates and representative people. Much time was given to supplication for the blessing of God upon the work. The religious services *The Northwest* were crowned with great outpourings of *District* the Spirit. The last night was a most marvelous and memorable meeting. It was the last meeting in the hall where the Nazarene people had worshiped for five years, and where the Church of the Nazarene was organized three years previously. Hence, it was full of holy memories and blessed expectancy, as well as very gracious anointings of the Holy Ghost. Dr. Bresee preached with great liberty and power. The testimonies were marvelous — clear, definite, unctuous. To quote from Dr. Bresee:

"As these men stood forth, redeemed, saved, transformed, lifted from the depths of sin, they were witnesses like the healed cripple, whose presence, well and sound, was a condition of things that they could say nothing against. Here are men from the depths of sin, whose lives were wrecked, every hope blasted, who were unable to break the chains that bound them, and yet were delivered, the bondage broken, a new life imparted, the years which the cankerworm had eaten restored — good citizens and good men triumphantly on their way.

"No wonder that police officers, city officials, and good citizens feel that this work is a benediction to the city. At the giving of the invitation, ten persons — eight men and two women — came to the altar as seekers for pardon or holiness. It was well along in the night when the warriors rested on their arms."

Just before the session of the District Assembly at Spokane, Dr. Bresee visited North Yakima, Washington. Of his visit here, he says, among other things: "It is here, at *North* North Yakima, that we have had the good for- *Yakima* tune to tarry for a little, and enjoy a few meetings with the saints. Here has recently been planted the Church of the Nazarene. It is really a child of that excellent work at Spokane. Here reside some of the relatives of our dear Sister Wallace. We have had the pleasure of being entertained at the home of her parents, Brother and Sister Marble. These friends came in contact with the work at Spokane, and wanted such a work here.

"It was arranged a few weeks ago that Brother and Sister Brown, assisted by Brother Kent and Sister Wallace, should hold a tabernacle meeting here, which resulted in the organization of a Church of the Nazarene. It was a very special providence that the Rev. J. B. Creighton had sought here the restoration of health, which has been shattered by excessive work in the Master's service, had found renewed vigor, and that he was here to unite with this work, and to take charge of the newly organized church. Brother Creighton is a man of excellent gifts, and greatly anointed with the Holy Spirit for the work. He has the conservative aggressiveness of the Holy Spirit upon a well balanced judgment.

"A hall has been rented and furnished, and regular services instituted. We were permitted to be with them for six services. Brother Kent came this way and tarried for a day, preaching once, and going on his way to Spokane. The meetings were attended with a good degree of interest, helping, as we believe, to establish in the minds of the people, a work which to them is new. The experience of the saints has been reinforced, and some souls have been blessed. We believe that under the experienced, able, and anointed leadership of Brother Creighton, the work will succeed. This seems to be the place for the planting of the work in this valley, and to be in the good providence of God, and it doubtless means much for His glory. Let the saints pray that this valley, which is to be an empire, may be filled with the spirit of holiness, which is the spirit of Jesus.

"The trip over the Cascades, up and down the dashing rivers, amid the beautiful mountain views, with its ever-varying scenery and coloring, never loses its charm. It is a matter of real regret to see the thousands of acres of timber devastated and ruined by the forest fires. But it is of small moment in comparison to the real condition of the country caused by the raging fires of worldliness. Oh, that through the springing forth of the river of life, the wilderness may become the garden of the Lord.

"We turn our eyes to Spokane, where the District Assembly is to meet, and then toward our much-loved people at home."

While in the Northwest, Dr. Bresee, in company with the Rev. H. D. Brown, visited Walla Walla, where he met a little company of saints, who were interested in the work *Walla Walla* of the Church of the Nazarene, and explained to them the plans, principles, and polity of the Church of the Nazarene. Leaving Walla Walla, he turned his face homeward, but stopped over a few days in San Francisco and nearby places. Of this, however, we will tell in the next chapter.

CHAPTER XXX

The Oakland Church — Berkeley — In San Francisco —
Another Eastern Trip —A Meeting at Topeka —Campmeeting Near Lewiston — Heroic People — Whisky Soaked Conditions — The Work in Canton
and Peoria — Meeting in Kewanee — The
Convention at Chicago — Some Glorious Realities — Holy Love.

On July 20, 1905, Dr. Bresee reached Oakland, California, where he was met by several of the brethren. He thus
described the conditions which he found

The Oakland there: "We were informed of an all-day
Church meeting for the day, that arrangements had
been made to open the work in San Fran-
cisco, and that our stay for the week was imperative. So
telegrams were sent, and the all-day meeting at once entered upon. The friends here have a large tent admirably
located, and finely seated and arranged.

"We found that a home campmeeting had been in progress for more than a week, and that the Lord had been very
graciously manifesting Himself in saving and .sanctifying
power; that already about forty persons had been at the
altar as seekers, either of holiness or pardon. This all-day
meeting was a peculiarly blessed one. There was a good attendance, much blessing upon the saints, and about twenty-
five seekers after God at the altar, most of whom were very
graciously blessed. Taking into consideration the difficulties which have environed the work here, and what the few
faithful souls have gone through, it seemed to us that this
day was one of the very best triumphs we have ever known.

"On Sabbath morning we were permitted to be with
these dear people again, to preach to a large audience, and
to stand around the altar with as heroic a band of about
fifty Nazarenes as the world ever saw, seven of whom were
received at this time into the church, the others being already members, some of them from other places.

"About eight months ago, a few earnest souls invited

Brother R. Pierce to come to them and open up more fully the work of the Church of the Nazarene here. He heard their call and came. Unforseen and unexpected difficulties have met them on every side, but God, in answer to their active and persistent faith, has at last opened up the way for them. Many people seem interested, and, best of all, many are being blest. The indomitable, heroic spirit of Brother Pierce, and his little band of helpers, is above all praise, but their record is in the book of life. Upon them the morning breaks, and it was a great joy to be permitted to help them shout on the battle, and rejoice with them in the tide of victory which had set in from the skies. May it abound more and more."

Quoting from Dr. Bresee as to the work in Berkeley:

"Berkeley is the mother of Nazarenes for this central part of California. It was here that the work was started *Berkeley* eight years ago, in perhaps as uncongenial soil as any place in this world well could be. Strictly a residence city, filled with churches, and overshadowed by the great State University, while there was great need of a church that would be faithful to the doctrine and experience of entire sanctification, yet all classes were intensely antagonistic. No one would have thought of attempting the establishment of a Church of the Nazarene here, but Brother E. A. Girvin and family resided here, and he, being at once a local preacher and the reporter of the supreme court, had 'the blessing.' The church to which he belonged, being unendurably cold, and his duties bringing him to Los Angeles, where he was greatly at home in the warmth and fellowship of the Church of the Nazarene, he determined, after much prayer, to have a church, at least in his own house.

"After a special meeting of ten days, a small church was organized, which has kept steadily on its way ever since. It has been environed by almost every difficulty. It has been subject to seemingly every form of attack by the Devil, yet a multitude have been converted and sanctified at its altars, and the seed of the kingdom sown far and wide. As at the early church at Jerusalem, and at the First Church at Los Angeles, there has been a continual scattering abroad, but this is doubtless a part of God's providence for the scattering of the seed.

"Brother Girvin has been continually its pastor. Some months ago Brother P. G. Linaweaver, of Illinois, accepted an invitation to become his associate pastor. Both of them have been pouring their lives into the work all around about. Especially have they given time and service to the beginning of the work in San Francisco.

"These heroes at Berkeley have demonstrated that this work of organized holiness can not be established and carried on, at least in most places, but by a strong conviction of faith and by continued sacrifice and devotion to this special work. It is a matter of great thanksgiving that, while some draw back, counting themselves unworthy, there are some who bear the tests, and are crowned victors at last."

After holding one blessed and fruitful service in the city of Alameda, just south of Oakland, Dr. Bresee went to San Francisco, where he preached five times, with some salvation. In speaking of this great center of population, Dr. Bresee said: *In San Francisco*

"There is a very great and pressing need of a great holiness church, which might be to that city what the Church of the Nazarene has been to Los Angeles — a great center of continuous revival fire, where multitudes would be saved and sanctified to God, with its strong reflex influence on the church life of the city. The workers in this part of the state, especially Brother Girvin, have been for a long time anxious to enter this field, but have been heretofore hindered.

"At last the work is begun, and, if not in the way that was planned, it has — we trust in God's way — been started. A hall has been rented and furnished on City Hall Square, which was opened with a good audience on Friday night, July 14, 1905. This was done largely through the agency of

Brother Girvin, especially assisted by Brother Linaweaver, and Brother and Sister Matthews. We had the pleasure of being with them at five services, and seeing some souls come into the kingdom. The arrangements are for Brother and Sister Hill to take charge of the work for a time. Let the saints pray that it may be an open door to a blessed work."

A general convention was held at the Church of the Nazarene, in Chicago, between September 5th and 11th, 1905. It was attended by the members of the Church of the Nazarene, and other friends of the

Another Eastern Trip work in Illinois and surrounding states. Dr. Bresee left Los Angeles on August 14th, stopping a day at Topeka, Kas., holding a campmeeting at Lewiston, visiting Canton and Peoria, and dedicating a church at Kewanee — the four last-named places all being in Illinois. We will let Dr. Bresee describe this eventful journey in his own terse, vivid language:

"Three nights and nearly three days lie between Los Angeles and Topeka. Going, going, going, and this fair city is reached, and the smiling face and outstretched hand of

A Meeting in Topeka Brother Mayberry bids me welcome. Taking me directly to his beautiful and hospitable home, his good wife adding her welcome also, makes me doubly welcome.

"By invitation the evening service was held in one of the Methodist churches, and the Wesleyan church adjourned its midweek meeting and came. There were a goodly number of their members, and four ministers of this church present — among whom was the Rev. G. B. Howard, who preached once for the First Church in Los Angeles, greatly to their delight, a few years ago. He was for several years president of the Kansas Conference. There was a good attendance, and an earnest, enthusiastic meeting, with the manifest presence of the King in the midst."

After leaving Topeka, Dr. Bresee proceeded to Lewiston,

Fulton County, Illinois. The campmeeting was in a beautiful grove, east of the town, and many friends of the movement were present from Canton, Maples Mill, Dunfermline, and the country surrounding Lewiston. The meeting lasted ten days, and the results were such as to cause the saints to rejoice. The last Sabbath, especially, was a great day. There had been a spirit of cumulative faith and victory for two or three days, and on Sunday morning at the love-feast, great blessings fell upon the people as they came forward in lines to the altar, and one after another gave their triumphant testimonies. At each service of the day the altar was partly filled with seekers, aggregating twenty-five during the day. Seven united with the Church of the Nazarene. The Free Methodist brethren were especially helpful all through the meeting. The Rev. W. B. Golden, the pastor of the Church of the Nazarene, had all the arrangements well in hand, and made everybody feel at home.

Camp Meeting Near Lewiston

Dr. Bresee thus describes the character of the people who had united with the Church of the Nazarene in the part of Illinois where this campmeeting was held:

Heroic People

"The Nazarene people in these parts — like those called to this work usually — are of the noble, heroic type. They have generally gone into this work because of their love for holiness, and the deep sense of the necessity of organization where there is full liberty Godward and heavenward, where holiness can be enjoyed, preached and testified to, without hindrance, and where the people can be led into the cleansing fountain. Many of them have the faith and devotion of the early church, and stand as pillars against the ungodliness of these times. Their homes are places of holy influence, and they are as salt in these communities where sin so sadly prevails."

I continue to quote from Dr. Bresee: "We were surprised, shocked, and appalled at the revelations made to us of the condition of this part of the country. We are not familiar with the laws of this state in reference to the sale of liquor.

Whisky-Soaked Conditions But it is licensed, the saloons in these parts paying $1,000 a year for the privilege of robbing and killing the people, and rapidly destroying civilization.

"I understand that the state has made at least a feint of setting some bounds of decency to the work of the saloon, but it is like setting bounds of safety to a licensed mad dog. Here it overleaps all bounds, breaks down all barriers, and pours out its liquid death all around.

"A young man dying from whisky nearby during the campmeeting, aroused my inquiries, and I was told that the same thing occurred during the meeting last year; that nearly all the young men in the country drink; that it is difficult to find boys in this section from twelve to twenty-four that do not drink. One good, reliable man told me that in the township in which he lives and knows the people well, out of forty or fifty boys whom he knows, there are only four who do not drink liquor; that many of the younger husbands and fathers are drunkards; that many of the young men are also drunkards, and that most of the boys are fast on the way. He states that the saloon-keepers sell to any boy that has the money, and that the older boys debauch the younger ones, until the boy that is not already in the way to drunkenness, is a rarity. This same brother told me of the sad condition of the family of an old local preacher; that his four sons were drunkards, and that his daughter's three sons were already drunkards.

"This is as fair and fertile a land as the sun ever shone upon, and to be thus bitterly cursed by the whisky demon, seems beyond endurance. If it can not be remedied by law or moral suasion, who would blame the mothers and wives, if they got Mrs. Nation's hatchet, and began a revival of destruction of the venomous serpents of hell? If the right of revolution is sacred, it certainly inheres to the homes which are being robbed of all their possessions, and from

268

which the dearest treasures of childhood are being sold into slavery and death."

After leaving the Lewiston campmeeting, Dr. Bresee held meetings in Canton, Peoria, and Maples Mill, in each of which places he found heroic bands of Nazarenes, and the

The Work in Canton and Peoria

same spirit of earnest intensity and holy victory which characterizes the Nazarene work wherever it is genuine. One elderly brother came to attend the meetings in Peoria, from a town twenty miles away. He said that he was so hungry spiritually, by reason of his inability to get gospel nourishment at any of the public means of grace in his town, that he determined to attend this meeting, if he had to walk. He was greatly blessed and refreshed, and united with the church, feeling that it would be a blessing to realize his union with the little band of Nazarenes in Peoria, and worship with them when he could.

Dr. Bresee tells in the following graphic manner, of his labors in Kewanee, Illinois:

"Dr. F. M. Swain, who with his family, spent nearly two years in Los Angeles, returned to this city

Meetings in Kewanee

something less than a year ago, and again took up his profession here — in which he evidently is a favorite. He at once began to gather together the broken and scattered remnants of people who had the blessing, and commenced to hold with them cottage prayermeetings. They determined to build a church, a very providential opportunity occurring for them to purchase a well located lot at a low price, considering its real value. This was done, and a neat, commodious building was erected. Dr. Swain did much of the work toward it, being greatly assisted financially by Sisters Wentworth and Thackery, and other devoted members of the little band doing heroically their part.

"I arrived here on Friday night, the 1st of September. They had been having meetings during the week, assisted by Brother and Sister Hoover, from our church at Chicago.

Sabbath was a great day, and from the love-feast in the morning, until the last amen at night, it was crowded with blessings. Several said that it was the best day they had ever seen. In the afternoon those desiring to become charter members in the organization of a Church of the Nazarene, stood around the altar — a noble, heroic band — and were received into the church. Next day the officers of the church board were elected, and the church duly organized.

"Monday, being a holiday, we had an all-day meeting, at which, according to His promise, the Master blessedly manifested Himself unto us.

"I greatly enjoyed the hospitality and fellowship of Brother and Sister Swain, whose home is a model of unostentatious piety and devotion to Jesus Christ. Brother Girvin, who is stopping for a little time at Chicago, cheered our hearts by coming on Saturday night, remaining, preaching, and helping in every way for the rest of the meeting.

"It was also a joy to have with us Brother Stuberger, who is also from our church at Chicago.

"While there is much to overcome, we believe that there is a rich harvest before the consecrated, anointed band of reapers here — may it be very abundant."

The following brief description of the convention and District Assembly at Chicago is from my own pen, as I was so fortunate as to be present throughout that historic meeting:

"I shall not attempt to describe in detail the great convention and District Assembly of last week, with its quiet conferences, holy joy, glorious victories, and scenes of salvation. To witness it was a benediction, *The Convention* to participate in it was a lasting blessing. *at Chicago* The prayers, and tears, and shouts, and songs, and sermons, and ringing testimonies, and salvation, of the five days ending with Saturday, September 9, 1905, culminated in the meetings of Sunday, which may be considered as the first anniversary of the Church of the Nazarene in Chicago.

"Let me begin with the briefest summary of the events of that great day, the greatest of the feast: Dr. Bresee preached in the morning, his theme being, 'The Divine Presence in the Church.' In the evening his text was: 'The path of the just is as the shining light,' etc. He preached to great congregations, the evening audience filling the house to overflowing. He spoke with unction, power, and pathos, and God owned the messages, and mightily moved the hearts of the people. In the afternoon Brother Danner, Secretary of the Iowa Holiness Association, preached with force and eloquence, and the gracious influence of the Holy Ghost accompanied his words. Following Brother Danner's discourse, Brother Martin, the pastor of the church, called on those who had been saved, reclaimed, sanctified, or in any way spiritually repaired at the altar of the church during the past year, to stand up. Fully half of those present arose, and lifted up their voices in thanksgiving to God. During the day ten persons united with the church, and eighteen seekers wept their way to the bosom of Jesus, and claimed either pardon or the fullness of the blessing. Hallelujah! In the afternoon Dr. Bresee led the people while they sang and shouted and marched and waved their handkerchiefs. It was an affecting spectacle, and when it was over, it was found that the brethren had made an offering of about $600.

"And now just a few words in the way of an effort to give a dim and faint picture of the glorious realities of the day, which was a veritable feast of tabernacles, that crowning, climacteric feast of the Mosiac dispensation.

"First. The Nazarenes in Chicago love God with an ardor and intensity that is indescribable. They give expression to this burning love in varied ways. They smile and laugh and weep, and clap and wave their hands, *Some Glorious* and sing and shout. They say 'Amen,' *Realities* 'Glory,' 'Hallelujah,' 'Bless God,' 'Praise the Lord,' and other things which have ample scriptural warrant and sanction. Sometimes when

271

they cannot help it, they leap for joy, and walk up and down the aisles or platform. Sunday morning, one sister, who is usually very quiet and undemonstrative, walked swiftly up and down the platform, clapping her hands and praising God. Her face was so radiant with holy joy, that my own heart was instantly filled with glory, and my eyes suffused with tears. Her husband told me afterward that she had been sick, and had besought the Savior to heal her, so that she might take part in the services and victories of the day. The Lord answered her prayer, and gave strength to her body, and raptures to her soul. Oh, glory!

"Second. They love one another with a warm, tender, and sincere affection, and do not permit differences of opinions to estrange them. All their meetings are sociable, and Sunday is a real campmeeting. Many scores *Holy Love* of people come to the church in time for Sunday school, at 9 a. m., and stay until 10 o'clock at night. They bring their food with them, and eat two meals in the church. Most of them bring enough to entertain one or two others. Between services, they have a real picnic to the glory of God. All are happy, and their conversation is in heaven, and not of a worldly character. Now and then, even at these times, a soul is brought to the altar, and saved and sanctified.

"Third. They love their pastor, and hold up his hands in every possible way. They encourage his heart by frequent expressions of appreciation and affection.

"Fourth. They love souls with an intensity created and sustained by the Holy Ghost. They have learned the sweet lesson that this is the central purpose and thought in the great heart of God, and that only by travailing for, and giving birth to spiritual children, can the church or its members retain their spiritual life and freshness, and constantly get deeper down into the fathomless depths of the love of God."

Dr. Bresee, in telling about the Chicago convention, stated that he was met at the depot in Chicago, after leaving Kewanee, by Brother Martin, Dr. Burke, and Sister Martha Curry; that during the various services conducted by him, nearly fifty seekers were at the altar; that at the convention proper, on September 6th and 7th, there were present representatives from the churches in the immediate vicinity, and some from greater distances, among the latter being Dr. Nye, from Michigan, Brothers Pattee and Harper, from Indiana, and the Rev. L. B. Kent, of Jacksonville, Ill.; that the General Superintendent was requested to organize that part of the country into a District Assembly; and that one happy peculiarity of the meetings was the presence there of Brother and Sister Ely, Brother Trumbower, and Sister Lynch, all of the First Church, Los Angeles.

After holding a largely attended meeting at Howard, Kansas, where Brother Brilhart was pastor, with a good tide of salvation, Dr. Bresee turned his face homeward, and for a time resumed his labors as pastor of the First church, in Los Angeles.

CHATER XXXI

This great Assembly met in the First Church, in Los Angeles, and its sessions lasted from October 11th to October
18th, 1905. Dr. Bresee presided, and his report of the pro-

*The Tenth
General Assembly*

gress made during the year just
past, was like a bugle call, full of
tender love, victorious faith, and a
courage unmixed with fear.

Among other things, Dr. Bresee said, in this great report:

"This year, like the preceding years, has been full of the

*General
Superintendent's
Report*

onslaughts of the enemy; the conflict
has been heavy, and in some places it
made the work peculiarly difficult. Indeed, we have demonstrated still further the fact that this work in which
we are engaged is a very difficult task; and that all of the
combined forces of darkness — ever opposed to holiness —
are especially enraged against this movement, which pro-
poses to fortify and hold the ground won. It is no easy
task in these days to reach men with the gospel of full salvation under any auspices; but, when it is determined to
turn every victory into a center of holy power, and maintain a fire which shall radiate continually its holy flame,
every carnal force is enlisted against the work; none seemingly more earnestly than the formal and worldly forces,
baptized in the name of Christianity. Herod and Pilate

274

make common cause against Him who baptizes with the Holy Ghost, sanctifying believers, and empowering them for testimony to the power of the cleansing Blood. Nevertheless, the presence with us of Him who says, 'All power is given unto me in heaven and in earth, go ye therefore, * * * lo, I am with you,' has given us the victory, and enabled us to move steadily forward.

"A large number of new churches and missions have been organized, largely augumenting the number over last year, and several able ministers have united with us. The Northwest District has been organized, to which the Rev. H. D. Brown was appointed District Superintendent, and he has been vigorously pushing the work in that great and inviting field. A Missionary District has also been formed, consisting of the Northern part of California, to which the Rev. E. A. Girvin was appointed. Recently a District, comprising a large area with Chicago as the center, called the Central District, has been organized, and Rev. I. G. Martin appointed District Superintendent.

"Even the looking after the work has become very considerable, and the larger amount of my time has been given to it — the correspondence and general touch being no small matter. I have been away from home, and my more immediate pastoral labors, nearly half the year. Over and above the constant care, I have twice visited the great Northwest, spending several weeks each time, and have again visited the East, giving as much time to the visiting of the churches and other work as has been possible. My associate pastor has greatly aided me in this work, not only visiting and preaching in adjacent churches, but visiting Bakersfield, Oakland, San Francisco, and Ashland, Oregon, in the latter place organizing the church, and rendering very helpful service generally in this superintendency. With thankfulness for the past — especially for the privileges of labor for another year — and for the many openings and great

Duties of the Superintendency

275

possibilities to which God has called us, we look up and say, 'What hath God wrought,' and how great His mercy in permitting us to be workers together with Him.

"To Him be glory forever and ever. Amen."

The writer was providentially permitted to be present on this memorable occasion, and the following description is from his pen:

Greatness of the Assembly "I would compare the General Assemblies of the Church of the Nazarene to the transition from plain to lofty mountain heights. The first General Assembly marked our ascent of the first little foothill. It was good to get above the common level of spiritual infirmity and worldly conformity. The hill was only a little one, but there was plenty of room for us, and we were glad and grateful for the view God gave us of the spiritual landscape. We could not see much, but what we did see was so much more and so much better than what our eyes discerned before, that we took courage and praised God. At that time we did not know much about ourselves, the work to which we were called, or its vast possibilities. But during the next year we climbed to the top of a higher and bigger foothill, and the Second General Assembly rejoiced and exulted in the progress made, and exclaimed, 'What hath God wrought!' It was my privilege to attend that Assembly. We hardly needed any committees. We were so small that we could have transacted business quite conveniently in committee of the whole. As the years went by we continued climbing, and God strengthened our hearts, for no one can climb with a weak heart. How glorious has been the upward and onward journey! How much higher and bigger and grander in every way has been each successive summit attained. How much more extensive and varied has been each succeeding view. And, bless God, between these heights there have been sweet valleys of humiliation, where we have had our souls refreshed by the flowing fountains of God, and have laved our spirits in the pure and rippling waters of the

276

rivers of Jehovah. And now, as we stop a moment and look back at the path which we have trod, we can scarcely discern the scenes of the old battles and the old victories. There are far greater battles and far mightier victories ahead. For, great and wondrous as has been our upward progress, we are still in the lower range of the mountains of our God. True, the character of the vegetation has changed, and we are getting glimpses now of evergreen trees, the pines of power, and the lofty cedars of spiritual Lebanon. True, the atmosphere is getting purer and more bracing, the view of the great sea of eternity more inspiring, and the ascending path so difficult that only hind's feet can scale it. God and the good angels are beckoning us upward.

"Yes, the little child is growing fast, the little cloud is overspreading the heavens, the air is being surcharged with divine electricity, and a mighty spiritual storm is gathering.

"I am deeply impressed with the spirit of this Assembly, the earnestness everywhere, the manifest confidence in the marvelous future of our movement, the love which keeps the discussions sweet, and the humility which *The Spirit* never forgets that our work is wholly of *of the* God, and that apart from Christ we can do *Assembly* nothing.

"Another characteristic of the Assembly was the marked distinctiveness of our movement, and the growing realization of this fact on the part of the members of the body. The movement at first was somewhat inchoate, but, as the years went by, it took a *Distinctiveness* more definite shape, and became more *of Our Movement* and more differentiated from all other phases of Christian organization and life. Doubtless the complete concept of our movement, with all its peculiarities, has been in the mind and purpose of God from the begining, but only dimly and gradually has the consciousness of this distinctiveness dawned upon us.

277

It is not within the province of this report to enumerate the characteristics which make and mark the Church of the Nazarene, except as they manifested themselves in the General Assembly. Prominent among them, however, may be noted our hopefulness, enterprise, and unflinching loyalty to the great dispensational truth of holiness.

"From the moment when the Assembly was first called to order, to its final adjournment, there was a marked and constantly growing tide of divine power. It seemed as if

The Tide of Power
God sought to manifest His presence at every opportunity, and to accentuate in every possible way the spiritual side of the work. In the midst of discussions and reports of committees, there would be blessed sounds of a going in the tops of the mulberry trees, and ripples of glory extending with lightning-like rapidity from heart to heart. Glad hallelujahs resounded, happy smiles irradiated faces, and eyes were filled with holy joy. Thus no business session was permitted by our good and kind Heavenly Father to become tiresome or tedious, or to descend to the level of the merely human and secular.

"The religious services with which each business session was begun, were filled with unction and sacred triumph. God gave the members of the Assembly very much of the

The Devotional Exercises
spirit of prayer and supplication, and prompted them to hearty praise. The leaders of these various services seemed to be especially prepared and anointed, and the Scripture messages given were timely and helpful.

"Rev. S. S. Chafe, of Cucamonga, preached on Thursday evening, his text being 1st John, 1: 7. The message was given with great force and unction, and in the power of the Holy Ghost.

The Pentecost on Thursday Evening
"It would be impossible to describe the scenes that followed the invitation to seekers to come forward. The altar was crowded with men and women in quest of heart

278

purity, or a fresh anointing of the oil of God. Waves of glory flowed over them in rapid succession. In answer to prayer and supplication, inspired by the Spirit of God, the holy fire fell just as truly as it did on the day of Pentecost, and bathed the heads and brows of those who had tarried long enough to be of one accord.

"This was a great day. Large congregations thronged and almost crowded the auditorium. There was a marvelous spiritual tenderness and warmth in the atmosphere.

The First Sunday "Dr. Bresee spoke with pathos and power of the work of the church since the memorable day ten years previous, when one hundred sanctified persons met in a hired hall on Main street, and organized the First Church of the Nazarene. Quite a number of those heroic charter members had gone to glory, and a very few had lagged behind and been gobbled up by spiritual bushwhackers, but most of them were still on the firing line, and doing valiant service in the great battle against sin. At the beginning God gave scarcely any vision of the future, but now we have reached a place where we can see something of the vast possibilities of our work.

"Dr. Bresee called upon the Rev. Lucy P. Knott, pastor of Mateo Street Church (now Emmanuel Church), and a charter member of the First Church. She spoke earnestly and eloquently of the work God had wrought, and pointed out that Dr. Bresee had been specially called and qualified as the anointed leader of this movement. She said that all the sounds in nature were in a minor key; that there was a note of sadness in the song of birds, the roar of the surf, the moaning of the sea, and the wail of the wind; but that in heaven the music was unmixed with melancholy.

"After the taking of the regular offering, which may be called the 'mite' collection, the people were invited to give as the Lord had prospered them toward the reduction of the church indebtedness. This may be termed the 'mighty' collection. Tables were arranged, and shouting and singing, the people marched down the aisles, and deposited their gifts upon the tables. In a few minutes they poured out nearly $4,000. This offering was made without preparation or pressure. Thank God, there is no begging in the Church of the Nazarene.

"Rev. H. D. Brown, Superintendent of the Northwestern Assembly District, preached in the afternoon, taking for his theme the small cloud that rose from the sea in answer to the prayer of Elijah. His sermon was strong and soul stirring, and the audience was greatly moved by the power of God. Rev. S. S. Chafe conducted the altar service that followed, and many souls were blessed. It lasted without intermission until the beginning of the evening service. Brother Chafe also led the young people's mass meeting, and ten seekers came to the altar in quest of pardon or purity.

"Rev. J. B. Creighton preached in the evening, his subject being, 'Death to Sin.' He spoke with unusual unction and clearness, and twelve or fifteen persons came forward seeking salvation.

"The day closed with shouts of praise, and glad testimonies of redemption, and will take its place in the records of our church as one of the greatest and most victorious in our history.

"One of the noticeable features of the General Assembly, was the vast amount of business transacted by the various committees, and the untiring industry of the men and women who constituted such committees. *Work of* The long sessions of the Assembly, and the *Committees* evangelistic services which were held every evening, made it absolutely necessary for the committees to utilize every spare moment for their labors. They did their work well and thoroughly, and in every case to the entire satisfaction of the Assembly.

"The Assembly accomplished much more than could have been expected during such a limited session. Its members had a mind to work, and were unanimous in their earnest purpose to do all that they possibly could to help the cause of Christ through the instrumentality of the Church of the Nazarene. They were also practically unanimous in their reliance upon the guidance of God, and in their belief, that, whether their individual views prevailed or not, somehow the Lord was having His way, and all would be well. The long sessions, the earnest debates, and the momentous nature of many of the questions that had to be decided, united to constitute a severe nervous strain upon the delegates; but they were divinely helped, and strengthened in their arduous labors.

"The matters which came before the missionary committee were vital and of the utmost importance. The report of this committee was very interesting, and was adopted unanimously by the Assembly.

The Missionary Committee "In conjunction with the consideration of this report, there took place one of the most unique and inspiring services of the entire session of the Assembly. Sister McReynolds, superintendent of the Spanish Mission in Los Angeles, which represents the church at large, took her place on the platform in the midst of quite a number of the men and women who have been saved and sanctified at this mission. She briefly narrated the series of wonderful providences by which God had made possible and opened up this marvelous work.

"The work of the educational committee was also of very great importance. Included within the scope of its action, are the Bible College, and the publishing interests of the church. The report of the committee was

Educational Interests able and exhaustive, and breathed a spirit of consecrated heroism and devotion to God, which made the blood tingle and the heart beat high.

"In connection with the consideration of this report, there occurred another service of wonderful interest and spiritual power. The students of the Pacific Bible College were gathered together on the platform, as noble a band of young men and women as it has ever been my privilege and pleasure to look upon. Miss Leora Maris, the principal of the college, led the service, and gave a brief but comprehensive and lucid history of the college. She told of how God had put it on her own heart, and the hearts of Mrs. Seymour, and Brother and Sister Johnson, and how, through prayer, faith, and self-sacrifice, the college had become a reality. She told of the missionaries and martyrs who have already graduated from its curriculum, and of the future preachers and missionaries who are now enrolled as its students. She told of its course of study, of its daily routine, of its atmosphere of devotion, and of the spirit of holy zeal and love which characterized and animated its teachers and students. And then the students gave their college yell of 'Hallelujah!' and sang and prayed.

"The work of the great committee on the state of the church, was truly soul-stirring and inspiring. It showed how our God is leading us on to victory in different parts of this continent, and how he is beckoning *The State* us upward and onward to further and *of the Church* more fruitful fields of spiritual usefulness. This report gave rise to one of the most interesting and helpful discussions of the entire session, and brought to his feet Brother Creighton, whose sanctified eloquence, varied experience, and bright and forceful way of putting things, have constituted one of the landmarks of the Assembly. With a few strong, striking words, he spread before us a vivid reproduction of the vision which God had given him of the divine origin, present status, and future destiny of the Nazarene movement, which he believed in the purpose of God would belt the globe with apostolic churches, and fight and win battles for God in every country in the world.

"Too much can not be said in favor of the work accomplished by the commission on legislation. It will prove to be historic, and much of it has been built into the organic

282

structure of our church. The commission came to the Assembly with matured ideas, armed with weapons forged in the fires of long and sustained reflection upon the needs and genius of our church. They perfected our profession of faith, elucidated and elaborated our statements of moral issues, strengthened and energized our ritual, and gave us a closely-knit, logical, and consistent scheme of polity and government. The report of the commission was very carefully scanned and scrutinized by the delegates, and on the floor of the Assembly its minutest details were subjected to painstaking analysis. With one exception, it may be said that the report was entirely adopted, and that exception dealt with the most pivotal point and vital issue which came before the Assembly, namely, whether the Church of the Nazarene should be Congregational or Episcopal in its polity, or whether a middle course could be found, free from the flimsiness of Congregationalism, and safe from the perils of Episcopacy. At last, that middle course was found, and it was decided by a large majority that the local church boards, after consultation with the General or District Superintendent, should call their pastors, subject to the approval of the General Superintendent.

"The new church hymnal, just from the press of the Nazarene Publishing Company, beautifully and appropriately called 'Waves of Glory,' is just what we all needed and wanted. Its name seems almost to be in-*The New* spired, and veritable waves of glory have *Song Book* swept over the people at the various religious services, held in connection with the Assembly and home campmeeting. This great hymn book contains one hundred of the glorious old battle songs of the church of Christ, the rich cream of all hymnology, the proved, tried veterans of centuries of song, the hymns our fathers and mothers sang, which inspired the devotions of our grandsires, and which wound themselves around our hearts in the dim, mysterious realms of infancy and childhood — the songs which speak to us with authority, and whose cadences march in might and majesty through all the halls and temples of our souls. It also contains those beautiful and thrilling peans of praise which mark the life and progress of the church of our own time; those songs of salvation which give us spiritual uplift. And in it are to be found a multitude of choruses which have proved their right to exist, and which fit into all sorts of occasions, requirements and emergencies.

"The singing has been a marked feature of all the devotional meetings.

"The reports of churches were encouraging, and showed the work is taking hold of the people in different parts of the country; that providential opportunities are presenting *Reports* themselves on every hand; that the Spirit of *of the* God is helping us to reach the masses, and *Churches* bringing them under conviction; and that He is leading us on to victory. These reports come from quite a number of states, and represent a vast area. The report of the committee on statistics shows that we have thirty-eight churches, classes, and missions, extending from Ohio, on the East, to Washington, on the Northwest, and Southern California in the Southwest. The aggregate membership of these churches is about 3,300; the total value of church property, exclusive of the Nazarene Messenger and Bible College, is $103,000, and the total amount raised by the churches during the past year approximates $35,000.

"Brother Coleman stated that a few years ago he carried the total issue of the paper to the postoffice in a market basket, but that now it furnished a load for an express wagon. *The* Too much can not be said of the consecrated devotion to this branch of the work of *Nazarene* Brother Kinne and Sister Ernest, and of *Messenger* their special fitness for the positions which they occupy.

"The most important legislation enacted by the Assembly

was the explicit bestowal upon the General Superintendent of the power of approving or disapproving of the pastors called by the local churches, the enlargement *Legislation* of the scope and power of District Assemblies, and the requirement that in future all applicants for church membership must be examined and recommended by the membership committees of the various churches. A legislative commission was formed, consisting of nine members, and to this commission was referred considerable proposed legislation. Conspicuous among the measures submitted to this commission is the proposal to create a board of three General Superintendents, each of whom shall preside at certain District Assemblies during the church year."

Dr. Bresee was re-elected as General Superintendent for another year. During the rest of the year, he remaind in Los Angeles, preaching every Sunday morning in the First Church, delivering a series of lectures on Isaiah in the Bible College, helping the work by his personal presence and preaching in the numerous towns of Southern California, where churches of the Nazarene had been planted, writing voluminously for the Nazarene Messenger, and through the means of correspondence, keeping in close touch with the work and workers in other parts of the country.

CHAPTER XXXII.

In January, 1906, Rev. C. B. Langdon took charge of the work in San Francisco, which up to that time was in a very weak condition. Brother Langdon, who was a converted locomotive engineer, was a man of the most heroic and self-sacrificing mold. He never asked about a salary, or the probabilities of receiving support, but seemed to delight in doing the hardest kind of pioneer work. He was one of the brightest, happiest men it has ever been my privilege to meet. He lived and thrived where most men would starve, maintained constant victory, and laid firm foundations for others to build on. His preaching was earnest, spiritual, and expository, and full of sparkling and strikingly original illustrations and applications of the truth. Under his leadership, the little church in San Francisco took on strength and numbers. Shortly prior to the great earthquake and fire in San Francisco, the Lord gave Brother Langdon a vision of the city as it was being destroyed by a mighty conflagration, and when a little later he saw it in flames, he plainly recognized many things that he had seen in his dream.

The Work in San Francisco

Brother Langdon did not often put his ideas in print, but in the issue of the Nazarene Messenger of February 22, 1906, I find an article from his pen, from which I quote in part:

"The Lord hath done great things for us, whereof we are glad. Praise His name; we have seen a few souls seeking the Lord, and a few real godly saints have united with us

286

to help push the battle on to victory; we also realize that 'Except the Lord build the house, they labor in vain; except the Lord keep the city, the watchman waketh but in vain.' But we feel safe, and confident, and can make no mistake while we preach repentance toward God, and faith in the Lord Jesus Christ, and holiness unto the Lord, a clean heart for believers, according to the sermon on the Mount. But many are running to and fro, seeking rest and finding none; others are feeding on all kinds of doctrines and new fads, until they have some sort of a spiritual grout, that keeps them from reaching their post of duty on time when they are most needed, resulting in Sunday headache, and unmistakable symptoms of backsliding in heart. Some, kin to Esau, run about hunting venison, while Jacob stayed home, swept his own door-yard, and received the blessing. So my own experience and work as an evangelist and pastor has been, wherever we find a humble little band of blood-washed saints, that love God with all their heart, and love one another out of a pure heard fervently, the Lord is always in the midst, and that to bless, always resulting in the conversion of sinners and sanctification of believers. We believe that we shall see greater things in the near future, if we go deep enough and keep humble. Pray for us."

Among others who united with the Church of the Nazarene at the General Assembly, in October, 1905, was Rev. J. W. Goodwin, now one of the General Superintendents of the church at large. He became the pastor of *Pasadena* the little band at Pasadena, and was greatly blessed and used of God in that work. In the Nazarene Messenger of February 22, 1906, he makes a glowing report of the presence and power of God in the services, convicting and converting sinners, and sanctifying believers.

Rev. H. Orton Wiley united with the Church of the Nazarene at the time of the sessions of the General Assembly in 1905, and in February, 1906, he was called to be associate pastor of the church in Berkeley. He was used of

287

God in this work, taking advantage of the opportunity to carry on his studies, taking a regular theological course, and at the same time familiarizing himself with other branches which were included in the curriculum of the state university.

At the end of three years, he left Berkeley to take charge of the little, struggling band in San Jose, California. After spending a year in this hard field, he became Dean of the Deets Pacific Bible College, a position which he filled with great faithfulness and ability for several years. Still later he was elected to the presidency of the Nazarene University.

On March 2, 1906, Dr. Bresee, accompanied by Mrs. Bresee, left Los Angeles for Oakland, to dedicate the new church building, and to hold a week of meetings in connection with the District Assembly of the San *On the Wing* Francisco District. I quote in part from his narrative of the trip:

"We sat down our full weight in the Pullman, and laid our head back and rested. No one but he who has experienced it, can realize what it means to have the line of separation drawn between you and the thousand things which call and press on every side both night and day. It is a great blessing to be full of cares for the precious work of Jesus, and for those who are His own. To be surrounded by open doors; with privileges and possibilities drawing on every side; to be impelled with the hope of comforting the afflicted, of bringing some ministry to the sorrowing; or to stand by the coffins of the dead; or to bid some stranger a glad welcome; or to put forth some effort to try to help students preparing for this great work; or to write some word of full salvation for some hungry heart; or to gladly delve into the Word for a fresh message from the heart of Him who continually says: 'Come unto me and I will give you rest.' To be separated from all this, and the multitude of things which continually press, by telephone, telegraph, and mail, and to feel that, though you love it all, for a little it is all separated, and that no privilege or possibility of that kind

288

awaits you, and that you can sit down, and for a short time abandon yourself to God and rest, is rest indeed.

"The fields and hillsides are delightfully green. It is the second day of March, but so far as appearances go, it might be a day in early June. The skies are deepest azure, flecked with silver clouds; the air is fresh and balmy. As we draw near the mountains and the tunnels, the rocks, melted and worn by rain and sunshine, are formed into curious, grotesque shapes, full of interest. For once, we go to bed early; if there may not be continuous sleep, this seems the way to make the most of the hours of rest. The morning dawns for us at San Jose, and at 9 o'clock we are at San Francisco, where Rev. P. G. Linaweaver, pastor of our church at Oakland, whither we go, meets us and conducts us through the fast falling rain, across the bay, and to his home, where we meet with the further loving greetings of his good wife."

After giving a striking description of the city, and touching briefly on its spiritual activities, Dr. Bresee continues:

"Several years ago we held the first meeting in this city under the auspices of our church. They were *The Oakland Church* well attended and were fruitful, a church being organized with Rev. W. E. Shepard, as pastor. After a few months he resigned his pastorate, and the little company was almost stranded, when Brother and Sister Armour, coming to this city, took up the work and gathered the scattered strands, and did heroic labor. Brother Ruth came and held a successful meeting, and, after the General Assembly of 1904, Rev. Robert Pierce was called, who came and served them for a year with heroic and successful devotion. But there was no place for meetings, and Brother Pierce held services in a tent, which he brought from Idaho.

"After the General Assembly of 1905, Rev. P. G. Linaweaver accepted the call of this church to be its pastor, he being at the same time appointed District Superintendent of the San Francisco District. For any advance, a house of worship was a necessity. Property was high, building dear, and the little band mostly poor. There was much prayer, and the way was made possible by the purchase of a lot by Mr. S. T. Allen, he personally making a payment of $500 upon it, and turning it over to the church. A church has been erected at a cost of something over $2,000, the pews in which had previously been purchased.

"The church is sufficiently commodious for present purposes, seating a good-sized congregation, and is neatly finished and furnished. It is at Ninth and West streets, a good part of the city for our work, and easily accessible. The dedicatory services were held on Sabbath, the 4th inst., the writer preaching morning and evening, and making an address in the afternoon on the work of the Church of the Nazarene, at which time the people laid a free-will offering of nearly $400 on the altar, toward the building, and an elect lady, Mrs. H. A. Stephenson, presented the church with a fine organ, after which the church was formally dedicated. There was a good attendance at all three of the services, and the presence of the Lord was manifest. Two souls sought the blessing of full salvation at night, and were blest. The joy of the long homeless people was very great. They felt as David did when he brought the ark of the covenant to Jerusalem. All felt that a new morning had dawned upon the church here."

The following account of this District Assembly is from the pen of Dr. Bresee:

"The first session of this District Assembly convened March 6, 1906, at the new church in Oakland, Rev. P. G. Linaweaver, District Superintendent. Dr. Bresee, General Superintendent, opened the Assembly, and Rev. C. B. Langdon, of San Francisco, led in a half hour of very precious devotional service. H. H. B. Ciprico was elected secretary, and a roll of the members was prepared, showing twenty-one members, a goodly number of whom were present.

The San Francisco District Assembly

"The General Superintendent addressed the Assembly,

discussing some things vital to the interests of the church, and reporting the work at large. The District Superintendent gave an interesting report of the District. The preachers in charge, and other preachers present, reported their work, and the characters of the preachers were passed.

"The Sunday school superintendents and delegates reported from the various charges, some of the reports running into personal experiences of the abounding grace of God, which caused the hearts of all to burn within them.

"The reports showed a good degree of prosperity, amid many difficulties and adverse conditions, with marked evidences of the presence and blessing of the Lord, with pentecostal anointings, and overruling providences. They also showed the clear call of the workers to this work of organized holiness, their heroic spirit, and that very substantial advance is being made in every way. Brother Linaweaver is doing excellent service; notwithstanding that he is a pastor, he is giving much time to the pushing of the work in other places.

"The recommendation of Brother C. B. Langdon for recognition of orders, was presented, and he was recognized as an elder among us.

"Much regret was expressed at the necessary absence of Brother E. A. Girvin, who is in the East, he being the first Nazarene in these parts, and having so firmly and efficiently stood for the work as pastor at Berkeley, which church for so long stood almost alone for the work of the Church of the Nazarene in this part of the state. He has earnestly sought its planting in the cities about the bay, and his sowing is coming to harvest. Scarce any one else could have rejoiced as he in the first District Assembly; but being absent, he will rejoice.

"There is a great field open to the church in this District — much land to be possessed. The planting of organized holiness work, which must stand on its own feet, make its own provisions and provide its own instrumentalities, is necessarily slow, but when once our feet are down, we can

291

run and not get weary. There is beginning to be felt the thrill of larger possible success.

"The workers go forth from this Assembly with new inspirations to win victory."

Dr. Bresee also spoke of the work in Berkeley and Alameda, saying, among other things: "Brother Wiley has been secured as associate pastor in Berkeley. He is giving great satisfaction, and under his earnest ministry the church is putting on further strength. We rejoice that so able and successful a helper as Brother Wiley has been secured.

"In Alameda we have a little band of heroic, devoted people. They have a nice little church, built on leased ground; built by two devoted Nazarenes, Sister Plummer and Brother Folsom. Brother Linaweaver has

Alameda it in charge, preaches for them Sabbath afternoons, and holds with them two week-night services. They are courageous and expectant.

"We have but recently entered this great field. The brethren have felt, as of old, that there was here set before them an open door, and that there were many adversaries. But the dawn of victory seems upon

San Francisco them. For every good work, about the first thing is agency. Get thee a man. In this case the Lord has provided the providential man in Brother C. B. Langdon. Earnest, patient, hopeful, he is pushing the work. We have here a pleasant rented hall, not as well located as Brother Langdon hopes to be after a time; but here souls are being saved and added to the church, and it is confidently expected that we will have before very long such a work as the needs of this great city demand. Let the prayers of the church go up for San Francisco, and the work in this part of the country."

"In the latter part of June, 1906, Dr. Bresee, accompanied by Rev. C. W. Raymond, and Brother C. E. McKee, made another visit to San Francisco, the especial object of their visit being to hold a service in the new building which had been erected by the church of the Nazarene in that city, as soon as practicable after the great ruin that had been wrought by the earthquake and the fire. Dr. Bresee, in the course of quite a lengthy description of the sad spiritual conditions in San Francisco, has this to say about our work there.

"The fires were scarcely out until Brother Langdon, through the generosity of Brother Girvin, of Berkeley, and the help of Brother Linaweaver, District Superintendent, had pitched a tent on the border of the burned district, and was holding forth the Word of life. A nice, temporary church has been built on a leased lot on Guerreo street, costing about $700. Considerable help for this has been afforded by the churches of Southern California. It was here that we had the pleasure of a very blessed service with a goodly number of the saints, re-enforced from Berkeley, Oakland, and Alameda. Our people about the Golden Gate are loyal, earnest, self-sacrificing, and expectant. They are joyfully pushing the battle, and they both have and expect victory."

On leaving San Francisco, Dr. Bresee and the brethren who were with him, started for the Northwest and the East, stopping over at Ashland en route. Dr. Bresee thus tells of his brief stay in Ashland:

Another "Here we stopped for twenty-four hours, to
Trip to the shake hands, preach, and pray with the dear
Northwest Nazarenes who stand for organized holiness, to
and East push the battle for Jesus. Rev. S. B. Rhoads,
the pastor, met us at the depot and took us in charge, providing for our needs. At night I had the privilege of preaching to a congregation that filled the hall. The Lord very graciously manifested Himself in power and glory. Here we had the pleasure of meeting Brother and Sister La Fontaine, who came from Portland on their way home, Brother La Fontaine staying long enough to preach at the 10 o'clock service the next morning. The Lord was present to bless and to save. Rev. P. G. Linaweaver, having come with us from Oakland, is to stay and carry on the work for a few days, and the people are looking for great

victory. There is much reason to expect that in this place there will be a center of spiritual power, which will fill this great valley with the light of heaven."

In speaking of his visit to Portland, Dr. Bresee, among other things, says:

Meetings in Portland "Our party arrived at Portland on Friday morning, June 29, 1906. We were met at the depot by Mrs. Whitesides, who has been for some time the very devoted friend of the opening up of the work of the Church of the Nazarene in this city, and for which she has suffered some persecution. Rev. H. D. Brown and wife, of Seattle, arrived about the same time. After rejoicing together, we were all taken to the home of Sister Whitesides, where we enjoyed real hospitality. Brother and Sister Brown were afterward claimed by Brother and Sister Baldwin.

"A few hungry souls here have especially desired the opening of a center of holy fire in this city; and to this end have turned their eyes toward the Church of the Nazarene. A few of our people are scattered over this country, one here and there. It is one of the strange things, how widely scattered are those whose hearts have been 'strangely warmed' at the altars of the old church at Los Angeles.

"A very good and commodious church building, which had been vacated by its congregation, had been hired and fixed up for these meetings. Among those present from a distance to help, were Brother and Sister Brown, and Brother Hubbard, of Seattle, and Brother Raymond and Brother McKee, of Los Angeles. Brother Hubbard is an enthusiastic and efficient leader of song. Friday was a cool, rainy day; overcoats were in demand. Saturday broke clear and warm. To the surprise of all, a tide of heat swept in upon us with great vehemence, which lasted for four days. The heat was almost unendurable. One day was the hottest, with possibly one exception, in thirty-four years. It was so excessive that it was almost impossible to hold meetings day or night. Still, some souls came to wait and pray and hear the Word of life. An all-day meeting had been announced for the 4th of July. On the evening of the 3d, prayer was offered that the heat might be assuaged, and cool air sent, so that it might be possible to hold the meetings as announced. The morning came with a fresh breeze and much reduced temperature. All day the little company waited, surrounded by the cracking and booming of firecrackers, and bombs, which at times made the continuance of the services almost impossible, but which the people surrounding declared were less a nuisance than the songs of worship which we sang. In fact, they seemed to encourage the hoodlums to fire them in front of the church for the purpose of annoying us. In this respect, the people residing in the vicinity of this church seemed to me to be the worst that I have met in any city, and I also felt that the police seemed to care the least as to the protection of the city's better class of people. All this shows the need of the gospel.

"At the afternoon service a goodly, enthusiastic company stood together to pledge their troth to God and to each other, that they would stand together as Nazarenes, lift the banner of holiness, and push the work in an organized way. At night a few more stood with them, and a church was organized with about forty members — earnest, devout, capable men and women, who can be relied upon to push the battle. Some who had been favorable to the work, and who seemingly desired a new opportunity, failed in the crucial hour, as is often the case, but others were raised up to take their place and crown. We believe that a very wide door has been providentially opened in Portland, and that there is to be another great light-house for God and holiness on this western coast.

"Mrs. Whitesides, by her constancy and heroic devotion, the coming to Los Angeles of Mrs. Eaton, with the Hindoo missionaries, and the presence of several who had been in touch with the work at the Home Church, helped to make the fine result possible."

Leaving Portland on the night of July 4th, Dr. Bresee

and the brethren with him, stopped long enough at Seattle to be welcomed by Sister Colburn. Continuing their journey over the mountains, they sojourned a little *North* while at North Yakima, and held some very *Yakima* blessed services there. Dr. Bresee describes the trip across the Cascades, and through the great Yakima valley in his usual pleasing and poetic way, and tells of the stay in North Yakima as follows:

"We were permitted to have two meetings with the dear Nazarene saints here. We can easily see solid advancement in the work since we were here a year ago. Brother Creighton, the pastor, is a man of excellent ability and deep devotion. At the first service it was a joy to baptize six children, four of them being the family of Rev. O. A. Clark, who, with his devoted wife, came to us from the Methodist Episcopal church. We then received nine persons into the church, after which I had the privilege of preaching the gospel, and many gathered at the altar to pray heaven down on our souls, and on the work of God. The following night, after the preaching of the Word, three promising boys knelt as seekers of holiness, with the whole church praying for the richer glory. At the close of the service, a very few moments sufficed for us to be on the train and in our berths, bound for Spokane."

Dr. Bresee thus narrates his coming to Spokane, and the conditions environing our work there:

"This work of organized holiness was begun here about five years ago. It is the vine that *The* creeps over the wall; it never ceases *District Assembly* to grow and creep on, until it will *at Spokane* stand in every place.

"It seems to be in the province of God that its enemies shall minister to its growth, only less than its friends. The sword with which they would smite it, leaves their own hands bleeding. It is the fulfillment of the promise, 'No weapon formed against thee shall prosper.' Every missile meant for harm, God makes the messenger of

296

good, and the seed is being rapidly sown through this great Northwest.

"We are here more especially to be present at this second annual Assembly of the Northwestern District, of which Rev. H. D. Brown, of Seattle, is District Superintendent. The session opened July 11th, and continued for four days. There was a good attendance, representatives being present from North Yakima, Garfield, Tipso, Seattle, Plainview, Medical Lake, Wilson Creek, and Spokane — all in Washington — from Portland, and Ashland, Oregon, and Boise, Idaho. The work as reported, showed a great advance over last year. New places have been opened, and new agencies have been raised up. There has been much seed-sowing, with some harvesting, much preparing of the way for oncoming conquests. There are many open doors. This whole northwestern country is open to this work of organized holiness. While the general strength of the work has been doubled during the past year, much greater victories await these heroic workers. The church at Spokane has secured very valuable property on the corner of Monroe and Sharp streets, not far removed from the center of the city, but in a good residence district, with excellent street-car privileges, the church being nearly free from debt. Their temporary building reminds one of the old tabernacle, in Los Angeles, and is well adapted to their present needs.

"North Yakima is moving for a church building, and has a fine outlook for the future. Garfield also has a church building, and is growing in strength. All rejoice over the newly-organized church at Portland, which they believe, in the providence of God, will be a great center of fire. Sister Whitesides represented them at the Assembly, and was full of enthusiasm and expectancy. Brother Rhoades has resigned at Ashland, desiring for a time to do evangelistic work. Brother Valjean, who has been serving at Boise, goes to supply Ashland. It was thought by the Assembly that there should be two strong evangelists in the field in this District, to open up and help push the work. Brothers

Creighton and Rice have been designated for this work, and, as soon as North Yakima can secure a successor for Brother Creighton, they will be in the field. Brother and Sister Brown are constantly at work, and have now arranged for two tabernacle meetings, the first being at Alberton, Washington. Brother Rice is to assist them. He has come among us during the last year, and like his friend, Brother Creighton, is a man of strength and power, who feels that he has discovered his people in the Church of the Nazarene.

"The home campmeeting at Spokane opened July 6 and closed July 15, 1906. The outpouring of the Spirit of God upon the people was especially blessed. I have rarely been in a meeting where the presence of *The Home* God was so manifest. Every meeting *Campmeeting* was victorious, and at nearly every service souls were converted or sanctified. At times the meeting rose to great heights of spiritual power, where everything seemed tossed upon its billows of holy power, and altars full of seekers were swept to the cross, while all about the house the wondering multitudes gathered. In the middle of the night three young men telephoned Brother Wallace, desiring him to come and pray for them, which he did, and they were blest.

"When the Pacific Bible School was being discussed in the Assembly, one brother, eighty-three years of age, walking on crutches, rose and said: 'The only thing which prevents my going and taking a course in the Bible College, is the lack of means.' Afterward he told me that he was like one of old, lame in his feet, always sitting at the King's table.

"On Sabbath thirteen united with the church at Spokane. Many said that for manifestation of divine glory and blessing, they had never seen anything like it. It did, indeed, remind one of the Mount of Transfiguration, and we all said, 'It is good to be here.'"

CHAPTER XXXIII.

Upon leaving the Northwest, Dr. Bresee and his party continued their journey toward the east, and in the editorial correspondence in the Nazarene Messenger, under date of August 2, 1906, I find the following from his facile pen:

The Kewanee Church "We were met at Kewanee by Dr. F. M. Swain, who soon took us to his beautiful home, where we found a most hearty welcome from his devoted wife.

"Kewanee is a thriving city of 18,000 inhabitants. A year ago I had the pleasure of organizing here a Church of the Nazarene, and dedicating the nice building which had then just been finished. The year has been one of continued going on, with a good degree of victory. A goodly number have been converted and sanctified, but a comparatively few of them have become identified with us.

"The prejudice consequent upon various forms of fanaticism among people professing holiness, has been such that people have not yet learned to discriminate between real and counterfeit. But this heroic band has gone steadily along the way of full devotement to God, with the blessing of the Comforter. They have liberally provided for the work among them, and for connectional interests. In this and all other work, the presence of Brother Swain and his family is a constant inspiration.

"I had the pleasure of one service with them. The following night in the testimony meeting, Sister Strahan had given her testimony, had lifted up her head in praise, and was just saying, 'Glory, glory,' when she sank in her seat, and was not, for she had ascended.

"We believe that the Lord himself will sweep away the

299

prejudices which have gathered because of the course of others, and will give to this faithful, heroic band His own victory."

Dr. Bresee continues his narrative as follows:

"Auburn is a town of 2,500 people, and is one of the old-est towns, I am told, in Illinois. I am *A Campaign* here for four days, to help push the battle *in Auburn* for organized holiness through the Church of the Nazarene. This is the home of Brother Patterson, who has been an earnest laborer in the interest of entire sanctification for a good many years. He especially desired to further it in Auburn, and to this end built a very nice and commodious church building in the center of the town, which he finally concluded to give to the Church of the Nazarene. This he did, and added to it the gift of a very comfortable cottage adjoining, for a parsonage. It was our privilege to conduct meetings here for these four days. The congregations were good; there were a few seekers after God, and a few united with the church.

"Here also there has been and still is, great prejudice against the work of holiness, because of the folly, or worse, of those who have had the work in hand. When Brother and Sister Walker began their work here four months ago, scarce any one would hear them, but they have so won their way by a reasonable and judicious course, and by their love for all the people, that they have gained their confi-dence, and gathered a good congregation. The church mem-bership is still small, but the people are being gathered, and by fidelity and honest work, ere long, many may be won to Christ."

Dr. Bresee thus describes the Chicago District Assembly:

"We arrived here from Auburn, of this state, on Tuesday evening, July 24, 1906, and were very pleasantly domiciled in the parsonage. On Wednesday morning at 9:30, the Dis-trict Assembly met, and continued in session every day until Saturday forenoon and afternoon. The reports were of deep interest, showing great advance during the last year. Five brethren were recognized as elders, and five were elected to elders' orders, four of whom were ordained, with very impressive service. Rev. G. C. Walker was elected District Superintendent. The night services were evangelistic, and about twenty seekers were at the altar the three nights, and nearly all were blest. Great spiritual power was manifest, both in the night meetings, and in the sessions of the Assembly itself. The reports showed that there are many open doors for the work of the Church of the Nazarene. Brother C. W. Ruth was present, and preached on Wednesday night. Brother Davis, of Warrenville, Ill., preached on Thursday night. Both sermons were good, and brought results in souls seeking Christ. Friday night was given up to a platform service under the guidance of Brother C. E. Cornell. A number of the preachers spoke and several souls sought the Lord, and great power from the skies swept the altar.

"Arrangements had been made for a baptismal service on Saturday afternoon, at the lake. The church having no baptistry for persons desiring the ordinance by immersion, *A Weird Baptismal Service* the lake is resorted to. Saturday came with wind and rain. For a time our going was a question, but candidates desired that there be no postponement, so those who had gathered at the church repaired to the lake, where many awaited them. Nearly three hundred Nazarenes gathered on the shore. A song was sung, prayer offered, a brief ritual service held, and the pastor and his helpers began baptizing the twenty-nine candidates. It was somewhat of a weird scene. The clouds had gathered blacker than before, the forked lightning was playing in every part of the heavens, the rain was coming down, and nearby was an upset boat, which had been overturned a few hours before, resulting in the drowning of the fisherman, whose body had not been recovered. As all mingled, pealing thunder, flashing lightning, descending rain, the presence of death, the song of the warriors, the vows of eternal devotion to Jesus Christ, the dashing waves, the gathered multitude, the anxious candidates, the officiating minister, the shouts of triumph — the scene was one not easily described, and not to be forgotten.

"The Sabbath was a day of great interest and power. The preaching of the day was done by P. F. Bresee, and G. C. Walker. The afternoon meeting was given to the baptizing of children and adults at the altar, the recep-

A Great Sabbath tion of members, personal praise to God, and prayer at the altar. At all three of the services

the house was crowded with earnest worshipers; and at night, when all whom it was deemed safe to admit were in, the people had to be turned away. It was remarkable that in the last days of July, when many are on vacation, and when even many of the churches are closed, this place of salvation should be crowded to overflowing through long services.

"Brother Cornell is throwing his wealth of boundless energy into the work, and is surrounded by a great company of most earnest and enthusiastic workers. As the pastor is to be absent during August, in campmeeting work, Rev. C. W. Rose has been engaged to supply the place.

"The new lots at the corner of Eggleston and Sixty-fourth streets, are very beautiful and finely situated for the work, and are not far from the present location. It is the firm faith of those whose brows are bathed in the light of this great movement, that this will be the greatest center of spiritual life in the land."

Continuing his editorial correspondence, Dr. Bresee says:

"On the morning of July 31, 1906, a four-hours' ride from Chicago brought us to Stockton, Ill. Brother Meek, the pastor and Brother Eade, who with his family

A Tent Meeting have spent the last two winters in Los Angeles, met us at the depot, and we were soon com-

fortably located in the beautiful home of Brother and Sister Eade, where they, with their delightful children — sons and daughters at home — keep open house for the saints.

"Stockton is a beautiful village of a thousand people, surrounded by a rich, thickly populated country. Everywhere here, a few miles apart, seem to be towns about this size, or a little larger or smaller. There are here five or six churches, and as many saloons — five — which pay $900 each per year license to carry on their destructive work. The whisky curse is the great woe of this country; in some parts the whole community is honeycombed with drunkenness.

"Near the center of town our people had pitched a large tent, and had it well seated and prepared for the meeting. Here for six days, three times a day, we were permitted to worship with the saints, and with the brethren, and to testify and preach the gospel. On the seventh day, Monday, the rain descended in such torrents, that a meeting in the tent was impracticable, but at night the people gathered in the hall, and the last service together was there held.

"A goodly number were present at the meetings from surrounding towns. Rev. Cass Davis, of Warren, twelve miles distant, was present with several of his people. Some also came from Apple River, Hanover, Elizabeth, and Mt. Sumner.

"One lady, who was sanctified at the altar, in giving her testimony, said that she was now one of three to stand for holiness at Hanover. I found that her husband and another

A Sanctified Family brother residing there, were sanctified four years ago, and had established a Saturday afternoon prayermeeting in their homes, and had maintained it until now, and that five or six persons attend. Now, as this sister testifies, there will be three of them. This breathes of a fidelity that will be surely owned and blest of the Lord. During the meeting several came to the altar and were blest, the saints were freshly anointed, and streams of holy blessing went out to the country round about.

"The people in these parts cherish the memory of Brother Linaweaver, who was stationed here for four years, and preached full salvation; during which time those here who now enjoy the blessing, and bear aloft the banner of holiness, were sanctified wholly. This country is being seeded down more and more with the Pauline-Wesleyan doctrine of entire sanctification.

"Rev. G. C. Walker, the recently elected District Superintendent, did excellent work, preaching with power, leading in song, and at the altar, and in every way pushing the battle.

"Our people have a beautiful hall provided for them by Brother Eade, without rent. It is centrally located, nicely furnished, and every way available. A great debt of gratitude is due and is rendered to Brother Eade.

"Rev. J. H. Meek, the pastor, came to us from the Wesleyan church. He is enthusiastic, and falls readily into the step of the Church of the Nazarene.

"There seems to be a large degree of prejudice and opposition, but the holiness people in this section appear to be doing what aggressive work is being done. No more heroic and faithful band is found than that of the Nazarenes in Stockton, Illinois."

After leaving Stockton, Dr. Bresee held one meeting at the Church of the Nazarene, in Canton, Ill., and participated in a great holiness campmeeting at Springfield, in the same state. This meeting was held under the auspices of the Illinois Holiness Association, of which Brother Kent was president. The regularly engaged preachers for the meeting were Rev. C. E. Cornell, and the Rev. Dr. McKaig. Dr. Bresee brought the message twice.

Dr. Bresee reached Topeka, on August 14, 1906, and in his editorial correspondence says:

"We came here for a specific purpose, and that is to hold a few meetings. There is resident here just one member of the Church of the Nazarene, Brother J. K. Mayberry, who has earnestly desired that there might be a center of fire in this city, where the work of real salvation might be carried on, and we had promised to stop here for a few days and hold a few meetings. A large tent had been arranged for, but did not arrive. A goodly number of commodious seats were placed under the trees, a platform erected, an organ brought into requisition, and the meetings were begun the night after our arrival, continuing twice a day, and all day on the Sabbath, for the eight days during which it was possible for us to remain. The attendance at first was not large, but it increased until the seats were full, and many stood around near, or at greater distances. This the people seem inclined to do whether there are seats or not. They seem to fear coming into close quarters. Some interest was aroused, and some souls found peace through believing in Jesus.

"Early in the meeting, Brother Martindale, and his daughter Hattie, both anointed workers, came from Moline, Kansas, to help push the battle, and were of very special service. Sister Ford, of Kansas City, led the singing, and Sister Crist gave us a glad surprise, coming home, and being at the meeting a couple of times. She with her mother and son are about to remove, perhaps temporarily, to Kentucky, and she was home making preparations. Brother and Sister Buffum came near the close of our stay, to take up the work and push the battle for a time. Brother Buffum preached, and that with great acceptability, before we left. Topeka, like every other city in America, needs a center of fire where the work of salvation is really carried on. As of old, there are wide-open doors, but many adversaries. The God who has brought us thus far, can lead us on, even to greater victories. We shall pray for triumph in this important center.

"The heart throbs with grateful emotions as one turns his face fully homeward, and is really on the train that he expects to bring him to see once more the faces of those so dear. Borne up in the covenanted faith of many, this trip has been one of peculiar favor. I have been very greatly blessed in my traveling companion, Brother C. E. McKee, who has been in every way helpful, both to the work and to myself. We have traveled more than 6,000 miles, in fifteen states and territories, and have held meetings in thirteen different places. It has been my privilege to preach over sixty times, usually with altar services, to hold lovefeast meetings, and other services, and to hold two District Assemblies, each necessitating several addresses, and each an ordination service, with baptismal services, etc. The heat has been at times intense, but the Lord has preserved in perfect health; and so we praise Him, and ask the prayers of the whole church, that as we begin in a new campaign, we may see more than ever the manifest power of God to save and sanctify."

CHAPTER XXXIV.

This great body met at the First Church in Los Angeles, on October 3, 1906. Dr. Bresee, as General Superintendent, presided. Rev. B. Pierce was elected secretary, and appointed as his assistants Rev. P. G. Linaweaver, and Percy W. Girvin, *The Eleventh* *General Assembly* then a student at the Pacific Bible College.

The report of Dr Bresee was very able and, among other things, contained the following:

"That our Lord and Savior Jesus Christ, who has called us into this work, has given us another year of victory, calls forth our highest adoration. That He is placing before us so many open doors, and that He is calling so many devoted and gifted men and women to join hands with us, and help to enter these open doors, fills our hearts with gratitude and joy. And yet, as we lift our eyes, according to the Master's command, and see the fields white for harvest, it is but to find that the laborers are few, and we take our place upon our knees, our hearts going out to the Lord, almost to the breaking, that He send forth more laborers into His harvest.

"We rejoice that, in spite of the onsets of the enemy, and that, though the world, the flesh, and the Devil, are violently over against us, and that, though we are attacked on one side by formalism, ceremonialism, and worldliness, and on the other by fads and fanaticism, that our churches and people have steadily held on their way, in truth and

307

righteousness, and have been generally able to push the battle on to victory.

"We rejoice to believe that the holy fire which God has given to our people, in which this precious work was born and has been carried out, has not burned low, but abides *Holy Fire* in deepening power and glory in the older churches, and is found in great blessedness in the new fields, as they have been opened, and that this gives everywhere a continued tide of salvation. While fanaticism in ever-changing form, continues to break out in different parts of the land, we rejoice that its attacks upon us have been from without. That we have not suffered from its inroads, would be too much to say, but it is a matter of great thanksgiving that our pastors and influential members have stood true to the truth of God, and have inquired diligently for the old paths, and have walked therein.

"We are thankful to recognize that there has been during the year a general strengthening of our stakes, and lengthening of our cords, and that this pavilion of organized holiness *Stronger Pillars* stands with broader arches, and stronger pillars than ever before. The churches are generally well manned, some new churches have been organized, and the demand for the work is constantly increasing. Some strong workers, preachers of the Word and laymen, who have been anxious to have a place to preach and labor for full salvation, have found a home with us; and others are also anxious to do so. We are more and more impressed with the great necessity of this work of organized holiness, and with the great difficulties with which it is beset. A great door is opened unto us, and there are many adversaries. The work calls for the greater unity of faith and effort, as well as the greater devotion, sacrifice and heroism. The difficulties are not few; the enemies are not such as the saints have not known in the past, but they come with peculiar force in these last days, and especially against a work of holiness that is not simply a skirmish line, or a flying battalion, but a conquering and possessing force, who propose to fortify and hold every position won. Against this work of the Son of Man, as of old, Pontius Pilate, and Herod have made friends — the enemies of holiness have united their power. The greatness of the work, and our littleness and lack of resources, make the advance less rapid than we wish, but evidently it is as fast as it can be healthily done. There must be homogeneity, and the spirit and step and swing of the movement maintained. Too rapid an amalgamation of elements might prevent this, and defeat the movement. We are sure that 'Our Father knows.' We rejoice that it moves steadily, and, for such a work, rapidly on, with ever-widening influence.

"I have been able to give to the different parts and departments of the work considerable supervision. The country is large, and our work is widely scattered, which makes *Superintendency* it difficult for a General Superintendent to give to the different parts of the movement that close and constant attention which it needs. It becomes more and more evident that we have been providentially led in the matter of the formation of Districts with District Superintendents, who can give more minute and constant care to the work in their Districts. It also makes it possible for them to co-operate with our evangelists, and assist in the organization of the results of their work. It seems evident that this arm of the service promises very great efficiency.

"I have been permitted during the year to visit the different parts of the field, consult with the District Superintendents, hold three District Assemblies, visit many of the churches, and keep in touch by correspondence with most of the ministers and churches, and to look after, to some extent, our missionary, educational, and publishing interests; as well as to help in some measure in the pastoral duties of the First Church of this city. In all of these various departments, I have been ably assisted by my associate pastor of the First Church, Rev. C. V. La Fontaine, and in each department by able and efficient workers."

In his report Dr. Bresee also reviews with satisfaction the steady progress of the missionary, educational, and publishing interests of the church. He states that the new song book, Waves of Glory, has met with a ready sale, and an enthusiastic reception, not only in most of the Nazarene churches, but in many other places, including some churches of other denominations.

It was again my privilege to attend and take part in a General Assembly of our church, and among the other duties devolving upon me, was that of writing for the Nazarene Messenger the following brief pen picture *An* of this really notable gathering: *Inspiring* "To one who saw the small beginning of our *Spectacle* work eleven years ago, and witnessed the first General Assembly of the Church of the Nazarene, a year later, the present Assembly of the church is indeed an inspiring spectacle. God's plan for us then was just as great, as far-reaching, and as glorious as it is now, but no prophetic vision of the grand and glowing future of the Nazarene movement was given to the little band of heroes who heard God's call, and met together in the upper room.

"I am glad that I was privileged to be there on the evening of the day of organization. What a meeting that was! At the very commencement the movement took on the form, color, and charactistics which have given it *A Moving* distinctiveness and individuality. Strong faith *Panorama* in God was the key-note of that meeting. The stirring events and moving panorama of the past eleven years, so familiar to us, were a sealed book to them. But their faith in God was supreme and triumphant. They sang and shouted, prayed and testified. They praised God and clapped their hands for joy. Dr. Bresee preached with power and unction, and the glory from the inner temple fell upon every heart. What smiling faces! What tears of joy were there! It was indeed a time of refreshing and victory, and the charter members of the First Church of the Nazarene shouted 'Hallelujah!' as God showed them his salvation.

"Since that glad day, how crowded with events have been the swift, encircling years! What hath God wrought! Many, very many of the saints, who put on their armor, and began the conflict on that day, have gone to their eternal reward, and are waiting for us at the eastern gate. But multitudes have taken their places, and the holy war is waged with unremitting vigor. Jesus, our great captain, has ever been in our midst. The sacred fire has always fallen upon us, and God has sent a constant stream of salvation to gladden our hearts. Holiness has been pushed to the front and kept there, and probably not less than 15,000 seekers for pardon or purity have knelt at our altars.

"Our growth has been marvelous. It was fifteen months after the organization of the First Church, before the second was organized at Berkeley, but since then churches have sprung into being all over this broad land.

"About the same time that the Nazarene work began in Los Angeles, another little band of holy men and women, organized in New England as the Association of Pentecostal Churches of America. Their object was *The* the same as ours, to spread scriptural holiness *Pentecostal* over the land. Their experience and methods *Churches* were practically identical with those of the Church of the Nazarene, and their growth has kept pace with ours. God has used them to preach and teach full salvation on the Atlantic Coast, as he has used us on the Pacific Coast, and in Chicago, and vicinity. These two bright, pure streams, starting on the opposite sides of the continent, have now flowed together. This General Assembly is the time and place of such confluence.

PHINEAS F. BRESEE

"The presence throughout its sessions of Rev. John N. Short, Rev. H. N. Brown, and Rev. A. B. Riggs, fraternal delegates from the Pentecostal Association, and the action of the Assembly, looking forward toward organic union of the two bodies, constitute the great, historical feature of the Eleventh General Assembly of the Church of the Nazarene. Brothers Short, Brown, and Riggs — who were pleasantly spoken of during the sessions of the Assembly as 'the three wise men from the east'— won our hearts at the holiness meeting immediately preceding the opening session of the Assembly. Their fervent, humble testimonies moved us mightily, and we felt that we were one in faith and love and destiny. How blessed it has been to hear them preach, and to see their smiling, tearful faces, when God, from time to time, has manifested His glory. They have been as one with us in the fullest sense of the word. They have preached, and prayed, and sung, and shouted, and labored with souls at the altar. They have met with us in committee, and taken an active and useful part in our deliberations.

The Three Wise Men from the East

"A committee on church union, appointed by the Assembly, met with these brethren on several occasions, and adopted a plan of union which was formulated by Dr. Bresee, and approved unanimously by the Assembly on the morning of October 6th. Dr. P. F. Bresee, the General Superintendent of the Church of the Nazarene; Rev. C. W. Ruth, one of our leading evangelists, who took the initiative in bringing about the union of the churches; Rev. H. D. Brown, of Seattle, Washington; and E. A. Girvin, of Berkeley, California, were appointed as fraternal delegates to visit the annual Assembly of the Association of Pentecostal Churches of America, in April, 1907, and represent there the Church of the Nazarene.

Church Union

"The scene, when final action was taken by the Assembly on this vitally important matter, was very impressive. All

312

felt that the contemplated union was a special providence of God, and that the occasion was epochal.

An *Impressive* *Scene* As Dr. Bresee, in impassioned and eloquent words, reviewed the origin and growth of the Church of the Nazarene, and told of the glorious future of organized holiness, all present felt their souls stirred, and gave expression to their joy by clapping their hands, waving their handkerchiefs, and shouting, 'Bless God,' and 'Hallelujah!'

"Much exceedingly valuable legislation was accomplished. All matters pertaining to the calling and arranging of pastors for churches, were left to the various charges, and the District Assemblies. Provision was made for a list of eligible ministers in each Assembly District, from which pastors are to be called by the church boards, or, in case churches refrain from making such call, chosen by the chairman of the District Assembly, with the approval of the Advisory board. Where churches make arrangements for the calling or retaining of a pastor, they must notify the Superintendent of their District, on or before the first day of the District Assembly. Provision was also made for transfers from one District to another, and other important legislation was enacted.

"This Assembly was larger than the last one, and more churches were represented. All those who took an active and leading part in the discussions on the floor a year ago, were present at this session, but the proceedings of this Assembly were characterized by much less debate than those of the last one.

"The work of the great committees of the Assembly was well done, and their reports were able and provocative of thought. The reports of the various churches were very encouraging, and showed revival conditions all along the line. The keynote of nearly all was growth in grace, salvation of souls, and increase in membership, and value of church property. The reports of the Publishing House, Bible College, and Spanish Mission, were especially inter-

313

esting and gratifying. All showed marked growth, and the continued blessing of God.

"Some notable addresses were given and sermons preached during the session of the Assembly. Among those who were especially helpful in this regard were: Rev. John N. Short, Rev. H. N. Brown, and Rev. A. B. Riggs, the fraternal delegates from our Pentecostal brethren; Rev. J. B. Creighton, Rev. W. C. Wilson, Rev. C. W. Ruth, Rev. J. W. Goodwin, Mrs. M. McReynolds, Mrs. De Lance Wallace, Rev. Lucy P. Knott, and Rev. Phœbe J. Epperson.

"The devotional exercises of the Assembly were fervent and refreshing. The young people's service was a glorious one, and Sunday, October 7th, the first day of the Home campmeeting, was marked by many and marvelous manifestations of the Divine Presence, with about fifty seekers at the altar during the day."

Thursday evening, October 4th, was devoted to the welcome and reception of the three visiting brethren, Brothers Short, Brown, and Riggs. Sister Libby Beach Brown, the noble wife of Rev. H. D. Brown, of Seattle, *The Victorious Host* sang with great effect an original song, written by her for the occasion, and entitled "The Victorious Host." Dr. Bresee said that the object of the meeting was to take the three "Wise Men of the East" to our bosom. Rev. C. W. Ruth, and Rev. W. C. Wilson, the latter at that time being pastor of the Church of the Nazarene, at Upland, Cal., spoke fittingly and forcibly of the providential features of the occasion. Brothers Riggs, Brown, and Short, expressed their appreciation of the unity of spirit, doctrine, and purpose which characterized both of the religious bodies represented, and made it plain that they desired the union of the two churches.

Rev. Robert Pierce thus summarizes the great revival service which was in progress during most of the period covered by the General Assembly, and continued several days afterward:

"Though God has given the First Church of Los Angeles a continual revival during the past eleven years, yet seldom, if ever, has there been such a turning to God as has been witnessed during the progress of the present Home Campmeeting. Not a service has been held without several seekers being forward, and several times the vast altar has been so overcrowded that the front row of seats has had to be called into requisition as a 'mourners' bench.' Without any singing or excitement, but in response to the tender invitation of Brother C. E. Cornell, the people flocked from all parts of the great tabernacle, and deliberately made their way to the front. Such sights made glad the hearts of the saints, and proved that the simple gospel, earnestly presented, has still power to convict and draw the multitudes. The Sabbaths were great days of victory, when at the morning and night services every chair in the large building seemed to be occupied, and the record for each of the Sabbaths was about one hundred seekers, who were graciously helped of God to receive what their hearts longed for. Time after time during the meetings, waves of glory swept over the audiences, and exultant shouts of praise came from men and women under the blessing of God.

"Brother Cornell, taught of the Spirit, knows how to put the great truths of the gospel in a simple, but earnest way. He is a wise leader, and knows how to handle immense congregations. His conduct of the altar services induces the seekers to plead with God for themselves, and as a result, many soon find the joy of salvation. Up to Wednesday night, fully 275 had knelt at the altar, seeking either pardon, reclamation, or entire sanctification, and many are gladly testifying that they received what they sought."

A Wise Leader

315

CHAPTER XXXV.

The writer penned the following in reference to the outpouring of the Holy Spirit in Berkeley:

"Ever since Sunday, September 30, 1906, when our dear

Revival in
Berkeley

Brother, Rev. H. N. Brown, of Everett, Mass., preached for us morning and evening, a revival has been in progress in our church. God helped Brother Brown to preach with special power and unction, and on that day several were reclaimed, and at least one sanctified wholly. Without any human planning, and undoubtedly by divine arrangement, there sprang into being a young men's class, of which Brother W. H. Girvin, my eldest son, became, by common consent, the leader. This class meets Sunday morning at 9 o'clock, and Tuesday evening at 7:30. It was not publicly announced, but more and more kept coming to the meetings, until last Sunday morning thirteen were present, the largest attendance since the beginning. Last Tuesday evening eleven attended and took part in the meeting, this being the largest number present at any of the evening meetings. At the first meeting of this class there was a marvelous outpouring of the Holy Spirit, and several were sanctified. Ever since, these meetings have been seasons of great joy, tenderness, and power, and the spirit of prayer prevails among the young men of the church as never before. There has been a marked quickening of spiritual life at all the services. Since September 30th, not fewer than five have been reclaimed, and ten or more have been sanctified. Seven have united with the church.

"There is a desire for similar work among the young

316

women of the church, and the providential indications are that it will soon begin.

"Rev. H. O. Wiley, our beloved pastor, who has done most of the preaching, and borne most of the burden of the work, by reason of my long and frequent absences from Berkeley, is being blessed in his ministry, and anointed of God as never before.

"For all these things we are praising God and giving Him the glory."

Dr. Bresee preached the dedicatory sermon at the Church of the Nazarene in Upland, California, on December 9, 1906, Rev. S. B. Rhoads preaching in the evening. At the close of Dr. Bresee's sermon, the friends stood and sang, and then came forward and laid $538 upon the altar, after which the building was formally dedicated to the worship of God. The church is a fine structure in mission style, with a good audience-room, and lecture-room. It occupies a prominent corner in the town.

Dedication of the Upland Church

The work which culminated in this society of the Church of the Nazarene, with its fine building, was begun as a mission, by Mrs. Pullman, and afterward carried on for some time by Rev. S. S. Chafe, under whose labors the church was organized. For more than a year prior to the dedication service, the church had for its pastor Rev. W. C. Wilson, who was greatly loved by his brethren, and held in high esteem as a man and minister by the people of the city generally. A preacher of marked ability, possessing special evangelistic gifts, and with excellent qualities of courage and endurance, he drew men, but, better still, he led them to Jesus, and to the cleansing fountain. Among those who helped the church very liberally along financial lines, were Brother and Sister Deets.

On January 13, 1907, the removed and remodeled Mateo Street Church of the Nazarene, in Los Angeles, was dedicated as the Compton Avenue Church, Dr. Bresee preaching the dedicatory sermon in the afternoon, when the spacious

317

building was filled with an enthusiastic congregation. The gratifying success of this Nazarene work was very largely due to the consecrated and indefatigable labors of the pastor of the church, Rev. Lucy P. Knott. During the dedicatory service, $1,000 was laid on the table as an offering. The people sang as they marched, and even the little tots, who had saved their pennies, took a happy part in the giving.

On April 4, 1907, Dr. and Mrs. Bresee left Los Angeles for Brooklyn, New York, their object being to attend the annual meeting of the Association of Pentecostal Churches of America. Dr. Bresee, in his editorial correspondence, thus describes their trip:

In Journeyings Oft

"It is a long way from where the rolling breakers of the Pacific ever beat upon the shore, to where the fiercer Atlantic dashes its spray upon the rocks.

"Our trip was in every way most fortunate. Leaving Los Angeles on April 1st, we pulled into the great Central Depot in New York City, on Saturday, having had twenty-four hours in Chicago. The sweet songs sung by a half hundred friends — college students, and others — at the Arcade Depot, in Los Angeles, alongside the train, seemed to go to the hearts of the crowd, and especially to fill the atmosphere of the crowded sleeper with a hallowed sense of spiritual verities, and to abide with us through the days of travel. Our train put in an appearance on time at each place, until it pulled into Inglewood station, Chicago, where it was entered by Brother Cornell and other friends, who hurried us off, before it started for the down town depot.

"We were taken directly to the home of Brother Cornell, where we had the pleasure of meeting, besides his own family, Brother and Sister H. D. Brown, from Seattle, Wash.; Brother C. W. Ruth, from Indianapolis; Dr. and Mrs. Burke, and others of our church in Chicago.

"A twenty-six hours' ride brought us to New York, where we were greeted by Brothers Hoople, Davis, and Mrs. Be

Vier, of Brooklyn; also by Brother E. A. Girvin, of Berkeley, Cal., who had preceded us by a few hours. We were conducted directly to Brooklyn, and taken to the hospitable home of Sister Be Vier, composed of herself, her son and daughter, both grown, and a young lady, a niece, all contributing to make a happy Christian home. Here we are for a few days, for the fellowship and service which may await us.

"The Pentecostal Churches of America have four organizations in Brooklyn. These are: The Utica Avenue, Rev. C. Howard Davis, pastor; the John Wesley, Rev. W. H. Hoople, pastor; Bedford Avenue Church, Rev. G. E. Noble, pastor, and People's Church, Rev. W. H. Raymond, pastor.

"The Utica Avenue Church has a good church building, fairly commodious. It is here that the annual meeting is to be held, from the 9th to the 14th of April. The other churches worship in rented halls, but the John Wesley Church has just purchased an eligible corner lot, and is arranging to go forward as fast as possible in the erection of a church building of ample size, to become a great place of gathering for the holiness hosts.

"I had, with Brothers H. D. Brown, and E. A. Girvin, the privileges of service with the brethren on the Sabbath day."

In the issue of the Nazarene Messenger, of April 25, 1907, there appeared an announcement as follows:

"Gratefully recognizing the merciful hand of God, in His overruling providences, and the guidance of His Holy Spirit; and having been authorized by our respective bodies, we hereby announce that the Church of the Nazarene, and the Association of Pentecostal Churches of America have both taken the necessary and proper action for the union of the two bodies into one organic church.

An Important Announcement

"We therefore hereby call a meeting of their united delegated bodies, heretofore known as the General Assembly of the Church of the Nazarene, and the Annual Meeting of the Association of Pentecostal Churches of America, to meet as one body, at the First Church of the Nazarene of Chicago, Ill., October 10, 1907, at 9 a. m.

"P. F. BRESEE, *Gen. Supt.*,
Church of the Nazarene.

"J. H. NORRIS, *Moderator,*
Assn. of Pentecostal Churches of America."

In the same issue appeared a long account by Dr. Bresee of the proceedings at Brooklyn, from which I quote:

"With us and the people whom we came to see, the interest has centered in the Annual Meeting of the Pentecostal Churches of America. The meeting is quite well attended by pastors, delegates, and visitors. It was called to order on Tuesday morning, April 9, 1907, by the Moderator of the past year, Rev. E. E. Angell, who is at the head of their educational work — the Pentecostal Collegiate Institute. The Rev. J. H. Norris, of Pittsburgh, was elected Moderator for the present year. The usual routine of business was attended to, the main interest centering in the proposed union of the two churches. The delegates present from the Church of the Nazarene, were introduced and asked to speak. They gave a few words of greeting, and Wednesday evening was set apart for their special reception, Brother J. H. Short being appointed to preside and say words of welcome. A committee was appointed to meet with the delegates from the Church of the Nazarene, and report on the basis of the union of the two bodies.

"On Wednesday night a large audience gathered, and Brother Short gave a happy statement of the going to the Pacific Coast of himself and fellow delegates, and of the royal reception by the General Assembly of the Church of the Nazarene. The report of the committee being ready, though it had not as yet been presented to the delegated body, was read to the meeting, which report stated the agreed

320

basis and recommendation of organic union. The report was received with the greatest manifestation of approval. The people sang and shouted and praised God. Addresses were then delivered by Rev. H. D. Brown, Rev. E. A. Girvin, Rev. C. W. Ruth, and Rev. P. F. Bresee. The meeting was most cordial, and full of enthusiasm.

"On the following morning the report was presented to the Annual Meeting, and unanimously adopted. The delegates were called out, and in the midst of their addresses, they began to sing the battle song of the Church of the Nazarene, 'Hallelujah, Amen,' and soon began a triumphant processional march around the church, praising God with great joy at the consummation of so desirable a work. All rejoiced, all were glad, believing that it marked a new era for the triumph of holiness through oneness and united effort. They also believed that it was the beginning of a wider union of our scattered forces, and that it was in the way of the more perfect fulfillment of the desire of the Master when he prayed: 'That they also may be one in us; that the world may believe that thou hast sent me;' and 'That they may be made perfect in one, that the world may know that thou hast sent me.'

"Not only has the Lord seemingly led in this whole matter, ruling and over-ruling, removing hindrances, moving on the hearts of the people, and opening up the way; but both in the General Assembly, in Los Angeles, and in the Annual Meeting here, when the matter has been favorably considered, there have been very great outpourings of the Holy Spirit, as an approving seal from the skies.

"The Sabbath was a great day. The love-feast at 9 a. m. was a time of very remarkable outpouring of the Holy Spirit. The preachers of the day were P. F. Bresee, John Norberry, and C. W. Ruth. Several people *A Remarkable* were at the altar, and blest of the Lord. *Outpouring* At 1:30 p. m., a great multitude marched to the corner of Saratoga avenue and Sumpter street, where the John Wesley Church has purchased a very eligible corner at a cost of $6,500, for a new church. There is a large dwelling house on it, and the multitude gathered in it as far as possible, and with prayer and song and suitable words, dedicated the ground to the service of God in this work. Rev. William Howard Hoople is the local pastor of this church. He is one of the very first in this movement. This church is to be a memorial to Rev. Charles BeVier, who was also one of the founders of this work, a very devoted and much loved man of God, who went home to glory nearly two years ago, but whose memory is full of fragrance. It is expected that this new church will seat 800 people, and it is hoped to have it finished by September 1st.

"These men and women, preachers, evangelists, and laymen, are an able, heroic, devoted body of workers, whom it is a joy to know, and whom it is a privilege to be yoked up with for the campaign.

"Some anxiety has been felt in various quarters as to the name of the united church. The joint commission considered it, and though there was no authority conferred *The Name* to fix a name, it was felt that it would be too great a loss to sink all that had been stood for in the past and that our names represented, and under which we had conquered, in an entirely new name. So it was concluded to recommend to the United Assembly that the name be the Pentecostal Church of the Nazarene. This the Annual Meeting unanimously joined in recommending.

"When the action had been taken completing the union of the two churches, Brother George W. Morse, known far and wide as Deacon Morse, arose, and proposed to give the new church a church building at Putnam, *A Wedding* Conn., known as the Morse Mission Church. *Gift* This church was bought by Brother Morse from the Episcopalians, about January 1, 1900. The building and lot originally cost about $15,000. This property he gave to the new church without any conditions.

322

Brother Morse has continued until now a member of the Baptist church, but will likely give himself, with his other gifts, to this new body, which will be more than all other gifts that he can make. He is widely known and universally beloved by the holy people.

"It is believed that this movement means multiplied possibilities, much added strength, reinforcement with new agencies, and enlargement of resources, and, above all, in the *The Outlook* approval of God, great Pentecosts of divine glory and power — the Lord's own hand tc open the doors, and opening the fountain of supply to give for His own glory, blessings more than we have asked or thought."

The following is the author's brief description of this memorable occasion:

"God has helped us to find a place where holiness people can unite. It is the middle course between the *Unearthly* extremes of Episcopacy and Congregational-*Power* ism. Now that we have found this due mean in the way of church government, it seems so simple and obvious that any sensible Christian ought to discover it almost immediately. And yet it has taken years for us to reach it, helped by the guidance of God.

"April 11, 1907, marked an important epoch in the history of the holiness movement in America. Then, amidst tears, and laughter, and shouts, and every possible manifestation of holy joy, the Pentecostal Association of America united with the Church of the Nazarene. It was a scene which time can not efface from the memory of the participants. This marks the beginning of the era of organic unity among the various branches of organized holiness in the United States. Christ's prayer was being answered, and God was pleased. He showed His good pleasure in the most unmistakable way. From that time on, the sessions of the Annual Meeting grew in power. God freshly anointed His saints over and over again, and the marvelous Pentecost culminated at the love feast on Sunday morning, April 14.

From the very beginning an unearthly power was felt. It was truly heavenly. Great tides of salvation rolled in and around and over us. The waves of glory almost swept us off our feet. We were immersed and inundated in rivers of love. I received the greatest anointing of my life. It seemed as if the Holy Spirit laughed within our souls. With me, during most of the meeting, it was really 'joy unspeakable and full of glory.' I was melted by the ecstatic, thrilling love of God, who so swept his fingers over the chords of my soul as to cause me to weep and laugh at the same time. With me, as I believe with most of God's people, this is the highest possible physical expression of the rapture caused by intimate fellowship with God.

"After the love feast, Dr. Bresee preached from the 6th chapter of Isaiah, with unction and force. The saints drank in the glorious truths of the message with the keenest delight. There was salvation at all the services of the day. Dr. Bresee, Brother Brown, and Brother Ruth were at their best, spiritually at least, during the Annual Meeting, and preached with power. They won the hearts of the Pentecostal brethren, and did much by their kindness and tact to make the union of the churches unanimous. The General Assembly will meet in Chicago, October 10th.

"From this time forward, we all belong to the Pentecostal Church of the Nazarene."

During the Annual Meeting of the Pentecostal brethren, at Brooklyn, the basis of union of the two churches was prepared by what was called the Joint Commission. This commission consisted of Brothers Bresee, Brown, *The Basis* Ruth, and Girvin for the Church of the Naza-*of Union* rene, and Brothers Hoople, Hosley, Norris, Short, Norberry, Bearse, and Riggs for the Pentecostal Association. The report of the commission was written by Dr. Bresee, acting as one of a sub-committee of four, and was adopted unanimously by the commission. As already stated, it was received with the utmost unanimity

324

and joy by the Pentecostal brethren at their Annual Meeting. The report is as follows:

"It is agreed that the two churches are one, in the doctrines considered essential to salvation, especially the doctrines of justification by faith, and entire sanctification, subsequent to justification, also by faith, and as a result, have the precious experience of entire sanctification as a normal condition of the churches.

"Both churches recognize that the right of church-membership rests upon experience, and that persons who have been born of the Spirit are entitled to its privileges.

"We are agreed upon the necessity of a Superintendency, which shall foster and care for churches already established, and whose duty it shall be to organize and encourage in the organizing of churches everywhere. We agree that authority given Superintendents shall not interfere with the independent action of the fully organized church — each church enjoying the right to select its own pastor, subject to such approval as the General Assembly shall find wise to institute — the election of delegates to the various Assemblies, the managing of their own finances, and all other things pertaining to their local life and work.

"It is agreed that any church of the Pentecostal Association, going into the organization, who may feel it imperative with them to continue to hold their property in like manner as at present, shall be at liberty to do so.

"It is mutually agreed that the further details for completing the union be left to the first meeting of the united body.

"Your committee recommend for your consideration that the name of the new body shall be the Pentecostal Church of the Nazarene."

Speaking of the reception of this report, the Beulah Christian, the leading paper of the Pentecostal Churches of America, said:

"The reading of this report was scarcely ended before the whole meeting arose like a mighty swell of the sea, and

325

vented its pent-up feelings in shouting, singing, waving of handkerchiefs, etc., until it was 'like the sound of many waters.' Those who were privileged to make one of that company, will never forget the auspicious hour when the Pentecostal Church of the Nazarene unfurled her banner to the breeze."

CHAPTER XXXVI.

In his editorial correspondence under date of May 2, 1907, Dr. Bresee says:

"On Tuesday morning, that great-hearted brother, pastor of John Wesley Church (referring to *Retrospection* Brother W. H. Hoople), conducted us, by sub-ways and other ways — certainly in ways that we could never have found — to the New Jersey side of the Hudson river, and saw us safely on the Ulster and Delaware railroad. It was a delightful ride, with beautiful scenery, up the Hudson river as far as Kingston, when we swept off among the hills, over the Catskills, and through valleys where villages, often half hid, nestle; then along the sparkling, sometimes dashing, streams, with the higher hills covered by the recent snows, and yet the buds of the trees so swollen as to make the hillsides in places bear a roseate hue of peculiar beauty. The small fields enclosed by stone walls in almost every imaginable shape, had a picturesque appearance.

"Here we are among the scenes of our childhood, to look once more upon the places where we played and worked and hoped; where we looked out upon life with childhood and youthful expectancy, and where, more than *Childhood* all, we found the pearl of great price.
Scenes "It brings a strange feeling to be a stranger in the land of one's childhood. The hills are here, the streams flow as of old, the same stars shine overhead, but the people are strange. Here are two villages, about three miles apart; each has a Methodist church. In one Mrs. Bresee was converted; in the other I was privileged to find the Lord. This was in our early youth. Both

of these churches are in one charge, preaching being at one at 10:30 a. m., and at the other at 1 p. m.; so that we were permitted to worship at both. The occupants of the pews were strangers, the pastor a stranger, all things strange. All that we could do was to find our way to the altars where we knelt so long ago, and with tearful memories and holy trust, and heaven-lit hopes, worship and adore, and preach the Word. As we closed our eyes, how the vanished forms seemed to fill the pews again, and the loved faces to smile anew. But, as we opened our eyes, there were the strangers; only God over all, who seemed even nearer and more precious than in other days. It was a joy, though shaded by many sorrows, to kneel again where the eternities dawned in divine love and pardon.

> There is a place to me more dear,
> Than native vale or mountain;
> A place for which affection's tear
> Springs grateful from its fountain;
> 'Tis not where kindred souls abound,
> Though that were almost heaven;
> But where I first my Saviour found,
> And felt my sins forgiven.

"But better than that, is to know Him now in the fulness of His love.

"Greater even than to be 'born again,' is to be born at all. To be *born* is the setting up of new forces, pushing off on the boundless sea of being an immortal soul. To have been created, to be alive, is the most wonderful of all *Nativity* facts. No wonder the German poet said, 'To me also has come the measureless glory of being alive.' Scarcely any thought comes to me with such unutterable meaning as: I am a living being in the eternities of God. In connection with this there comes to me, from the lips of God, bringing unspeakable joy, 'I have made and I will bear.' I am not left to find my destiny in this boundless sea; but He bears me up with the certainties of His revelations and the riches of His grace.

"A good livery team and two hours of drive, bring us

to the place. No vestige of house, or mark that any house had ever been; but here it is, surrounded by these hills, covered by these skies. Right here is the place where, sixty-eight years ago, I opened my eyes to the light, and God laid me upon the bosom of a mother who never ceased to love and care for me. Five years ago in a real translation, God took her to Himself, but I am sure that her love still abides.

"When one year old, my parents moved to what was the real home of my childhood, nearly three miles away. Thither we go.

Childhood "The gentleman and his wife could not have been more courteous. The house was thrown open to us, and we were conducted to everything reminiscent. From here the first things in memory rise. Occurrences come up distinctly from the time I was one year old, through childhood. Here is the same beech-tree under whose shade I rested; the same flowing spring, from whence the water still flows; the two great twin rocks upon which my sister and myself played. But the house was most replete with memories. I asked to see the chambers, and was conducted thither. I went directly to the little room which was mine own. There in one corner was my bed. How vividly I remember, when my mother used to put me to bed, and then knelt by the bed and prayed. The echo of her voice is still in my soul, and the touch of her vanished hand still on my brow.

"In these parts God gave me my richest blessings. Here I was born, here born again. Here God gave me my wife, who by her loving devotion has comforted, cheered, and blest me through these years, and to whom is largely due what little I have been able to do. To cherish these memories, and to see the few who linger, we have turned aside for a few days to make this pilgrimage, that with new vigor and fresh anointing we may tell out the story of infinite love.

"Thursday, April 25, 1907, we once more said good-by to our native New York hills, and getting the midnight

train, arrived in Chicago the following evening. Such great
cities, where millions of people abide, and multi-
Other tudes more are ever coming and going, are to the
Scenes strangers great deserts. There is no place more
lonely and desolate than a very great city, to a
stranger within its gates. It was with joy that we beheld the
familiar faces of Brother Cornell and Brother Girvin, as
we tarried on the platform of the depot.

"Such a place as the Church of the Nazarene is a real
oasis. It was our privilege to spend the Sabbath amid the
praises of this wonderful church, and enjoy with them the
mighty spirit of victory, which trembled on so many lips,
and filled the place with glory.

"This is really one of the greatest churches of America.
Great in the number of people which it reaches, in the tide
of salvation which continually flows, and in the strength
of Christian character into which the redeemed
The are brought, as well as efficiency for the Lord's
Chicago work in every way. They are in very great
Church need of a building, where the multitudes who
throng this place of gathering may be accommodated, and more and more the people be brought to the
Cross. They have purchased very eligible lots, and propose as fast as possible to move in this direction. We believe that it would be very pleasing to the Master, if some
man or woman who is a custodian of His money, would
make it possible for them to move on at once by a gift so
large and generous as to inspire this faith, and open up
for them the way. Of course, the enterprise must be of
some magnitude, and must be done soon. The church is
very fortunate in having for its pastor one so versatile,
active, and conservatively aggressive as Brother Cornell,
and aided and supported as he is by so good a body of
intelligent and heavenly-appointed men and women. All
things which are within the Lord's pattern, are possible.

"We were glad to greet at the service Brother and Sister

J. M. Harris, and hear them once again sing in their almost matchless way. Brother Harris has long been very ill, but seems himself again, and they anticipate being soon in the midst of the battle once more.

"No more delightful home can come to the weary wanderer than we had the pleasure of enjoying with Brother and Sister Bohart. We had the privilege, with a dozen of the saints from this church, to go to Hammond — a suburb of the city — where Brother A. T. Harris has a flourishing young church, which has meetings every night the month through. The rain was pouring down in torrents, but the house was full, and some souls prayed through to the dawn.

"Brother Hoover has a flourishing church organized at South Chicago, which we had hoped to visit, but were not permitted at this time.

"Here we have again met Brother and Sister Brown, of Seattle, and with them turn our faces toward the Northwest."

Dr. and Mrs. Bresee made the long trip from Chicago to Spokane in company with Rev. H. D. Brown and wife. They spent one Sabbath in Spokane, Dr. Bresee preaching in the morning, and Brother Brown in the evening, and found the Church of the Nazarene there in a flourishing condition. In his editorial correspondence, Dr. Bresee says:

The Northwest

"We left Spokane on Tuesday morning in company with our traveling companions, Brother and Sister Brown, reinforced by a good delegation from Spokane. Among them were Brother and Sister Wallace, and several representatives of the church there; also Brother Little, pastor of the church at Garfield. We arrived at North Yakima about 2 o'clock in the afternoon.

"Our church here feels the tide of general prosperity. During the last year a nice corner lot has been purchased, and a good church building erected. Such provision has been made that it will be unencumbered by debt. The membership has increased, and there has been prosperity. Much of this has been due to the careful planting of Rev. J. B. Creighton, who was the first pastor, and to the management of Rev. William S. Rice, the present pastor. The church here has also been greatly indebted to Brother O. A. Clark, who, with his family, came to our church about a year ago. He is one of the leading business men here, and at the same time a wise, careful laborer in the kingdom of God. But, above all, the people — at first but a little band — have been true to the dispensational truth, that Jesus Christ baptizes believers with the Holy Ghost; and the fire has rested upon their Assemblies and homes, and the work has gone steadily forward.

"The night preceding the Assembly, an earnest prayer-meeting was held, and the seal of the Lord was upon the gathered people. At 9:30 a. m., Wednesday, the Assembly *The District* was called to order, and it remained in session four days. The attendance was remark-*Assembly* ably good, the reports were of great interest, and the open doors seemed to be multiplying. The Lord is raising up laborers to enter the various fields. A great advance has been made during the past year, and the promise is of much greater things in the near future. The preaching was in the Spirit, and owned of the Lord, and a good spiritual condition was dominant. Some souls were at the altar, which on the last night, the Sabbath, was well filled with those seeking the Lord, all of whom were blest. During the Sabbath sixteen persons were taken into the church. They were good representative people, among whom was Rev. T. E. Webb, a superannuated member of the Northwestern Indiana Conference of the Methodist Episcopal church. Dr. Webb is an able preacher, and a man of evangelistic spirit, and indomitable energy. He has a place on the street where he preaches every Sabbath afternoon, which he calls his church. He is a clear teacher of entire sanctification, and felt that his place was among the people who stand for this precious doctrine and experience. These additions were a great reinforcement to the local church here, and there are evidently more to follow. The promise of the church in this city is bright.

"The old home church at Los Angeles is well represented in the ministry of this District, among whom are Brother and Sister McIntyre, and Brothers Valjean, Henricks, and Dilley, all doing valiant service. Rev. H. D. Brown was re-elected District Superintendent for the coming year, and has, with Sister Brown, a warm place in the hearts of the laborers in this great Northwest. They have given themselves unstintedly to the work, providing largely for their own necessities.

"An empire is being sown down for our work in this vast field. This District will doubtless average five hundred miles square, and these heroic workers go forth to take it for the work of holiness.

An Imperial Field   "The orders of four elders were recognized, and two, Rev. De Lance Wallace, and J. S. Parkins, were elected and ordained elders. The ordination service was held on Sabbath afternoon, and was of peculiar interest.

"Some of the young men who are in the oncoming tide of preachers for this Northwest country, hope to be in the Pacific Bible College next year."

After spending a night and a day in Seattle, at the hospitable home of Brother and Sister Brown, Dr. and Mrs. Bresee, with Sister De Lance Wallace, went to Monroe, about fifty miles north of Seattle. They *The Work at Monroe* were met by Brother Parkins, the pastor of the church, and entertained by Brother Pierce. Dr. Bresee preached to good gatherings in the afternoon and evening. Six preachers were present, with whom he became sufficiently acquainted to have sweet fellowship, and the field seemed to give promise of future harvests.

Returning to Seattle, Dr. and Mrs. Bresee called upon Sister Hervey, of the First Church in Los Angeles, who was ministering to her brother, Rev. Best, of the United *Seattle* Presbyterian church, who had been very seriously injured by an automobile. Communion with these saints at the throne of grace, was peculiarly refreshing. At night there was a delightful service at the Church of the Nazarene, the house being well filled, and the Spirit of the Lord resting upon the people. At this service, Dr. H. W. H. Reece, pastor of the First Methodist Episcopal church, of Seattle, and a friend of other years, was present, and testified to full salvation. At an after meeting the brethren welcomed Sister Wallace, who had been called as pastor of the Seattle church.

Of his visit to Portland, Dr. Bresee wrote:

"We arrived at this beautiful city on Friday, May 17th, late in the afternoon, accompanied by Brother and Sister *Portland* McIntyre. We were met at the train by friends who took charge of us, Brother and Sister McIntyre finding a home with Brother and Sister Whitesides, and Mrs. Bresee and myself with Brother and Sister Eaton.

"Our church here is, of course, to us the center of interest. We were permitted to organize it on the Fourth of July last. We were disappointed in reference to the pastor, whom we had expected to take charge of it, and the church was without a pastor for nearly four months. The wolf — sometimes having a sheepskin thrown over him — did all that he could to destroy the flock, and there was a falling away. But, in October, Rev. A. O. Henricks was appointed to take charge. The faithful ones who had stood heroically by the guns through the months, rallied, and they have had a constant tide of victory. God has made

334

the wrath of man to praise him, and the rest He has restrained. They are without a church building, and worship in a rented church, which is commodious, but also quite expensive. Hence, they are looking for a way to secure a house of their own. We had the privilege of preaching to them morning and evening, with good audiences, and found them earnestly pushing the battle. They have an earnest, enthusiastic, intelligent people, who know the fulness of the blessing of Christ, and great and greater victories await them."

Dr. Bresee wrote at some length of Selwood, a suburb of Portland, where Brother and Sister McIntyre were about to take charge of a new work, with only two members to begin with, but with a good church building.

On their way south, Dr. and Mrs. Bresee spent an afternoon and night at Ashland, stopping with Brother and Sister Mills, preaching in the new church building, and encouraging Brother Valjean, the faithful pastor, in his work.

The Southern California District was organized Sept. 4, 1907, at which time preachers and delegates from the various churches of the southern part of the state, met at the First Church, in Los Angeles. It was large-*Southern California* ly attended, and a great gathering in *District Assembly* every way. Dr. Bresee said in his opening address:

"I might say in calling this Assembly to order, that it would seem that the 'first should be last' in the matter of organization. It would have been fitting to have the Southern California District Assembly the first to be organized, but it seemed to be essential that we have the General Assembly, which was composed mostly from this District, and, therefore, it was not felt necessary to have a District Assembly. The time, however, has come when the church has spread, and as a result of the union with the Pentecostal Church, it is now found necessary for a District Assembly

335

to carry on the work. We have thus called you today just to do the necessary things which God has called us to do.

"God is opening the way before us, and we expect many outside organizations to be present with us at Chicago. We expect that the holiness ranks will flow together and become one mighty army to push the gospel of a full salvation. It is not the multitude of people, but the kind of people we are, which tells. Thus, we must have perfect love and self-abnegation. We should be a people filled with the thrilling, anointing power of the Holy Ghost, and be all aglow with the love of God.

"I rejoice that the great body of our people have stood firm to the real experience for which we stand. If we have the impulse of an indwelling Christ, we shall hand-pick the hungry hearts and lead them to God. This is the highest evangelism of the twentieth century. We are here to make centers of fire, and God will open the way and give us the victory."

Rev. R. Pierce was elected as secretary. He chose Brother Fred C. Epperson as his assistant. About one hundred lay and ministerial delegates answered to their names.

Among other business transacted by this Assembly, was the adoption of resolutions providing for the institution of a campmeeting within the bounds of the District, to be arranged for by a committee of three pastors and two laymen, with the District Superintendent as chairman. Rev. C. V. La Fontaine was elected unanimously as District Superintendent. The reports of the various committees and pastors showed the work to be in a healthy, aggressive condition. There were frequent downpourings of precious spiritual anointings, and the hours given especially to prayer and praise were times of victory. The sermon by Rev. L. H. Humphreys, the ordination service and altar gathering, were all crowned with holy triumph.

CHAPTER XXXVII.

On Thursday, October 10, 1907, the first General Assembly of the united churches held its opening session at the First Church, in Chicago.

Among other things in Dr. Bresee's report, which was a strong and exhaustive paper, the reading of which aroused constant outbursts of enthusiasm, were the following: "Dear Brothers and Sisters of the Assembly:

First General Assembly of the United Churches.
Dr. Bresee's Report

"It has been the custom of the General Assembly of the Church of the Nazarene, to expect that the General Superintendent would present to them some account of himself and the work committed to his hands. As we meet for the first time in our united capacity, I may not be able to speak in any comprehensive way of the whole work as represented here, and, while others doubtless will in some general way represent other branches of this united brotherhood, yet it still may be expected that I would say a few words in reference to the stream which flows from the west, to mingle its waters with the stream from the east, and lose itself in this blessed confluence, to create the enlarged stream of salvation to flow on forever. And we are all here to say:

> Flow, wondrous stream, with glory crowned,
> Flow on to earth's remotest bound;
> And bear us on thy gentle wave,
> To Him who all thy virtues gave.

"And, first, I desire to congratulate myself and you all, that we are permitted to see this blessed, auspicious day.

337

When Achsah, the daughter of Caleb, was married in the land of Canaan, though she had received an inheritance in the Southland, yet on that day she sought a blessing of her father, and he gave her springs of water, the upper and the lower springs. So we feel that in this marriage, God has enlarged our inheritance, and given us the eastern and western springs of enlarged love and fellowship.

"It was my privilege, in connection with the other fraternal delegates and members of the General Commission from the Church of the Nazarene, to attend the annual meeting of the Association of Pentecostal Churches, at Brooklyn, and not only to enjoy their brotherly greeting and fellowship, but to witness and enjoy with them the loving and enthusiastic work of completing the union of the two denominations, and their concurrent action in calling this meeting and joining in the appointment of a commission to prepare and report to you disciplinary regulations for our united body. I regarded the performance of this duty, together with all the personal blessings which it brought, as one of the most gracious privileges of my life.

"I regard the action there taken, together with the previous action of the last General Assembly of the Church of the Nazarene, which have led to the bringing of us together here in this united Assembly, as most momentous, and in the good providence of God, opening the door in a remarkáble way for the unification of the holiness forces in this country, and their organization for its more efficient promulgation in all lands.

"I rejoice also that God is putting into the hearts of the holy people in all parts of the country, a hunger for a wider fellowship, and seemingly a willingness to put aside, or in its proper place, anything not essential to holiness, for the sake of the greater usefulness of united co-operation. This seems to me to promise, if not a new era, a very greatly enlarged possibility for the work to which God has called us. We are evidently as yet in the early morning of what God intends in reference to this organized work of holiness, and it becomes us to walk very softly before Him in love, looking for His way and His guiding hand in the way.

Let your light
so shine
before men,
that they may see
your good works,
and glorify
your Father
which is
in heaven.

Matthew 5:16

that in what is more especially ... now united work, there has ... he good hand of our God upon ... g of the streams of salvation, ... w rivers in the wilderness, and ... has continued to give salvation ... here is a greatly enlarged de- ... e messengers who can establish ... rches have been organized, and ... ing that I am led to emphasize ... cy and organization.

e together. The doors are open- ... ultiplied rapidity. It must be ... e to see that they are entered, ... ches organized, and proper pas- ... provided for them. This must ... one quite largely through the ... of the General and District Su- ... s will help, and especially Dis- ... y be found practicable to put in ... er, who should have all the ele- ... ganizer, to co-operate with and ... . This work is very great, and ... devotion of some of our very best

ing this work in every consider- ... rom which it may radiate to vil- ... about, and the doing it as soon ... necessities. Our Lord has called ... hand beckons us on. He opens ... ur one business to enter this land ... for Him and His glory. By His

339

strength and through His leadership we shall be fully able to go up and possess the land.

"In the western part of our work, for which I of necessity more especially speak, we have four Districts organized: the Chicago Central, the Northwestern, the San Francisco, and the Southern California. Some of them are very large, covering immense stretches of country, and the great distances have made them difficult to care for. But our work has been scattered, and these large Districts have been a necessity. Nevertheless, large and unwieldly as they have been, with our efficient Superintendents and District Assemblies, they have been of incalculable service to the work. In this, like all the other departments of the work, we are yet in the early morning, but the day has dawned. The country must be covered with Districts, with able men at the head of them, and we will soon be able to have a center of fire in every city in America, and will be able to enter foreign fields in a way that will promise good and efficient work.

"Time emphasizes the fact that our first great mission field is this country. That God has called us to help reinforce the religious forces of America, and thus help to save *Missions* it from the paganism with which it is so strongly threatened, and which the worldly churches are so powerless to resist. No doubt but the reflex influence of this movement upon the older churches is good, and every church that can be impelled, inspired, or provoked to deeper spirituality, is so much of an asset to this work. But there is a very great need everywhere of this church — not narrow, nor partisan, nor sectarian, but in a spirit of love as broad as the gospel — to preach holiness, and organize the results of our ministry for aggressive and continuous work. No mission work at this time is so essential for the redemption of this world from sin, as the preaching and establishing of holiness in America. Every holiness center established, is the springing forth from the skies of rivers of life to men. While in these days the distinction between home and foreign missions has vanished, and the world is at our doors, yet a wise, discerning eye will see that a new movement like this, must in order to efficiently serve the whole, spend the greater force in creating the very largest possibilities. Whatever else we may be able to do, we *must* possess this land, both for its own sake, as well as for the conditions of service to every land. I fully believe, with the accelerated momentum given by our union of holiness forces, that only a few years will be necessary to give to this work a thousand centers of holy flame in this country, and that from them the streams will flow to the world. The reports of the missionary boards will show some organized effort; though the great amount of the work has been done by the people directly, preaching and testifying the gospel of the grace of God. Our work has been new, and with but small aggregations of people and means, but I believe to a considerable extent the scattered people have gone forth testifying to this great salvation."

The remainder of the report dealt largely with the organized mission work carried on heretofore by the Church of the Nazarene; its publishing interests; and the great educational work represented by the Deets Pacific Bible College. The report closed as follows:

"In coming into this union we find ourselves possessed of societies and corporate boards, brought into being to carry out in each of our previous organizations, the same
Adjustments purposes, such as missions, publishing interests, and education. It will be our work to so adjust these societies and boards, that they may work in the best ways, co-operating and assisting each other until such times as it may be found advisable to unify them.

"With unspeakable thankfulness for the way God has led us in the past, and for the gracious outlook as we turn our eyes toward the future, and with earnest prayer for divine guidance, we enter upon the duties of this providential Assembly. May His anointings be upon us, and His wisdom direct us in all things."

The work done by this commission before and during the sessions of the Assembly, was very great and far-reaching. It was composed of the following fourteen brethren, seven of them representing each of the two *The Joint* great organizations whose union had been *Legislative* so blessedly brought about: P. F. Bresee, *Commission* J. C. Bearse, W. H. Hoople, C. E. Cornell, H. B. Hosley, J. H. Norris, H. D. Brown, J. N. Short, E. E. Angell, T. H. Agnew, John Norberry, C. W. Ruth, L. B. Kent, and E. A. Girvin. C. V. LaFontaine was added to the commission at Chicago.

I quote the following from an account of the Assembly written by Rev. Isaiah Reid:

"Never in all the great holiness gatherings in the middle west, have we had such a representation. Certain-*Blessed* ly the time is nearing when the Savior's prayer *Unity* 'that they all be one,' shall be true of the holiness people. At any rate, here meet and mingle in blessed unity and fellowship, a multitude of people once divided in many ways, but now merged into a harmonized body of saints. Bless God for His marvelous doings among the children of men!

"Here, as not manifest in any of our Association gatherings, is the 'missing link,' we have so long felt the need of — spiritual and suitable, heaven-born, organic unity. This is for ever impossible in our interdenominational association plan, as in the association there necessarily remains the 'tie that binds' us to the inimical ecclesiasticism, and by which we are necessarily limited.

"Take into consideration with these, the unctuous experiences, the anointed lives, the splendid conquering faith, the real spiritual freedom, the Wesleyan theology, the middle ground organization polity, the flowing together of men and women of like faith from fields of great usefulness in many denominations, and, added to all, the deep-rooted conviction that without the real baptism of the Holy Spirit, nothing can be wrought, we have in fact, already in motion and on victorious march, God's best human agency for the promotion of the conquering gospel. I came away from the Assembly younger than I went."

This great service, on October 11th, was full of holy joy and triumph. The flood of divine joy swept high, and the saints were filled with the rapture that comes only from the heart of God. The occasion was the reception *The* *Opening* *Service* of the fraternal delegates from the different holiness bodies from Texas and other parts of the South. Sister Libbie Beach Brown, sang a song, written by herself and entitled, 'Holiness is Moving On.' The other delegates from the Northwest united with her in the chorus in such a way as to take the vast audience by storm.

Professor John W. Akers, of the Chicago church, made the address of welcome, which was admirable in every way. Among other trenchant utterances of this powerful address, were the following:

"A few years ago God raised up a man and surrounded him with a little band of faithful men and women. He was a man of necessity. Things born to universal necessity can not be put to death. The world is still hearing the strokes of the hammer made by Martin Luther; and later when the church was given over to fanaticism, God put forth a John Wesley, and millions were swept into the kingdom. The Pentecostal Church of the Nazarene comes forth at the call of God, as a necessity, to answer formalism, higher criticism, and worldliness. Persecution will sweep along this movement as it swept along Methodism. The same spirit which put Joseph into the pit, has driven these men here today. We did not know when we started this work in this city, that God would make it the place where the East and the West would come together to lay solid foundations.

God is going to make this church the mighty power to over-come scepticism and error."

Sisters Carrie Crowe, and Lulu Kell, sang the "Meeting in the Air," and all present were deeply moved. Addresses were made by Rev. P. G. Linaweaver, of Oakland, Cal., and Rev. H. B. Hosley, of Washington, D. C. Rev. C. B. Jernigan, who with six other brethren from the South, was present as a fraternal delegate from the Holiness Church of Christ, made a thrilling address, full of telling points. Among other things he said:

"There will only be one when we get through. We shall never see two again. This is the biggest live thing we have ever seen. Thank God, holiness is rolling on. For the past five years I have been hunting something like this. We have heard Jesus say, 'You must all be one.' And you can't be one without us, and so we are here. This is a big thing, and Texas is not afraid of big things. We are here, and we are here to stay."

Dr. Bresee was called upon. I quote but a little of his weighty words: "There are things which can not be said. When a little band in Los Angeles, we never thought we should see this night. We are here at this hearty welcome, but another General Assembly we may be at the eastern gate. Thank God, we are here — here to rejoice; here to gird up our loins to girdle the earth with the gospel. God calls us to new conquests. Will you attend to the job! Will you be true? Will you be true?"

Dr. Bresee presided at the Assembly with his usual skill and fairness. Rev. R. Pierce was secretary. It was decided to elect two General Superintendents, and when the time came for their election, Dr. Bresee was chosen unanimously by a rising vote, and Rev. H. F. Reynolds, of Massachusetts, by a majority of all the votes cast. Brother Reynolds was also elected General Missionary Secretary of the united body.

Rev. R. Pierce wrote a very able and comprehensive re-

344

port of the proceedings of the Assembly, which is of great historical value. In speaking of Dr. Bresee, he said:

A Tribute to
Dr. Bresee

"The venerable face of dear Dr. Bresee was seen everywhere, beaming a smile of greeting upon the strangers, and a hearty welcome to the delegates from all quarters. His inspiring messages, his great sermon on Sabbath morning, his God-given wisdom and grace in presiding over the Assembly, and his wise counsel and help in the different committees, were a great benediction to this great gathering. We thank God that He took him in His arms, and strengthened him for this great work.

"One of the interesting and pleasant episodes of the Assembly was the presentation, through the First Church of Chicago, of a beautiful bust portrait of our General Superintendent, Dr. Bresee. The donor did not desire the name to be known, but we hear that it was the work of a talented artist, who is a member of Brother Cornell's church. The gift was highly appreciated, not only by our venerated leader, but by the whole Assembly."

The following is a brief summary of my own impressions of this General Assembly:

An Epoch in Our
Movement

"It marked an epoch in our movement, and was in every way the greatest General Assembly I have ever attended. In numbers, in interest, in importance of the work accomplished, in its representative character, in the manifest presence and unmistakable guidance of God, it stands in a class by itself, and far surpasses all its predecessors.

"I was not permitted to attend many of its public sessions, but was engrossed in committee work. It was my privilege to take part in the numerous meetings and prolonged deliberations and discussions of the legislative commission, and the committees on superintendency and church relations. The work of these committees, which was very important, was accomplished in a spirit of mutual concession and brotherly love. Although there were often sharp differences of opinion, a way was always found to attain unanimity, and thus avoid a minority report, or any contention on the floor of the General Assembly.

"The legislation enacted by the Assembly was comprehensive and far-reaching, and the polity of the united church is one which will commend itself to holiness people everywhere. The statements made in the declaration of doctrine in regard to Baptism, the Second Coming of Christ, and Divine Healing, were satisfactory to both sides of these much mooted subjects.

"The tide of salvation and divine glory ran high at all times, but there were a few episodes of the Assembly which were especially prominent. Among these were the great communion service on Thursday, October 10th, the address of welcome by Professor J. W. Akers, of the Chicago church, on Friday evening, the sermon by Dr. P. F. Bresee, on Sunday morning, the march and table offering, on Sunday afternoon, the re-election by acclamation of Dr. Bresee as General Superintendent of the Pentecostal Church of the Nazarene, and the presentation of his portrait, and the adjournment of the General Assembly with great joy, on Wednesday night, October 16th.

"Among those present were seven fraternal delegates from the Holiness Church of Christ, representing more than one hundred churches, and 3,000 members, in Texas, Arkansas, Indian Territory, and Oklahoma, and two fraternal delegates from the Holiness Christian Church, having a membership of 1,800 in Pennsylvania and Indiana. These brethren left the Assembly with the determination of doing their utmost to effect a union of their bodies with our church.

"Thirty states and territories were represented, many leading holiness evangelists were there, and the gathering was essentially a national one.

"The government of our church is a mean between extremes, thus avoiding the vices and weaknesses of Episcopacy on the one hand, and Congregationalism on the other. Its doctrinal statement is one which ought to receive the approval of every man and woman who enjoys the experience of holiness. That the first General Assembly succeeded in bringing about this condition of things, is proof positive, to my mind, of the special leadership and direction of the Holy Spirit.

"The missionary work of the united church was put upon a new basis by the adoption of the envelope system, and the creation of a great central missionary board, with auxiliaries in the various Assembly Districts and local churches. Rev. H. F. Reynolds, who was elected one of the General Superintendents of the church, was also chosen as General Missionary Secretary. He has had years of experience in this work, and is better qualified to carry it on successfully than any other man in our church.

"As a result of this General Assembly, the eyes of lovers of holiness all over the American continent are fixed upon the Pentecostal Church of the Nazarene."

The following is Dr. Bresee's summary and characterization of this historic gathering:

"The great General Assembly of the Pentecostal Church of the Nazarene for 1907, has gone into history. *The Breath of God* Not to be laid away upon the shelf, and dry up like a mummy, and be forgotten, for, though past, it lives, and will live for ever. We expected a great meeting. The coming together of the two churches in their representative capacity; the perfecting of the government for the new church; the arranging and adjusting of the various interests and agencies for the carrying on of the work; the drawing together of many people deeply interested in this movement; and, above all, the deep, earnest, wide-spread spirit of prayer which was upon the holy people — really the breath of God upon the hearts of

men, as a mighty inspiration to ask largely of the Lord —
had assured us in advance of great things.

"The Lord never disappoints, but He does surprise us by
the greatness and richness of His gifts. It has been so in
this Assembly. While many things have been as we expected, and in no part less, yet there has been
Glory from through and about, environing it, such mani-
the Skies festations of the providences of God, such evident divine guidance, and, above all, such a
sense of His presence and approval, as to be an unspeakable
benediction and joy. We could only wish that the whole
church could have been present and felt directly the impulse
and glory from the skies. It was not in the number of
people brought together — great gatherings are frequent —
nor in the religious enthusiasm — this is often at fever heat
in great gatherings. There were many present, about two
hundred delegates, and I think probably nearly as many
more friends, who came from far and near to see and mark
the epoch-making gathering of earnest people with a purpose, besides multitudes of earnest people, only numbered
by the size of the house. At one call it was shown that there
were representatives from thirty-four states and territories,
besides Mexico. There was religious enthusiasm, though we
have often seen more demonstration. We have seen greater
tides of seekers, yet at every opportunity we were permitted
to witness, some were weeping their way toward the Lamb
of God. All these often come and go at various gatherings,
and are blessed, and they spend themselves as water poured
upon the parched earth. The sun rises upon the spot where
they were, and there is little to tell that they ever were.

"Though we may not be able to tell men who do not feel
it, the burstings forth of glory in this Assembly — the
Divine Presence and His leadings, which are not with observation, are difficult to delineate — yet there are some marks
that men must see. "They were a people conscious of the
special call of God to gather the holy forces into or-

348

ganization, and create and arrange for permanent centers of fire throughout the land, that the world might know His glory. These people seemed under an awe-inspiring conviction that God had called them, and in this day of need, to this great work. This sense of a divine call to this great and definite purpose, would of itself have glorified this Assembly. There is so much indefiniteness in the holiness work, and when there has seemed to be an aim, it has usually been only far enough to lead into deeper uncertainty, so much aiming at nothing definite, and hitting it, that to find a people with a great, definite purpose, clear and evident before the gaze of men, thrilled all hearts.

"That these people had received the promises, and like Abraham, did not stagger under them, but were looking all difficulties and sacrifices, and sufferings, and even impossi-

The Vision of Seers bilities in the face, knowing that with God all things are possible, and counting all things but loss for the excellency of being conformed to the purposes of His death, not only in their own experience, but in the salvation of the world, glorified the Assembly. The coming of so many noble men and women with the vision of seers, especially from the Southland — many sections being represented, and different organizations — all with radiant and satisfied faces, that the Lord was leading in the way of unity and enlarged victory, was inspiring.

"There was no note of doubt or doubtful questioning, but only arrangements and adjustments for the forward march. The enthusiasm was that of men who see the certainties of

The Special Call things in divine light, who distinctly hear the voice of God calling to heroic duty. The Assembly excelled in the elements which usually enter into large gatherings of holiness people, the preaching was full of the strong meat of the gospel, the hours of prayer were seasons of holy triumph, the altar services were full of victory, souls were converted and sanctified, and believers were edified; but underneath and over, and emphasizing all these, and sweeping on, was the special call and inborn purpose, the prophetic outlook, and manifest divine guidance which made this meeting peculiar unto itself.

"We have been told about 'every good and perfect gift.' It seems that among good gifts there are some which are more excellent. So it is of the blessings which come to the world through the gatherings of saints.

Blessings Which There can be no gathering of holy people
Abide for worship, but there will be prayer and praise, with the Word and the divine blessing, and more or less souls will be refreshed. God has promised that He will pour water upon him that is thirsty, and floods upon the dry ground, and I fancy that there can be no such gathering of the saints, but what this promise is fulfilled. We have seen many meetings when the parched earth was moistened, and sometimes there were floods enough to change the face of things somewhat. But the shower passes, the flood sweeps over the earth, the sun comes out, and, while many remember the rain, it is only a little time until things are as dry and parched as ever. There is another class of promises, such as tell us of more permanent things, that He will cause waters to break out in the wilderness, and streams in the desert. These represent blessings which abide. 'I will open rivers in high places, and fountains in the midst of the valleys,' tells us of blessings which abide to pour their richness for ever. This Assembly was not gathering blessings from the skies for the day, but to open ever flowing rivers of love and salvation to the ends of the earth, and as long as time endures."

In closing his account of his homeward journey from Chicago, Dr. Bresee pays this touching and noble tribute to Rev. Joseph Knotts, his closest, dearest friend, of whom so much is said in preceding chapters: "As I approach El Paso, there is a shadow upon my soul. Here alone, among strangers, died the best friend I ever had. And yet to know that a man can go steadily on, doing that to which he feels called, expecting any time to lie down and die, and yet not waver, give his dying word to a stranger, and pass on as he would have gone to another day of toil, glorifies human personality. It was from these valleys that such a soul, with such a large capacity, such gentleness, heroism, and unconquerable courage, went up to God."

CHAPTER XXXVIII.

In some sense the General Assembly of 1907, marked perhaps the greatest epoch in the illustrious career of Dr. Bresee, and I take it that this will be an appropriate place *Characteristics* in the narrative of his life to tell some- *of Dr. Bresee* thing of the impressions which I gathered of his real nature and personality during the many happy years that I was privileged to enjoy his friendship and confidence.

His noble brow, strong, regular features, large flashing black eyes, and firm but restful mouth, were an appropriate index of the great soul that dwelt within. His complexion *Appearance and* was dark, and until his later years, his *Manner* hair was black. His habitual expression was one of strength and repose. Benevolence and benignancy shone in his countenance.

He was a loyal and self-sacrificing friend. Those who were thus favored, were always sure of his hearty support and unwavering devotion. In his greeting of friends he was *As a Friend* very warm and cordial, and loved to have them visit him, and accept of the hospitality of himself and his good wife. Although manifold in his labors, and always busy, he gladly took time to converse with all who came to see him. He was the soul of hospitality, and when his friends or brethren were sick and needed a home, he welcomed them with the cordial concurrence of Mrs. Bresee, to their abode. Though his toils and responsibilities were never ended, he was always glad to meet a friend and have a chat with him. His face would light up with pleasure, his greeting would be hearty, and his whole manner would show that he was really pleased to see the caller.

He did not dwell in inaccessible heights. He made no pretense of being superhuman, never patronized others, and was entirely free from that sanctimoniousness which mars the character of some really good and giftd men. Plain and unassuming, he was easily approachable, and had a rare knack of putting people at their ease, and making them feel at home. About him there was nothing forbidding or austere. He was intensely human, had a keen sense of humor, and greatly enjoyed a good joke. In the midst of the cares and responsibilities that rested so heavily upon him, he would frequently relax and tell a funny story. He would laugh very heartily at anything which was really witty or humorous. On these occasions he would often purse his lips, smile, bow his head a little, nod two or three times, and then laugh aloud, sometimes until the tears came to his eyes. I shall never forget his ringing laughter on these occasions.

Great as he was, he entertained a poor opinion of himself. He was unusually modest. I never knew him to boast. Always underrating his own ability and attainments, he felt

Humility that he had accomplished very little for the Savior whom he loved so fervently, and served so devotedly. He seemed to enjoy talking of his own deficiencies, laughed over the difficulty which he had ever experienced in spelling, acknowledged that his method of preparing sermons was bad, insisted that he had a poor memory, and deplored the fact that his religious experience fell far short of the spiritual life of many of his brethren.

He was an example of industry, a tireless worker. Possessed of great physical strength, he was able to endure almost unremitting toil. He habitually did the work of three ordinary men. I once asked him many years ago:

"Why, Brother Bresee, when do you rest?" His laconic reply was, "Nights."

He had remarkable intensity of purpose. Having once determined upon a course of action, he pressed on toward the goal, undaunted by opposition, undeterred by difficulty. He learned early in life the value of desperation in bringing things to pass. And yet he was not stubborn, or unduly set on having his own way. He valued highly the counsel of those whom he esteemed.

I never knew another man who had such perfect control of two things that are most difficult to manage, time and money. I take it that our ability to dominate these, and to prevent them from getting away from us *Control of Time* without being fully utilized, is in a large *and Money* degree the measure of our strength.

Dr. Bresee was hardly ever in a hurry, or greatly pressed for time. He carefully planned to meet all his appointments on time. He possessed singular precision. He saw a long way ahead, and allowed himself ample time for preparation. It could be truthfully said of him that he was never late at a religious service, and never missed a boat or other public conveyance. He allowed himself a sufficient margin, and enjoyed his spare time, not before he started, but after he had boarded his train. I have been in his home when the time came to start for church. He would say: "Everybody who is going to church get ready." Then he would put on his own hat and overcoat, and stand in an attitude of brisk expectancy until the others were ready. If they showed any signs of lagging, he had a pleasant but effective way of stirring them into action.

Although extremely generous and freehanded, he so managed his financial affairs as always to have a little money on hand. When taxes were due, he had the funds to pay them. When a trip was to be made, he had the requisite means to make it with. When a friend was in dire need, he was always able to put his hands upon the amount required to meet the emergency. I could give many instances of this latter trait that came within by own observation.

He was gifted as a writer, and had a literary style of rare purity, power, and originality. In some of his editorials he reached a height of nobility and grandeur which will bear comparison with the greatest utterances of Milton, Bunyan, and our own Lincoln. He had a marvelous genius of expression, and coined many phrases which came into very general use in holiness circles. Among these are: "The quick to-morrows;" "bring things to pass;" "we went out under the stars;" "Holy Ghost intensity;" "get heaven open;" "the sun never sets in the morning;" "the eastern gate;" "the inner temple;" and "the unseen holy."

Gift of Expression and Literary Style

He loved nature, was in touch with her in all her moods, and could truly interpret them. Although entirely unconscious of the fact, he was a real poet. He never made a study of versification, or attempted metrical composition of any kind, but his sermons were full of true poesy, and many of his writings were poetical gems. He was a master of pathos, and instinctively knew all the avenues that reach the human heart. The following are a few of the almost innumerable passages that I could quote from his writings and sermons, which are fragrant with the sweetest flowers of poetry:

A Poet in Soul

"Have you nothing but earth, no love, no joy, no hope that flows from the upper springs, that never dry up? A great inheritance awaits you. Come to the Father's house. Infinite love and home and heaven may be yours."

"A word fitly spoken, a joyous, happy word, that scatters sunlight all around. A word that is a seed of truth in a human heart, that will live and grow and be a beauty and a joy forever. A word that will point to higher ways and greater success, and some blessed triumphs. A word that should live in the memory — a golden band to the heart

355

that uttered it for ever. How great the privilege to speak kind, sweet, loving words, to bless human hearts and make the world seem bright. But words not fitly spoken — how sad, how keen, how cruel they are."

"It must be back to Christ — the Christ of the dusty highways; the Christ of sorrows, and acquainted with grief; the Christ of the poor, the downcast, the friendless; the Christ who reached out to the 'woman who was a sinner;' and then the Christ who, in that last prayer, cried for His church, 'Father, make them holy through thy truth.' "

"You are so absorbed in your own thought or experience, or in the special work that the Lord has given you to do, that you forget to stretch out your hands and speak a kindly word to that one you pass by. Not that you do not feel kindly toward him or her, but you are absorbed. There are those who have heard your testimony, who have been drawn to you, and are willing for you to say some sweet word out of your heart to them — but you pass on, and they are disappointed, and finally grieved. They are disappointed in you, and you have become a trial, and possibly, a stumbling-block in their way. That kind word and sweet look which were not given to them, personally become your loss for ever. I beseech you, dear friends, to be careful and break the bread of life through your own care for hungry ones, the hunger of whose souls you have not seen. Those whose hands you have not pressed, and into whose eyes you have not really looked."

"One life is ours. One transient life. Yesterday we were not here; tomorrow we will be gone. We are heavily freighted with intelligence, conscience, moral obligation, clear light, a knowledge of right and wrong, all the responsibilities of destiny. God over all has revealed Himself to us. Eternal life and glory are our inheritance in holiness."

"Horeb's bush is the figure of a heaven-baptized soul, whose fruitage is the flaming glory of the Divine Presence.'

"Repent. That word dawns upon thy soul like the star of Bethlehem upon the vision of the Eastern Magi. It means

356

to thee that a new King is born. It means to gather thy store and away — out of the country — to pour thy treasure at His feet. Repent. It means that thou hast seen the vision of God. That cross which Constantine saw beneath the sun bearing the inscription, '*In hoc signo vinces*,' thou hast seen, with its bleeding, dying victim bearing to you the inscription — 'In this hope' — thou hast seen in it a new possibility; it may be but ·dimly, but thou hast seen; and written beneath it was pardon, freedom, purity. Thou hast seen an opening beyond it, in the blue ether, a jeweled portal, and over it inscribed, 'Life, abounding life, eternal life.' Something of this vision has come to thee."

"The indwelling Holy Ghost will bring about our personal transfiguration. He makes the place of His abode all glorious. I see human faces that shine with a glory like the rainbow around the throne. We need not wonder at it. He has made man for his own abode."

"This cripple was, in many things, well surrounded. He lived in a favored land of beauty and blessing. Sky of deepest azure bent above him. A landscape of more than ordinary attractions met his gaze. Works of rarest art were all about him — he lay at the beautiful gate of the magnificent temple — and more than all, he was at the entrance of the house of God. But none of these things availed him aught. It was the name of the Nazarene — that name and the power of the Holy Ghost — that made him whole.

"There are many who live within a few minutes walk of the house of God, who never enter. Oceans of selfishness and mountains of prejudice lie between them and the house of the Lord."

"Brethren, we have the pry under a thousand souls, and every one must lift! Lift every pound of strength! Lift till we see stars! Lift until we see beyond the stars! But, Brethren, we may lift till every eyes is strained from its socket, and it will do no good, if Jesus of Nazareth walk not in the midst. When Peter lifted, almighty power wrought."

"Peter hastened to assure them that not any power of

their own had wrought it — it was not in them or of them; but *'The Prince of Life,'* who was dead and is alive forevermore. The marvel was, the mystery was, the glory was, that the Holy Ghost took that Name, that uplifted Name, and smote the hearts of men, and gathered them to the bosom of God."

"There is not a text in the Bible three feet away from Calvary. God has put nothing in His book that is not within easy reach of His dying Son. Nothing will come into your life that will not be under the outstretched hand on the cross. So in everything, through everything, tell men of 'The Prince of Life.' "

"The whole Christian movement sprang out of the old conditions like a bird out of its shell, and yet was persecuted to death by the old church. But, finding new life in death, springing up out of its own ashes, rising out of its own blood, it conquered its way. There is something marvelously strange in the history of the Christian church. Persecuted, bleeding, dying, she draws strength as from her own blood, and, by the hand of God, puts on power in the midst of weakness. But, becoming strong, powerful, influential, she in turn, becomes the oppressor, and persecutes the same truth for which she has been persecuted. Her triumph becomes the strength of the oppressor. Thus, has history over and over again repeated itself."

"A sanctified man is at the bottom of the ladder. He is but a child — a clean child. He is now to learn; to grow; to rise; to be divinely enlarged and transformed. The Christ in him is to make new and complete channels in and through every part of his being — pouring the stream of heaven through his thinking, living, devotement and faith. The divine battery — His manifest presence — is to be enlarged. The truth of God is to be revealed, and poured through the soul and lips, with holy fire and divine unction, more and more aboundingly. I am convinced that a lack of the conception of these facts has been the death warrant to many a soul. A lack of personal realization of the fact that

I, myself, must stir myself up, has brought wreck and ruin to many. God will stir him up who stirs up himself, until he comes 'unto the measure of the fullness of the stature of Christ.' "

"It must be made possible for man to be forgiven, and reconciled unto Him, and the first work of Jesus was the making of the atonement, but in doing that He contended with the powers of darkness; Satan gathered his emissaries; hell poured forth her legions; the heavens were black with the power of darkness; the earth trembled under the tread of the mighty contending forces. But that wounded, bleeding hand; that broken heart, held the hosts of hell at bay. For dreadful hours billows from the pit broke over Him.

"At last, He lifted His eyes, and looking out into the darkness and beyond, said, 'It is finished;' and when the cloud of the darkness of the conflict passed away, there waved above the cross in holy triumph, the banner of salvation, and streams of heavenly light and human hope sprang out from it."

"The Son of God has made the darkest place of human history the most luminous place in this universe. Everything is dim beside it. Ten thousand suns gathered into one, would be blackness itself compared to the unspeakable glory of the cross of Christ. The cross is the great, suffering, infinite, crowning glory of God. It is the mighty, struggling, dying effort to do what omnipotence can not do; to accomplish the impossible; to cause infinite justice and infinite mercy to kiss each other over the brow of a doomed man, and folding their arms about him, lift him to a new possibility. To the amazement of a moral universe, it is done. Infinite love, infinite suffering bring it to pass. A door of hope is opened for man. A possibility is set before us. There is light for darkness, purity for impurity."

"There is no top to the divine heights; there is no bottom to the divine depths; there is no shore to the ocean of God's perfections. The soul bathes and drinks, and drinks and bathes, and yet I stand awe-inspired in the presence of the infinite glory, which, though I come nigh, is ever unapproachable; though I bathe my soul in it, and am filled with its measureless heights and depths and lengths and breadths, overwhelms me."

"Out of the great ocean of eternity, out of the great depths of the infinite, mysteriously comes the divine message. Love brooded over the depths, and mercy and justice found new relationship in atoning favor. On the wings of love and power, the redeeming forces were borne to the altitudes of Calvary, where they were compressed by dying agony, and the Holy Ghost came to scatter, like showers, love and mercy and power upon the hearts of men. And these showers and tempests of love and salvation, these irrigating streams from the mountains of His holiness, find their way as a divine utterance to human hearts.

"There is, to me, in this, one marvelous — almost awful thought. Back of the rain and snow, the gentle showers and storms and water brooks, are all the forces of the infinite God. God does not fail. The rain and the snow come, and the earth is made fertile and productive, and no man can stop Him in His work. A man might undertake to thwart God's purposes. He might, by incessant labor, succeed in keeping some little spot from producing, and yet, a few feet away, the grass would spring up to mock him. Every shower that falls, every murmuring stream, every blade of grass, every flower, every head of grain and waving harvest, laughs him to scorn; vegetation still goes on; rain and snow come, and the earth buds. God is not dead. A man may not work with Him, and thus starve himself, but the great purpose of God goes on. So it is with His utterance to men. Out of the depths of the heart of God, by infinite power and love, it comes, borne on the wings of the Holy Ghost, to human hearts."

"Worship rises high above all forms. If it attempts to find utterance through them, it will set them on fire, and glow and burn in their consuming flame, and rise as incense to God; if it waits to hear His infinite will and eternal love, it spreads its pinions to fly to His bosom, there to breathe out its unutterable devotion."

"It is true then, there is a baptism with fire. My friends, no man can have the baptism with God, which means the entrance of the Divine Presence into the soul as its abiding King, enthroned for two worlds, who does not receive the heart of the infinite into his being. Talk about a further baptism than the indwelling God! Oh, no; he who needs that, needs all; he who could desire it, does not know the billows of glory which His fulness of presence is."

Dr. Bresee was a man of dauntless courage. Threats and intimidation had no effect upon him. He regarded them not, and pursued his purpose with unyielding tenacity. He *Courage and Gentleness* feared no one but his Maker. Nothing could induce him to compromise the essential principles of truth and righteousness, in order to avert trouble, or gain a selfish purpose. Naturally resolute and determined, his will was somewhat imperious, but, as the years went by, and he was melted and moulded by the Holy Spirit, he became one of the meekest and gentlest of men. He frequently quoted the verse, "the servant of God must not strive," and insisted that, in yielding our own rights, privileges, and preferences, we most truly conquer. He freely forgave those who injured him most, and gladly restored them to the fullest friendship and fellowship, when they acknowledged their wrong-doing, and asked for pardon.

And yet in a very marked manner he combined the lion and the lamb. In his late years the lamb greatly predominated, but occasionally, when his indignation was aroused, those deep, mysterious eyes of his would seem to flash fire, and his stern denunciation of sin would remind one of the roar of the lion.

He was hesitant about judging the motives of others. He knew the weaknesses and infirmities of men, and expected less from them than he did in his younger manhood. He made full allowance for human frailty. In this connection,

I note that he marked with approval this statement by Gladstone:

"Nothing grows upon me so much with lengthening life as the sense of the difficulties, or rather the impossibilities, with which we are beset whenever we attempt to take to ourselves the functions of the Eternal Judge, (except in reference to ourselves where judgment is committed to us), and to form any accurate idea of relative merit and demerit, good and evil, in actions. The shades of the rainbow are not so nice, and the sands of the seashore are not such a multitude, as are all the subtle, shifting, blending forms of thought and of circumstances that go to determine the character of us and of our acts. But there is One that seeth plainly, and judgeth righteously."

Feeling this, Dr. Bresee was exceedingly slow to condemn one whom he regarded as a brother in the Lord. While admitting that the word or action was ill-timed, in bad taste, or perhaps essentially wrong, he would not readily conclude that the person at fault had committed an actual sin. He gave full weight to ignorance, weakness, thoughtlessness, foolishness, unconscious prejudice, etc. When a man had been fortunate enough to be admitted into his friendship and confidence, he would loyally defend and support him until he was absolutely convinced that he had been deceived, and that the person thus trusted was a willful offender.

His heart went out to those who were more or less outcasts, and who had lost the confidence of Christian people generally. He still hoped for their spiritual recovery, and did his utmost to help them back into the *Sympathy for* kingdom. For instance, if a preacher fell *Outcasts* into open sin, such as drunkenness, or other immorality, and afterward professed repentance, Dr. Bresee would, not only give him temporal help, but would offer him an opportunity to preach. I will mention only one instance of this nature, although I am cognizant of several.

Many years ago an extremely eloquent and brilliant minister came to Los Angeles. He had been a drunkard, and for that reason was compelled to withdraw from the ministry. But he professed repentance, and restoration to the favor of God. He gave some glowing testimonies of the work of grace in his heart. That was enough for Dr. Bresee. He took the stranger to his home, gave him a comfortable room in the upper story of the barn, and had him eat with the family. Without formally employing him as assistant pastor, he gave him an opportunity to preach in the First Church, and for some time the returned prodigal ran well. He was a genius in the pulpit, and the people were delighted with his eloquent, able, and expository sermons. He presented the great truths of holiness in a most spiritual and delightful manner. But after a few months, he fell from grace, and suddenly disappeared from the community.

Because of this charitable attitude to professedly penitent sinners, and this earnest desire to assist them into a useful position in the church and community, Dr. Bresee was often accused of covering sin. Many times I have heard him exclaim, with a smile: "They say that I am the friend of every scallawag." Truly, his great heart was overflowing with love and sympathy for all who were in especial need. His hand was never raised against the backslider and the fallen, but, on the contrary, it was held out to succor them. He hated sin, but he loved the sinner. He recognized modern phariseeism, and realized the ravages which it has wrought in the holiness movement; and yet he had great charity for those servants of God who fell into that awful delusion of Satan, who, instead of tenderly loving the backslider, and doing their utmost to win him back to Jesus, held themselves aloof from him, or, worse still, pushed him further into the mire of sin. He knew that they, too, were backslidden, and needed to be restored.

The general trend of his conversation was serious. He knew the world, and how cruel, hollow, and superficial it was. He realized the condition of the great body of the professing church. But, while he was usually serious, he was invariably cheerful. Of course, always his chief interest was in the deep things of God, and in the prosperity of the kingdom of Christ on earth. During the last years of his life, he came to have an extremely vivid apprehension of the paramount importance of the manifestation of God in men; and he insisted more and more that, in order to live up to our highest possibilities, and do the work that God had given us, we must have frequent and mighty revelations and demonstrations of the Holy Spirit. This was the keynote and under-current of nearly all the great sermons of his later years. In this connection I will relate an incident which occurred about three months before his death.

It was Sunday afternoon, shortly after his return from the morning service in the First Church. He was in the sitting-room, engaged in conversation with Mrs. Ella Palmer *An Impressive* and myself. She asked him what he thought *Incident* of the second coming of Christ. He replied that, while he devoutly believed in it, yet since God had shown him his exalted privileges here and now, as a regnant soul, dwelling in the heavenlies in Christ, and filled with all the fulness of God, he had not given the subject much thought. Knowing as I did, what was back of these few simple words, and how much they signified, I was profoundly moved, and a tide of holy rapture thrilled my being, and suffused my eyes with tears.

He laid constantly growing emphasis upon soul life, the spiritual progress of the Christian after he was sanctified, and the vital necessity of a constant walk with God. He *Soul Life* felt that with nearly all of the holiness people, the standard of spiritual life and victory and fellowship with God, was too low. Let me quote from his wonderful sermon called "The Lifting of the Veil;"

"The great thing is Christian life — soul life. There is some Christian experience in this earth. We thank God for what there is. But I am more and more convinced that anything like a creditable article of Christian experience is now, and always has been, a scarce commodity. Men and women who have passed the first and second stations of initiatory work, in whom carnality is destroyed, who are crucified to the world, in whom Jesus Christ lives His life on earth, who go on with steady victory through the blood of the Lamb and the word of their testimony, are not numerous.

"I have examined with a good deal of interest, Charles Wesley's hymns on consecration and sanctification, as given in the Methodist Hymnal — about sixty of them. Their teaching is very clear in reference to the doctrine of entire sanctification. Over *The Hymnology* and over is repeated the deep, impassioned *of the Church* cry, the promise of God, and the way to enter in. That men are to enter now, by faith, is plainly taught. These hymns give rare, little glimpses of experience which comes after one has entered, but viewed more as a hope.

"One of these hymns, 'Wrestling Jacob,' thought by some to be the greatest ever written, not only delineates the way, but dwells upon the glory and triumph of the obtained experience. But why the fact that all, or nearly all, of those hymns deal only with the transitional period, if it be not that this was the place where the church at that day largely lived?

"The hymnology of the worship of holy hearts is scarce. The great hymns — those most familiar to us, which the fathers and mothers have sung — are mostly a cry out of the darkness, a cry for help, the cry of need. 'Rock of Ages,' 'Jesus Lover of My Soul,' and among another class of singers, 'Nearer My God to Thee,' and 'Lead, Kindly Light,' are all prized, but are they not chiefly a cry out of the darkness for light and help?

"I hardly know where to turn for singable hymns of real devotion. We have what is called a rich hymnology. But the hymns are so largely, simply sentimental, or descriptive, or the cry of an imprisoned soul for deliverance, or an endangered one for help! I admit, good in their places, but hardly the songs to be sung by holy hearts at the feet of Him whom we love better than all else. The songs of worship and adoration — where shall we find them? Now, why this scarcity, except it be from the scarcity of soil out of which such hymns spring? Much longing, hunger, struggle, theology, but little real adoration.

"This is why we delight in such songs as that of Mrs. James:

Since my eyes were fixed on Jesus,
I've lost sight of all beside,
So enchained my spirit's vision,
Looking at the crucified.

"And that other little chorus, 'Hallelujah, Amen:'

How oft in holy converse
With Christ my Lord alone;
I seem to hear the millions
That sing around His throne.

"We have but little triumphant literature. It is true that we have more of this than we have of hymnology, in the same way that there is more of life than of genius. We have biographies which burn and glow, not alone with service, but with red-hot devotion of soul to God. And now and then utterances have come down through the ages, which are the thoughts of God, melted and recast in human souls, but they are not plentiful.

"We have testimony and living in these days — manifestation of hearts which are burning furnaces unto God, sending out their utterances like red-hot fire balls, and their lives are rivers of life in this world — but there is not much of it.

"There are churches which are pentecostal, not simply in name, but in the presence and power of the Holy Ghost, where men and women walk in His fellowship, and are filled with His heavenly comfort, to whom earth is a little antechamber to the skies, a little standing-place to stretch their pinions for immortal flight — churches unworldly, heavenly-minded, divinely-filled — but they are evidently scarce.

"Our apprehension of religion, which gives to us our type, is low, almost, if not altogether, unworthy of Him who emptied Himself of the infinite glory to take our place; who, though He was rich, became poor, that we, through His poverty might be rich—of Him who wrought out our redemption in pain, in infinite heart agony, in sacrifice for sin, in the manifestation of the divine power; who reinstated and re-endowed our humanity with eternal glory, and to make it effectual, came as the Eternal Spirit to make men holy, 'that they might know Thee the only true God, and Jesus Christ whom Thou hast sent.'

"We linger this morning near the gate-way of this most excellent glory, to say to men — the King invites."

Much might be said, and with profit, on the subject of Dr. Bresee's methods and ability as a preacher. He told me that for several years of his ministry, he chose a text as a site

Pulpit Preparation

for a sermon, and with little idea of developing the portion of Scripture thus chosen. He would treat it rather as an appropriate setting or background for his discourse, and explore the universe for material with which to construct his homiletic edifice. As he thus built, he kept getting farther away from his scriptural foundation. As the years went by, God showed him a better way, and he came to regard his text more as the entrance to an inexhaustible mine of truth, or as the opening into illimitable rivers of oil, from which it would gush forth in greater volume and power as he continued to bore his well.

During the twenty-six years that I knew him, he did not habitually search for his themes, but he treasured the faint and gentle intimations that came to him from time to time regarding his pulpit subjects. He took these as coming from God, and carefully noted them, for he well knew how quickly these winged messengers from the Lord took their flight and disappeared. When a theme came to him in this manner, he would mediate upon it, and talk about it to his wife and friends. He would often discuss with me these inchoate sermons. He would usually begin in some such way as this: "Brother Girvin, I am trying to prepare a sermon on such and such a text, and I would like to have you help me. There are some difficulties, and I need your suggestions." While I knew that he was perfectly sincere in this, I was also aware that my proper attitude toward him was that of a learner. Nevertheless, I sometimes permitted myself to make a suggestion.

In this way, he accomplished two things. First, his preaching was always in line with his intellectual and spiritual development, and the subjects chosen were evidently revealed to him by the Holy Spirit, as best suited to his own needs, and those of his hearers. Second, he never lacked a supply of fresh, new sermons.

Let me say at this point that his sermons were thoroughly prepared. He did not trust his ability, skill, or experience. He did not rely on the inspiration of the moment or the occasion to carry him through. He always did his best, and gave his best in sustained, prayerful thought and study.

Having let the sermon saturate mind and heart, the next step in his process of preparation, was to take his pen in hand and prayerfully write a sermon outline. These outlines were quite full, containing perhaps one-quarter of the discourse, as afterward preached. One characteristic of his sermons was their remarkable fulness of thought. Some of them could easily be expanded into books. They were marvelously rich in ideas, illustrations, and imagery. He was gifted with historical imagination in a high degree, and would begin with a vivid picture of the scene of the text.

The final stage of the process of preparation was what he called "soaking" his sermon. For the last twenty-five years of his life it was his custom to go to bed for this purpose. He would then close his eyes and review over and over his sermon outline, until he had committed it to memory, not exactly verbatim, but sufficiently to enable him to repeat it substantially from beginning to end. He admitted that this was very slavish work, and that it would probably have been better if he had adopted a less laborious method in his early ministry, but stated that he was too old to change.

His eloquence was of a high type, and sometimes so fiery and impetuous that his hearers were carried away, almost forgot where they were, and were seemingly transported into realms of glory. His sermons abound-
His Eloquence ed in lofty climaxes, and, as he rose in the scale of inspired and impassioned utterance of the sublimities and infinitudes of the grace of God, he took on in his personal appearance much of the glory and grandeur of the mighty gospel which he proclaimed. His eyes seemed to burn, his face shine, and his whole being glow, as with all his physical, mental, and spiritual power, he preached a salvation which destroyed sin, and lifted the pardoned culprit from the lowest depths of degradation to the shining summits of the mountains of God.

Few men had such unction as he. The fire of God seemed to burn through his being, as he proclaimed with all his might the glorious message of full salvation. His flashing eyes, rich and vibrant voice, and compelling
His Unction presence, all heightened the effect of his fiery eloquence. As we listened with rapt attention to the fervent appeals of this "regnant man," we felt that his great soul was all ablaze with the love of God shed abroad in his heart by the Holy Ghost.

I heard him first in the summer of 1889, at Beulah Park campmeeting, in Oakland, California. He preached on the divine Presence in the pulpit. I do not remember much of what he said, but all around him there seemed to be an atmosphere aglow with heavenly radiance, and palpitating with the very life of God. I was moved as I had never been before by the preaching of any man.

His sermons were always expository, and his comments on the sacred text were analytical, comprehensive, interesting, illuminating, and full of a divine unction that opened the deepest fountains in the hearts of his hearers. Most of his illustrations were drawn from the Word of God. His entire ministry was evangelistic, his preaching was greatly blessed by the Lord, and the history of his pastorates is one of unbroken revivals. Thousands of persons in this land today, who were converted and sanctified through his ministry, rise up and call him blessed.

He was a consummate master of all the noble arts of oratory. Although slow, deliberate, and apparently not perfectly at ease, at the beginning of his discourses, he soon gained a complete freedom, and displayed a thorough command of gesture, his style of delivery being at once natural and pleasing, impressive and bold.

CHAPTER XXXIX.

His Use of Music — Family Relationships — His Reading — His Cordiality — Two Pictures — Strong Faith — Free From Fanaticism — A Man of Prayer — A Marvelous Illumination — His Public Prayers — His Knowledge of Ritual and Hymnology — Love of the Bible — As a Leader — A Wise Counselor

Dr. Bresee was very fond of music, but lacked tune. He had a wonderful voice. It was strong, vibrant, resonant, rich, and unusually musical. I never heard a more perfect voice. In range, compass, volume, tone, and flexibility, it was exceptional. Its quality was very fine, and it was so expressive as to respond to every demand made upon it to convey delicate shades of feeling and thought. It matched the man.

The following characterization is very apropos; it is from the pen of Miss Clemie Gay, who for many years has taken a leading part in the song service at the First Church in Los Angeles.

"Dr. Bresee was greatly appreciative of spiritual singing. He realized that good spiritual poetry, combined with fitting and expressive music, often makes half the worship of an individual or a congregation. He felt that it was necessary to the spiritual uplift of the meeting that every one take part in the singing; and he often told the people to sing whether they could keep the tune or not. He said that as each person took part in the prayerful song, or the outburst of praise, and was thereby blessed in his own heart, so the meeting took on new power, and the Holy Spirit could get an opportunity to work on hearts, as otherwise He could not.

"Dr. Bresee disliked very much to have a few paid singers 'up on the shelf,' as he expressed it, to do the singing for the people. He would just as soon have some one else eat his dinner for him. He loved singing from the heart, and in the Spirit, and often called on one or more with the gift of song, in solo, quartette, or duet, to give a message to the people.

"He loved the old-time songs of praise and prayer, and yet liked many of the newer ones also. While not a leader in singing, there were a few songs and choruses which he sometimes would venture to start, trusting to others to catch it up and carry it through. Who that ever heard him will forget the way he would start 'Rock of Ages, cleft for me, Let me hide myself in Thee,' with such devotion in it, or that lively chorus, 'Oh, glory, glory, glory, Oh glory to the Lamb,' or that other one, 'There is power, power, wonder working power, In the blood of the Lamb,' and how he would emphasize 'power.'

"But it was in the testimony meetings that he especially appreciated good singing interspersed with the testimonies; and, when pastor of the First Church, if he had Brother R. F. Shaw as song leader, and Miss Lettie McKee (now Mrs. David Moncton), or Miss Esther Killinger (now Mrs. Carpenter), at the organ, he felt that he was amply reinforced for a good, spiritual meeting. He was a peerless leader of testimony meetings, never seeming to shut a person off, yet so directing, exhorting, and encouraging, that people seldom took advantage of him. He was especially courteous to old people, saying sometimes, 'They'll not be here long.' He believed in enthusiasm in religion, was very set against formality and coldness, and was an adept at arousing fervor, and stirring up the people to devotion."

He dearly loved his parents, and saw to it that they had a home with him for many years prior to their death. During the more than fifty-five years that intervened between his marriage and his death, *Family* *Relationship* he was most devoted to his noble wife, and she to him. Their union was ideal. He was a fond father, and was greatly loved and revered by all his children.

Although to a large extent self-educated, he was a man

of ripe culture, and very extensive reading. He generally bought the books that he read, and thus gradually accumu-

His Library lated a valuable library. Surrounded by the books which he had acquired during all the years of his ministry, and which represented his intellectual, and to some degree, his spiritual growth, he prepared his sermons, pursued his studies, and conducted his voluminous correspondence. His library was rich, of course, in theological works, sacred history, and the biographies of the great men and women in the kingdom of God through all the ages. It was well supplied with books which sought to explain and elucidate the inspired writings of Isaiah and the apostle Paul.

He was fond of poetry and philosophy, and appreciated the importance of historical studies. He read with relish, and enjoyed discussing the works of Carlyle and Emerson, the former of whom had a marked influence on his life and literary style. The sermons of the mighty preachers of his own and other times occupied a conspicuous place in his collection of books.

Prominent among the many volumes which contributed to his culture in the earlier years of his ministry, and constituted measurably his literary and theological equipment, were the following: Delineation of Roman Catholicism, by Charles Elliott, D. D.; Illustrations of Biblical Literature, by James Townley, D.D.; Butler's Analogy; The Laws of Figurative Language, by John Lord, and Beacon Lights of History, by D. N. Lord; Meditations on the Actual State of Christianity, by M. Guizot; Mental Philosophy, by Joseph Haven, D.D.; The Cosmos, by Alexander Humboldt; The Immortality of the Soul, by Hiram Mattison, D.D.; Lectures on the English Language, by George P. Marsh; Works of Dr. Stephen Olin; Ecce Deus; Ecco Homo; Credo; Rev. James Saurin's Sermons, translated from the French; History of the Christian Church, by Philip Schaff, D.D.; History of the Reformation, by George P. Fisher; God in Human Thought, by E. H. Gillett; Horace Bushnell's Works; The Influence of

Jesus Christ, by Phillips Brooks; Boston Monday Lectures, by Joseph Cook; Modern Doubt and Christian Belief, by Theodore Christlieb, D.D.; The Theistic Conception of the World, by B. F. Cocker, D.D.; Endeavors After the Christian Life, by James Martineau; Wonders of the Deity, by M. Schele de Vere; History of the Eastern Church, by Arthur Penryn Stanley, D.D.; Rush on the Voice; The Life of Edward Irving, by Mrs. Oliphant; and Doomed Religions, by Rev. J. M. Reid.

He prized most of these highly, and they doubtless had much to do with the trend, at least, of his intellectual and spiritual development. Throughout his ministry he read and studied persistently.

A work called "The Preacher's Lantern," consisting of four large volumes, was very helpful to him for several years, and among his treasures were "The People's Bible," by Joseph Parker. In middle life, he acquired and deeply studied, "The Life and Epistles of Saint Paul," by Conybeare and Howson; "Hours With the Bible," by Cunningham Geike, D.D.; and the works of Rev. Daniel Dorchester, and Bishop Randolph S. Foster. A little later, he became interested in the writings of George Adam Smith, and made a careful study of his works on "Isaiah" and the "Book of the Twelve Prophets." Other favorite volumes found in his library, were the works of Fletcher, John Wesley, Watson, Puncheon, Spurgeon, Millman, Henry Ward Beecher, Gilbert Haven, Henry White Warren, Hugh Price Hughes, William W. Newell, John Hall, and Bishop J. M. Thoburn.

Among his especial favorites were the History of the Reformation, by Merle D'Aubigne; The Throne of Eloquence, by Paxton Hood; the historical works of Bancroft and Motley; Keith on the Prophecies; Channing's Works; Frederick W. Robertson's sermons; Curiosities of Literature, by Disraeli; The Land and the Book, by W. H. Thomson; Max Muller's Works; ten large volumes on Modern Eloquence; and Science and the Bible, by H. W. Morris.

He owned and read with interest, a complete set of Maclaren's sermons, and a prominent place in his library was occupied by the works of Gibbon, Macaulay, Buckle, Prescott, Emerson, and Carlyle.

In the last few years of his life he derived intense pleasure from the writings of W. M. Ramsay, J. H. Jowett, Lewis O. Brastow, Harold Begbie, Charles Silvester Horne, W. K. Fleming, and others. He was especially delighted with the works of Ramsay and Jowett, and I think he bought all their books.

He subscribed for and read two or three of the leading papers of other denominations, as well as the "Homiletic Review," and kept in close touch with the best religious literature of the day.

Dr. Bresee's religion did not make him unhuman, superhuman, or abnormal in any way. He did not hold himself aloof from his fellows, either because he was too good or too busy to have intercourse with them. He *His Cordiality* was approachable, cheerful, congenial, and sociable. All who associated with him, could feel the atmosphere of love and sympathy which he had about him. There was genuine warmth in his greetings, and his face lighted up with manifest pleasure on these occasions.

During the stirring scenes of his long, eventful, and useful life, there were almost innumerable incidents which, if it were practicable to depict them in a volume such as this, would be extremely interesting, but I can not follow him in all of these.

Two pictures, however, still present themselves vividly to my memory. I can see him yet driving his old white horse, not only to and from church, but all over the city of *Two Pictures* Los Angeles, as he diligently visited his people, accompanied generally on these occasions by Mrs. Bresee.

The picture of him still lingers in my mind's eye, as he stood in front of the tabernacle and cordially greeted the people. During the many years that he was able to devote himself to the pastorate of the First Church, he made it a practice to come to the church a little after 9 o'clock every Sunday morning, take his post at the front door, and shake hands with every man, woman, and child who entered the building. He would welcome the folks so heartily, and show so keen an interest in their welfare, that his very greeting was a benediction. He shook hands with from 500 to 1,000 persons every Sunday morning, and, although this involved a considerable expenditure of energy on his part, he was able immediately afterward to go to the platform and begin the morning service. This practice was one of the things that so greatly endeared him to his people.

He thus records a Sabbath in June, 1900: "Sabbath was another day of triumph. It would gladden the heart of an angel to stand at the door of the First Church, and welcome the pilgrims, as they gather on Sabbath mornings; the aged expressing their thanksgiving that once more they are permitted to come to the house of the Lord; and the same joy and gladness in the hearts, and on the faces of the young that it is theirs to be fully given up to God and His service, and to have a place in His house; and the strangers often telling how far they have come to be with us this morning, or that this is their first opportunity to be with us, etc. I count it one of the richest privileges to stand and take them by the hand as they come; and I often pray that I may be permitted to welcome all of them at the Eastern Gate of the New Jerusalem. 'Oh, what a gathering that will be.'"

He had well learned the lesson of emphasizing the things essential to holiness, and minifying those which were not essential. He realized the fundamental importance of oneness among the disciples of Christ, and *Emphasized Unity* knew that, in order to secure and maintain such unity, it was absolutely necessary to accentuate in every possible way our primary and vital points of agreement, and to just as sedulously ignore and overlook our little differences.

He was a man of strong faith. He simply took God at

His word, and waited restfully for the answers to his prayers. His definition of faith was "heartfelt, trustful loyalty to God." He believed that the Lord

Strong Faith had in hand everything that pertained to the welfare of His kingdom; that He would care for and shape the destinies of His saints; and that in some way, He would bring things to pass. One of the passages of Scripture which was especially impressed upon his heart in the last two years of his life, and which he often repeated, was the sixth verse of the sixth chapter of the Gospel of John: "And this he said to prove him: for he himself knew what he would do." The last six words, "he himself knew what he would do," were the portion of the text which he most emphasized. In the midst of the most trying difficulties, and when the responsibilities connected with the various great institutions of the church pressed most heavily upon him, he would smile, and say with joyous emphasis: "Jesus knows what He will do."

I never knew a man who was freer from all forms of fanaticism, and from that presumption which so often masquerades under the guise of faith. He insisted upon our using all the means which were placed at our

Free From disposal, trusting God for the outcome, and
Fanaticism giving Him all the glory. While he frequently prayed for the healing of the sick, and his prayers were marvelously answered in many cases, he never anointed any one with oil. He would pray with and for those who desired to be anointed, but would invariably have some one else do the anointing. His exegesis of the passage in James, referring to anointing the sick, was that the oil was used as a kind of medicine, and that we complied with that requirement when we gave to those who were ill the best remedies at our disposal. He claimed that God healed in all cases, whether means were used or not, and that healing was always divine healing.

He was unusually gifted in prayer. On one occasion, at

a prayermeeting in the old tabernacle, he led in prayer, and the power of God came upon him in a very marked manner.

A Man of Prayer

It seemed as if he led us up and up until we could almost see the jasper walls, and hear the songs of the redeemed. It seemed as if we entered the eastern gate, and were approaching the vast multitudes of angels and men who surrounded the throne. We could almost see the inner temple, and for a moment were in an atmosphere which was full of spiritual power and celestial fragrance. But gradually, with our gifted leader, we receded from the city of gold, and realized that we were still on earth.

On another occasion, not more than two years ago, as Dr. Bresee was leading in prayer at the Sunday school service in the First Church, at Los Angeles, I had a very remark-

A Marvelous Illumination

able experience. We knelt close together on the platform in the Sunday school room. I do not remember what he said, but during his prayer, the Holy Spirit suddenly flashed upon my mind and heart an intense realization that it was my privilege to here and now anticipate and possess in my own being everything that was in heaven — the tree of life, the fountain of life, the river of life, the crown of life, and the glassy sea. It was one of the most wonderful and glorious illuminations and revelations of the deep things of God that I had ever been permitted to enjoy. I immediately spoke to Dr. Bresee about it. He said what I had been shown was the exact truth, and one that had been made plain to him in recent years. I went home with him to dinner that day, and we had a long conversation upon the new truth that had been revealed to me. As a result of this experience, and our talk in regard to it, in which he set forth his convictions upon the subject of our having a real heaven within and around us, I devoted much time to the prayerful study of the Scriptures bearing upon this phase of truth, and was amazed at their teachings. I discovered that the portion of the 12th chapter of Hebrews, which speaks of our coming "unto Mount Sion unto the city of the living God, the heavenly Jerusalem, to an innumerable company of angels, to the general assembly and church of the firstborn, which are written in heaven, to God, the Judge of all, to the spirits of just men made perfect, to Jesus, the Mediator of the new covenant, and to the blood of sprinkling, that speaketh better things than that of Abel" — was in the present tense, viz., "we are come." I next learned that Paul, speaking by inspiration in the first chapter of Ephesians, locates the saints of God in the heavenlies in Christ, in these sublime words: "Blessed be the God and Father of our Lord Jesus Christ, who hath blessed us with all spiritual blessings in heavenly places, in Christ." I found many other Scriptures along the same line, and the uplift of that glorious experience has been permanent in my spiritual life.

He prayed much, and was nearly always in the attitude of prayer. He lived habitually in communion with God. Of his private devotions he spoke little, for he was singularly reticent in regard to the things that were most sacred to him as an individual. Not long since, a stranger gave his testimony in one of the Sunday afternoon meetings at the First Church in Los Angeles, and told an incident of Dr. Bresee's life. He said: "I met him long before this work was started. Our first acquaintance was at a campmeeting at Bennett, Nebraska. When he came on the grounds, the first thing that he said, after greeting the brethren, was: 'Where can I get alone before the meeting?' They showed him the nicely furnished tent that they had prepared for him; but he said that he wanted to be alone. They then refered him to the large tent where the men were to sleep, with nothing but straw in it. He replied, 'That is all I want.' I had heard so much of Dr. Bresee that perhaps I should not have followed him as I did, but I was so anxious to know what he would say and do, that I was guilty of eavesdropping. He went to the tent, parted the flaps, and fairly dove into the straw. For half an hour he prayed as

379

I had never heard any one pray before. The first thing that he said was: 'Lord, keep Bresee out of sight.' He pleaded with God to pour out His Spirit upon us, and Oh, how the fire did fall on that meeting!"

The following prayer was offered by Dr. Bresee at the First Church, in Los Angeles, on Sunday morning, July 9, 1911, the writer taking it down in shorthand:

His Public "Oh, God, our Heavenly Father, we worship and adore. Glory be to the Father; glory be *Prayers* to the Son; glory be to the Holy Ghost. As it was in the beginning, is now, and ever shall be, glory be to God.

"Oh, how we thank Thee, our Heavenly Father, that we are permitted to be in Thy house once again. For many years some of us have been privileged to tread Thine earthly courts. We have walked with the saints of God, who have slipped away from us, and gone sweeping through the gates into the unseen holy; but, Lord, thou hast permitted us to tarry and press our way on and up for a little longer, until our time shall come to ascend and be forever with the Lord. Thou hast been calling other men and other women to join our ranks, and they have held up our hands; they have put their arms of faith about us, and we have been brought along the way until this Sabbath morning, in this month of July, 1911.

"Glory be to Thy Name! Thank God that we ever obeyed Thy call. Thank God that this gospel, sent of God, ever became a living reality to us; that Jesus Christ came by where we were, spoke to our hearts, called us to his bosom, took us in his arms, and said, 'Peace, be still.' Thank God that, though our sins were like mountains, Jesus took them all away. Thank God that, though the billows were about us, he breathed upon them, and the tempest was stilled. Thank God, He took us into the vessel with Him, and brought us safely to the land of perfect love.

"Glory be to God, the time came when the depths of our hearts cried out to the depths of His infinite love, and He showed us the way of a complete consecration to God, and entrance into the Holy of Holies, where the Shekinah spread His glory over us.

"Glory be to God that we have come to know that the blood of Jesus Christ, His Son, cleanseth us from all sin. Thank God that Jesus now is revealed in us, and we have peace, and joy, and victory. (Shouts of 'Hallelujah! Glory to God!) That we have them through the blood of the Lamb, and the word of our testimony. Oh, Lord, we praise Thee that we have been lifted out of the pit. Thank God, our feet are upon the rock, a new song has been put in our mouth, even praise to God, and we are runing up the way, shouting the praises of the Lamb that was slain.

"And now, Lord, we are here this morning to worship Thee, here where we would rather be than any place this side of heaven, here where the smile of Thy love is upon us. Lord, make this the best hour that we ever saw. Let the heavens open upon us in richest benediction. Let the glory of the Lord fall upon every heart this morning, and may we rejoice together in the covenants of Thy love.

"I pray God to bless our dear brother, the pastor. Put upon him the anointings of God. Let heaven break loose around him this morning. Give him a depth of unction, and a breadth of spiritual power greater than anything that he has ever known. Sweep down upon him, Oh, thou Shekinah of God, this morning, until he will not know himself.

"We pray God that the Word may be in the power of the Holy Ghost, that all our hearts may be filled with love divine, and that we be lifted nearer to the great white throne. Oh, Lord, we pray that Thy people may be united in their cry, with the cry of the prophets and apostles and saints and martyrs in all ages. Hear our united cry, as we put it in the name of Jesus this morning, and open the windows of heaven upon us. Lift the everlasting doors, and let Thy glory fall upon every heart.

"Oh, Lord, we pray for Thy coming everywhere, for all the churches, for all who preach the fulness of the gospel of the Son of God, for all who are sick and dying and bereaved — for all our sick and dying and bereaved ones — Oh, Jesus, come and walk among us.

"We pray for our missionaries in foreign lands, that God may abundantly rule and overrule with mighty power in the work of Thy love.

"We pray, Oh, God, for our university. Oh, Lord, we are looking to have it grow to the pattern shown us in the heavenlies, where there will be a fire burning up to God, the red hot lava of divine love, flowing on and on, through the oceans, and over the mountains, to the glory of Jesus Christ.

"Lord, we are waiting for Thy mighty leadership to lead us on. Oh, hear our cry this morning, and answer, not according to our feeble asking, but according to Thy riches in glory; for Thine own sake let it come to our waiting hearts.

> And when the mighty work is wrought,
> Receive Thy waiting bride;
> Give us in heaven a happy lot,
> With all the sanctified.

"Lord, we are coming; we know the mansions will be ready, and that Jesus will come and take us to His own divine abode. Bring us on in triumph, that we may be forever Thine."

He closed with the Lord's prayer.

The following is a transcript of my notes of the prayer offered by Dr. Bresee at the First Church, Los Angeles, on Sunday morning, March 15, 1914:

"Oh, God, our Heavenly Father, we praise and adore Thy holy name this morning. Praise shall employ our nobler powers while life and thought and being last, or immortality endure. Glory to Thy name! Oh, God, we wait with reverential awe before Thy throne. This morning, with uncovered face, we gaze into Thy glory, and adore and worship Thee.

"Oh, Lord, we thank Thee that we are in Thy house this morning. We would rather be a door-keeper in the house

382

of the Lord than to dwell in the tents of wickedness. All the week long we have looked forward to again standing within the gates of Thy sanctuary, and joining with Thy holy people in songs of praise and thanksgiving. And Thou hast spared us. The dawn of this blessed Sabbath is upon us, and we once again tread Thine earthly courts. One thing we have desired of the Lord, and that will we seek after, that we may dwell in the house of the Lord all the days of our life, to see Thy beauty, and to inquire in Thy temple.

"We are here this morning with great thanksgiving. Glory be to God, we are not left in darkness. We are not left shut up to ourselves. We are not left to struggle on simply with human intuitions, and human longing and hunger, but Thou hast met us with Thy revelation, with Thy light, with Thy power, opening our ears and our eyes. Thou hast broken the long night of our senses. Thou hast come into our being. Thou hast made us new creatures. We know what it is to feel and realize the second birth. Thank God, that we have come into the divine family, and our whole being, as though stretched out in flowers, opens its petals to and in the life and light of God.

"Glory be to God, we are at Thy feet. We see no man but Jesus only. We are looking into Thy face. We are here today for divine manifestation. We have something of form and ceremony, but that does not amount to anything with us, only as it may help us to see the King this day, to behold Thy glory, and to be metamorphized into Thine image, and transformed into Thy beauty, that we may tread Thy courts with great delight, that we may hear Thy voice, that we may be thrilled with Thy touch, that we may be transformed by Thy presence.

"Lord, we are here for Thee to open upon us the windows of heaven, according to Thy covenant, and to bind us up in the bundle of Thy everlasting covenant, and to fill us with Thy divine glory. Thou knowest that we are in harmony with Thy purpose, that we may be transformed before

Thee, and filled today with heavenly light, life, and power. Oh, Lord, not our way, but Thy way. Not according to our thinking, but according to Thy thinking, for Thy thoughts are higher than our thoughts, and Thy ways than our ways; and, as the heavens are higher than the earth, Thy ways are higher than our ways. Let the chariots of Thy glory swing down here this morning, and the messages of God be like heaven to our hearts.

"Oh, God, bless Thy servant as he preaches the Word. Be Thou with all his ministry. We praise Thee for the success that the Holy Ghost has given him. Let him be anointed afresh this morning. Let fire fall on the pulpit. Oh, for divine unction! Oh, God, we want to see Thee through human agents today, and catch the glory through Thy Word of Thy voice and Thy heart. Speak to our hearts today through Thy Word.

"God bless Thy saints. In some way lift us up a little higher. In some way deepen our experience. In some way enlarge our being. Oh, God, make this a day of fire from on high, when Thy saints shall be lifted and filled as never before.

Oh, Lord, bless the unsaved ones and draw them to Thyself. Let the mercy drops come to their hearts today. Bless Thy people that have not found the depth of Thy love. Help men and women to plunge into the purple flood. Let this be a marvelous time and a glorious place all the day long. May Thy fire be mighty enough to burn up to heaven.

"Lord, bless all the churches; bless all the people; bless all the institutions of Thy kingdom; bless our university; bless all the members of the faculty; bless all the students; bless all its matters of business. Lord, put fire more abounding upon that institution. We pray again for the great publishing interests of our church; abundantly bless them with an outpouring of Thy Spirit and wisdom and grace.

"And now, Lord, we pray for all our loved ones, and our brothers and sisters and friends, and for all this poor human race, with which we mingle. God bless them all. The sick

384

ones — Oh, Lord, comfort them. God bless the nurses in the sick rooms. God bless the physicians, these ministers of Thine, who assuage human pain and help men and women back to health and strength. Bless them in their ministry this and every day.

"Oh, God, we pray Thee to bless this poor, suffering world. Bless our city, the mayor and council, and all in authority. God bless the president of the United States. Bless Congress and all in authority in the state and nation, in this land in which we live. While for all mankind we pray, we pray for America especially, the land that we love best.

"God, let Thy hand be upon us and Thy guidance with us, and keep us, dear Lord, until that day. May none of us miss the goal. May we go sweeping through the gates into the unseen holy.

"Answer us, we pray, not according to our feeble asking, but according to Thy riches in glory, for the sake of him who taught us to pray." The petition closed with the Lord's prayer.

Dr. Bresee knew more thoroughly the ritual and hymnology of the church than any other man I have ever met. He had not merely mastered their letter, but was inbued with their spirit. The choicest of the *His Knowledge of* grand old hymns were his possessions, *Ritual and* and he interwove them at will with his *Hymnology* prayers, exhortations, and sermons. In his advice to young preachers, he stated that part of their equipment should be the commitment to memory of at least two hundred of these majestic spiritual songs.

His use of the ritual was not slavish, and he did not feel constrained to follow its exact letter. Although perfectly familiar with its phraseology, he felt free to so vary its order or modify its contents, as to suit his purpose. He would blend and mingle the sonorous diction of the ritual with his own statements, thus interlacing the new and the old, and making the service exactly fit the occasion.

The marriage ceremony, as conducted by him, was exceedingly beautiful and impressive. He strove to make it a real means of grace to all that were present, and to imprint spiritual truths indelibly upon the minds and hearts of those who were united in holy wedlock.

The Scriptures and paragraphs of the ritual which were most perfectly adapted to the burial of the dead, were peculiarly his own, and he conducted these services with touching pathos, and deep solemnity. To those who mourned the loss of loved ones, his ministrations were like healing ointment. These occasions he always regarded as sacred opportunities to present the gospel in its saving and sanctifying power.

His conduct of the baptismal service was especially helpful and edifying. He emphasized the duties and privileges of parents in rearing their children in the nurture and admonition of the Lord, and gave a beautiful exposition of the real spiritual significance of the ordinance of baptism. After performing the actual rite, he would take the little children in his arms and kiss them. This he did so lovingly that the hearts of the parents were always moved.

Too often ministers conduct these services in a formal and perfunctory manner, evidently having no thought of making them a means of grace; but Dr. Bresee was never more sympathetic and earnest than on these occasions.

He had a profound love of the Bible. It was the subject of his deepest meditation, and the theme of most of his conversations. He realized that in the holy Scriptures are contained and presented the vital, inspired truths, *Love of* without which salvation would be impossible; *the Bible* that these living truths are absolutely needful to every degree of spiritual life, growth, and activity; that they are essential to our guidance throughout our earthly pilgrimage; and that one of the surest signs of growth in grace, is a deepening interest in and a widening knowledge of the Word of God. And yet he insisted that the truth was like the wire which is the conduit of the mysterious and mighty electric current, and that, as the wire without the current was dead, the truth without the very life and personality of God was inert and powerless. In this view he felt that he was borne out by the declaration of Paul that "the letter killeth, but the Spirit giveth life." He declared that it was possible to proclaim the truth in such a way that it would be entirely disassociated from the Holy Spirit, and utterly valueless as a means of grace; but that, on the other hand, it was our privilege to preach it with such unction, inspiration, and faith, that it would be "quick and powerful, and sharper than any two-edged sword"; that it would be overflowing with the divine nature and energy, "the power of God unto salvation."

Isaiah and Paul were the inspired writers whom he most admired. In his younger manhood and ministry, the latter was his favorite, and he was glad to give the name Paul to one of his sons; but for the last twenty years of his life, he came to regard Isaiah as the greatest prophet, poet, and saint that God had ever raised up in Israel. He declared that all the glorious truths of the gospel were to be found in the book of this wonderful Old Testament seer. He never tired of pondering over its sublime teachings, of treating them in an expository manner, and of presenting them to the students of our different educational institutions.

He was not led to give especial attention to the dispensational aspects of the Bible, or the almost innumerable questions that are involved in the study of eschatology. He belonged to no particular school of prophetic thought. He was neither a premillennialist, nor a postmillennialist, and, while he told me at different times that he was inclined to believe that premillennialists were right in their general conclusions, he humbly admitted that he did not know enough about the subject to be dogmatic regarding it. Feeling thus, however, he had no criticism for those of his brethren who made special investigations in this department of scriptural truth.

All that he demanded was that the great fundamental doctrines which are essential to regeneration, sanctification, growth in grace, usefulness in the kingdom of God, and a final and glorious triumph over all the power of the enemy, be kept well to the front. He knew full well that his especial and divine call was to experience, preach, and push holiness in life and doctrine. He found this subject such a vast one that it afforded full scope for the constant and most strenuous exercise of all his powers. His conception of holiness was not that of those who stop at its portals, and feel that they have done their whole duty when they have led a soul into the experience, but he had a burning desire to enter himself, and to lead others into all the vast ranges and limitless vistas of the fulness of the blessing of the gospel of Christ. He was in favor of every belief that would melt into holiness, as he put it, and opposed to every teaching which would not thus mingle and harmonize with it.

He had great executive ability. His was a consummate knowledge of human nature. He was a born leader of men. In his various activities in the Church of Christ, he invari-

As a Leader ably bore in mind the essentials, and bent all his energies to obtain them. He never ran the risk of losing these by too strenuously insisting on the things which, though desirable, were non-essential. By freely giving to others the non-essentials, he generally succeeded in securing that which was really indispensable. Although possessing a genius for details, he was no stickler for petty things. His views were broad, and his plans practical and sagacious.

I never knew a wiser counselor. His judgment was eminently sane, and his conclusions were dispassionate and free from bias and prejudice. Though burdened with many and heavy responsibilities, and in the midst of incessant toil, he was always glad to suspend his labors, listen with interest and sympathy to the troubles, perplexities, and life problems of his friends, and give them the benefit of his counsel. God truly gave him the word of wisdom in such junctures as these, and he often seemed to speak as the very oracle of God. Taking a real interest in the embarrassments and predicaments of those who thus sought his counsel, he gave his best thought to the solution of their life problems. Confidences reposed in him were sacredly kept. His advice in emergencies was invaluable.

CHAPTER XL.

I had hoped to be able to include in this volume a few of
the greatest and most notable of Dr. Bresee's sermons, but
feel that to do so would be to unduly extend the book. In
this chapter, however, I give the outlines of his two most
brilliant and powerful addresses, one called "Regnant Manhood," and the other entitled, "The Unchanging Purpose."
I also give the outline of his sermon on the text, "Be still,
and know that I am God," as preached at the Southern California District Assembly, in June, 1915. In addition to this,
I have set forth the greater part of another sermon outline,
which he prepared from the same text, with the intention of
preaching it at the General Assembly, at Kansas City, in
October, 1915, but which he was unable to preach because of
his feeble physical condition. This last and revised sermon
was probably the greatest that Dr. Bresee ever prepared.

"The address "Regnant Manhood," was delivered at the
Nazarene University, Pasadena, California, on Commencement Day, June, 1913, and is as follows:

Man is not always on the throne. He is sometimes in the prison
cell. He does not always wear the diadem. Sometimes he wears the
chain. It is not environment that makes man king or slave. He is
crowned or bound in his very being. One of the finest little poems
on liberty which I ever heard or read was written on the walls of a
slave den in Charlestown, South Carolina, by a slave awaiting the
auction block. He wrote of soul liberty, higher than prison walls,
and though but a few days afterward, in the effort to escape, he was
torn to pieces by bloodhounds, yet his soul was free.

There was a man in the first century who wore a chain of bondage, and yet at the same time wore the fairest and brightest diadem

A PRINCE IN ISRAEL

of any man of that time. The luster of its jewels was so bright that the atmosphere of this world in eighteen centuries has not been able to shake out its radiance. Men assume to occupy kingly places and to sway scepters, and yet their every movement clanks their chains.

To be a man is a marvelous verity. A man is not a result achieved by matter and motion. There is but one tenable theory of man's origin, which also somewhat defines his being, and that is in the Book of Wisdom: "And God said, Let us make man in our image, after our likeness. So God created man in his own image, in the image of God created he him; male and female created he them." A man, even in his physical being, is a marvelous creature, with sight and hearing and sensation; with unseen capacities of sensation, and possibilities of pleasure and pain. To have measureless possibilities of the accumulations of knowledge, with a moral nature, with a sense of right and wrong, with a strong somewhat or someone within his being that always pronounces upon the rightness or wrongness of the choice of motives, with a mysterious capacity of communion with his fellows, and a still more mysterious capacity of communion with God — he is a very marvelous being.

King David, the poet-prophet, in one of his times of deepest meditation, looked upon man in wondering awe, and said: "What is he? What is man, that thou dost spend so much thought upon him; that thou dost have so much care about him and visit him?" He expressed the greatest astonishment. He had been looking at the universe. He had traced system after system of worlds. He had looked upon Orion and Caseopia and Perseus, the wonderful suns and their systems. Then he looks at man and sees a thousand times more attention and care bestowed upon him. Worlds and systems of worlds might be thrown off from the end of God's fingers, but here is a frail being upon whom constant and infinite care is spent. Almost as if he would absorb the Divine mind and heart, the thoughtful poet begins to go into careful research about it. He takes up the history of things. He says: "Thou hast made him a little lower than the angels," or "For a little time lower than the angels." I find myself doubly interested as I stand before this Being so strangely affecting even the Divine thought and ministry, as I stand with this student of his place in the universe of intelligent beings. In what or how was he lower for a little than the angels? He was made in the Divine image and likeness. In that he was not lower. In moral purity he bore his image. He had no reason to think that in possibilities of thought or knowledge and affection man was made lower than the angels. For a time his sphere was closer, narrower; he was a denizen of much narrower quarters; his knowledge and intellectual grasp and power were much less. We do not know what angels were when first created, in the babyhood of angelic existence; but when man was born, angels seemed to have excelled in strength. "Bless ye the Lord, ye his angels that excel in strength," as with Sennacherib's army. "The angel of the Lord went forth and smote in the camp of the Assyrians one hundred and four score and five thousand; and when they arose in the morning they were all dead corpses." "The Assyrians came down like a wolf on the fold," etc. Man seemed to have been lower than the angels at this time in his great difficulties of environment, as well as in the possibility for wrongdoing. In early

391

angelic being and ministry there were evidently no outside influences for evil. Whatever temptations were possible to them must have come from the eye or ear, or outer senses directly to themselves or from themselves. But when man was created, evil spirits were already in the universe to tempt and press evil upon him. In this sense, for a little at least, he was lower than the angels, but here the comparison ceases.

Imperial Dignity. There is nothing commensurate with the Divine grace pertaining to man. "Thou crownest him." To invest with imperial dignity, peace, and power, to be crowned, is to be perfect in the state or type, to be the acme of his kind. God crowns manhood with the perfection of glory and honor. It is this crowned or regnant manhood that we would consider this morning. I am about to speak of his crowning, of his excellence and perfection. We can properly consider man, only as we regard him divinely accredited and crowned. Man without God can have no valuable excellence or glory.

Atheism is necessarily pessimistic in reference to what is, and its own plans for something better are utterly futile. An ancient atheistic philosopher says: "It would be right and admirable to sacrifice all men actually existing, if it were possible thereby to organize a stronger species." But, if there was no Divine being, no immortal life, this super-humanity would only see more clearly the misery and futility of existence.

We rejoice to be able to consider man in connection with his Divine creation and coronation, in that God made man in His own image and likeness of thought and volition and moral nature and sense of right and possibilities of glory; and, notwithstanding the awful incident of sin, God is not defeated, but the preparations for His coronation have been carried on just the same. The arrangements for his perfection and excellence have not been stayed. Man is before us with his marvelous powers, and the day of his coronation has come; the time and possibility of man's imperial glory are come — regnant manhood, not at the judgment, not in heaven, but now, in the earth, for this, for all worlds.

Man's Coronation. It is with this crowning that we have to do. Man is divinely crowned. Such a being, created in the Divine likeness, can never come to his excellence but by Divine power and glory. It I were to say of what this crowning of glory and honor consists, I should say possibilities and opportunities. But when I have said that, I have drawn but a faint outline — scarcely that. I have only indicated the encircling but retreating horizon, that which enters into and makes up the landscape — hills and valleys and rivers, and forests and plains, with God-given light within the horizons of possibility and opportunity revealed. The crowning of manhood, the giving of royal excellence to a human soul, begins with the advent of Jesus Christ into this world — begins by the revelation and manifestation of His Divine power, by the Virgin conception and birth.

Taking upon Himself our nature, becoming not a being filled with God simply, such as John the Baptist, but a God-man, Jesus took up into His Divine nature our nature, and began to open the wider, higher possibilities. This was wrought out through His sacrificial death, by His triumph over death and the grave, by His resurrection and ascension. He took humanity up into a God-man,

392

that man might be filled with God. He took human nature by a new creation out of the old, into the womb of the Virgin, uncontaminated by sin, that He might lift men out of sin. And that was not all; but that man might be filled with God. His coming in the Holy Ghost was man's coronation. By it man is filled with the Divine presence, and crowned with the excellence and glory of God. When we really see this, we begin to see the landscapes, and mountains, and hills, and valleys, and oceans of human possibilities and opportunities.

He is crowned with glory and honor, the glory of transformed personality. Whatever really adds to the glory of a man, must be in his personality. Place, environment, laudations, coronets, scepters, waiting courtiers, control of human forces — these do not glorify a man. They may only display his littleness and poverty of being. Many a man has been surrounded by the pomp and pageantry of a throne, only to show how little and near a nonenity he was. Real men are not made by conditions. They change or make conditions. We prize little the momentary environments and conditions which surround a man, especially such temporary things as simply tend to earthly aggrandizement and power, which a breath of air may dissolve, or a stroke of the clock may end.

Real Regnancy. Real regnancy comes into personality. Divinely imparted regnancy comes only in the prescribed way of Divine personality, bursting forth in human personality. The crowning is the supernatural making a man pure and strong and luminous. The coming upon a human soul of the Holy Ghost is coronation. No diadem ever rested upon a human brow like the tongues of fire. Fading leaves, or the tinsel of rubies and diamonds, which seem to be fitting to the cold brow of a mummy, or the ghastly skull of a skeleton, are nought.

The man of whom we speak today, God crowned with glory and honor in his very being. He already reigns with Christ. He is come unto Mount Zion. In his unity with the risen Christ, he is raised up with Him and made to sit in heavenly places with Christ Jesus. In all things this regnant one, crowned with the glory of the indwelling Christ, is more than conqueror. Over against the enemies of the love of Christ there comes up the shout: "For I am persuaded that neither death nor life nor angels nor principalities nor powers nor things present, nor things to come, nor height, nor depth, nor any other creature shall be able to separate us from the love of God which is in Christ Jesus our Lord."

Enlarged Empire. To the regnant man there is always the possibility of enlarged empire. For him are all things and to him all things come. Such a life is so deep that it is a river flowing toward and into the sea of glass, mingled with fire.

A river never competes with other streams; it opens its bosom and takes them into its life, and bears them to the great sea. "Unto him that hath shall be given, and he shall have abundantly." For him the generations past have lived and labored. For him all noble words were spoken, and all heroic deeds done. For him Moses lived and wrought. For him three hundred perished at Thermopolæ. For him Demosthenes spoke words of matchless eloquence. For him Columbus sailed the untraveled seas. For him Gallileo gazed on the starry vault. For him the Savior died. For him poverty and difficulty and opposition and persecutions have lifted their heads that he might be lifted into the depth of greater love and lowliness and strength. The regnant soul is crowned with peace. To be kind, gentle, patient, to be buffeted and bear the burdens of men; to weep with them that weep and love and care for them for whom nobody else cares; to come unto the woes of men and gaze into the heavens until he can see over all the stars, until he ascends the throne of Christ's own standard of greatness — and becomes the servant of all.

The Diadem. Thus man is crowned with a diadem of brightest jewels, purity, humility, gentleness, patience, long suffering, faith, hope, and love. His heart, his deeds, his words fulfill the highest ideals of greatness. His heart bears the Divine image, and throbs with abundance of love. His deeds and words are filled with the kindness and gentleness of Christ. As eloquence and rhetoric are trash, tenderness and love are regal. Thus the regnant man fulfills God's own ideal. He says: "A man shall be as a shadow of a great rock in a weary land"— a sheltering rock in the desert, a rock that makes a sheltered place, that makes possible a green place when all is fear — a garden in the desert. A man shall stay, or hold back the trend of a sin-cursed civilization, and make it easier for men to be good.

The Drift of Sin. Sin is a long, heavy drift, sweeping on, burying everything in its cursed course. But a man stands forth with the anointing of God, withstands the drift and at last turns it aside. He is a shelter to some souls. Such was Abraham. He turned his back to the idolatry of his forefathers, lifted his brow to heaven, and worshiped one unseen God. When Judah was rushing down the hot steeps of politics, carried off by the two great powers, fear of death and greed to be on the side of the strongest, Isaiah turned his back to the drift and said, "In greatness and in continence shall be your strength; in returning and rest shall ye be saved." When the tide of Judaism was about to sweep over the church so that even Peter and Barnabas and all of the apostles seemed to have been swept away, Paul stood up and turned back the drift. When the Roman empire, checked a little by the efforts of the reformers, gathered itself and rose in one awful front, cardinals, priests, and rulers determined to bury supernatural things for ever, Luther arose and said, "Here I stand. I can not do otherwise, so help me God."

God's ideal is far more than this. It is not only or chiefly staying the drift of evil. This regnant man goes forth as a new creature to create in the earth the kingdom of God. He is as rivers of water in a dry place. He is not a reformer simply. He is the avenue of God for a new earth. The reformer has a great work. He is a grave-digger, and stands to welcome the superstitions, errors, poisons, customs, tyrannies, and cruelties to bloody hands and ready graves. But this regnant man goes forth to recreate and make new. He is never a pessimist. He never blights the budding hopes or breaks the bruised reed. He lifts up the fainting heart. He pours oil and wine into the wounds of the poor pilgrims who have been wrecked by the Devil on the journey from Jerusalem to Jericho.

John Brown was a reformer. It was a dark day when he stood on the scaffold, that December day; but he was more than a reformer. He poured his life into the future and his soul went marching on. Henry Ward Beecher was more than a reformer, and Abraham Lincoln was more than a reformer. Dr. Grenfell said recently: "Do not pity me. Do not talk of sacrifice. This is my job. I like it." So with everyone who stands in the regnant, conquering place that God plans for him. Such men wear the crown of the Lord. One may say: "But you speak of *great* men?" God has other measures. The microscope is as great a revelation as the telescope, and God cares as much for the atoms as for the constellations.

The following is Dr. Bresee's outline of his great address, delivered at the Nazarene University on Commencement Day, 1915, the last occasion of this kind at which he was permitted to participate:

There are stadia in the lives of men, crisis points, birthdays of new departures, arrests, and startings which awaken reflection. We have reached such a point today. Slowly, with toilsome effort, we have reached this place. We tarry to look back down along the valleys by which we have come, and to turn our eyes and look up along the hillsides, hoping to catch, at least, some vision of the city that hath foundations, whose builder and maker is God.

Life is not all sunshine. There are to most people, some days, at least a few, of mildness and calm, of freshness and beauty, like a bright, early June day, when the sun laves the landscape in golden beauty, when valley and stream and hill and mountain and azure and flecking cloud all seem to combine like a variegated jewel reflecting the golden light, and our spirit seems to respond to it all with unfettered delight; and for a little moment it seems a luxury to be alive. There are times when love and friendship and home are about us, and we feel a sense of peace. There are some Elims in this wilderness with palm trees and springs of water.

Then there are days of storm with some, many days — when the beating tempest is upon us, when the winds blow cold and chill, when the tornadoes sweep, when the thunder shakes the earth, and the forked lightnings are athwart the heavens, when our hearts and brows are beaten, and there seems no refuge.

There are some human crafts on life's ocean which, like the boat that bore Paul and his fellows toward Rome, get along very well with sunshine and a favorable wind, but are only driven before the euroclydon that comes down from the mountains, or the cyclone that comes from the great deserts.

There are other souls, like the great steamship, not dependent on or controlled by outside forces, moving steadily through storm and tempest, on toward its destined port.

There may be no absolute safety outside the gates of pearl. There may be the artillery of the world, the icebergs of the forces of darkness, or the submarines of the arch-demons; but there may also be the power within that does not swerve.

When Jesus, our Lord and Master, was in the midst of the swellings of the billows of the most terrific storm that ever raged upon the ocean of human life, as He stood before Pilate, who asked, "Art thou a king then?" He answered: "Thou sayest that I am a king. To this end was I born, and for this cause came I into the world, that I should bear witness unto the truth." There was one unchanging purpose. Neither mockery, nor buffeting, nor the scourge, nor the cross, nor the deeper darkness, nor the untold agony of utter suffering could swerve Him from that purpose. There was but one end, the regnant end, to bear witness to the truth.

This is the crucial purpose of every human life. To this end was I born, and for this cause came I into the world. Man's being in this world has but one purpose, and that is the same as the unchangeable purpose of our Lord: to bear witness to the truth. Man's fore-ordained and true destiny is the same as His of highest destiny. Every man can say, and in the clearest light must say, "To this end was I born," etc.

God's Plan. God has planned every human life. How carefully God planned everything! How careful is the plan for the building of a world! How exact the balance with a million other worlds! It is said that He weighs the mountains in scales and the earth in a balance. How carefully it must be weighed against every other particle in the universe! How particular the measurements of force and attraction! How careful the adjustment of it all with every other body of matter in the universe! How carefully planned is all animal and vegetable life, and all their adjustments! So it is with a tree or a flower. Take an oak; see it springing out of an acorn. Not less is this plan manifest in the rose, the violet, the creeping vine. Every house, temple, and cathedral is carefully planned. A human life, so much greater than them all, is not left to chance. God has the plan of every life fully wrought out in the outline of its magnificent possibilities. They are not all after the same pattern. They are not all great oaks or towering pines, or redwoods. But each one has his place in the Divine plan, and one part is as great, as beautiful, as glorious as the other, being in the Divine plan and purpose. The one great end being the manifestation of the Divine glory; that end being in every man, as in the Lord Jesus, to be a witness to the truth. The manifestation of Jesus' regnancy, His highest kingship, was in His being a witness to the truth.

What Is Truth? When Jesus declared that He was a king, to this end was He born, and for this cause came He into the world that He should bear witness unto the truth, Pilate was aroused a little, enough to say, "What is truth?" But he was so overwhelmed by the conditions, that he did not wait for a response, but turned to go out and say to the people: "I find in him no fault at all." But he asked the great question. Jesus' mission was in it. His kingdom was in it. His knowledge was in it — also the being and destiny of every one who hears His voice. Had Pilate tarried, Jesus might not have undertaken to tell him. It might not have been possible to have told him. That one touch of the Christ was as a flash of lightning. For an instant, strange landscapes seemed to flash before him, far distances seemed to come nigh; towering mountains stood like specters; far-off worlds glimmered. But a flash of lightning scarce reveals the universe; it needs the day, and the morning had not dawned upon Pilate. But to us the Day Star is risen, the sun is in the heavens. We ought to be able to see more clearly. What is the great end of man? To glorify God and enjoy Him for ever. Yes, that is the catechism. That is great. But what does it mean? What lies underneath it? What is it to glorify God? It seems now very evident that we are to be with Christ, in Him, filled by Him, our personality mingled with His personality.

One Face. What is truth? Not a statement of fact, not a principle, not a science, not a philosophy. Truth is infinitely more than

396

all this. Truth is personality. Righteousness is personality. Power is personality. Love is personality. God is personality, divine personality, which embraces all this in an unthinkable comprehensiveness and completeness. Jesus said, "I am the truth." Righteousness, justice, mercy, compassion, power all blended, every part melted, into the indescribable beauty of love. As I look, I see many lineaments. As I continue to look I see one face — Jesus Christ, the embodiment of the Godhead. God is love. Jesus Christ is God incarnate, manifest for and unto the salvation of men.

The Infinite Verities. His testimony was not just an utterance, even by Himself. It was not the utterance of a man in reference to Him. John bore witness unto the truth, but Jesus said, "I receive not testimony from man." God testified to Him, and in Him, and of Him, and through Him. So He was that faithful witness, being Prince of the kings of the earth, who loved us and gave Himself for us, and makes us kings and priests unto God, having loved us and washed us from our sins in His own blood. He testified to the infinite verities — God righteous and holy, just and glorious in holiness; God infinite and eternal in love, blessed for ever. To man in sin and exile, wrecked and dying, in chains and dungeon, He testified in love and power, in dying agony and resurrection power, rending the veil in twain, bursting the prison doors, breaking the chains of sin, bringing the captive back to the bosom of God. He bore witness to the infinite verities. For this cause came He into the world.

A Witness to the Truth. It is enough for the servant that he be as his Lord. What is the divine plan for man? Why is he here? That he might bear witness to the truth. He seems to have little of mission or message or vocation other than this. The truth is divine personality, manifest by an incarnation, made radiant and more fully revealed by the unlimited spiritual manifestation of divine personality. To this truth man is a witness.

I wish to mark some of the possible elements, the necessary elements, the practical elements, essential to his being a witness to the truth.

The truth is the divine Christ. Barnabas exhorted the people at Antioch that with purpose of heart they would cleave unto the Lord, only this, etc. We hear much in this day, of comparative religions. I question whether there is any such thing. There are differences and contrasts; but there is nothing to compare to the religion of Jesus Christ. Whom can you compare with Jesus Christ? Buddha? Zoroaster? Mohammed? There is no religion to be compared with the religion of Jesus Christ. There is none that can re-make men, cleanse the inside of the cup and platter, and clothe the outside with humility, gentleness, long suffering, and hope.

Christ is the truth, and the highest human ideal is to be His witness. This is the divine purpose for us. This is the inwrought purpose created in us by the Holy Ghost.

Sainthood. The necessary soil, the essential conditions, the ensphering environment of this purpose, the atmosphere in which it lives, is sainthood. I use this term with aforethought. It is not much used in these days. The church sheers away from it. It seems a part of that letting down, both from experience and confession, resulting partly, perhaps, from misunderstanding as to Christian perfection. But the Bible is full of sainthood. Perhaps no term is so often and so lovingly used for God's people. Nearly one hundred times His people are called or referred to as saints.

But what are some of the constituent elements of sainthood, in which this purpose finds its springs of life and power?

1. Unswerving loyalty to conscience. Conscience is the voice of God in the human soul, pronouncing upon the rightness or wrongness of the choice of motives. What I mean by loyalty to conscience is unflinching determination to be right at any cost, which Christ always approves. It does not tell us what is right. It does not point out the way. It only smiles at the irrevocable determination to be right. This is the fountain of the great power. This is the rock from which the waters of life burst forth. Saul of Tarsus was smitten in his inner being by what was to him the most momentous question, of having the prophetic religion (which was to fill the earth and lift up the nations) hindered or perhaps overthrown by an imposter. Every element of his being was aroused. He purposed to throw himself in the way of what to him was an awful catastrophe. It was this which impelled him to hale men and women to prison and to death. And when the divine Christ met him in the way, and there came to him the heavenly vision, that Jesus is alive, He is the Christ, his purpose was not changed, and the Jewish religion was lifted to a new plane. It was not now a higher ethical and moral condition, but a message of life, of transformation, of glory, with the same loyalty to conscience, but with a brighter glory through Christ Jesus.

2. *The Vision of God.* The next element of sainthood in which unchanging purpose abides, is the vision of God. It is not enough that I mean to be right, that I am determined to be right. I must know the right. I must see the truth. I must catch a glimpse at least of Him who is the truth: I must see God. To hold steady to this unchanging purpose, there must be reality of spiritual experience, not simply a mechanistic intellectualism, under which spiritual life grows atrophied, as Darwin felt that his musical and poetic instincts did — not fanatical and incoherent things to excite sensibilities; but spiritual realities and experiences.

There is to be the receiving of the intellectual, the broadest and completest of human thinking, together with that which might — even without deep thought, stir the heart and mingle the whole in the fiery crucible, the experience of the Divine, God manifest in the soul, until it fills our being and gives unspeakable impulse to the one purpose, to be and bear witness to the truth.

It is this which pushes back the shadows of the world, and gives steady and resistless power to the hand which guides life's great purpose. It is this which lifts and glorifies personality, whether it be genius or mediocrity, learned or unlearned, and presses men steadily toward the mark of their high calling in Christ Jesus, filling their hearts with power and touching their lips with fire.

To fulfill our mission, is to be a witness to the truth, is to be a witness to Christ. How great, how all-comprehensive this is! It is difficult as a theory to comprehend. It is only as an experience, that we know how all-embracing it is, how it presses everything, from motive to destiny, into one all-pervasive and controlling purpose.

It is here that Paul stood, when he said, "This one thing." It is all-embracing, all-comprehensive, all-controlling. He looked out

398

upon every opposing force, and in the greatness and intensity of his purpose, cried out: "None of these things move me. . . . So that I might finish my course with joy, and the ministry which I have received of the Lord Jesus, to testify the gospel of the grace of God." To testify, that is to be a witness to Jesus Christ.

The Great Motive. This one great motive filled the lives of patriarchs and prophets and of martyrs and heroes all down the ages. Enoch purposed in his heart, etc. Abraham staggered not at the promises of God, but purposed in his heart to stand as a witness and pillar for the ages. How clear and strong the purpose of Moses, Elijah, Isaiah, John the Baptist, Polycarp, Savonarola, etc. These were all in heroic mold, when the battle waged hard about them.

The battle was never heavier than it is today. The church today is smitten with weapons more subtle and effective than the sword of Herod or the fires of Nero or Trajan. We are smitten with mildew. We are paralyzed by worldliness. We are buried under forms and pretenses, until the vision is lost, and the testimony in the power of God by manifestation is lost. Men will preach holiness, if there is a place for them. Luther was asked, Will the princes defend you? He answered, No. "What will you do," etc.

Our Aim. Piety that is intelligent, and intelligence that is pious. When I began to think specifically about this matter, I was led to suppose that these two, piety and intelligence — at least when they were once acquainted, and especially when betrothed — would ever, almost increasingly, walk together. But we find instead that there is a continued tendency to separation, with frequent divorce courts, with sad results.

By piety we mean much more than religion. There are religions many. Different religions have many devotees, and almost everybody has one. There are several different classes of religion, and in them are many different kinds. When we speak of piety, we mean the Christian religion in its spirit or mystical meaning, and in its activities incarnated in a human soul and life, controlling reverence toward God and loving conformity to His will. We scarcely mean mysticism or pietism; and yet in their best forms we might mean both. We are led almost to say that such piety must be intelligent. It would seem so, and yet there is a constant tendency to draw apart — for piety to draw back and undervalue various activities, as well as different branches of knowledge, to shun or draw away from investigation, to become introspective, and find its standards in its meditations and experiences, and its ends in the ecstacies of its own being. Thus, its tendency to quietism, or to extremes and fanaticisms.

On the other hand, intelligence, or, as we sometimes express ourselves by that word which seems to us broader and fuller, culture, seems to have a tendency toward being self-contained and self-efficient, and irreverent of its own ideas and to draw away from the humility, devotion, and spiritual intensity of piety, and set up its own esthetic forms and ceremonies. This has been the history of the ages. This is the difficulty today. But for this we should scarcely have been here today.

Places of Cleavage. Our colleges and places of learning are largely places of cleavage in this matter, and have such a tendency to divide the one from the other, and are at the same time such a power in fixing and controlling the lives of students, thus tending to turn culture against piety, when they ought and need to be melting pots in which piety and knowledge blend.

The first great end in this world is piety. See the old confession of faith. Saintliness is infinitely above scholarship; yet without scholarship, it is shorn of much of its possibility, and runs constant risks, which it ought to be protected against.

Culture without piety is bright and cold and selfish and worldly. To educate a man without piety is likely to make him worse. The gleam of light is brighter and shines further, but it leads into the wilderness of doubt and despair. We can ill afford that the boys and girls of the church shall be spoiled in the making.

We have built this place. May God let the strands drop down from heaven and call us to take their ends and weave them into an institution where the Holy Ghost with infinite glory can mold culture into young life after the pattern of the heavenlies, where men like Enoch shall have the testimony that they are pleasing God; and like Abraham will get visions of a city that hath foundations. Like Moses may they see the bush of truth all aflame with the divine Presence. May it be a place where men shall be filled with the message of Chrysostom and Savanarola and Jerome and Luther and Whitefield. This is a sacred trust given us from the skies. For it we pour out our lives, as David poured out the water brought him from the well at Bethlehem.

The following outline of a sermon preached *"Be Still"* - by Dr. Bresee, at the Southern California District Assembly, at Pasadena, Cal., in June, 1915, is perhaps the most comprehensive and far-reaching in its scope of any that he ever preached:

"Be still and know that I am God" (Psalm 46: 10).

The greatest question of all ages, in every department of human thought, is the question of God. The deepest scientific questions involve it. It fills human philosophy.

The deepest longings of the human heart, and all the great problems of life are involved in it.

My text is a most comprehensive and startling utterance. It is a command embracing all thinking, experience, and life.

Of the existence of God all thoughtful creatures agree. The great, necessary thought of Cause, efficient and sufficient, drives every man to the thought of God. Everything that would stop man on his way breaks down. Spontaneous generation stopped man a little while. Evolution did so also. Every one comes soon to stand in the midst of the universe and say, "The heavens declare the glory of God." The necessities of our being reach out to know this. Our thinking stretches out its hands toward Him. Here is the history of all philosophy. Here is the basis of all religions. Here are heard the deepest outcries of the human soul. Here men have builded hierarchies and ecclesiasticisms, have reared magnificent cathedrals, and builded innumerable altars; here they have made their costliest sacrifices, and paid their richest devotions; and here their most appealing cries have found utterance. Here Job cried, "O, that I knew." It is the deep, the deepest, cry of every human heart.

When the mystery of our being is upon us; when the struggles of life are about to overwhelm us; when we feel near the borders of desperation, how there comes up a cry to God!

An Unholy Being. We can scarce put ourselves in the place of a heathen, who has seen the sun and moon and stars, and built an altar and offered sacrifices upon it. We are Christians. We are born into the light of a divine revelation. From the time we have opened our eyes in this world, we have been taught of God, infinite in holiness, power, wisdom, love, and mercy; of His incarnation; of His redeeming grace; of His eyes of glory, looking through and through us; of His loving longing for us. We have been taught to look for His presence, to listen to His voice, and to feel His touch. And yet all this teaching does not satisfy us. We cry out with St. Augustine, "Thou, O God, hast made us for Thyself, and the heart is restless till it rests in Thee." An unholy being can not love or abide in a holy being. A holy being may love an unholy being, for he may conceive of him outside of his sinfulness, in his possible separation from evil. But a sinner in his very being is in antagonism to holiness: he can neither love it nor dwell in it. As an intelligent being, there may be to him things which have their source and inspiration in holiness, and that he admires. There may be heroism, unselfish devotion, deeds of valor, benevolence, altruism, things of sentiment, artistic and poetic things, which he admires, and which his sentiment responds to.

It is in this field that a worldly church operates. Here are the intellectual and moral activities of an unspiritual ministry. Into this field are brought the altruism, the benevolence, the unselfishness, the service for others, of the Christ and apostles. Into this comes the service for men, and the heroic doings of men, with their achievements in art, poetry, hierarchies, the winning of influence, position, etc. It is in this field that we find social Christianity.

The Divine Presence. But the door is not opened into the divine presence. While these may have their fountain in divine personality, they are separated from divine manifestation, grafted into human experience. They become a man-centered religion, and divine manifestation is not sought or desired.

There is in all of this no soul salvation, no meeting the needs of the human soul. In it are many things, human things, beautiful things; but there is no coming to the mountain brow, where the fires of the divine presence burn; no coming to the Mount of Transfiguration, where the glory glows in the face of Jesus Christ, until the heart cries, "It is good for us to be here"; no lifting of the veil, amid the perfume of incense and the merit of the sprinkled blood; no coming where the Shekinah shines.

Every person, now and for ever, goes where he is prepared to go. The world seeks its own — gross minds, gross things, refined minds, refined things. Those who know the Spirit, and are transformed by the Spirit, seek for and enter into the glory of divine manifestation. Every man seeks his own, and goes where he is prepared to go — now and for ever.

Their Own Place. Men coming to this city, go to their own place. "Who shall ascend into the hill of the Lord? or who shall stand in his holy place?" (Psalm 24: 3) "Who among us shall dwell with the devouring fire? who among us shall dwell with everlasting burnings?" (Isaiah 33: 14, 17).

I speak today more especially to those whose hearts are fixed on

God, "whose delight is in the law of the Lord, who long to know God, who count all things but loss, who are in the house of the Lord with great delight, saying, "One thing have I desired of the Lord," etc. I speak to my own soul, to my brothers and sisters in Christ Jesus. God is our great desire, delight, and joy. We have escaped from the heresies of our early teaching and the chains of conditions. Some of us from the very dawn of our thinking were impressed with the most unreal, untrue, if not the most outrageous, things, in reference to Him — not by the intent of those who taught us, but by the way it was done. We came to regard Him as a monstrous being, who knew everything, was ever near us; who seemed to be on the watch to catch us and punish us, and hold things against us; who knew our thoughts, especially to upbraid and censure, until we wished there was no God, and would get away from Him if we could. I well remember my own early experience in this regard.

I sometimes hear men preach of the necessity of our meeting God, and of the punishment of the wicked, in a way that seems to carry with it a vindictiveness in God, that fills me with sorrow, but also with thanksgiving that the spirit of the whole thing is false.

The great need of men is God; and while sin can not desire God, yet human need is such that under the helpful, illuminating power of the Holy Spirit they would see how He only can meet their needs. It seems to me that if He were properly presented and manifested, and the scales removed from their eyes, men would run to Him like a famished child to its mother's arms, like the prodigal to his father's bosom.

Tumultuous Seas. At any rate, hearts set on holiness long to know Him, and it is to such that He says today, "Be still and know that I am God." He speaks this to us gently and earnestly, amid the conventions and confusions of earth, amid the roaring of tumultuous seas, and the removal of things from their foundations. He speaks of His presence as a quiet and secure place, amid earth's confusion and desolation. He calls on us to hear and know Him. He would have us learn what we may from the temporary, dissolving things of earth. Some voice of His is in it all, and yet no clear, divine utterance. Not in the whirlwind, or in the tempest, or in the earthquake. Job says, "Lo, these are the outskirts of his way, but how small a whisper do we hear of him." There must be the direct, divine utterance. "He that hath my commandments and keepeth them, I will manifest myself to him" (John 14: 21).

It is to this point that we have come. In obedient trustfulness we wait the divine utterance. We hear Him say, "Be still, and know that I am God." "Be still" is an expression here strangely used. Hebrew scholars tell us that this is the only time that this word "Raphah" is used for "being still," and that it is in the active voice, an act of silence for a purpose, a mental and spiritual activity for an end. It indicates:

ATTENTION. It is an intensely active condition, but a silent activity. Silence is the condition of activity. While I speak, I demand attention, etc. This active silence indicates:

RECEPTIVITY. To listen and receive. An excited condition, which grasps every word. As David declared of himself, "I was as a dumb man, that openeth not his mouth" (Psalm 38: 13). As Job

402

said, when the Lord spoke, "I lay my hand upon my mouth." No question, no argument, etc.

Not only the silence of my own soul, but the silence of environment. My attention must not be distracted. My listening is so active toward God that my attention is withdrawn from other things. Other things are of small account, and have little attraction. One seeking for amusement or entertainment will hear nothing from heaven. If our ears are filled with the sounds of earth, the message from beyond will not get through. I call long distance, etc. I am told that the wire is busy, etc. In silence we come to know ourselves.

We may live so much in outer things, in their noise and tumult, that our real self is lost. We become external and shallow. I need to be still and hear the cry of my own soul. I need to get below society. I need to get below a sociological religion, down into the desperation of my own being. This is on my way to hear God, and brings me where God can talk to me.

Thus, in my own need, attentive, receptive, with all noises shut out, in the activities of intense silences, I hear His voice. I am enamored to hear His voice. I am delighted to hold the receivers of His truth, and listen to His own utterance.

Silences of the Soul. The divine conditions are that I must be silent, alert, hushed, quiet, intense, hearing no other voice. Then God speaks, etc. This all-prevailing silence of the soul, listening to and hearing divine verities, is a state of desperation. There may be a silence which is meaningless — an absence of thought and feeling or emotion. When thought begins to act, and feeling to come in, there is usually an outcry; but when thought becomes strong and concentrated and feeling intense, outcry ceases. When there is the beginning of determination, and feeling begins to work, there is effort to give it expression, but when it becomes all-pervasive, it takes on the awful quietness of the depths. Such do not declare; they are; they do.

We are through with arguments, at the end of appeals. We are waiting upon the Lord, gazing to see the glory of His face, to feel the thrill of His utterance; stretching out our hands to touch the hem of His garment, etc. We are in one mighty effort of discovery: to see the unseen, to know the unknown. We hear Him say, "Be still, and know that I am God."

What does this mean? I confess that I am overwhelmed. I am not in the full sense confounded, but I am in the sense of being overwhelmed. As I think, I tread giddy heights; I go down into unexplored depths. The horoscope of finite things has lifted, and the infinite eternities press me.

The King of the Palace. I have discovered the King of the palace of earth and of the ages. How long and how vainly I sought Him in the palace itself, and through the ages! I sought in the cities and in the solitudes. I inquired diligently. I was shown the print of His feet and His finger prints; but Him I found not. I traversed the ages. I saw strange, marvelous things. I made diligent inquiry, and I was shown many things that were intimately associated with Him; but Him I found not.

In my longing I went into the solitude of my own being. My eyes began to feel a new anointing, and I began to see that the

PHINEAS F. BRESEE

Author of my being must be Spirit, infinite Spirit, and that He could be discerned only in the Spirit, by the Spirit. I felt a strange touch on my ears, and I heard a strange word, "Ephphatha," and I heard, "Be still." The light flashed through my own being, and the heavens were aflame with light. As in the twinkling of an eye, I became a new being. With the rising of the sun, I was filled with light. And I began to see God. In the beginning, God; in the end, God. In time, God; in eternity, God. God over all, blessed for ever. God in His Son, Jesus Christ. God in the Holy Ghost.

He breaks the chains and makes us free. He cleanses us, and makes us pure. He empowers us, and causes us to walk in His commandments.

Nothing transforms men but the manifestation of the divine presence. It is this that makes us men, worthy men, Christly men; that lifts us out of contaminating conditions, and regulates our relations to the universe.

To Know God. To know God as God is to know Him in fellowship. Moses in one of his trying days, cried out to God, "I beseech thee, show me thy glory." There had been great sin; the tables of stone were broken. God had talked with Moses, and had said, "My presence shall go with thee, and I will give thee rest." The experience of Moses as set forth in Deuteronomy 34: 10 and other Scriptures, belonged to Canaan, into which He was leading them.

In preparing his sermon for the General Assembly at Kansas City, the last he was permitted to attend, Dr. Bresee took the same text. "Be Still, and know that I am God,"

His Last Sermon and wrote a new outline, in which, however, he incorporated nearly everything contained in the foregoing outline. He elaborated, changed the arrangement and order of thought, and enriched the illustrations. The sermon thus diligently and prayerfully prepared was never preached. I shall not set forth the full outline, but will simply give what was not included in the former outline, or was so changed as to be practically new. It is as follows:

Carlyle said: "As I get older, and I am now near the borders of eternity, there comes back to me with increasing force what I learned from the Catechism — that the chief end of man is to glorify God and enjoy Him for ever."

We are so taught as to be filled with misconceptions of Him. Heresy is rubbed into us from our childhood, and often preached into us, or at us, all through life. I well remember when I was a little child, these facts led me to wonder whether I could escape Him and the hell that I was to be punished in, if I were to crawl into the fire and burn myself up now and end the whole business.

The Lord himself says to us, "Be still, and know that I am God." He speaks thus gently and earnestly to us amid the conventions and confusion of the world; amid the removal of things from

404

their foundations; amid roaring, tumultuous seas; amid the overwhelmed and sinking mountains. Amid all this He hides away in a quiet, protected place, and says, "Be still, and know that I am God." He evidently desires us to see it, and know what an uncertain thing it all is. He may, and probably does, desire that we hear some voice of His in it all, and yet there is in it no clear, divine utterance. The clear utterance is not in the whirlwind or earthquake or fire. The clear utterance is the clear voice of God. There is a great utterance in Job. After describing one of the wildest of manifestations, he says, "Lo, these are but the outskirts of his way, but how small a whisper do we hear of him." All nature, all history, are but a small whisper of Him. To know Him, there must be direct manifestation and revelation to human consciousness.

There must be silence about us. Dr. McClarren, writing of Dr. Joseph Parker, in the days of his great power at the Temple, in London, and his magnificent work in so many ways, speaks of the necessity of his living much alone, isolated from society, giving himself to hearing the voices and seeing the visions of divine truth.

A Peculiar Necessity. This is a peculiar necessity. The voices of the world must not charm or confuse us. They must not fill our ears, or clutter our souls. There must be solitude unto God.

Silence here is unutterable desperation. The man who is declaring his determination, who is giving voice to his feelings, who can find words for his passion, who can give utterance to his intensity, is still dealing with surface conditions. There is passion too deep for utterance. The deepest depths are unmoved by surface currents. There is a silence that is meaningless. Silence from the very absence of thought or feeling or emotion. When feeling begins, there is usually an outcry; but when feeling gets deep, the outcry ceases. I have often marked this at the altar. You are at the end of things. You are through with arguments, through with appeals — simply gazing, with every power of the mind alert, with every avenue open. The eye is strained, the ear is open, the hand outstretched. I am in one mighty effort of discovery. I am looking for the unseen. I am open to visions of the infinite. I am stretching out my hand to feel the robes of divine personality. I hear Him say, "Be still, and know that I am God." From the depths of my soul I am gazing toward horizons. I am looking to the hills.

My mind is open to the avenues of His revelation. I look at the environments about me, the universe in which I find myself. I am as one awakened in a great palace. I walk up and down the halls. I open the doors and enter the great rooms. I look upon the magnificent pictures upon the walls, and the fine sculptuary in the niches. I roam through the great library. There are couches here and there, and I sit down to rest. I begin to wonder where the owner is. I admire the skill, the thought back of it all. I lie down and rest, and wake and wonder. My curiosity is excited, and I press on. The rooms are cleanly swept and everything is freshly dusted. I will find Him soon. I press on into the parlor — a book lies open upon the desk; He can not be far away. I come to the dining-room; the table is freshly spread with viands. I sit down and eat. So in this world: there is plan everywhere; marks of His skill everywhere; footprints everywhere; prepared food; lighted fires; handiwork, care, and planning everywhere.

PHINEAS F. BRESEE

The Ages. I turn my eyes out along the ages. Surely God is in His temple. I am unable to catch up with Him in Nature, but surely I will find Him among men. Man is His masterpiece in creation — man, the thinker, the reasoner, the seeker after the cause of things, the moral being with a sense of right and wrong; man with the ages for the platform of his activities; man working out his destiny. Surely, here I will find God. I have sought Him there. I have walked slowly through a hundred generations. Men have told me of Him. Men have told me that He had been among them; that He veiled Himself in flame; that He hid Himself in light; how He manifested Himself in flesh; that they beheld His glory; how He spoke in terrifying tones and in gentle whispers which soothed and blessed; how He had overturned empires and kingdoms, and brought things to pass. But Him I found not. I have cried out with Job, "O, that I knew him!" and with David, "As the hart panteth after the waterbrooks, so panteth my soul after thee, O God."

Footsore, weary, and worn, I have sat down under the stars, with the shadows of the ages upon me, and closing my eyes, I have said: "O, where is He whom my soul desireth to know? May I not know Him in Agnosticism, the end, after all?" And I have heard clearly the voice, "Be still, and know that I am God."

In Spiritual Realms. It began to come in upon me that God is Spirit; that He will be found in spiritual realms; that He is to be known in the Spirit; that it is vain for me to search for Him among the mountains, or to march through the centuries to find Him; that, if I found Him, if I came to know Him, it would be in the depths of my own Spirit. It was then that I heard these words of revelation, "Be still, and know that I am God."

There is knowledge which does not come through the eye, or ear, or sense of touch; that does not come from sense or memory, or imagination, or conscience, or judgment. I do not say that it comes without them, or any one of them. But no one of them seems to be the real avenue of it.

There seems to be a direct way to human consciousness — a way by which the Spirit-man comes to know spiritual personalities. How much sensuous and mental faculties may be avenues, it is difficult to tell. How much a super-sensuous and intellectual avenue is opened up to the human spirit, may be difficult to tell. But that into our consciousness comes knowledge of Spirit personality — other than self — there seems no room for doubt.

When the child Samuel heard again his name called, it was not the ear that caught and conveyed the sound. When Isaiah saw that vision and heard those words, there was something more and other than eyes and ears and sense of touch, which revealed it to his inner consciousness. The same was true when Moses stood on Sinai, or on Pisgah's brow, and saw the promised land; when John saw heavenly visions on the Isle of Patmos; and when Paul was lifted to the third heaven, and heard words that were unutterable.

An Open Vision. God has a way of manifesting Himself directly to the spirit of man. The pure in heart shall see God — not as a matter of the future; but the very condition of a pure heart is an open vision of Him.

The knowledge of Him is as mysterious as the way of knowing Him; it is even more so. How those who have known Him have

406

tried to tell it! They have only been able to say, "The mystery so long hid, has been made known unto me by the Spirit."

The longing to know Him finds large expression. David cries out, "As the hart panteth after the waterbrooks, so panteth my soul after thee, O God." Paul said, "I count all things but loss, that I might know him." Augustine said, "The heart is restless till it rests in Thee." Charles Wesley said, "In vain thou strugglest to get free, I never will unloose my hold."

But when men come to tell what the knowledge itself is, they are silent. John says of that supreme manifestation of Him, "We saw his glory." Paul says, "I heard." There are some things we know that we can give expression to, or describe. There are other things which we can only describe by telling their effect upon us. The knowledge of God seems to be of this class. When men undertake to tell us, they merely begin to describe how they themselves felt.

Job says: "I have heard of thee with the hearing of the ear, but now mine eye seeth thee. Wherefore, I abhor myself." Isaiah says, "I saw the Lord." John Wesley says, "I felt my heart strangely warmed." Charles Wesley says:

> " 'T is love! 't is love! Thou diedst for me!
> I hear Thy whisper in my heart;
> The morning breaks, the shadows flee;
> Pure, universal love Thou art."

Samuel Medley said:

> "O could I speak the matchless worth,
> O could I sound the glories forth,
>   Which in my Savior shine;
> I'd soar and touch the heavenly strings,
> And vie with Gabriel while he sings,
>   In notes almost divine."

CHAPTER XLI.

During the year 1908, Dr. Bresee, in addition to his pastoral and editorial work, his duties as General Superintendent, and his labors as president and lecturer of the Deets Pacific Bible College, found time to take
Principal Events in 1908 part in a great holiness convention held at the First Church, Los Angeles, by Rev. Bud Robinson, Rev. I. G. Martin, and Rev. Will Huff, in the month of March. About the same time he dedicated the Grand Avenue Pentecostal Church of the Nazarene, in that city.

A few days later, he started on an extensive trip of nearly three months' duration, through some of the Southern and Eastern states, including New England and the northwest. During this journey he presided over several great District Assemblies.

In July he was the principal preacher at the Beulah Park campmeeting, in Oakland, California. About the same time he held the District Assembly for the San Francisco District.

Shortly after the adjournment of the General Assembly of 1907, the Holiness Church of Christ, representing more than 3,000 members in the Southern states, decided to unite
The Holiness Church of Christ with the Pentecostal Church of the Nazarene, and requested that a joint session of the General Council of that church and the General Assembly of the Pentecostal Church of the Nazarene be held at Pilot Point, Texas, in October, 1908.

Pursuant to this request, and the formal call of the Gen-

408

eral Superintendents of the Pentecostal Church of the Nazarene, the General Assembly met at Pilot Point, on October
8, 1908. The sessions were held in a large
The General tent, with a seating capacity of 1,000.
Assembly At the opening of the Assembly, Rev.
At Pilot Point J. D. Scott arose, and on behalf of the
Holiness Church of Christ, stated that
the time had come to open the joint Assembly. He said:
"We have been called together by this joint Assembly of
churches, and have here present the representative heads of
the two churches." He then called Dr. Bresee, Rev. R. B.
Mitchum, and Rev. H. F. Reynolds to the front of the platform, at the same time moving that Dr. Bresee, as the senior General Superintendent, be given charge of the Assembly.

Rev. R. Pierce, and Rev. J. D. Scott were elected joint
secretaries of the Assembly.

The report of Dr. Bresee was as follows:

Dear Brothers and Sisters: It is with me a matter of thanksgiving to God, that in His good providence I am permitted at the end
of the first year of our life as a united church, to render up to you a
brief account of my stewardship as your humble servant, acting as
one of your General Superintendents. Last year, as in the years
preceding, in the narrower limits of the work, I undertook to report
in reference to the varied forms of organized activities within the
church. But since the blessed union accomplished a year ago, I
have been permitted to co-operate with Rev. H. F. Reynolds, we
being by your election of us to this position, associated together in
this General Superintendency; and, the various agencies being in
such position as to report directly to this body, it is only necessary
that I make some brief references to such personal services as I
have been able to render. Allow me to say that my relationship
to my colleagues, and all of the brethren of the ministry, has been
a blessing and refreshment to my soul. Also that I have rejoiced
in the precious fellowship which I have been permitted to have with
the churches in the different parts of the land.

Labors as Superintendent. That I have not been able to do
more, and give more constant and undivided attention and service
to the church at large, has been my regret. It has been necessary
for me to give some time and strength to heavy pastoral services, by
and through which my general service has been made possible. I
recognize that this is not the most desirable method, and that it
gives more or less opportunity to the enemy at both ends of the
service, which might be impossible if the gates could be more perfectly guarded and defended. If it shall be possible for you to find

some one who can give more full and better service in this office, it will be your duty to do so, and will be a relief and joy to me. But I have been permitted, in addition to pastoral duties, and a large correspondence, and some editorial and educational work, to make a brief visit to this Southland, in which I had the privilege of visiting Peniel, Texas, and I hope doing for them some little service; at least, having with them pleasant fellowship in the work; and then visiting the brethren here at Pilot Point, to plan with them and somewhat arrange this larger union and enjoy with them some ministry of the Word. Then I visited and labored a little at Indianapolis and Seymour, Ind.; Louisville, Ky.; Johnstown, Pa.; and Washington, D. C., on my way to the District Assemblies of the East — all of which: Washington, New York, New England, and Pittsburgh — I had the pleasure of assisting in holding. All of these Assemblies were remarkable for unity and holy fellowship. The blessing of God was greatly upon them, great unction being upon the ministry of the Word, and even the business sessions at times overwhelmed with the glory of the manifestation of the divine presence. Some of them were peculiarly blessed with tides of salvation. I shall always thank God for the privileges of the sweet fellowship and communion that I enjoyed in this my first visit and ministry among these dear brethren and sisters.

Brother Reynolds. Accompanied by Brother Reynolds, with whom I had been associated from the time I reached Washington City, we went by the way of Chicago, Greeley, Boulder, and Denver to Portland, Ore., where we held the Northwest District Assembly, which was the occasion of the bringing together of a host of that fine division of the army toiling so heroically in that great and growing Northwest, to kindle fires of true holiness in its cities and towns. It was also a time of the outpouring of the Holy Spirit, and during the Assembly, and at the home campmeeting which followed, a goodly number of people found the Lord.

After visiting and holding some meetings at Seattle and Everett, both Brother Reynolds and myself attended the campmeeting and District Assembly of the San Francisco District, at Oakland, Cal. These were seasons of spiritual power and profit. The campmeeting was a very gracious season of salvation, a multitude of people finding their way to the altars as seekers and finders of pardon and purity. The District Assembly was held in connection with the campmeeting, was well attended, and the business well done, and showed good work and a hopeful outlook. Afterward the District Assembly of Southern California District was held at Pasadena, Cal., which was a large and earnest body, and there were business, blessing, and salvation.

Since leaving home to attend this General Assembly, it has been my privilege to hold a three days' meeting in Denver, Colo., and organize a church with forty charter members, with every prospect of victory before them. I have also been permitted to join with Brother Reynolds in holding the Chicago Central District Assembly, at the First Church, Chicago, Ill. This was the last of the District Assemblies of the year, and was a great occasion. Not only was a large amount of important business attended to, but great blessings were upon the people. At the three great services of the Sabbath, about twenty-five persons were at the altar; besides, at every service

410

during the Assembly there were some seeking the way of the Lord, and many found the truth of the Master's words, "He that seeketh, findeth."

So, by the grace of God, we have come to the close of another year with thanksgiving, trust, and hope, asking only that we may go on in the way that the Lord himself may appoint, until we find the outer gates and the loving Master's welcome home.

Professor E. P. Ellyson, President of the Texas Holiness University, was elected as General Superintendent, and Dr. Bresee and Rev. H. F. Reynolds were re-elected to the General Superintendency.

The Union   Rev. R. Pierce thus describes this glorious event:

As Brother R. B. Mitchum, president of the Holiness Church of Christ, spoke in a tender way of the gracious leadings of God up to that moment, and moved that "The union of the two churches be now consummated," followed and seconded by Rev. C. W. Ruth, John N. Short, J. B. Creighton, H. B. Hosley, and several others who spoke to the motion, amid great joy and gladness brethren of the South hugged brethren from the North, East, and West. As Dr. Bresee put the motion, he said that this is an epoch-making time, and is the answer to our Lord's prayer; but it is only the early dawn, and we are going forth to victory. The motion was put and carried unanimously by a standing vote, amid great enthusiasm.

The burst of holy joy continued for some minutes, the brethren embracing each other, at the same time singing a new hymn written for the occasion by L. Milton Williams and I. G. Martin, to the tune of "Dixie." Soon the inside of the tent became too small for the freedom of such a joy, and the glad people began the march outside and around the great tent, waving their handkerchiefs amid shouts of joy, eventually forming an immense, compact circle on the grounds, where Dr. Bresee mounted a chair and addressed the multitude in words of inspiration which moved the hearts of all. Surely the Lord was pleased with such a manifestation of holy love."

Battle Hymn of the Assembly. This hymn, the singing of which aroused so much enthusiasm, was as follows:

> The holiness bands from over these lands
> Are fast coming in and all joining hands.
>   Praise God! Praise God! Praise God for Jesus!
> With the Blood and the fire of the Holy Ghost
> We'll rout the foe and his black-winged host,
>   March on! March on! March on with Jesus!
>
> CHORUS:
>   With forces all united,
>   We'll win! We'll win!
>   We'll preach a gospel o'er the land
>   That fully saves from sin.

411

PHINEAS F. BRESEE

Praise God! Praise God! Praise God!
For Full Salvation!
Praise God! Praise God! Praise God!
For Full Salvation!

With the Nazarene hosts and the Pentecostal band,
And all our folks from the old Southland —
　　Look out! Look out! Look out for vict'ry!
This Gideon band unitedly stand,
And are determined to conquer this land
　　Right away! Right away! Right away for Jesus!

These Nazarenes are a happy host,
Equipped with the fire of the Holy Ghost —
　　Amen! Amen! Amen! Hallelujah!
While others sleep they are wide awake
To rescue souls from the burning lake —
　　Praise God! Praise God! Praise God for vict'ry!

And when the battle here is o'er,
We'll sing and shout on the other shore —
　　Praise God! Praise God! Praise God for Jesus!
And when around the throne we meet,
We'll cast our crowns at Jesus' feet —
　　And shout: Praise God! Praise God! Hallelujah!

Dr. Bresee's Impressions. Dr. Bresee thus characterizes the Pilot Point General Assembly:

As was expected, this Assembly has been momentous and historic. It has been another epoch ushering in an era of still greater things. It has been said that "there is no clock in the horologe of time to strike the passing from one era to another." When history is being made and great things are coming to pass, those who are in the often hard and difficult places, struggling for the birth of the greater things, are so taken up with the burden of toil which taxes their being to the utmost, that they little realize new heights which are being won. Some one or a few may have the vision of what is really being done; but mostly the actors are covered with the dust and smoke of battle. But they whom God leads build better than they know, and when the years reveal the unveiled structure, they are as much surprised as any — possibly the most surprised. Both Napoleon and the Iron Duke were eagle-eyed, but probably none were more surprised at the results of Waterloo in history.

"God leads in a mysterious way
His wonders to perform."

And it is only as we get a perspective that we can see His marvelous work.

This has been true of this providential movement, in all its confluent streams. The work began — east, west, south — at about the same time. In no place as an ecclesiasticism, but in each case men were thrust out to preach full salvation and raise up a holy people. And each obeying the divine impulse, and following the pillar of

412

cloud, they did not realize what they were doing. This impulse to unity — this answering of the Lord's prayer that they may be one — from the coming of the "Three Wise Men of the East" to the borders of the western sea, and the subsequent happy union of the East and West, and now this confluence of the South: turning us all like the rivers of the south; pouring much of the holiness movement into an organic whole: no one knows or can realize what it means; but one thing seems certain,

"Our God is marching on."

A Representative Body. The preparations for the Assembly were on a large scale. A tabernacle that would seat probably one thousand people, a boarding tent, etc., had been provided; the school building was made contributory, and the people of the town had thrown open their houses. There was a large attendance, not only from the Southland, but the North was much more largely represented than it had been feared was possible, a large number of the representative people of the church being present. From the beginning it was very evident that things were in the divine order. At the first session, which was opened with the Sacrament of the Lord's Supper, the manifest presence of the Lord was marvelous. The service occupied a considerable part of the time of the session, with wave after wave of heavenly glory sweeping over the hearts of the people. From that time the melted hearts began to flow together, and it was soon evident that nothing could prevent, not only organic, but the soul unity of the gathered forces.

Complete Unity. As the Assembly progressed, it was found that there were no serious hindrances to be overcome in polity, and the faith being common between the churches represented, and the experience and purpose one, things were rapidly adjusted until, on Tuesday, October 13th, at 10: 40 a. m., the fact of complete unity and oneness of the Pentecostal Church of the Nazarene and the Holiness Church of Christ was declared by a unanimous rising vote.

A Great Shout. The scene which followed was beyond description. Amid songs of praise and victory, the people shouted a great shout; until finally it burst over all bounds, and they began to march through the aisles of the great tent, until that could not hold them, and they began to march out and around the tent, until at last they gathered on the campus, a great company of nearly a thousand people, who sang and praised the Lord, with a brief address, emphasized by ebullitions of shouting and singing between paragraphs. It was declared by all to be the greatest occasion they ever witnessed. There was no holding back, no opposition, no criticism, but one mighty wave of holy victory and triumph, which was probably never excelled this side of Pentecost. All said, We have seen great things today.

What God Hath Wrought. People were here from Nova Scotia to the Gulf of California, and from Puget Sound to the Gulf of Mexico; and all agreed that it was twice worth crossing the continent to be present. The Sabbath and other specially devotional services were times of great blessing and a good tide of salvation. Many were present to study the movement, and rejoiced with us at what God has wrought, and are turning their steps this way.

It seems now a foregone conclusion that the holiness forces of this country will be very soon largely united in one organic body.

413

Many things have gone before to prepare the way, and now this movement, at each progressive step, seems so providentially ·led, that one incoming wave seems to prepare the way for another. The work moves on with great strides, not according to any human forecast, but by a divine impulse, to the great joy of the bloodwashed host.

Greatness of the Assembly. Rev. Allie Irick, in a vivid and discriminating analysis of the Assembly, says among other things:

It was remarkable for its sound, cool, sane, and smooth business deliberations. Dr. Bresee presided with ability, grace, and favor. He can dispatch more work in less time and in tenderness and love than any man, doubtless, of our day. All the brethren and holy sisters did loyal, faithful work in their various allotted places.

Perfect harmony and Christian love and grace prevailed throughout this entire assemblage. The union was deep, sacred, sweet, close, real, thorough, fitting, satisfying, and eternally sealed by the Holy Ghost. It was more than glorious for the work of salvation in all the services. The power of God increased, the tides rose, conviction seized the throngs that attended, and salvation rolled in upon us from on high.

It was during the year 1908 that Dr. Walker, the well known holiness evangelist, one of the mightiest preachers of full salvation in all the Church of Christ, cast his lot with the Pentecostal Church of the Nazarene, *Dr. E. F. Walker* and became pastor of the First Church at Pasadena, California. He helped the Bible College greatly, and contributed illuminating and inspiring articles to the Nazarene Messenger. Dr. Bresee gave the following tribute to this man of God: "Dr. Walker is in the front row, and that a very short one, in ability to preach the Word. We know of no man in the holiness ranks who is his superior as a preacher. He is a humble, devoted, anointed man, and we rejoice in the strength he brings us."

Home Campmeeting. A great holiness meeting was held at the First Church, in Los Angeles, in the early part of December, 1908, conducted largely by Rev. Seth. C. Rees, and Rev. I. G. Martin.

CHAPTER XLII.

The close of the year 1908 found the Pentecostal Church of the Nazarene with eighteen Districts, and the following District Superintendents.

Eighteen Districts   H. D. Brown, R. M. Guy, C. B. Jernigan, E. Dearn, H. H. Sumlin, H. W. Hoople, A. B. Riggs, C. A. Bromley, H. B. Hosley, A. M. Bowes, J. D. Scott, W. F. Dallas, J. H. Norris, T. H. Agnew, J. W. Goodwin, H. G. Trumbauer, P. G. Linaweaver, and W. E. Fisher.

There were from 250 to 300 churches, with a total membership approximating 11,000. The educational interests of the church were represented chiefly by the Texas Holiness University, the Deets Pacific Bible College, and the Pentecostal Collegiate Institute. The missionary activities of the church extended throughout many heathen countries. Three publishing houses were actively engaged in promulgating holiness doctrines and literature, and pushing the work of the church in every possible way.

On December 4, 1908, speaking of Christmas, Dr. Bresee said: " 'Hail the heaven-born Prince of Peace.' Hail the day that saw His birth. With joy we welcome the day we celebrate as its anniversary. His coming *Christmas* thrilled the universe of angelic life with a new song.

" 'Quick through the vast expanse it flew,
      And loud the echo rolled;
    The theme, the song, the joy, was new —
      'Twas more than heaven could hold.'

"The joy of that coming fills the earth more and more. The chorus of that song of good will and peace and glory

415

to God in the highest, finds echo in innumerable hearts. Through His coming, the company around the great white throne is such as no man can number, and a vast company on earth walk with Him in white.

"No fairy story so affects childhood as these marvelous realistic tales of the angels and heaven-born song, the glorious light on Bethlehem's valleys, the finding of Him with Mary, His mother and Joseph, the star guiding the wise men, and their worship, with offerings of gold, frankincense, and myrrh. No other facts so affect the most thoughtful as these spectacular things, reinforced by the virgin birth, the preceding prophetic utterances, the succeeding revelations of His personality in His life, death, and resurrection, and the effects produced upon the race. With joy we hasten to celebrate His day, and worship at the feet of Him 'who has lifted the gates of empires from their hinges, and turned the stream of human history out of its course,' and who is giving us a new earth by bringing down into it the New Jerusalem.

"Wait! We shall see it all later. Water will blush and turn to wine; waves will cease their commotion and make a rocking cradle for tempests. Funeral processions will stop at His command, and the house of sorrow will be rehabilitated with the voices of love."

During the first half of the year 1909, Dr. Edward F. Walker became one of the pastors of the First Church, in Los Angeles, Dr. Bresee remaining the senior pastor of the church. In the months of May and June, *Progress of the* Dr. Bresee presided over the District As- *Movement* semblies of the San Francisco and Southern California Districts. These Assemblies, as well as those held in other parts of the country, showed a constant advance, and manifested the conquering spirit and trend of the movement.

In August, Rev. W. W. Danner, for many years an honored member and officer of the Iowa Holiness Association, and an able preacher, educator, and executive, accepted the

416

position of dean of the Deets Pacific Bible College. Dr. Bresee was re-elected president, and Dr. E. F. Walker became a member of the faculty. The following additional officers were also elected: Leslie F. Gay, vice president; Lily D. Bothwell, recording secretary; Fred C. Epperson, treasurer. The trustees besides the foregoing were: Rev. Isaiah Reid, Leora Maris, Martha L. Seymour, Rev. H. S. Johnson, C. E. McKee, Rev. John W. Goodwin, Andrew Adams, F. E. Crawford, Jackson Deets, Rev. W. C. Wilson, and Rev. E. A. Girvin.

It was in August, 1909, that the first District campmeeting was held in Southern California. It was a time of great victory and salvation. Among those who preached were Dr. Bresee, Rev. W. W. Danner, Rev. H. J. Elliott, Rev. P. G. Linaweaver, and Brother Fred St. Clair, the well known evangelist.

Describing his journey across the continent in September, 1909, Dr. Bresee says: "The long trips across the continent never lose their exhilaration. To go anywhere as even the lowliest of His messengers, would be sufficient joy. Bishop Taylor used to say, 'The Lord does not need to give me a second invitation to go with Him to any country or any world.' In this trip, as in others, the mountains and deserts and clouds have been full of ministries of pleasure. I enjoy with peculiar pleasure the cloud formations. Nothing in art, and few things in nature excel in beauty their fantastic and often almost lifelike scenes. The deserts and mountains have each their own peculiar charms. The earth and skies are full of magnificence and beauty, which has been spread before us all. Incitements to worship seem to come from all things about us, but none can really worship in the beauty of holiness, but he who sees the riches of glory of divine love, as manifested on Calvary."

Communion With Nature

Rev. Alpin M. Bowes, writing to the Nazarene Messenger in regard to the first session of the Rocky Mountain District Assembly, at Denver, Colo., said: "We especially rejoiced

417

in the high privilege of the presence and ministry of our beloved Dr. Bresee. He proclaimed the Word with great unction and power, and delivered such advice and instruction as will strengthen the cause and encourage the laborers. God was with us in much power, and a deep spiritual atmosphere characterized the entire meeting."

We next hear of Dr. Bresee at the Chicago Central District Assembly, in October. Rev. J. F. Harvey said: "Dr. P. F. Bresee, our senior General Superintendent, was present and presided. His very presence was *His Presence a* a benediction. His sermons and addresses *Benediction* were all under the anointing of the Holy Spirit. He has the fire and the glory, and, though three score and ten, his natural force does not seem to be abated. May God give him strength for many more years to push this work that is so dear to his heart."

While in Chicago, Dr. Bresee presided at important meetings of the General Missionary Board, and the Board of General Superintendents. It would be interesting to tell of his trip to Ponca City, Okla., where Brother and Sister McIntyre were leading a faithful band, of his dedication of the new church building there; and of his great meeting at Oklahoma City, where he first met Dr. H. H. Miller, later of Berkeley, Cal.; but other events crowding each other in his busy, strenuous life, demand attention. His homeward journey was brightened and cheered by the companionship of Brother and Sister Leslie F. Gay.

During the closing weeks of the year, Dr. Bresee devoted much of his energies to the rapidly expanding missionary interests of the church.

The Nazarene University. In the course of a somewhat extended editorial in the Nazarene Messenger of January 20, 1910, Dr. Bresee says:

This year is the best of the years thus far for "The Nazarene University and Deets Pacific Bible College." The larger attendance, the new dean, Rev. W. W. Danner, who is doing especially excellent work, with a fine corps of professors; and the added Academic Course, with Miss Professor Cora Snider, an especially cultured and adapted preceptress, with exceptionally excellent professors, have brought us on a goodly way.

A still further advance is now planned. It has seemed providential to change its location. After careful and prayerful study and examination into possibilities, a large and beautiful tract of land has been purchased at Pasadena — a city of about forty thousand inhabitants, which is far-famed, its attractions being world-wide, because of its beauty and healthfulness, the people loving to emphasize what its name suggests, that it is "The Crown of the Valley." It is a suburb of Los Angeles, and seems to have every advantage for such an institution.

What seems to me to be the most beautiful location in or about it for such a purpose has been purchased for this university. A plat of land of one hundred and thirty-four acres, within a few minutes' ride from the center of the city, lying almost under the shadow of the beautiful Sierra Madre mountains, on the eastern side of Hill avenue, overlooking the city and valley, said to be one of the most beautiful valleys in the world; causing Bishop Gilbert Haven, as he looked upon it, to call it "The Damascus of America," perfectly level only as it slightly slopes toward the south. At the upper end is a kind of palatial residence, with other buildings, with finely ornamented grounds and great trees, all facing a beautiful palm avenue. It is where the frosts do not nip the most delicate flowers or foliage, with a climate all the year most salubrious and healthful; a place that charms every beholder, and which is universally admitted to be ideal. Though the purchase price was $165,000, yet it was providentially cheap, and offers largely in advance were almost immediately made for it. It is expected that about thirty acres will be reserved for a campus, and that the rest will be converted into residence lots for those who may desire to live near the university.

Here it is expected that the school will be opened next year, such additional buildings as may be necessary for the housing of the school being erected. It is expected also that a College of Liberal Arts and other departments will be added, and that comparatively soon the pressing need of a real university, under the most reverent, sacred, and holy influences, will be at hand.

It should be stated in this connection that Brother Fred C. Epperson, the treasurer of the University, secured an option in his own name for the purchase of this magnificent property, during the course of his real estate business, and gladly turned it over to the University, without any profit or compensation, except a moderate commission. For some time Brother Epperson continued to act as financial agent for the University.

During the remainder of his life, Dr. Bresee devoted much of his prayer, thought, and toil to the furtherance of the interests of this University.

PHINEAS F. BRESEE

In April, May, and June, 1910, Dr. and Mrs. Bresee made a very extended trip throughout the central, eastern, and New England States, where he presided over many District
An Extended Trip
Assemblies. If space permitted, I would rejoice to quote fully from his vivid, sparkling reports of the scenes, incidents, and victories of this journey, some of which were thrilling in a high degree. I will, however, give his account of the pilgrimage of himself and his wife to the scenes of their childhood.

Among the Hills. These are the words of Dr. Bresee:

A day was to be spent in central Vermont, and a few days among the hills of New York. A trip along the rivers — Merrimac, Connecticut, White, Deerfield, Hoosick, and Susquehannah — amid the mountains and hills, and through the valleys, with here and there beautiful lakes, at this season of the year, when the buds are just bursting into leaf, with all the variegated hues which the transition reveals, with fruit trees in full blossom, some as white as snow, with green grass everywhere, and country roads, unhindered and unprotected by fences, winding their ways in most enchanting places, into glen and forest, crossing dashing brooks, and through the meadows, with the constantly recurring farmhouse, usually painted white, with outbuildings red, mostly with an air of age and comfort, with so many indescribably beautiful landscapes — arouses in one a sense of beauty, the thrill of which is not soon forgotten.

The cemeteries impressed us, many so large and all seemingly so full. Here the generations rest. Life, struggle, and toil and sorrow, and fitful joy, are over; friend and foe and lover lie quietly side by side. Already in some instances, the stone or board, or marble slab, is crumbling or falling, and one involuntarily says, "Whence? Whither? Where?"

It was in this immediate vicinity that both Mrs. Bresee and myself were children, were reared, and were converted. It was here that I came from the West, a youthful preacher, for my bride, and bore away from her home and friends, one who has fulfilled in largest measure, in all the difficult places through which we have passed, as well as the more open paths, all that can be meant by that sacred name, wife.

But one person is alive out of a large company that was at our wedding, and scare any whom we knew in our youth are here. The hills and the rocks and the streams abide; many houses are just as they were; but the people are gone hence.

In Our Childhood. As in our childhood, the two Methodist village churches about three miles apart, constitute a circuit or charge. There is preaching at the one every Sunday, at 10:30 a. m., and at the other at 1 p. m., and alternately at night. At the one Mrs. Bresee was converted; at the other I bowed at the altar and found peace. ·I was very willing to accept the invitation of the pastor, and preach in both places. Several times we have returned from our western wanderings and looked at these, to us, sacred places; but the memory of the saving grace of our Lord was never more sweet than now. Though all who gathered here are gone, the experience and comfort of the grace of God abides.

One thing is impressed upon us, that all these lands are simply camping grounds for the people as they march to the grave. How they need to hear with heaven-born energy the words from the lips of Jesus, "I am the resurrection and the life."

A Memorable Day. Upon his return to Los Angeles, Dr. Bresee preached a great sermon at the First Church on the resurrection. The scene is thus described by Rev. J. P. Coleman: "The Sabbath, June 12th, at First Church was one of the greatest days we ever saw. Dr. Bresee's sermon was a masterpiece of unanswerable argument for the resurrection of Christ from the dead. It was attended with a power and unction that moved the assembled multitude as trees swept by a tornado. And such it was, though sent from heaven. The people shouted and wept for joy until the noise could be heard afar. At the close they broke forth with our hallelujah song of triumph, with waving of handkerchiefs and great rejoicing. It was worth a lifetime to be permitted to witness what our eyes saw, and to feel the thrill of immortal joy that welled up from overflowing hearts. Our hearts burned within us as we waited in the presence of God with awe and holy triumph. This was truly a milestone in the history of our church."

Great Events. Great events followed one another swiftly during the rest of the year. Some of them were: a glorious home camp meeting at the First Church, Los Angeles, conducted by Rev. Bud Robinson and Rev. J. W. Pierce; the commencement week at the Nazarene University, full of good things; the Southern California District Assembly, presided over very ably by General Superintendent E. P. Ellyson; victorious reports from the foreign missionaries of the church; the Southern California District Camp Meeting, with Rev. C. B. Jernigan, superintendent of the Oklahoma and Kansas District, as the leading preacher: a trip by Dr. and Mrs. Bresee, in October, during which he presided at the annual meeting of the General Missionary Board, held the Chicago Central District Assembly, and preached at Mansfield, Ill., and St. Louis, Mo.; dedication by Dr. Bresee of the new church in Fresno, Cal., of which Rev. C. B. Langdon was the pastor; and, in December, a brief campaign by Dr. Bresee in the Nazarene churches around San Francisco Bay.

Tides of Glory. The year 1910 closed with the Christmas love-feast at the First Church, where, as the meeting went on, the tides of glory passed over it like the rolling waves of the great deep. This was the twenty-fourth successive annual Christmas love-feast conducted by Dr. Bresee.

CHAPTER XLIII.

Rev. C. E. Cornell — Important Happenings — Resolutions of Appreciation — Other Events — Special Bible Edition — A Marvelous Camp Meeting — The Nashville Assembly — Interesting Debates. A Great Tide of Salvation — Brotherly Love — Work of the Assembly — The Great Church Boards — The Work of Missions — Statistics — Dr. Bresee's Report of the Assembly — Its Personnel. The Interest Manifest — The Coming Host — In Memoriam — Loyalty.

Rev. C. E. Cornell. In January, 1911, Rev. C. E. Cornell, after serving for five years with remarkable success the First Pentecostal Church of the Nazarene, at Chicago, resigned his pastorate there, and accepted a call from the First Church in Los Angeles, coming to the latter city with his family and beginning his pastoral work in April. This was made necessary because of the constantly growing labors of Dr. Bresee in the general superintendency, the presidency of the Nazarene University, and the editorship of the Nazarene Messenger, causing him to withdraw entirely from the pastorate of the First Church, the membership of that church reluctantly acquiescing in his decision. These circumstances created the vacancy that was so fittingly filled by Brother Cornell.

Important Happenings. Passing hastily over most of the events which preceded the great General Assembly, at Nashville, Tenn., in October, 1911, I will summarize the most important of them, regarded, of course, from the viewpoint of Dr. Bresee's biographer, as follows:

Resolutions of Appreciation. Just before Dr. Bresee began to preach at the First Church, Los Angeles, on Sunday morning, March 19, 1911, Rev. J. P. Coleman arose and read the following resolutions:

WHEREAS, We have had the rare privilege of the continued pastoral relation of the Rev. P. F. Bresee, D. D., with this the mother church of the denomination, from its organization until the present time, who under God became the leader in the founding of this church; and

WHEREAS, With the increasing responsibilities devolving upon him as General Superintendent, together with his work in connection with the university, and as editor of the Nazarene Messenger, with other duties pertaining to his official relation to the church, he finds it a necessity to resign the pastorate of First Church; and

WHEREAS, We recognize that through the instrumentality of his faithful preaching of the Word, enforced by his upright and blameless life, he has been made a great blessing, not only to us as a local church, but through him, aided by the divine Spirit, influences have gone out in streams of blessing to multiplied thousands of people throughout the length and breadth of the land, which in ever widening circles are sweeping around the world, bringing hope and encouragement to sin-burdened hearts; therefore, be it

Resolved, By the First Church of the Nazarene of Los Angeles, California, that we hereby render to Almighty God profound thanks for His great mercy in sparing to the church one so peculiarly gifted for the work, who has been to us not only pastor, but a true helper, a tried friend and brother indeed; that during these years he has gone in and out among us, visiting our homes, comforting the sick and dying, burying our dead, and out of the fulness of his great heart, performing innumerable deeds of kindness and benevolence, known only to Him who takes cognizance of each act done in His name.

Resolved, That while we shall miss him in the more intimate relation of pastor; and, while we feel keenly the necessity placed upon us to part with him, yet, recognizing his call to fields of greater usefulness, and that the time has come for the enlarging of the work of organized holiness, not only in the homeland, but throughout the world, we bow to this overruling providence, knowing that He doeth all things well.

Resolved, That in accepting this resignation, we wish to record our unbounded confidence in him, and also to express our great love and profound respect for him, and shall ever cherish among the many precious recollections of his long and faithful pastorate, his wise counsels, his holy example, his self-sacrificing devotion, and Christlike interest in our welfare.

Resolved, That we commend him to the ever watchful care and guiding hand of our heavenly Father, and also to the church at large, and to all lovers of holiness, as one especially qualified by his spirituality and experience to unify the forces in the holiness ranks, and to inspire them by his faith for the great battle against sin and worldliness.

Resolved, That we extend to him as our General Superintendent at any and all times when it shall be possible for him, a glad welcome to our pulpit, and we assure him that our hearts and our homes are always open to him. And we trust that we shall be permitted to share together our mutual church home until called to the church triumphant.

Resolved, That we tender to Sister Bresee, the devoted wife and faithful companion, who through toil and sacrifice has ever shown the heroic spirit of true Christian womanhood, our highest esteem and Christian affection, and assure her that her kindly ministry, her gentle nature, and true devotion have won a place in our hearts never to be erased, and our constant prayer shall be that her useful life may be spared to us for many years to come.

Resolved, That we express our high appreciation to the family for their uniform kindness, loyalty, and generous support toward our cause, and we cherish the hope that together we may continue to share in our church home; and when toil and conflicts are done, we may all come to the "Eastern Gate" to go out no more for ever.

J. P. COLEMAN
L. F. GAY
J. W. GOODWIN
T. A. ASBRIDGE

After a few appropriate words by Rev. J. W. Goodwin, district superintendent, the resolutions were adopted by an enthusiastic, rising vote.

Other Events. Brother Cornell commenced the work of his pastorate at the First Church, Los Angeles, on Sunday, March 26th. During the month of March, Dr. Bresee resigned the presidency of the Nazarene University, and Rev. E. P. Ellyson, D. D., was elected to fill the vacancy, with the understanding that he would enter upon the duties of his position at the beginning of the ensuing college year. Some time previously Rev. W. W. Danner had withdrawn from the office of Dean of the Bible College, and Rev. H. O. Wiley had been elected in his stead.

Special Bible Edition. On April 13, 1911, the Nazarene Messenger appeared as a special English Bible number, and in that issue appear the following noble utterances from the pen of Dr. Bresee:

For three hundred years the eyes of men have been looking upon this excellent version of the Bible known as King James Version. How many eyes now closed in death have carefully scanned its pages! How many hearts have thrilled with unutterable rapture as they have laid hold of the marvelous truth, and the light of God has come streaming through the Word to their souls! How many weary, worn pilgrims have tarried by the wayside to drink from this fountain of living waters, to be refreshed and strengthened for the rugged climbing! How many burdened hearts have gazed into its promise until they have seen Him whose brow is marred more than the sons of men, and at the sight their burdens have rolled off, like that of Bunyan's pilgrim at the sight of Him who hung on the cross! How many as they have come into the valley, and it seemed as if they might be overshadowed, have marked the lights along the way hung out by this Word; and as the waters have been about their feet, and the spray on their brow, have heard God speak through the words of this Book, and have been comforted and strengthened into triumph! How our language has been purified, and human utterance uplifted, and social life made luminous, by the clear, tender, lofty tone of this great Book of sacred history, poetry, and salva-

425

tion! How the English-speaking nations have drunk in its ideals of liberty and brotherhood and jurisprudence! It has passed through almost every conceivable crucible, and has come forth as gold tried in the fire. Every test has added to its luster. It has gone forth conquering its way, and still goes on to conquest. No book has been so assaulted; none has been so vindicated. No book has been so widely read; none held in such sacred confidence and love. No wicked human hate has been able to destroy or even mar it. It is still a lamp shining into the dark places, guiding the feet of men into the way where there is full-orbed day. Men still find that in the way of these testimonies is great delight, and through them is transformation and hope. Many still whisper with sacred awe, "I will not forget thy word."

In May Rev. C. W. Ruth and Rev. Seth C. Rees held a great meeting in First Church, Los Angeles; and in the same month Dr. Bresee presided at the San Francisco District Asembly, held in the Oakland Church, of which Rev. E. M. Isaac was pastor. A little later Dr. Bresee presided at the Northwestern District Assembly, and held a gracious meeting at Boise, Idaho. The Southern California District Assembly, at Ontario, beginning June 28th, was a memorable gathering, Dr. Bresee presiding with patience, tact and skill, and Rev. Fred C. Epperson performing the duties of secretary with exceptional efficiency. Rev. J. W. Goodwin withdrew from the district superintendency to take, in conjunction with Brother J. F. Sanders, the financial management of the Nazarene University, and Rev. W. C. Wilson was elected in his stead. At that time no one present had any thought that the time would soon come when both Brother Goodwin and Brother Wilson would be members of the Board of General Superintendents of the church.

Shortly after the adjournment of the Southern California District Assembly, Dr. Bresee and Brother Goodwin journeyed through northern California, the Northwest, Utah, and Colorado, in the interests of the Nazarene University, in connection with the district assemblies.

A Marvelous Camp Meeting. The Southern California camp meeting, held at University Park, Pasadena, from August 24th to September 3d, was the greatest that I have ever attended. It was my privilege to attend, and I thus characterized it at the time: "I take it that this mighty manifestation of Jehovah in His shekinah glory is fraught with the deepest and profoundest significance. It indicates to me that in this Nazarene movement God is going to shake the world. Never before have I witnessed such streams of holy fire, such constant heavenly breezes, such great overpowering tides of salvation. In the place made sacred by such marvelous displays of unearthly power, hundreds of souls have been born into the kingdom and reclaimed, or sanctified wholly, and the disciples of Christ have learned lessons of prayer and faith of which they were never cognizant before. This unspeakably glorious work will go on and on, crossing continents, leaping mountains and inundating the isles of the sea." Rev. Seth C. Rees, Rev. C. E. Cornell, and Rev. Guy L. Wilson were the preachers. We were fortunate, also, in having Brother and Sister Bresee with us. The very presence of the former was an inspiration to us all, and the smiling, happy face and cordial greeting of Sister Bresee gave us a constant uplift.

One day was set apart for the Nazarene University, and Dr. Bresee in a brief address summarized the great events that had culminated in the Nazarene movement. He said that the supply of men who could preach and spread Scriptural holiness was entirely unequal to the demand, and that we would be compelled to make our own preachers; that the other great religious bodies of the country had largely gone out of the business of making holiness preachers; and that, in order for us to do it, we must have a great holiness university.

Before the close of the camp meeting Dr. and Mrs. Bresee started on an extended tour of large portions of the West and South, attending several district assemblies, over which he presided, and arriving at Nashville, Tennessee, a little before the opening of the General Assembly in that city, on October 5, 1911.

The Nashville Asembly. The writer was privileged to be present as a member of the Southern California delegation, and so will take the liberty of giving his own impressions as they were written on the ground, and those of Dr. Bresee. My first report, published in the Nazarene Messenger on October 19, 1911, was as follows:

Several cars filled with happy, shouting members of the Pentecostal Church of the Nazarene, reached the city of Nashville, Tenn., at different hours, beginning with the evening of October 4th, and ending with the morning of the 6th.

All the delegates were met by representatives of the Pentecostal Mission, and were escorted to the mission, which occupies a large brick building on Fourth avenue. Here they were assigned to the place where they were to be entertained. Too much can not be said of the thoughtful, loving hospitality shown by the members of this mission, and especially the head of the mission, Rev. J. O. McClurkan.

The sessions of the Assembly are held in the large auditorium of the mission, our committees are meeting in the chapel and other rooms of the mission, and most of our delegates are taking their meals at its dining-hall.

About two hundred delegates are in attendance, a considerable proportion of whom are women. Their spirituality and intelligence are of a very high order.

Rev. Fred C. Epperson was elected secretary, with Brothers F. H. Mendell, E. J. Fleming, and C. A. Kinder as assistant secretaries. Their work has been extremely efficient.

Interesting Debates. Many stirring and interesting debates have occurred, giving opportunity for the display of forensic ability and parliamentary skill. Thus far these debates have been brought forth in connection with the admission of delegates more or less irregularly chosen, and the adoption of the report of the joint Commission created for the purpose of reaching a basis for the union of our church and the Methodist Protestant Church of Louisiana, having a membership of three thousand. Finally the report of the Commission was referred to the Committee on Manual Revision.

The Committee on Publishing Interests has already agreed to recommend the establishment of a great, centrally-located publishing house, under the management of a board of seven members. The Committee on Manual Revision has refused to recommend any change in the name of the church, and is now wrestling with other exceedingly difficult questions.

Victory is in the air, and our God is leading us on to new conquests. The singing has been especially good, and the musical part of the services has been greatly helped by our Peniel University orchestra.

Our beloved senior General Superintendent, Rev. P. F. Bresee, was quite ill when the General Assembly convened, and he is still a very sick man. Nevertheless, he has presided at the different sessions of the Assembly, ably assisted by General Superintendent Reynolds. Dr. Bresee was unanimously re-elected as General Superintendent; and Rev. H. F. Reynolds was re-elected by a good majority. Dr. E. F. Walker was chosen as the third member of the Board of General Superintendents.

A Great Tide of Salvation. From the first session there has been a great tide of salvation. Already many have been saved and sanctified. The first day was practically wholly devoted to worship. Evangelistic services have been held every evening, with great congregations. In fact, the large auditorium is not sufficiently capacious, and on Sunday, October 9th, the services were held in the great Ryman Auditorium, erected years ago for Sam Jones to preach in. During the day, the congregations ranged from two thousand five hundred to three thousand, and God gave us glorious victory. Dr. E. F. Walker preached a mighty sermon in the morning from John 17: 19. Rev. Bud Robinson gave a characteristic message in the afternoon, and Rev. Seth C. Rees preached with unction and power in the evening, taking for his theme, "The Cross of Christ."

In the Nazarene Messenger of October 26th, appeared the following from my pen:

Brotherly Love. Now that the Assembly is over, it is possible to see it in its general outlines, and discern its great distinguishing characteristics. These may be briefly summed up as follows:

1. The spirit of brotherly love prevailed. While there were wide differences of opinion on many points, and earnest debate on the floor of the Assembly and in the different committees, there was no bitterness or harshness. The sincerity of all was unquestioned, and in everything that transpired there was nothing which caused me for one moment to doubt the earnest purpose of every delegate to promote the prosperity of the church and the upbuilding of the kingdom of God.

2. A very large proportion of the delegates were men and women of exceptional ability. They showed this in their discussion of important questions before the Assembly, in the character of the work which they performed on the committees, and in the able and luminous reports that emanated from these committees.

3. The spirit of the body was progressive, and yet not too radical. While the Assembly kept fully abreast of the onward sweep and growth of the church, it turned its face against everything which seemed to be speculative and visionary, and refused in nearly every case to restate doctrines, or make fundamental changes in legislation.

Work of the Assembly. Much of the time and energy of the leading men of the Assembly was taken up with the two closely connected subjects of tobacco and secret societies. At Pilot Point, three years ago, the brethren from Texas and Oklahoma united with the Pentecostal Church of the Nazarene under the impression that the paragraphs of the Manual dealing with these subjects were legislative, and, hence, a test of membership. When they learned that this was not the case, but that the matters referred to came merely under the head of Special Advices, they insisted upon having the Manual so amended as to put these paragraphs under the head of General Rules, thus making them obligatory, instead of advisory. Their delegates were successful in effecting these changes.

Closely related to these paragraphs was a provision put into the Manual to the effect that the local churches may adopt a probationary system.

As a result of this action, and of a change in our legislation to the effect that all the acts of the District and General Superintendents shall be subject to the respective vetoes of District and General Assemblies, it is probable that a large majority of the three thousand members of the Methodist Protestant Church of Louisiana will unite with the Pentecostal Church of the Nazarene.

The Great Church Boards. The greatest constructive work of the Assembly was the creation of four great boards, known as the Board of Publication, the Board of Education, the Board of Church Extension, and the Board of Rescue Work and City Missions.

The Board of Publication consists of seven members, and will have its headquarters at Kansas City, Mo. It will there carry on a general publishing house, and, as soon as possible, will conduct a great central church paper. Rev. B. F. Haynes is the president of this board; W. T. McConnell, of Texas, its secretary; Rev. A. S. Cochran, of Kansas City, its treasurer; Rev. C. J. Kinne, of Los Angeles, its manager. Rev. DeLance Wallace, L. D. Peavey, and W. M. Creal are the other members of the board. Negotiations are already under way for the purchase of the good will and property of the *Pentecostal Advocate*, the Nazarene Publishing Company, the *Beulah Christian*, and the *Pentecostal Era*, having valuable printing presses and equipment, and an aggregate weekly circulation of about sixteen thousand. Rev. Bud Robinson has donated to the board $4,200 of his stock in the Pentecostal Advocate Company, and Rev. H. B. Hosley has given to the board the subscription list of the Pentecostal Era, numbering four thousand. During this Assembly it was announced that $50,000 would be needed for the establishment of the publishing house and paper; and in a short time $20,000 of this amount was subscribed.

The Work of Missions. Quite a number of missionaries were present at the Assembly, and much interest was taken in missions. The General Missionary Board was reconstructed under the name of the General Foreign Missionary Board, so as to consist of the three General Superintendents and twelve other members — six ministers and six laymen. For the purpose of selecting these twelve, the country is divided into six great divisions, and one minister and one layman are chosen from each. Rev. William Howard Hoople, of New York, is president of this board, and Rev. H. F. Reynolds is the General Secretary. Rev. Lucy P. Knott and Mr. Leslie F. Gay represent California on the board.

The Board of Church Extension hereafter will do much of the work which heretofore has been done in this country by the General Missionary Board.

The great holiness university of Peniel, Texas, representing an investment of $100,000, has been turned over to our church. Henceforth it and all the other educational institutions of the Pentecostal Church of the Nazarene will be under the general control of our Board of Education.

Statistics. The report of the Statistical Secretaries showed a total membership of more than twenty thousand, and nearly a million dollars worth of church property. Our church has practically doubled in membership and property during the last three years; and during the last year we have devoted about $25,000 to missions.

A PRINCE IN ISRAEL

The General Assembly at Nashville marks a great historical epoch in our movement. It was great in its personnel, great in its spirituality, great in its purpose, great in its work, and great in its influence upon the future. Dr. Bresee's report, in part, was as follows:

The third General Assembly of the Pentecostal Church of the Nazarene, held at Nashville, Tenn., is not to be soon forgotten, especially by those who had the privilege of being present and taking part in its work. It was far from being a holiday. The eleven days were full of toil and devotion. Great questions were grappled with, the best methods possible devised, and the Lord's own way of carrying on the work most carefully sought.

That all personal training, sectional prejudice, and individual notions melted into perfect oneness as easily as would have been ideal, might be too much to say; but that there did prevail an overmastering spirit of love and unity that did melt all before it, is true. All seemed filled with the one desire: to find the Lord's pattern for the work, and to carry it out in the earth. That perfection was reached, or the very best possible results found in everything, might be too much to claim; but the work done forms a body for the great spirit and purpose of the church to work in and through for the next four years, to which all agreed, and the promise and expectancy of great success rests upon it.

Some things pertaining to the Assembly impressed us.

Its Personnel. It was a striking assemblage. In it were many men of power. One could easily count up more than a dozen men of national reputation as preachers, and while many more of the same class could be counted in the denomination who were not present, yet it seemed remarkable that so large a number should be gathered in the Assembly. As a result, the preaching was mostly excellent, some of it touching the very highest line of pulpit effort. And yet there was nothing for show, or for literary or oratorical effect; and God crowned His Word at every service with the salvation of souls. The secret of the holiness movement in developing great preachers, lies in the fact that it has a message to men. The absence of this power among a people, when the gospel is emasculated, is because there is no real message.

The Interest Manifest. The local interest was great, the large hall where the Assembly was held being usually crowded, both at the business sessions and at the weekday religious services. We were told that no church or religious gatherings ventured to take the great auditorium for their Sabbath services; but great audiences were gathered there both Sabbaths. The daily papers said that no religious gathering had so affected the city since the great meeting of Moody and Sanky. We were told by a thoughtful observer that the joy of our people made a great impression. Many people were present from long distances. Some wondered "whereunto this thing would grow," and others rejoiced that there was a "sect of the Nazarene," where not only those driven from their churches because of holiness could find a home, but that there was an organized agency to push full salvation and hold the ground. It was a time of seed sowing for the whole Southeast.

The Coming Host. The Old Guard are firm, united, and invincible. They stand East, West, North, South, with banners flying. But, as Wellington rejoiced in the coming of Blucher, they rejoiced in the constantly gathering reinforcements. Almost every District has an oncoming crop of promising young men. We were impressed with this in the Districts that we have recently visited. The president of Oklahoma Holiness College told us that he knew eight or ten young men in that District who gave large promise of great excellence in the pastorate. Abilene and Dallas Districts have a host of young men that promise well. There has been among them an undue tendency toward being evangelists, but a hopeful reaction has set in toward the pastorate, which that great field so much needs. Kansas District is also bringing its young men to the front. God is raising up holiness schools to train as many of them as possible for larger service. We have reason to believe that what we say of these Districts is true of many.

In Memoriam. The Assembly was more than startled, early in its session, by the announcement of the death of Rev. Isaiah Reid, so well and long known as one of the leaders in the holiness work in this country; who by pen as well as voice had so earnestly uttered the message. It seemed to us peculiarly sudden, as it had been but four weeks since we parted from him at the close of the Kansas District Assembly. He had recently found his way back into the Pentecostal Church of the Nazarene, and an open door to what seemed a wide field of usefulness as teacher of theology in the Kansas Holiness Institute. The District Assembly had recognized his orders, he preached with much liberty, and seemed especially happy, loving, and hopeful. We little thought that we should see his face no more. We trust that he has gone to join that division of the army to which he seemed to more especially belong, represented by such of our brethren as Inskip, McDonald, Wood, and Kent, who have preceded him.

Loyalty. To be fully loyal to a church there must be a deep conviction that it is doing the will and work of God, and that we are built into it by divine grace and power. The men and women who are really of this work known as the Pentecostal Church of the Nazarene, have had its life begotten in them by the Holy Ghost, and its work is brought forth as a holy service unto God. As Jesus was the Son of man, born by divine love and power, through human necessity, so this work is born of the Spirit through the deep necessities of men, and is the spiritual child of these devoted hearts. To simply say that they love it, seems to lack fervency. Their very being has gone forth into it. Anything that would seem to threaten to divide or mar it, seemed to send a thrill of agony. It was the heartless woman who was not the real mother, who could consent to see the child cut in twain and divided; the real mother was ready for any sacrifice rather than the severing of the child of her life. There seemed very generally this sacred sense of motherhood in the hearts of the Assembly, in reference to this precious work. Many, we believe most, felt, "This is God's work, born by the Spirit through my soul." This was the keynote of its unity and strength and the promise of its future.

CHAPTER XLIV.

It will not be feasible within the limits of this volume to
narrate in detail the stirring events of the last four years
of Dr. Bresee's life. He traveled much as General Superintendent, presiding over District Assemblies,
His Last explaining as no one else could, the distinc-
Four Years tive peculiarities of the Nazarene movement,
holding conventions, assisting in the organization of new churches, dedicating new church edifices, preaching with all his might the glorious possibilities of the sanctified life, inspiring his brethren by his example, his voice, and
his pen, to heroic and lofty Christian ideals, and doing his
utmost in every way to promote the work of organized holiness. He devoted much of his time and thought to the management and upbuilding of the Nazarene University. During the comparatively brief seasons that he was permitted
to dwell in his home at Los Angeles, he busied himself with
an extended correspondence, attended numerous meetings of
the Board of Trustees of the University, and preached
nearly every Sunday in the various Nazarene churches of
Los Angeles and other cities in Southern California. It was
during this period that Professor A. J. Ramsay, a man of
rare culture, ability, and spirituality, became dean of
Deets Pacific Bible College and Brother C. E. Jones, an
experienced and capable business man, was appointed Financial Agent of the Nazarene University.

As the time sped by, Dr. Bresee's health gradually failed,
and the condition of his heart made it impossible for him to
endure much physical exertion. And yet, strange to say, he

was able to put as much energy as ever into his sermons, without the slightest physical inconvenience. Because of his heart trouble, he was accompanied by Mrs. Bresee in the numerous journeys required for the performance of his duties as General Superintendent. With her loving care and delightful companionship, he was enabled to engage in the strenuous activities involved in traveling from state to state, presiding over and planning for the highest welfare of District Assemblies, and preaching almost daily, and sometimes three times a day, without apparent injury.

On December 30, 1911, some sixty members of the First Church of Los Angeles, met at the residence of Dr. and Mrs. Bresee, the occasion of their gathering being the seventy-third anniversary of his birth. This oc-
Seventy-Third curred on Sunday, December 31st, and
Birthday hence it was decided to celebrate the evening previous. The gathering was a genuine surprise to Brother and Sister Bresee. By common consent, Rev. C. E. Cornell took charge, and called upon Brother T. A. Asbridge to lead in prayer. Several hymns were sung, Brother Cornell made a few appropriate remarks, and Brother and Sister Bresee both expressed their appreciation of the love and thoughtfulness of the brethren. The former spoke at some length of the providential circumstances connected with their coming to California. Several presents were handed to Dr. Bresee, among them being a purse of fifty-five dollars.

A Tribute in Verse. On this occasion E. A. Girvin read the following stanzas, written by himself:

I know a man whose walk has been with God
   For nearly threescore years, who gave his youth
To Jesus, and, without reserve, at home, abroad,
   Has served right royally the cause of truth.
A man of brilliant gifts, of eloquence
   That thrills the heart, of logic that persuades
The reason, for it is without pretense,
   Or sophistry, whose power never fades.
A man with great and splendid intellect endowed,
   And yet with vast capacity of soul;
With simple trust in friends, and never proud,
   But humbler ever as he neared the goal.

A PRINCE IN ISRAEL

I see him in life's morning, as he rode
    A fiery messenger of grace divine,
And preached in church and school and rude abode,
    While on his soul the heavenly light did shine.
A noble spirit his, a strong, undaunted soul;
    Ah, fearlessly he pushed the battle on;
For thus he aimed to reach the glorious goal
    That he had set before him in life's dawn.
While others earthly wealth and honor sought,
    His quest was souls, as trophies for his Lord;
While others with mere carnal weapons fought,
    He served his Captain with the Spirit's sword.

Where'er he preached the Word, revivals blazed,
    And guilty sinners found a gracious peace,
Rejoicing in salvation, and amazed
    That inner tempests should so quickly cease.
But, as the years passed by, he had to fight
    A strange, mysterious principle within,
Suggesting doubts and fears — the foe of right,
    The friend of every form and phase of sin.
One day God suddenly met all his need,
    And in a moment made his spirit whole;
The blood of Jesus set him free indeed;
    The Holy Ghost indwelt and filled his soul.

Thus filled and thrilled from heart to fingertips,
    He preached with burning unction from on high,
And everywhere, with heaven-anointed lips,
    He told of Jesus' power to sanctify.
God gave him souls, and multitudes he led
    Unto the fountain that makes wholly pure,
While to the hungry he gave heavenly bread,
    In Jesus' name, and taught them to endure.
At last God called him in a wondrous way
    To follow Jesus as the Nazarene;
And organize His people for the fray
    With sin and Satan and the hosts unclean.

A hundred other holy heroes knelt
    Around him on that great, momentous day,
And formed a band in whom the Savior dwelt,
    And mightily His power did display.
By voice and pen and constant sacrifice,
    This man of God the holy battle waged,
While sympathy he gave and counsel wise,
    To those who with him in the war engaged.
The movement spread, prospered by power divine,
    From California to the Atlantic's shore;
And multitudes of saints sprang into line,
    Both North and South, and all the country o'er.
But in the thickest fight I see this man,
    And hear his clarion voice denouncing sin;
While looking heavenward he leads the van,
    And trusts in God the victory to win.

435

PHINEAS F. BRESEE

His erstwhile raven locks are silv'ry now;
  His form is not as sturdy as before.
For seventy years and three have touched his brow,
  And brought him nearer the eternal shore.
All thro' the long, long years of holy strife,
  He ever found encouragement and cheer
From her who in his youth became his wife —
  A noble woman, one who is the peer
Of all the heroines of Holy Writ,
  Of Hannah, Esther, Deborah, or Ruth,
Those saintly souls, who, thro' the ages sit
  Enthroned on high, exemplars of the truth.

We hope and pray that Phineas F. Bresee,
  And she who all his joys and woes has shared,
May linger with us long; that they may be
  For many years to church and children spared.
God grant that they may yet with joy behold
  A hundred thousand heroes of this fight,
As soldiers of the Nazarene enrolled,
  With holy ardor warring for the right.

"Thou Hast Well Seen." On Sunday morning, February 11, 1912, Dr. Bresee gave the message in the First Church, at Los Angeles, his theme being "Thou Hast Well Seen," Jeremiah, 1 : 12. The following is the writer's report of the sermon in metrical form:

What was it that the prophet saw,
  When God declared, "Thou hast well seen"?
Was it the old Mosaic law,
  Designed to make God's people clean?
Or was it visions of the glory
Set forth in sacred song and story?

Did Jeremiah really see
  The mighty truths of saving grace,
Embodied in an almond tree?
  And could he from this vision trace
In Christ the river of salvation,
Which reaches every tribe and nation?

Ah! yes, for God had poured the light
  Upon him; he could understand.
What was it that thus gave him sight?
  The fingers of the wounded hand,
So gentle, and withal possessing
Such power in the way of blessing.

He saw the budding of the rod,
  Betokening Jehovah's choice;
While rebels fell before the God
  Who made His people to rejoice.
He saw within the place most holy,
A man whose mein was meek and lowly.

436

It was the great high priest, who came
   Close to the sacred mercy seat,
And for the people's sin and shame,
   Brought forth an offering complete;
And, with a faith that did not falter,
Sprinkled with blood the golden altar.

He heard the ringing of each bell
   Upon the priestly robe, and knew
Its ringing meant "Emmanuel,"
   For God's shekinah came in view,
While everywhere throughout the nation,
Resounding horns announced salvation.

He saw, far down the flight of years,
   The mighty Savior, full of grace,
With agony and groans and tears,
   Lay down His life for all our race.
'T was thus that faithful Jeremiah
Foresaw the glorious Messiah.

Again he looked, and saw the tomb
   Where Christ, the crucified, had lain,
And knew that Death had lost its gloom,
   And ne'er could touch the Lord again;
For on the third day He had risen,
And burst the doors of Satan's prison.

On April 17, 1912, the HERALD OF HOLINESS, the new official organ of the Pentecostal Church of the Nazarene, made its first appearance, as a beautiful 16-page paper. It was then as now, published in Kansas City, Mo., with the following staff. Editor, B. F. Haynes, D.D.; Office Editor, C. A. McConnell; Agent of the Publishing House of the Pentecostal Church of the Nazarene, by which the paper was published, C. J. Kinne. The HERALD OF HOLINESS gave very bright promise of the future — a promise which it has more than fulfilled. In looking over the files of the paper, I find many notable articles by Dr. Bresee.

The Herald of Holiness

He thus begins a thoughtful discussion of the mission of the Pentecostal Church of the Nazarene, in the issue of December 18, 1912: "The day does not begin with the noontide fulness of light. No great vision is born full-orbed. There is first the gray twilight, the azure in the heavens, then the golden beam on the mountain tops, the retreating pur-

ple of the valleys, and the fulness of light." He then goes
on to speak of the origin, growth, and development of the
Nazarene movement.

International Holiness Convention. In October, 1913, a
great gathering of holiness workers from all over the world
was held in Chicago. Among those who delivered addresses
was Dr. Bresee, his theme being "The Necessity of Organization." He spoke with a clearness of statement, strength of
logic, and keenness of philosophic insight that carried conviction to those who heard him.

A Partial Survey. In the issue of the HERALD OF HOLI-
NESS of January 7, 1914, Dr. Bresee says among other things:

> As a whole, the work is going forward with a good degree of
> rapidity. We have closed up the eighteenth year since the Church
> of the Nazarene was organized, and the other branches have gener-
> ally near the same length of history since their beginning. It seems
> questionable whether any other compactly organized movement for
> the spread of evangelical Christianity, since the days of Constan-
> tine, has made at the beginning, in eighteen years — in evangelism,
> in organization, in general upbuilding, in educational provisions,
> and in institutons — so great an advance. It has had the difficul-
> ties, struggles, and discouragements of infancy; the ostracism, per-
> secution, and mistrust of being new in the world; it has known the
> coldness of friends and the blows of enemies; it has had to create
> the beginnings of all kinds of institutional life; it has been obliged
> to create and test leadership, raise up workers, build churches, get
> people saved and sanctified, overcome prejudice, and opposition of
> many kinds; and yet it has passed the empirical period, established
> its right to life, and is enjoying the privilege.
> We are not like other people: we are to sing our shouts and
> shout our songs, and shout without our songs, and maintain and re-
> joice in our separation from the world, and unto the Lord, to be His
> own peculiar people — made peculiar by His manifest presence, and
> the holy fragrance of hearts and lives filled with His love.

Dr. Bresee continued in the harness until the end. Occasionally when his health would fail, or his physical strength
would flag for a few days, he would relax his labors, but as
soon as he recovered his wonted bodily pow-
In the Harness ers, he resumed his activities. He preached
his last sermons in the First Church of Los
Angeles, in August, 1915. They were masterly in every way,
and full of high thought, unctuous utterance, and impassioned eloquence. During the months of July and August,

he wrote several articles for the HERALD OF HOLINESS. In another chapter I have given the outline of his last commencement day address at the University of California.

On September 2d, an interesting program was given at the Nazarene University, in connection with the beginning of the new college year, and Dr. Bresee delivered a
His Last Address at the University strikingly original address, in the course of which he set forth the fundamental principles involved in Christian education. He took for his text
2 Timothy, 3.17: "That the man of God may be perfect, thoroughly furnished unto all good works."

The following is a very brief epitome of his discourse:

The Work of Education. The work of education lies deep in the foundation of the work of this dispensation. The very last words of the Old Testament, as the last prophet stood on its crumbling beach, looked out over four hundred years of trackless waters, and discerning the hilltops of the unseen ages, caught a glimpse of the light of the Sun of Righteousness purpling the hillsides and valleys of the new era, were: "He shall turn the heart of the fathers to the children, and the heart of the children to their fathers, lest I come and smite the earth with a curse." And when the Son of man trod the earth, and opened up with His bleeding heart the way, he said, "Go, disciple and teach."

Human Personality. The greatest thing of which we know in all the creation and movements of God, is a human life. A human personality, with a few brief years, and yet eternal in its destiny, is like a star blazing across the sky, leaving a flame of glory to burn for ever. I know that a human life may not be luminous; that there may be no light; that it may cross the area of being, sink beneath the horizon, and be all dark. Of such a life I do not speak. It is not God's plan. His call is, "Arise and be luminous, for thy light has come." A man filled with goodness and truth, shines like the stars for ever.

In a great school, one department might be working at this, and another at that, but all are to fit into a personality after the pattern. As the Lord said to Moses in reference to the tabernacle, and all the wondrously typical things pertaining to it, "See, saith he, that thou make all things according to the pattern shewed thee in the mount."

The Pattern. The pattern is "a man of God." We have no ambition or desire to turn out from this institution men other than men of God. When Dan Crawford was coming out of Africa, he brought a party of his native friends to the railroad, and while they waited by the locomotives and cars, he was beguiled into the European habit of boasting of modern science, and its achievements. He told his black companions of automobiles, submarines, aeroplanes, wireless telegraphy, etc. They listened, but it was evident

439

that they were not impressed. The spokesman of the group of Africans said: "To be better off is not to be better." We are here to be better off, but to be sure also that we are better.

We labor for the certainty that every product of manhood from this institution shall be a man of God; that his desires, purposes, volitions, longings, and loves shall be Godward; that his being — whatever there be to it; his life —whatever there be of it; that his possibilities and destiny — are all surrendered to Jesus Christ; that he has written his name beneath the crimson folds of the banner of Calvary; and that for him to live is Christ.

A Man of God. We expect him to be — we shall undertake to help him to be, on the highest line — a man of God, perfect. But we are told that this is folly; that none are perfect. And yet Paul, writing to the boy Timothy, that young preacher, who was yet in his apprenticeship, said, "That the man of God may be perfect." There is a perfection amid much imperfection. Listen to the voice of the Lord, "Be ye therefore perfect, even as God is perfect."

"Thoroughly furnished unto every good work." Every part of his redeemed and purified being needs furnishing. His body needs to be inured to intellectual toil. College and university athletics, as a matter of physical development, are a grotesque humbug. A few men get muscle at the expense of brains, and many get harm. We make no center of attraction of athletics, which creates a few bullies, hinders intellectual excellence, and destroys spiritual ideals.

We would have such exercise as would strengthen and train the body to be the efficient servant of a clear brain, noble heart, and pure soul. A subjected and trained body, with good food, plenty of sound sleep and sufficient exercise, will create conditions favorable to spiritual devotions, clear, strong intellectual effort, and such service as may be possible.

Mental Furnishing. But especially are we here for mental furnishing. The first thing which we prize is a royal atmosphere, full of intellectual and spiritual ozone. A pure atmosphere, reinforced from ocean breadths and mountain tops, means much for intellectual and spiritual conditions. Men and women are to be so trained as to be immune from intellectual and spiritual diseases. It is sought that intellectually and spiritually diseased men shall be debarred from creating influences here. Men and women who exude the microbes of worldly or low ideals, or of doubt, or of fanaticism, or of phariseeism, or of selfishness, are to be excluded. We want nothing second-rate or doubtful here. This platform is not a free forum, except in the sense of freedom toward the best, the purest, the noblest. The vagaries of such abnormalities as I have mentioned are not expected to find a place here; but truth, saving truth, luminous with the light of love and the glory of God.

These are not the groves of sectarianism. Any students, or others, who may be of any church, will we trust, find no effort here to proselyte, but to help each of them to be "a man of God, perfect, throughly furnished unto every good work."

But we mean that there shall be a strong, pure, healthy denominationalism. We have no sympathy with the twaddle which attempts to express the desire that all people be of one denomination. We believe that such is neither providential nor desirable. We are lovingly, earnestly, intensely denominational. If any one wishes to criticize his own denomination, this is a poor place for him to do it.

A Pure Atmosphere. We seek to make an atmosphere, pure, unselfish, full of divine love and holy thought, which shall be a spiritual and intellectual tonic to every one who is so fortunate as to draw breath in it. To this end, in the name of the Board of Trustees, I ask all who come in touch with this institution, to help us.

But we do not live on atmosphere alone, vital as it is. In this atmosphere we have arrangements for intellectual nourishment. First, there is the Word of Life. Here the standard is the Word of God. It is appealed to, honored, studied. It is the standard of experience, morals, life.

We have not forsaken the old classics. We do not fear philosophy. We delight in mathematics. We cultivate the sciences. We undertake to know what we may of the Word of Life, to learn here to be learners, that God may teach us what is best for us to know.

His Last Editorial. Dr. Bresee's last editorial — and which was never published — was written by him in the month of September, 1915, and was as follows:

Loyalty. Love, reverence, and devotion enter into loyalty. There are some things, such as country and church, which demand loyalty. Any one who can be easily turned aside, is not likely to be of much value, and any one who has not the spirit of loyalty is likely to be of as little value elsewhere, as where he now is, and to have as low a rating.

A true patriot can not easily change his fealty to the flag which to him has meant so much in emblems and ideals. But, when the way is made clear, and he is providentially led in conviction and sense of duty to do so, and writes his name under a new flag, all the possibilities of his being go with him in loyalty to the country whose protection he seeks, and of which he becomes a part.

Those foreigners who sought privilege, protection, and home under the Stars and Stripes, who in the days of this country's trial, turned back in their loyalty to the country from which they decamped, and against the home of their adoption, were never worthy to be American citizens. They should return to the land from whence they came, take upon themselves anew the vows of the old land, and there abide. Naught but selfishness had led them in the past; if possible, something better should be sought in the future. None among whom they now dwell can have any respect for them in their present relations. Their room is necessarily more desirable than their presence.

In the church, where the relation is still more sacred and delicate, where men, of their own volition, have taken on connections which embrace relations to each other of fellowship, friendship, and common duties and obligations, those who can treat it lightly, or sever the relation easily, are evidently where they are only for what they can get out of it, and are a weakness to the body of which they claim to be a part. A church of such persons would have no reliability or strength.

It is impossible to think of Paul as possessing or harboring for a moment any such qualities. Those who have lacked loyalty to a cause have failed it in its time of need. Demas may have had many good traits. He may have done some service, and Paul does not

441

multiply words against him; but his lack of supreme loyalty to Jesus Christ, has doomed him for ever tō the contempt of men. Benedict Arnold had done good, heroic service, but his loyalty being weaker than his love for British gold, he was stamped with infamy. The man upon whom inspiration pours its darkest woe, was the friend, acquaintance — a guide, an equal — with whom there was sweet counsel and communion on the way to the house of God. But he lacked loyalty at last, and Judas became a name with unutterable meaning for ever.

Those who injure the church most are not out and out enemies, nor those who are simply weak and fall into sin; but men who are disloyal, who sell their birthright — the confidence of their brethren — for price, or for naught.

CHAPTER XLV.

Serious Sickness —The General Assembly — General Superintend-
ents' Address — In Retrospect —The Quadrennium Past —The
Spiritual Life — Union of the Pentecostal Mission — Church
Literature — Missionary Work — Education —The Ministry
Deaconesses —The Duty of the Hour —The Sacramental
Service —The Rules of Order —The Election of General
Superintendents —Tribute to His Wife — Last Days
A Touching Scene — Finished His Work — Victo-
rious Death — In His Zenith — A Regal Soul
The Funeral Service —The Floral Tribute —
The Burial.

During the month of August, 1915, Dr. and Mrs. Bresee went to Catalina, a beautiful island off the coast of Southern California, where two of their children have summer homes; but the change of climate, or the *Serious Sickness* exertion, had a very serious effect upon his health, and as soon as possible they hastened to their home in Los Angeles. Dr. Bresee gradually rallied, but never became as strong as he was before. His heart performed its functions imperfectly, and he had constant difficulty in breathing. This respiratory trouble was aggravated at night, and caused him to lose much sleep. He had no appetite, and took very little nourishment.

But he never gave up his purpose of attending the General Assembly, and whenever I saw him he expressed the belief that the dear Lord would enable him to go to Kansas City, and take his part as one of the General Superintendents in the deliberations of that body, which he felt would be the most important in the history of the church. He had made all his preparations, which included the writing of the General Superintendents' report to the General Assembly. This he had drafted several months before and sent to General Superintendents Reynolds and Walker, who made slight changes, and returned it to him with their approval.

On the evening of September 5, 1915, **Dr. Bresee and the** writer attended the **Emmanuel Pentecostal Church of** the Nazarene, and heard an excellent sermon by Rev. J. Proctor

Knott. I spent the evening of September 20th, at the residence of Dr. Bresee, which time he was feeling somewhat stronger, and was profoundly grateful to God for giving him the physical ability to start on the long trip across the continent.

On September 22d, accompanied by Sister Bresee, Miss Sue Bresee, and Mrs. Paul Bresee, all of whom were delegates to the General Assembly, he turned his face toward Kansas City; but on the way there his respiratory trouble grew rapidly worse and his condition soon became alarming. In the same car with him and Mrs. Bresee were nearly all the Southern California delegates to the Assembly, and everything possible was done to alleviate his sufferings; but several times it was feared that he would not survive the trip. Earnest prayer was offered for his recovery, and his condition so improved that he reached Kansas City alive. Shortly after his arrival there, Mrs. Paul Bresee wired for her husband, a skillful physician and surgeon, to come to Kansas City at the earliest possible moment. Dr. Paul Bresee answered this summons with the utmost promptitude, and was in Kansas City shortly after the time of the opening of the Assembly, on September 30th. Dr. Bresee was fortunate in having a son who so thoroughly understood his physical condition, and whose treatment and administration of restoratives so strengthened him that he was enabled to attend all the business sessions of the Assembly, and take part in the proceedings:

The General Assembly. Dr. B. F. Haynes, the editor of the HERALD OF HOLINESS, in the course of an article descriptive of the Assembly, said:

The session of the Assembly on Friday morning was a marked success. Dr. Bresee was graciously strengthened by the Father, sufficiently to be present and read the quadrennial address of the General Superintendents. The General Superintendents gave us a good account of their stewardship in this paper. The Assembly was delighted to see that our venerable and able senior General Superintendent was able to read it in so clear and strong a voice. It was his own personal composition, though, of course, the voice of the entire Board of Superintendents.

A PRINCE IN ISRAEL

I quote the following from the report in the HERALD OF HOLINESS: Friday morning, Dr. Bresee, although weak in body, manfully read the address of the General Superintendents. Forty-five minutes were consumed. It is a well-written and comprehensive document, and should be read by each Pentecostal Nazarene. Just before this great paper was read, Dr. John Matthews gave an impassioned address of welcome." The address was as follows:

Superintendent's Address

Brethren and Sisters Beloved; Members of the General Assembly of the Pentecostal Church of the Nazarene:
It seems fitting that your General Superintendents, who, by the arrangements of the last General Assembly of our church, have had general charge and oversight of the work during the last quadrennium, and whose duty it is to preside over your deliberations, should more especially introduce the important duties upon which we now enter, with some more formal words in reference to the work.

We rejoice to greet you in the name of Him whose we are and whom we serve, and humbly pray that "The God of peace, that brought again from the dead our Lord Jesus, that great shepherd of the sheep, through the blood of the everlasting covenant, make you perfect in every good work to do his will, working in you that which is well pleasing in his sight, through Jesus Christ; to whom be glory for ever and ever." Amen.

IN RETROSPECT

Four years have elapsed since the last General Assembly, at Nashville, Tenn. They have been eventful years. A church as young as this makes history fast. This length of time, in the early years of the movement, may mean more than a much longer period when things have become more settled and mature. The work in which we are engaged, and in which we believe we have been providentially led, for the propagation and establishment of the experience of Christian holiness in the earth, which has been the confluence of various streams that have sprung up in different parts of the wilderness of human need, bringing together people of different schools of Christian thought and theology as well as of various methods of church government and forms of Christian service, all meeting and mingling in the one great necessity of our being — holiness unto the Lord — has presented a peculiar condition of hope and of possible peril. These years have been a time when we have been put into the melting-pot together, and the real question seems to have been whether the holy fire of the glory which Christ has given, would be able to melt us into the sacred unity for which He prayed, that we might be one, that the world might know His power to save unto the uttermost.

We desire to congratulate you that it now seems that, while there may have been here and there a little slag, the great body has melted as pure metal into a more and more perfect unity. Preconceived ideas, notions, and educational colorings have been given

445

up or held in abeyance by an intense loyalty, that we may be one for the salvation and sanctification of the people. We believe that which would not coalesce has been, to a large extent, eliminated, and that more and more the spirit of unity has prevailed. We regard this as the result of the large liberty which we all enjoy, and the fire of the Holy Spirit which has so blessedly glowed in our midst. In this we congratulate you and rejoice with you.

We need scarce call your attention to the sacredness of the great and responsible duties which are upon us in this Assembly. Within providential limitations and restrictions, we are vested with supreme powers, both to make and interpret laws, and to initiate new, or modify existing, measures and methods of church economy and work. The greatness of the interests involved must impress us with the weight of the responsibilities which rest upon us. When this Assembly adjourns, we may not be able to change the record or remedy mistakes. The wisdom or folly of our acts will either bless or injure the church which has entrusted us with these great and vital powers. To walk humbly, carefully, prayerfully, devotedly, and unselfishly before God, behooves every one of us. Our utterances and deeds may bless the ages, or may retard the kingdom of God. By our words and acts we shall be justified or condemned. The God of history will write the record. We, your General Superintendents, feel that you with us will wait in earnest prayer. Let us humble ourselves, and be sure that there is no selfish way in us; and seek earnestly that there may be given unto us the illuminating and guiding Spirit, and that He will so fill us with abounding love that we may be sufficient for the perfect will of God, so that no word or act of ours shall be a hindrance or stumblingblock in the way of any human soul, to the end that if in anything we should not see eye to eye, we shall abide heart to heart, to patiently wait and be led by Him in His own way; if it is not our way, that it may be His way, and He glorify Himself in the unity of our love to God and to each other, and in our devotion to the work to which He has called us. While each one of us may have convictions, as well as judgments, as to what is best, and may not be able to see that ours is not the wiser and better way, yet let us not be too certain, or assume that we are either better or wiser than the majority of our brethren. Let us remember that humility and regard for the best judgment of others becomes us, and that it is always a pitiable sight for any one to stand out and oppose, or forsake the fellowship of his brethren, because he is, in his own judgment, better or wiser than they. God always has a way for each one of us, and holy people are to find His will, and in accord do His service. "The glory which thou hast given me, I have given them, that they may be one, that the world may believe."

There are places of vision — temporary surveying stations — in the lives of men and institutions — crisis points, places of arrival and departure, which awaken reflection, and from which we look back upon the way already trod, as well as toward the path of the future. This is such a place; and our thought goes back, not only over the four years since our last General Assembly, but over the two decades since this work began more especially to take form in different parts of the land. It is with no little sadness that we mark the absence of so many of the heroes who went forth with us into this work. And yet even this fact awakens our thanksgiving, that they wrought with such fidelity, and that in holy triumph they have ascended to God.

It is with special gratitude that we recognize the large numbers of devoted and able men and women whom God has called from the East and West, from the North and South, as well as those whom He has raised up from the stones of this New Jerusalem, to lift the banners and carry on this work. While our hearts are sad for the absence of so many regnant spirits, who have been called from us, we lift our eyes to look upon the re-enforced army pressing on for greater victory. We weep: but the wounded hand is wiping away the tears and cheering our hearts by the visions of the heavenly.

Not only is the battle the Lord's, but those who finish their course with fidelity are crowned among the victors. So the conflicts here and the glories there come close together. Great and noble spirits who have labored with us have gone on before, but their work abides. They wrought even better than they knew. They laid foundations deeper, broader, stronger than their most sanguine hopes ever conceived. We have inherited the sacred trust. It remains for us by holy zeal, devotion, and heroism, by broad, manly statesmanship, by unswerving fidelity to Jesus Christ, to show ourselves worthy of being their successors in carrying forward the work left to our hands, and to meet the demands which are upon us in these times.

THE QUADRENNIUM PAST

We have reasons for rejoicing and for thanksgiving that the four years now closing since our last General Assembly, has been a time of signal prosperity in all the various departments of our work both at home and abroad, and that there have been so few regretful things.

The lives of your General Superintendents have been preserved, though serious illness has come to both Doctors Walker and Reynolds. Yet in answer to the prayers of the church they have been raised up. We have been able to present and perform the duties given us to do, at most of the District Assemblies, and to go in and out among our churches in overseeing and evangelistic ministry. Doctor Walker visited Scotland and England, doing some evangelistic work, and especially looking after the prospective work of our church in those countries. Doctor Reynolds made a trip around the world, especially visiting our missions, and inspecting as far as possible the mission fields.

Our District Superintendents have usually been preserved in health, and have generally wrought with heroic devotion in their exacting, and often difficult, fields. Our pastors have usually been untiring in their devotion and toil, and the membership has largely held up their hands by prayer and sacrifices, so that in most places success in winning souls and leading believers into the fulness of the blessing of Christ has been given us. We return to you after four years of service, to render our report with joy and thanksgiving. The work has been difficult and strenuous, but not more than we could bear. There have been demands upon our wisdom and skill, often beyond our ability, but through your prayers we have been helped of God. One of our members, Doctor Reynolds, has, in con-

447

nection with his other duties, acted as our General Missionary Secretary, and the other two have supplemented the work of holding Assemblies, by visiting and ministering to the churches, as has been possible, and as there has seemed need; organizing churches, dedicating church buildings, doing the work of evangelists, meeting educational, missionary, and other boards, and in every way possible laboring to build up the kingdom. We have not been able to respond to all of the calls upon us, but have done what we could.

THE SPIRITUAL LIFE

We rejoice to believe that the fresh glow of spiritual life, which attended those who first went out under the stars to preach holiness and gather together a holy people, has not been lost, nor has it departed from us; that with the foundations laid of all our people declaring in unmistakable terms their belief in entire sanctification, and all of our preachers clearly confessing their experience of the blessing, and the constant insistence that all men seek and obtain it, there has not been, as a rule, loss of spiritual life; but the manifest presence of God among us abides, and the scenes of Pentecost are often repeated. It is a favorable omen that our people, more and more, seek not simply times and seasons of revival, but look for constant tides of salvation, so that in many of our churches, a week when there are not conversions and sanctifications is of rare occurrence; and there are added to the church daily such as are saved. As a result, there is an increase of the spirit of unity among us, with intensified loyalty to each other and devotion to the work. There have been no serious schisms among us, but a growing and intensifying of the unity and thankfulness that the Lord has raised up a people where the gospel of entire sanctification is clearly and continuously preached, and where there is liberty in its confession, and in seeking and manifesting the fulness of the divine indwelling.

We also rejoice that the statistics are likely to show a good increase in the membership of our churches, as well as the strengthening of the various agencies of Christian service.

UNION OF THE PENTECOSTAL MISSION

One of the most auspicious occurrences of the quadrennium has been the union with us of the holiness movement known as the Pentecostal Mission. It will be remembered that it was this people who invited the last General Assembly to hold its session at their headquarters at Nashville, Tenn., and who so magnanimously entertained it. It was a season of precious fellowship and much thought was given to the union of the two bodies; but no definite steps were then taken. After a time to the sorrow, not only of the Pentecostal Mission people, but of many others, including our whole denomination, Rev. J. O. McClurkan was suddenly called to his reward in heaven. After he had gone, the necessity of union seemed more pressing, and after proper conference and arrangements, it was consummated at Nashville, in October, 1914. By this act, a body of considerable size and influence came into organic union with the Pentecostal Church of the Nazarene, bringing with them a missionary force of considerable strength, doing work in India, Cuba, and Central America. The Pentecostal Church of the Nazarene and these heroic people of the Pentecostal Mission had long been one in spirit, and it was a matter of special joy to be one in this closer organic union and fellowship, as well as service.

CHURCH LITERATURE

At the very beginning of this work, in the different parts of the country, it was found necessary to create avenues for the propagation and conservation of our work, and to make known to men that for which we stand. Thus, in the East, West, and South, papers were established. These were generally individual enterprises, created at large personal sacrifice, to serve and advance the work. The task of publishing a Sunday school literature had also been entered upon.

The General Assembly, held at Nashville, in 1911, thoroughly considered the whole matter and provided for the church to establish a publishing plant, which should be owned and conducted by the church itself. To this end, a Board of Publication was appointed, with powers and instructions. This Board has gone forward in accord with the instructions given it, and has with remarkable success inaugurated a Church Publishing House. It has been greatly handicapped by lack of funds, but the results seem to be marvelous. Full reports will doubtless be made to you by them of this great work. This is one of the most important interests that will come before you, and will demand your most careful thought to plan for its largest development.

MISSIONARY WORK

Our whole work is missionary. A few people went out from old church affiliations, to begin again the raising of a holy people. For some cause, the work was greatly discounted, if not worse, by the large body of professedly Christian people of the country, which made it peculiarly difficult. To raise up a people and create new centers of fire, with the general sentiment of so-called Christian people against the work, and continued opposition from them to the central truth and experience of Christian holiness, which we teach, made the work largely missionary, often as difficult, or more so, than the establishment of Christianity in a heathen country. To do this has brought forth a degree of heroism and sacrifice on the part of ministers and the little bands of laymen, rarely excelled. So that our field of missionary work has been quite largely in the home land, to help as best we could, directly and indirectly, to Christianize Christianity, and let loose the tides of holy power to awaken and save America. This must in great measure still be our work, until at least a great center of holy fire is created in every city in the land.

But, while we have been doing this, our people have lifted up their eyes, and looked upon the fields so white for the harvest, where there are few, if any reapers. This has led to the sending of missionaries to Mexico, Japan, India, China, Africa, and islands of the sea, as well as to people of other nationalities within our own coasts. We are thankful to report that a good degree of blessing has been upon the labor of our brethren and sisters in these lands — proper reports of which will doubtless be before you, calling for your thanksgiving as well as challenging your thought and prayer.

EDUCATION

While the evangelization of men and their building up in holiness is our great commission and our first work, it also inheres in our commission to train and educate those, who, through our labors, are brought into this great salvation. In this country the state usually makes provision for the rudimentary instruction of children. Yet, often our people find the religious ideals. or the absence of ideals, are such that it is a great grief to them. and in some instances, church or parochial schools have been attempted. A few such have attained to great excellence and some success. But the cost is so great, and our people usually being poor, no great advance in this direction has been made. In the meantime the public schools should be zealously guarded from abuse, and the religious home and church teaching and training be strict and full. But higher education is of such a nature, that the church which turns such work over to the state, or to others, will soon find itself robbed of its best inheritance. Especially is it necessary for us to educate our own youth. Spiritual religion is quite usually dispensed with, and often worse, in the colleges and universities of the land, and almost entirely holiness is tabooed and a seeker after it, or a professor of it, is regarded as a crank. At the age when the truth should be fixed in the mind and the experience developed toward maturity, their convictions are undermined, and their experience blasted. Academies and colleges are to us a necessity. Our young people will go forth to our pulpits, our counting houses, our farms, and our homes, full of the hallowed fire of the indwelling Spirit, only as they have been dwelling under the shadow of the Almighty in the classroom, chapel, and social life of their college years. We should not yield to the temptation of attempting to establish too many schools of higher education, as we may not be able to give them a proper degree of efficiency. The establishment of a college is a great work, demanding men and women of culture, and much money for its support; and should not be entered upon unadvisedly or without provision. We rejoice that we already have a number of schools which are doing good work, and which bid fair to obtain permanent and large usefulness. They are most, if not all, in great need of money, and should receive the careful thought and help of our people, especially of those to whom the Lord has committed some of His money. There should be great care in reference to the creation of more schools, until those already established are much better provided for. A little further travel to get a properly equipped institution, is a small matter, in comparison with building, equipping, providing Faculties, libraries, and so forth, for a school. We are especially pleased with the intense spiritual life generally found in our schools, which, with the exaltation of the Word of God, together with the molding hand of the cultured personality of sanctified teachers, promise well for prepared labor to enter the field.

THE MINISTRY

God has greatly favored us by leading to our communion men of rare gifts, who have loved holiness, and the privilege of preaching it unobstructedly, more than they have loved ecclesiasticism, or even pleasant associations. He has also raised up among us many with hearts aflame to tell out the divine message.

Our Superintendency — General and District — is one of the most vital and important parts of our simple, but necessary, machinery. Our pastors are an absolute necessity. It is very desirable that our ministers' hands be strengthened in every practicable and proper way, that they may lead us on to the greatest victory.

The calling of pastors and their continuance in a charge demands your careful consideration. Evangelists are of great service and usefulness among us. In some parts of our church too much is expected of them, and they too largely take the place of pastors. This should be carefully avoided, and only such employed as are loyal to the church, and who assist in gathering up those reached, that the work may be subserved, and the results cared for, and who are ready to assist in the dissemination of the literature of our church.

Our licensed preachers should be pushed out into the byways, to preach and pray with the people, and should be given opportunities to preach and develop their gifts for still greater work.

DEACONESSES

There has come to be a large class of these workers. They are making a strong and effective arm of the service. Many consecrated and intelligent women are finding in this work a wide open door for useful service. They minister to the sick and the needy, visit the homes of non-church goers, and invite to the house of the Lord, welcome and look after strangers, and in many ways strengthen the hands of the pastor and build up the church of God. We commend to your attention the importance of more exact provisions for their careful selection, licensing, public recognition, training, and government.

THE DUTY OF THE HOUR

No Assembly of our church has ever gathered for greater work, and none has ever needed more to be imbued with the prudence and wisdom which come from above. The times are distracting; many conditions make our work difficult; we are generally misunderstood and often misrepresented; the work is great; the resources are limited; the fields are ripe for the harvest, but the laborers are few. A careful outlook will surely impress us with the solidarity of the enemy, the general opposition to holiness, and especially to any effective way of its obtainment, and will surely fill us with seriousness. God has put us in a place of great responsibility. We are the representatives and guardians of a church, which holds as its central purpose the bearing to men of the message of the power of the blood of Jesus to cleanse from all sin, and the readiness of the Christ to dwell in holy hearts, thus especially revealing and manifesting Himself for the salvation of the world. A realization of the great work to which God has called us, will awe us into reverence, and impel us to seek closest unity with God and with each other, that we may prove worthy of our high calling. What we do can scarcely fail to be fraught with mighty consequences. If we shall be able by wise counsel, by unreserved sinking out of sight for ever all selfish or personal aims as well as preconceived notions, and give ourselves unreservedly to divine guidance, we shall doubtless be able to command already existing forces, so as to add to their efficiency, and devise new plans and arrange for new agencies for larger work. Unity and divine guidance are to be especially sought.

The manifestation of a selfish or arrogant spirit by a few, or even only one of us, with a determination to have our own way or

451

no way, might immeasurably harm the cause of holiness in the earth. Let us realize that we tread holy ground, with eternity gazing upon us. A sense of our responsibility will certainly humble us, and fill us with seriousness in the performance of our present task.

We have the uttermost confidence in our brethren and sisters — ministers and laymen of the Pentecostal Church of the Nazarene — with whom we have solemnly covenanted before God, to be true to Him, to each other, and to His cause as represented by this work. We have every reason to believe that our people, generally scattered over the lands, are with one heart and mind enthusiastically loyal to their vows, and rejoice with unutterable thanksgiving that God has raised up unto them, and allows them to be a part of, a veritable Church of Jesus Christ, which He so delights to honor with His presence and so crown with the salvation of men. Each has the right to expect of every one of us, fullest loyalty to the work which we have unitedly undertaken and to Him who is Head over all, blessed for ever.

Fortunately, we are not here to settle matters of doctrine. On the great fundamentals we are all agreed. Pertaining to things not essential to salvation, we have liberty. To attempt to emphasize that which is not essential to salvation, and thus divide forces, would be a crime. An unwillingness for others to enjoy the liberty that we enjoy in reference to doctrines not vital to salvation, is bigotry, from which the spirit of holiness withdraws itself.

We are not here to quiet disaffections or allay strifes, as we have never been in greater peace, or in better temper of loyalty throughout our borders. It would be sad indeed, should any word or act of any of us magnify any slight condition or affair which might occur, into dissatisfaction. A dissatisfied soul is already injured, and there is no telling how vital to that soul, and possibly to others, it may become. A general work of God may not be largely injured by individual dissatisfaction, but to the individual it may be fatal. We are here for continued answers to the prayer of our Lord, that we may all be one, and to know the satisfaction of those who have awakened in His likeness. We rejoice that there largely prevails among us that love which melts not only into accord, but into oneness.

The question before us is greater efficiency, the girding for vaster results in the great work to which we are called, especially to find a way for us as a people to more effectively help fill the earth with the spirit of holiness.

We rejoice that there are others to share the work with us, and we claim blood-relationship with every holy person in the universe, and would strengthen the hands of all. But we are especially concerned to do our part of the work, and to acquit ourselves worthily in the mighty struggle. More and more we must realize that it is not of man, but of God. Closeness to the Almighty leader is our hope of victory. Our brethren and sisters, let us reverently say: "No hindrance shall be in, or through me, and, God helping, all possible help shall be given by me."

We have written the adorable Name on our banner, and lifted it to the gaze of men. Some are looking hopefully toward us, let us not disappoint them. Let us not waver. We are sure that our dear Redeemer is looking. Let us be true. Forward: — calmly, thought-

452

fully, prayerfully, and with eyes steadily fixed upon the Master for direction and strength. Let us so do that the Church which we love, may approve, and we at last may hear the Lord's own, "Well done."

The Sacramental Service. On Friday afternoon, September 30th, Dr. Bresee conducted the sacramental service, which Rev. H. H. Miller characterized as follows:

It was an event of a lifetime. Dr. Bresee was in charge, assisted by Dr. Walker and Dr. Reynolds and other elders of the General Assembly. Dr. Bresee, though feeble in health, in his old-time way, with unction from heaven on him, delivered a marvelous communion address. His base was the Scripture read (the last three verses of Isaiah 52 and all of Isaiah 53). Who can ever forget his description of "My servant"? He brought us all up where we saw that "Surely he hath borne our griefs, and carried our sorrows: yet we did esteem him stricken, smitten of God and afflicted." The effect was tremendous, as this mighty man's words, in the words of the Word of God, gripped every heart by the power of the Holy Ghost. One of the oldest of the ministers remarked to the writer that in all his lifetime he had seen no such a communion service; and never expected to see such another one. It is doubtful if he or any one else will see a greater one, "until we all drink it new with him in his Father's kingdom."

Rev. Fred Mesh said:

There is here a united affection for Dr. Bresee in his illness. It is not idolatry for a man, but affection for a man of God used for our blessing. The spirit is exhilarating in its fervor of feeling. Sometimes a word of testimony touches a fountain of holy joy to flowing. Then a song lifts the congregation literally to its feet. Then a tribute of affection offered for Dr. Bresee in his illness upsets the bowl of tears.

The Rules of Order. These rules, which were adopted by the Assembly in their entirety, were prepared by Dr. Bresee several months before, with the most scrupulous and prayerful consideration. They were very comprehensive, and contributed much to the expeditious transaction of the business of the great gathering.

Election of General Superintendents. Dr. Bresee, Rev. H. F. Reynolds, and Dr. E. F. Walker were all re-elected General Superintendents. Rev. E. P. Ellyson was also elected to the general superintendency, but resigned, and Rev. W. C. Wilson, of California, was elected in his stead.

The Assembly was great in attendance, in spiritual life, in the manifestation of brotherly love, in the intellectual

453

power of the delegates, in the fervor of the prayers, in the unction of the preaching, in the beauty and effectiveness of the singing, and in the great tides of salvation at all the evangelistic services.

Dr. Haynes said:

> The session has been one of intense interest, and we believe will eventuate in great blessing and profit to the church at large. There was a very full attendance, and nearly all the delegates remained faithfully to the close. The spirit of the body was very good. There was much very earnest debating, but no unbrotherliness, or rancor or acrimony. God was manifestly with the evangelistic services throughout the Assembly. The Spirit was in the Word from night to night, and put His seal to the salvation and sanctification of many souls.

It was my privilege to see much of Dr. Bresee during the twenty-nine days that elapsed between his return from the General Assembly, and his passing away.

Tribute to His Wife   I was permitted to spend forty minutes with him and Sister Bresee on the evening of Saturday, November 6th. He was sitting on the edge of his bed, seeking in this way to breathe with greater ease than he could do in a recumbent position. I spoke of the marvelous manner in which the dear Lord had blessed him during the nearly sixty years of his ministry. He did not reply directly, but, as he turned on his right side, he said: "The greatest blessing I have ever had is my wife." Sister Bresee gently demurred to this, but I heartily agreed with Dr. Bresee, who then said substantially as follows: "Position is nothing; reputation little. True godliness is the only thing which has any value."

Last Days   I last saw him for just a moment on Sunday evening, November 7th, and told him that I was going to the 6 o'clock upper room prayermeeting at the First Church. He said: "Tell them all that I love them, and that I pray that the glory of God may come upon them, and that they may have victory through the precious blood of Jesus." He was sitting on the edge of the bed, and I shook hands with him and said good-by, not knowing that it was the last time on this side of the eastern gate.

On Thursday evening, November 4th, he sent for all his children, as he felt that his end was very near. First he spoke to his four sons — Ernest, Phineas, Paul, and Melvin — and then called for his two daughters, *A Touching Scene* Mrs. Bertha Parker, and Miss Sue Bresee, and his daughter-in-law, Mrs. Paul Bresee, whom he loved as a daughter. As they all knelt around him, with his faithful wife among them, he prayed for them and all the absent members of his family, mentioning each by name, and commending them to the mercy of God. He thanked the Lord for the great love and kindness of his children to him, and besought the Savior to bring them all to heaven. As he prayed in a way which Sister Bresee characterized as wonderful, and something that would be indelibly impressed upon the memories of every one present, the tears rolled down his cheeks, and were wiped away by his eldest son, Ernest.

During these long and weary days of suffering, he said many sweet and precious things to Sister Bresee. He frequently rallied, and spoke at different times to quite a number of the brethren, among them many of the leaders of the Church and University. He gave them wise and loving counsel, addressing them with the utmost love and tenderness, not only about the different phases of the work, but about the importance of freely and fully forgiving every one that had ever injured them, and dwelling and working together in the divine love and the unity of the Spirit.

While waiting for death, he finished every detail. He forgot nothing that pertained to the welfare of his family, the Nazarene University, and the Church which he had loved so well and served so faithfully. Like *Finished His Work* the apostle Paul, he fought a good fight, finished his course, and kept the faith.

His last days were crowned with complete victory. He

455

was very tender and solicitous for the spiritual well-being
of all his family, friends, and brethren, and faced death, not
only fearlessly, but with glad anticipation.

He passed away at 1 o'clock Saturday afternoon, November 13, 1915, loved and lamented by a vast multitude of
those who had been helped by his ministry, and blessed by
his life. At last the busy hands were still;
Victorious Death   the clarion voice silent.

His brethren paid him many beautiful
tributes, all of which I would rejoice to include in this volume. In most of these expressions of love and appreciation, he was spoken of as "A Prince in Israel," and so I
have chosen those words as the title of this book.

At the time of his translation, he was in the zenith of his
intellectual and spiritual powers. He was a man of genius,
a prince among his fellows. For sixty years he followed
Jesus, and proclaimed the glorious gospel
In His Zenith   of the Son of God. For nearly two-score
years he was a fearless evangel of holiness.
During each successive year he laid increasing stress upon
the essentials of salvation, the fundamentals of holy living,
the primary elements of godliness. He realized with growing intensity that the disciples of Christ must have more
and more of the divine manifestation, of the revealed personal presence of God; that they must be lowly and loving
and loyal in all the relations of life. But, more than this,
his life corresponded with his teachings. His faith was simple, his love tender, his hope buoyant.

A Regal Soul. His was a regal soul. A true Christian,
a noble man, a good citizen, a loving husband, an affectionate father, a faithful friend, a real brother in the Lord, he
has left us with saddened hearts and tearful eyes, but with
a lively hope of meeting him where the many mansions are.

All that remains for me to do in bringing to a close this
labor of love is to briefly describe the funeral service of him
who won so high a place in our affections.

The last sad rites connected with the death of Doctor

A PRINCE IN ISRAEL

P. F. Bresee, our beloved senior General Superintendent, occurred at the First Pentecostal Church of the Nazarene, Los Angeles, on the afternoon of November 16, 1915. Long before 2 o'clock, the hour set for the beginning of the service, the auditorium was crowded, and in a short time there was no longer standing room, and probably two hundred people unable to gain admittance, were gathered in the street. The beautiful casket containing the remains, was placed in front of the altar of the church between 10 a. m. and 2 p. m., when it was closed. During the period indicated, two thousand men, women, and children took advantage of the opportunity to view the lifeless form of him whom they loved so well. Some twenty or more seats were reserved for the family of the deceased, immediately in front of the pulpit, all of which were filled. The display of floral offerings was remarkable, not only for the number of pieces, but for their beauty of design and the loveliness of the flowers which composed them. The largest, from First Church, was a representation of the Eastern Gate, surmounted by a beautiful white dove. The Sunday school, Young People's society, and Dorcas society, were also appropriately represented among the floral offerings, and a large and exquisite floral emblem, bearing the word "Papa," was the last loving tribute of the children of Dr. Bresee. In another paragraph there appears a more detailed description of the floral pieces, which completely filled the space between the altar and the platform, and surrounded the twenty or more elders of the church who occupied seats back of the pulpit.

At 2 o'clock the family and relatives of our beloved leader walked down one of the central aisles, and took their seats, whereupon Rev. C. E. Cornell, the pastor of the church, opened the sweetly solemn service with a few words of prayer.

Rev. J. P. Coleman read some appropriate Scriptures, after which Rev. Howard Eckel, Superintendent of the

Southern California District, led in prayer with much tenderness and unction.

The writer read a terse biographical sketch of Dr. Bresee, and the male quartet of the Nazarene University sang with much expression, "Lead, Kindly Light."

Rev. John W. Goodwin, then pastor of the Pentecostal Church of the Nazarene, at San Diego, Cal., and since elected as one of the General Superintendents of the church, paid a glowing tribute to the memory of him whom he had loved so well.

Brother Goodwin was followed by Dr. E. A. Healey, dean of the theological department of the University of Southern California, who was present, and asked the privilege of speaking a few words, and of bringing a tribute of affection to Dr. Bresee, who twenty-nine years before had been his pastor in Pasadena, California.

Rev. C. E. Cornell, the pastor of the First Church, then gave a brief but luminous exposition of Psalm 37 : 37, and spoke feelingly of how, during the five years of his pastorate in the First Church, Dr. Bresee had put his arms around him, and helped him in a difficult situation.

William M. Jones, professor of music at the Nazarene University, then sang, in a touching manner, "In the land of fadeless day, lies the city four-square."

Rev. H. O. Wiley, president of the Nazarene University, closed the service with a few words of fervent prayer, and pronounced the benediction.

Mrs. Lilly D. Bothwell, an old and warm friend of Brother and Sister Bresee, thus describes the floral tribute on this occasion. "As a tribute of love and honor to our beloved Dr. Bresee, the flowers at his funeral *The Floral Tribute* at First Church, Los Angeles, bespoke the hearts best fashioning for him.

"Tribute was laid upon the finest bloom of our Southland, and, as though God had thought upon His servant for this speechful phase of offering, beauty and form and color and fragrance and profusion, conspired to make the floral tribute to this good man replete with the best that could be offered. Under their tender touch chancel and pulpit were transformed into a mass of breathing beauty.

"At the front of these the form of our great, good pastor-friend lay in a casket which bore upon it two palm branches — the inspired offering of his sons. For what could better symbolize the character of this hero of God, who had entered 'the Unseen Holy?' — 'This thy stature is like to a palm tree.'"

At the close of the service in the church, the still form of him whom we all loved so well, was taken to Evergreen cemetery, accompanied by a vast cortege, in automobiles, and street cars chartered for the occasion. Here *The Burial* in the midst of the greensward, all that was left of Phineas F. Bresee was laid to rest. His grave was in the lovely spot where his sainted parents were buried. As the weeping family, relatives, and friends stood about the grave, Rev. C. E. Cornell gave the committal; Rev. H. H. Miller, Superintendent of the San Francisco District, uttered words of earnest prayer; and Rev. Arnold Hodgins pronounced the benediction. The scene was impressive and beautiful. We left him in the midst of the grass, the trees, the flowers, and the singing birds, beneath the sunny California sky — all of which he loved so well — to wait with his father and mother for the resurrection morn.

APPENDIX

Expressions of esteem by the First Methodist Episcopal Church, of Los Angeles, California:

At the meeting of the last Quarterly Conference, held at the Fort Street Methodist Episcopal church, September 13, 1886, the following resolutions were read and unanimously adopted by the Conference:

WHEREAS, The polity of the church demands at this time the removal of our pastor, Rev. P. F. Bresee, D. D., it becomes our pleasurable duty to give, to some extent, expressions to our appreciation of his work and worth. Three years ago he came to us a stranger, having left the fruits of an average lifetime behind him. Under circumstances of peculiar difficulty, with a cosmopolitan membership numerous and widely distributed, he at once mastered the situation and took position in the front rank of the clergy of Southern California. By an unusual combination of the factors essential to the successful teacher and pastor, he has during his administration won the affection of our whole people and of a wide circle beyond, while he has commanded the respect and confidence of the entire community. With a rare ability for the management of details, the prosperity of the varied interests of the church has been steadily progressive under his direction, so that our Sunday school, class meetings, prayermeetings, local and general benevolences, measure up to the standard of a high type of Methodism. Therefore, be it

Resolved, (1) That his ministry among us has been characterized by a noble, self-sacrificing service.

(2) That he has been bold in the proclamation of the truth and fearless in the denunciation of evil.

(3) That he has been tender and devoted in his ministrations to the bereaved, the suffering, and the dying.

(4) That in all his work we have found him a man of tireless energy, with a resistless purpose to please God and help his fellowmen.

(5) That while the church has been built up by his effective preaching, it has been established by his equally effective pastoral care, and the exalted example of a holy life.

Resolved, That in Mrs. Bresee we have found a model preacher's wife, who, by her lively interest in every department of the church and by a hearty co-operation with her husband in all possible ways, has added largely to his efficiency.

Resolved, That we will follow them with our prayers for long years of increasing usefulness, and that we will welcome them to our hearts and homes whenever, in the providence of God, they may be in our midst. N. S. AVERILL, *Secretary*.

At the meeting of the Church Board of the First Pentecostal Church of the Nazarene, of Los Angeles, California, held on the first Monday evening of December, 1915, the following resolutions were unanimously adopted; and on the following Sunday morning, they were likewise adopted by a unanimous rising vote:

WHEREAS, Rev. P. F. Bresee, D. D., the greatly beloved senior General Superintendent and founder, under God, of the Pentecostal Church of the Nazarene, and the first pastor of this church, after finishing his course, fighting a good fight, and keeping the faith, has been crowned with final victory and glory, and taken to the bosom of the Savior, whom he so devotedly loved, and so faithfully served; and

WHEREAS, By his preaching, teaching, prayers, admonitions, godly example, and loyal, self-sacrificing friendship to all of us, as individuals and as a church, he was greatly used of God in strengthening our faith, deepening our piety, and intensifying our love for God and humanity, and in very many instances, was our real spiritual father; and

WHEREAS, By his dauntless courage, heroic devotion, sweet simplicity of character, and deep insight into the Word of God, as well as by his consecrated eloquence, rare powers of exegesis and exposition, saintly life, and tireless labors in the kingdom of Christ, he was enabled to spread organized scriptural holiness directly all over the American continent, and indirectly, throughout the world; and

WHEREAS, In journeyings oft, in weary vigils, in good report and ill report, by voice, by pen, by self-denial, by the sword of the Spirit, this peerless leader has led the people of God in many a victorious onslaught against the citadels of sin, thus defeating hell, and causing heaven to rejoice; and

WHEREAS, We as a church were most benefited by his sacred ministry, and stimulated by his holy example, we desire not only to place on record our tender love and reverence for the memory of this Prince in Israel, but to pledge ourselves to so follow Jesus in righteousness and holiness, that when our work is ended here, we shall all meet dear Brother Bresee at the Eastern Gate; therefore, be it

Resolved, That we extend to precious Sister Bresee — whose close walk with God has been an inspiration to us all — and to every member of her family, our heartfelt sympathy and prayers in this time of sorrow; and, be it further   ,

Resolved, That these resolutions be adopted by a standing vote of the members of this board; that they be read next Sabbath morning to the congregation, and put to a standing vote; that they be inscribed upon the Minutes of this board, and that a copy thereof be sent to the HERALD OF HOLINESS, with the request that these resolutions be published therein.

At the session of the Southern California District Assembly, at Pomona, California, June 21-25, 1916, the following resolutions were unanimously adopted by a rising vote:

WHEREAS, He who for many years was our leader in the Lord, and who was wont to be among us in our District and General Assemblies, is no longer in our midst, to guide us by his wise counsels, and to inspire us by his saintly and holy example; and,

WHEREAS, Phineas F. Bresee was raised of God as an evangel of holiness, and especially anointed and fitted to conserve the results of holiness teaching and preaching by the promotion of organized holiness; and

WHEREAS, He was truly a prince in Israel, a mighty preacher of righteousness, a gifted and able leader in the great holiness movement, and withal, a man of the deepest simplicity and humility of spirit, having a heart of tenderest love, which always beat in sympathy, not only with those who were perfect in love, and had their robes washed in the blood of the Lamb, but with those who had fallen, who were cast down, discouraged, and forsaken; and,

WHEREAS, He adorned the doctrine of Christ by gladly forgiving his enemies, praying for those that despitefully used him, and making a point of going the second mile, thus leaving us the priceless heritage of his example and teaching, and the precious influence of his holy life; therefore, be it,

Resolved, That, though we deeply deplore his absence from among us, and miss more than words can tell his personal presence

461

and wise leadership, we can not but exult in the consciousness that he is now basking in the heavenly light that shines around the throne of God, and rejoicing with joy unspeakable and full of glory in the presence of the Savior whom he loved so well, and served so faithfully during the nearly three score years of his ministry; and, be it further,

Resolved, That we sympathize with Sister Bresee and all the members of her family in their very great bereavement, and assure them that our earnest prayers ascend to God to keep and comfort them very tenderly in this time of sadness and loneliness.

The following resolutions were adopted by the unanimous vote of the Board of Trustees of the Nazarene University, shortly after the decease of Dr. Bresee:

WHEREAS, Our dearly beloved and honored brother, friend, leader, and General Superintendent, Dr. P. F. Bresee, having finished his course with joy and triumph, has been called to his heavenly home, and has received his crown of final glory; and,

WHEREAS, In labors more abundant as its great burden bearer, faithful founder, and loyal supporter, he so devotedly served this institution, with his wise and far-reaching plans, and able and paternal counsel; and,

WHEREAS, By his courage and Christian heroism, as the great leader for organized holiness, he unfurled a banner around which have gathered the united forces of the Pentecostal Church of the Nazarene; and,

WHEREAS, Looking into the future, as a wise builder, he foresaw the urgent necessity of an institution which should make possible a higher education, crowned with the glory of the divine presence, thus perpetuating his ideals of holy life and experience, in a church filled with divine intensity and power; and,

WHEREAS, It was for those ideals and the conservation and perpetuation thereof, that Dr. Bresee gladly gave his all, and sacrificed his life; therefore, be it

Resolved, That we express our great sorrow and deep sense of loss in the departure of this holy man, whose life was eminent for spiritual power; that we also express our sincere appreciation of his godly example among us in this institution known as the Nazarene University, of which he laid the foundation for the coming days better than he knew; and that, as a loving father in Israel, a true scholar and an able teacher, with deep insight into spiritual truth, his memory will ever send forth the sweetest fragrance among the faculty, the student body, the patrons, and the friends of this institution; and be it further

Resolved, That we pledge our loyalty to his lofty ideals, and our fidelity to the Pentecostal Church of the Nazarene, which has been his chief joy and crown; and that we also pledge our most devoted efforts for the realization of the vision given this great hero of the Cross, until from the doors of this University, like burning lava from the mouth of a blazing volcano, young manhood and womanhood, sanctified and empowered, shall be poured forth to destroy evil and to bless the world; and be it further

A PRINCE IN ISRAEL

Resolved, That we express our deep sympathy for the sorrowing wife and family; and direct that a copy of these resolutions be spread upon our minutes, and published in The Herald of Holiness, and that a copy be sent to the bereaved wife and family.

J. W. Goodwin,
C. E. Cornell,
Committee on Resolutions.
A. O. Henricks, Sec'y. of the Board.